THE
ELEMENTS OF
SUCCESSFUL
TRADING

DEVELOPING YOUR COMPREHENSIVE STRATEGY THROUGH PSYCHOLOGY, MONEY MANAGEMENT, AND TRADING METHODS

ROBERT P. ROTELLA

Library of Congress Cataloging-in-Publication Data

Rotella, Robert {date}
    Comprehensive trading strategies : combining risk/return analysis,
trading methods, and psychology / Robert Rotella.
        p. cm.
    Includes bibliographical references and index.
    ISBN 0-13-204579-6
    1. Futures market. 2. Options (Finance) 3. Speculation.
I. Title.
HG6024.A3R675 1992
332.64'5—dc20   92-4244
                                                                    CIP

© 1992 by New York Institute of Finance
Simon & Schuster
A Paramount Communications Company

Printed in the United States of America

10 9 8 7 6 5 4 3 2 1

This book is dedicated with love to my family:

To my father **Joseph** *and my mother* **Theresa,** *who taught me the value of perseverance and provided the foundation of love necessary to pursue a dream.*

To my sisters **Mary Beth, Diane,** *and* **Rosemarie,** *and to my brother-in-law* **Chris.**

Contents

Preface

The Elements of Successful Trading is for those traders and investors who want to develop a realistic and comprehensive trading strategy. Trading is a deceptively simple yet complex process of developing a trading method, applying money management concepts, and understanding yourself. This book should help novices as well as seasoned traders in any area of speculation such as futures, stocks, bonds, or any trading enterprise. The examples represent futures, but the principles and concepts are the same for any market.

This book is partly the result of courses I teach at New York University and the New York Institute of Finance, but it is much more a description of my actual trading experiences.

It was written for easy access to important ideas. Toward this end, the chapters contain topical segments so that areas the reader is familiar with may easily be skipped without loss of continuity. Important definitions appear in boldface type, and significant concepts are shown in italicized print.

A common question arises when writing a book: Why give away trading secrets? The answer will become clearer as you continue with the book. Trading places tremendous demands on a person. There are few easy trades. Trading, as much an art as it is a science, demands certain qualities that many people may not possess. There will always be magical ways to make fortunes in the perpetual search for the perfect trading method, but this book is intended for the individual determined to work hard and to learn trading. I hope this book will encourage at least as many questions as it may answer.

ACKNOWLEDGMENTS

Writing a book is a difficult process akin to trading, but there were special people along the way who helped in many ways. The constant love and support received from my family was essential in helping me write this book—starting with my father and mother Joseph and Theresa Rotella, my three sisters Diane, Rosemarie, and Mary Beth, and my brother-in-law Chris Aquino.

Don Converse provided excellent suggestions and help in many areas, and read parts of the text. His keen insight into people and trading proved invaluable, and many of his thoughts echo throughout this book. Bob Ward read parts of the text and was generous in providing suggestions and help. His insight into people and trading proved beneficial as well. Jim Lillard's help, particularly in computer support, proved quite valuable.

Audrey Sanders provided the spark to write this book, and her help and encouragement are greatly appreciated. Thanks to Sam Lentine for his creative ideas and irrepressible enthusiasm—though he is no longer with us, his spirit lives on. My cousin Richard Rotella was helpful in getting the book started. Thanks to Eric Nadelburg and Robert MacArthur at Merril Lynch for the use of their office equipment. And last but not least to Donna Barriero for the photo of me, and for her unwavering support and understanding; and to all the creators—artists and scientists alike—who have inspired me.

Robert P. Rotella
New York

There is a tide in the affairs of men,
Which, taken at the flood, leads on to fortune;
Omitted, all the voyage of their life
Is bound in shallows and in miseries.

William Shakespeare, *Julius Caesar*

Chapter 1

Developing a Trading Strategy

There is nothing more difficult to take in hand, more perilous to conduct, or more uncertain in its success, than to take the lead in the introduction of a new order of things.

Niccolo Machiavelli, *The Prince*

Which trading method is better: technical or fundamental analysis? What type of risk should I take, and what reward should I expect when trading? Why don't I have more confidence in myself when actually trading? These are frequent questions asked by novice as well as experienced traders. This book will address these questions and many others, but we will soon learn that simple questions may not always be explained with simple answers.

To answer these questions it is perhaps best to ask another question: What is trading? There are many ways to describe and think about the process of trading. For many the economic definitions of speculation and hedging and the existence of a marketplace comes to mind. For others, trading is a game in which the key is simply finding the right trading method, applying it, and then sitting back to relax and watch the money pour in. But trading is much more than this.

This book is about trading. Trading is a deceptively simple yet complex process of developing a trading method, applying money management concepts, an inquiry into crowd psychology, and an understanding of yourself. Trading is really a study of people as reflected in their actions in the market but also the search for ourself—what we truly desire and how we react during good and bad times. Trading is much more than simply trying to make money. Trading is:

1. An analysis of the market and the development of a good trading method.
2. The application of proper money management principles.
3. An understanding of yourself and determining what you expect to achieve from trading.

This triad is depicted in Figure 1.1.

FIGURE 1.1
The triad of trading method, money management, and the psychology of the trader are essential in developing a sound trading strategy

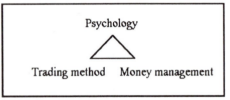

TRADING METHOD

A **trading method** *refers to the way the market is analyzed and how a trading decision is reached.* The two most popular trading methods are technical and fundamental analyses. These two forms of analysis are becoming more blurred in their distinction but a generalization can be made.

1. **Fundamental analysis** *is the study of the underlying factors of supply and demand that affect the price of the commodity.* For example,

the demand for stocks is partly a function of the supply of money and confidence people have in the economy. The supply of coffee is related to the amount produced each year, which can depend on weather factors such as rainfall and frost in the growing regions. After reviewing many of the factors affecting a market, the fundamentalist often makes predictions on the price of the commodity. *In essence fundamental analysis is concerned with the cause and effect of supply and demand, or why things happen, and predicting possible outcomes.*

2. **Technical analysis** *generally refers to analyzing market data or data that correlates with the market to choose the appropriate time to buy or sell.* The most commonly used data is market information such as open, high, low and close, volume, and open interest. All kinds of calculations can be done on the data, but some of the more popular include moving averages, oscillators, and stochastics. Other forms of analysis embody chart patterns such as head and shoulders formations, pattern recognition and artificial intelligence, market sentiment, astrological patterns, and so on. *In essence technical analysis is concerned with the timing of the market or when things might happen.*

MONEY MANAGEMENT

Money management *is the evaluation of risk and reward in a trade, which is the essence of trading, and the measure of how efficiently investment capital is used.* Anyone making a trade must fully understand the amount of risk incurred for the possible reward. Trading methods are often heralded for their potential rewards but the issue of risk is seldom addressed. Yet risk and reward are integral to trading. The opportunity for profit is always balanced by the ever present potential for risk. Successful trading is impossible without understanding these concepts.

An efficient use of capital provides the highest return for a given level of risk. For trading this means determining the amount of risk and reward taken on any trade, diversification of markets, holding time of a position, and type of trading method used. Combining money management with the proper trading method is crucial to developing a successful trading strategy. *A trader may develop a profitable trading method but may still lose money if proper money management techniques are not followed.*

PSYCHOLOGY OF THE TRADER

Psychology *refers to the state of mind of the trader and how the trader is involved in the entire trading process. Psychology is the crux of trading because your choice of trading methods and money management techniques will be based on your psychology and outlook on life.* Why choose a technical trading method over a fundamental one? What money management techniques should be applied? No method will guarantee success, so why do some traders believe in one method while other traders swear by another?

Psychology is the most important but least understood aspect of trading. How a trader deals with winning and losing periods will be crucial in developing a sound long-term trading strategy. A trader may have one of the finest trading methods and superb money management methods but still may not possess the psychological traits requisite for successful trading. The trader may not be able to take the stress involved in trading or have the self-control necessary to carry out the trading plan. The trading process is extremely demanding of your mind, body, and soul, so it is essential to know what you expect to attain from trading. Why do you want to trade?

TRADING IS AN INTERACTIVE PROCESS OF THE THREE ELEMENTS

Many traders are often bewildered by the myriad number of trading methods and money management techniques available. Most continually wonder which method is the best. It is generally inaccurate to think one method is better than another but instead the choice is often dependent on the individual's psychology and philosophy on life. You must be able to live with your choice of methods and believe they work.

Most traders focus on only the first aspect of trading methods, trying to find the magical trading system that works and guarantees fortunes, but their search is often disappointing. *All three elements are integral and essential to successful trading.* Combining trading methodology with money management techniques and psychology is an interactive procedure. You can progress at one level but will not be able to trade effectively and enhance your skills unless progress occurs at all levels. For example, you may believe you have the best trading method available but if you cannot convince yourself to trade on the signals you will never be able to trade. A trader who is weak in one area will be held back in the other two areas.

PHILOSOPHY OF TRADING

Trading is both an art and a science. The artist and scientist both seek to understand and express their ideas about the universe through different means. Trading is a study of the market and oneself. The trader may use the knowledge of any discipline to seek a better understanding of the ways of the market. The only limitation imposed on a trader is his or her own creativity and ability.

This is a book about theory and application. Many books deal with theory, but trading demands application. Any theory, no matter how eloquent or convincing, is meaningless unless proven in trading. Unlike many subjects, theories in trading can be quickly tested and easily proven right or wrong with sometimes brutal efficiency. This is a book about applying many different concepts to the process of trading.

There are many books written on trading methods, which are an important aspect of trading. However, the process of trading is much more difficult and involved than simply applying a trading method and naively believing you can instantly make money. There is far more to trading than just using a trading method or desiring to make money. The use of a trading method is actually one step in the long evolutionary process of trading.

No other endeavor depends so strongly on the immediate results of just one person in such a nebulous environment. Many other occupations require precision and results, such as medicine, but often the outcome is in cooperation with others. Physicians must go to school and follow rules and procedures that are developed and generally accepted by their peers. The artist works in a nebulous environment but the results may not be judged for years, decades, or lifetimes. Trading is different. There are few rules, less instruction, and little guidance, but the outcome is always definite—profit or loss.

APPROACH TO TRADING

I take a probabilistic view of the market. No technical or fundamental trading pattern is infallible in making or losing money, but various patterns have a higher or lower chance of making money in different times and markets. Trading is a business. You should make trades only when the probabilities are in your favor. Trade when you have an advantage and not out of boredom, hoping to make money, wanting to get back money previously lost, or the host of other poorly conceived reasons for trading. What is important is not the outcome of one event, but rather whether the correct trading decision was made in the first place.

CONCLUSION

Trading is a process that requires the development of a successful trading method, good money management techniques, and the understanding of yourself. This is a long and involved process, but it the trader is successful, the many rewards may well justify the time and effort expended.

PART ONE

TRADING METHODS

If a man will begin with certainties, he shall end in doubts; but if he will be content to begin with doubts he shall end in certainties.

Francis Bacon, *The Advancement of Learning*

Chapter 2

Fundamentals of Markets

By nature, men are nearly alike; by practice, they get to be wide apart.
Confucius, *The Confucian Analects*

It were not best that we should all think alike; it is difference of opinion that makes horse races.
Mark Twain, *Pudd'nhead Wilson*

PURPOSE OF MARKETS

Markets are integral to a modern society, serving many purposes.

1. The efficient transfer of goods or services.
2. Price discovery.
3. Transfer of capital to productive areas.
4. Transfer of risk.
5. Exchange of ideas.

1. *Efficient transfer of goods or services*: Markets provide a place to conveniently buy and sell goods and services. Buyers and sellers can go to or call one location and trade large quantities of the product.

9

2. *Price discovery*: One of the most important functions of a market is to establish a "fair" price—one on which buyers and sellers agree. Markets allow buyers and sellers to agree on a price for a good. A fair price implies the best price for the general welfare of all the people. Highly competitive markets have typically been the most efficient and fairest markets. If there is greater demand, then prices go up; if there is greater supply, prices go down. This has proved far better than other systems, such as bumbling bureaucrats trying to determine the right price.

3. *Transfer of capital to productive areas*: The debt and equity markets allow the transfer of money to more productive uses. For example, a corporation may issue debt or equity to buy assets that will allow it to expand or become more productive. Entrepreneurs can realize some of their ideas by raising money through these markets and creating wealth for society. Investors with capital, but without the vision of the entrepreneur or the necessary time, can channel some of their funds into these new enterprises. The debt and equity markets have been essential for the growth of economic prosperity for everyone through capitalism.

4. *Transfer of risk*: Capital is often exchanged for risk in a market. A byproduct of the transfer of capital to productive uses is the transfer of risk. For example the buyer of stock becomes part owner in a company and assumes some of the risks of the company in exchange for potential profits. The purchase of a bond does not usually entitle ownership in a company as an equity purchase might, but the debt buyer does take partial risk in exchange for potentially less reward. Another market designed for the transference of risk is the futures market.

5. *Exchange of ideas*: Markets have become an increasingly important way to exchange ideas. The needs of buyers and sellers can be presented in a market, which helps to improve the existing market and also create new ones.

EQUITY AND DEBT MARKETS

The debt markets are among the biggest in the world. *Debt* is an obligation to repay an amount (called the *premium*) at a stipulated price (called the *interest*) for a predetermined time (*time to maturity*). The government is one of the biggest issuers of debt, and corporations are also an important part of this market. A debtor borrows money and a creditor lends it. The government is usually a huge borrower, and the people may often be the creditors (but not always). The equity or stock markets are also some of the largest markets in the world. An important distinction between equity and debt is that equity usually confers ownership and/or the ability to participate in the wealth of the company. The creditor can only make a profit on the interest received, but the equity owner may share in the potential prosperity of the company. In return for this reward the stockholder usually takes on more risk, especially if the company suffers economic hardship. Another distinction between debt and equity is in the repayment of income to the stockholder. The equity owner's reward is usually less definite and may occur through dividends and often through capital appreciation of the stock and so is not guaranteed. Since equity is considered more risky than debt, many investors feel the reward should be greater for equity than for debt.

A **future** *or a* **commodity** *is an item or good which is indistinguishable from a similar good.* The term "future" is a newer term but is essentially synonymous with the word "commodity" and will be used interchangeably. An example of a commodity is a certain grade of wheat or crude oil. Once the grade is established, the good can be traded and considered a commodity. Items which vary, such as wine or artwork, are not commodities (although one wonders sometimes) because they change from year to year as well as from the same producer.

A **futures contract** *is the obligation to buy or sell the underlying physical or cash commodity at a specific price and time.* Assume it is March and you feel the price of gold will rise so you buy one December gold contract presently trading at $400. In April the December contract drops to $390 yielding a $10 loss but you decide to hold for higher prices. The market rallies in May and you end up selling out the position at $405 for a $5 profit. This is an example of a futures transaction.

HISTORY OF FUTURES MARKETS

Commodity markets have been in existence for approximately 5000 years. The ancient Sumerians recorded commodity transactions beginning around 3000 B.C. Active markets existed in China, Egypt, India, and Arabia as long ago as 1000 B.C. The Roman and Greek civilizations developed markets similar to present day commodity markets. The Japanese had a futures market that traded rice in the 1600's. The concept of the modern futures market and exchange began in the 1800's in Chicago. The present-day domestic exchanges are located in Chicago and New York with important foreign exchanges in London and Tokyo.

REASON FOR A FUTURES MARKET

One of the main reasons for a futures market is to transfer price risk. Futures markets allow one group to hedge or transfer price risk to another group willing to accept the risk. For example, a farmer growing soybeans which will be ready for harvest in August wants to sell the beans in March to lock in August prices. The farmer can sell soybean, futures which will help to protect any drop in price between March and August.

Another important function of the futures market is price discovery. What should the price of a commodity be? **Price discovery** means determining the proper price for a commodity. In a capitalistic economy the fair price of a commodity is determined by the market forces of supply and demand. In a communist or socialist economy prices are arrived at by bureaucrats or other government agencies. Historically the capitalist system has been much more efficient and fair in both price discovery and social welfare than the corresponding communist system.

A benefit of the organized futures market is that it provides a centralized location with consistent rules for buying or selling the commodity. Anyone wishing to make a transaction need only look at the prices on a screen, pick up the phone, and call a broker to execute a trade. This is much more efficient than calling different locations to obtain a variety of prices and then finally making a transaction.

Another benefit of the futures market is that it provides for more stable pricing over the long term. Any realistic study has concluded that futures markets tend to dampen price fluctuations and reduce the volatility of prices. This is clearly beneficial to society.

PLAYERS OF A FUTURES MARKET

The two major players in the futures markets are:

1. *Hedgers:* **Hedging** *is the process of transferring risk to protect against a loss.* Hedging is an important economic function and is integral to certain businesses such as insurance and banking. The futures market began out of the need for hedgers to transfer risk. Hedgers can be farmers, food processors, oil refiners, banks, and many other types of people and businesses that face price risk. Hedgers fall into two basic categories:

a. Risk associated with the price going down. Producers or any business long inventory of the commodity are at risk if the price drops.

b. Risk associated with the price going up. Distributors or any business which has a contract to deliver the commodity at a specific price and time are at risk if the price goes up.

2. *Speculators:* **Speculation** *is the business of taking on risk in expectation of a profit.* The speculator hopes to profit (but is by no means guaranteed a profit) by taking on price risk which the hedger does not want. This transfer of risk is shown in Figure

FIGURE 2.1
The futures markets function as a way to transfer risk from the hedger to the speculator.

2.1. The speculator also provides depth and liquidity to a market which makes the market more efficient. Speculators fall into two basic categories:

a. *Floor traders* provide an immediate market and liquidity for hedgers and off-floor traders.

b. *Off-floor traders* provide depth and liquidity for the market.

One of the arguments against speculation is that some people believe speculators cause markets to be more volatile. Virtually any unbiased study has concluded that speculation actually tends to reduce volatility. It may be possible that speculators do exaggerate some market moves at certain times. Nevertheless they more than compensate for this by providing depth and liquidity, which are essential for any market to exist. Liquid markets are the backbone of capitalism and are integral to the well being of society.

HEDGING EXAMPLES

Hedging If Prices Go Down

One of the easiest examples of hedging, and probably one of the first ways futures markets were used, is in the agricultural area. Homer is a soybean farmer considering using futures.

In March Homer notes the price of the August soybean future contract is $7.00 a bushel. He can make a reasonable profit if he sells his beans at this price but he is concerned that prices may head lower between March and August. However, he cannot sell his beans in the cash market because his crop will not be ready for harvest until August. He can instead use the futures market and sell soybean futures for August delivery at the prevailing price of $7.00 a bushel. He will have to calculate the number of bushels of soybeans on his farm and then sell the proper number of bushels in the futures market. This will lock in the August price so that he no longer faces the risk of the price dropping. He decides to sell the futures contracts so one of the following three possible scenarios will result:

Scenario 1: The price declines to $5 in August. Cash soybeans and the August future are quoted at $5.00 a bushel. Homer will sell his beans in the cash market for $5.00 and buy back the futures contract for $5.00. Therefore:

1. Loss from cash soybeans = $5.00 − $7.00
   = − $2.00
2. Profit from futures contract = $7.00 − $5.00
   = $2.00

The loss from the prevailing cash price will be negated by the profit from the futures contract.

Scenario 2: The price rises to $10.00 in August. Cash soybeans and the August future are quoted at $10.00 a bushel. Homer will sell his beans in the cash market for $10.00 and buy back the futures contract for $10.00. Therefore:

1. Profit from cash soybeans = $10.00 − $7.00
   = $3.00
2. Loss from futures contract = $7.00 − $10.00
   = − $3.00

The loss from the futures contract is offset by the profit from the prevailing cash price.

Scenario 3: The price remains at $7.00 in August. Homer will obtain $7.00 for his cash crop and breakeven on the futures contract.

Homer has been able to sell his crop of soybeans at his intended price irrespective of where the market trades through the use of the futures market. In all the examples the futures contract offsets the profit or loss from the cash crop. Homer has foregone the possibility of greater profits when prices rise for the protection against severe losses when prices decline. He has stabilized or eliminated a portion of the risk in his business. This stabilization has a profound effect on the economy and the consumer because it provides lower prices for the consumer and reduced risks for the producer.

Hedging If Prices Go Up

Many businesses are at risk if prices go up. Let's meet Rose, who is an oil refiner selling gasoline.

In May Rose agrees to sell gasoline to a retailer for $0.50 a gallon for December delivery. The price of the December futures contract is $0.45 a gallon so she expects to make a $0.05 profit on the deal. If December prices rise she will end up losing her profit and possibly even losing money on the deal. Is there a way to hedge the risk? Yes, she can buy December gasoline futures at $0.45 a gallon and lock in a $0.05 profit now. Three possible scenarios may arise:

Scenario 1: The price of gasoline rises in December. If the cash price rises to $0.50 a gallon then she will pay $0.50 for the gasoline and the futures contract.

1. Break even on the gasoline $= $0.50 - 0.50
$\qquad\qquad\qquad\qquad\qquad\quad = 0

2. Profit from the futures $\quad = $0.50 - 0.45
$\qquad\qquad\qquad\qquad\qquad\quad = 0.05

Whatever price the gasoline rises to will be offset by the profit from the futures contract.

Scenario 2: The price drops in December. If the price of gasoline drops to $0.40 a gallon then she will:

1. Profit from the gasoline $= $0.50 - 0.40
$\qquad\qquad\qquad\qquad\qquad\quad = 0.10

2. Loss from the futures $\quad = $0.40 - 0.45
$\qquad\qquad\qquad\qquad\qquad\quad = - 0.05

If the price of gasoline drops then she will make a $0.05 profit but forego making an even larger profit because of the loss from the futures contract.

Scenario 3: The price remains the same. Rose will make a $0.05 profit on the gasoline and break even on the futures contract.

This is an example of risk associated with prices going up. The farmer sold futures to lock in a price or hedge the risk of the price decreasing. In the second example the refiner bought futures to lock in a price and hedge against the price increasing. Note that in both examples neither hedger took possession of the actual commodity in the futures market.

RISKS IN HEDGING

Although hedging eliminates one kind of risk, it does not eliminate all kinds of risk. There are risks associated with hedging and using futures:

1. *Loss of product:* In the first example the farmer must realize he faces another risk if his crop is destroyed. Prices may rise and he may lose money on his futures position but not be able to offset this loss because his crops are gone. This is a frightening prospect and unfortunately possible. There are ways to get around this by using options, but there is always a cost or tradeoff in reducing risk that someone must pay.

2. *Forgoing favorable price moves:* By hedging the farmer has forgone any profit in prices going any higher but has protected himself and his business if prices go lower. The farmer's main concern is not to make big profits if the price goes higher but to be sure he can make a living and protect himself if prices should move lower. If prices were to drop too low it could mean the difference between being in or out of business. All hedgers forego the possibility of profits in exchange for the safety and continued profitability of their business.

3. *Basis risk:* Another risk in hedging is the basis risk. The two examples assumed the futures price followed the cash price but this does not always occur. If the futures price is significantly above or below the cash price, then the futures may not adequately protect the hedger from price risk.

4. *Margin calls:* The hedger must put up money if prices go severely against the position. The hedger may still have to put up more money even though the cash position offsets the price move.

5. *Quality risk:* The future represents a certain grade and quality in the commodity. The hedger may not have the same grade of the commodity, so there may be differentials in price.

SPECULATION EXAMPLES

Floor Traders

The floor of the exchange is the immediate and actual futures market where buyers and sellers come together for most futures contracts. The floor trader (market maker) makes a market by providing a bid at which the person may sell and an ask at which the person may buy. This **spread**, or difference in the bid and ask, is how the floor trader attempts to profit in speculation. Many people believe this is an easy way to make money but in fact it is very difficult. What may have been the bid just a second ago may not even be an offer anymore and the trader may have a big loss when a small profit was expected.

Market makers are essential for liquid markets. The floor trader takes on the risk of others who wish to enter or exit the market. Some question the need for market makers and feel a market of hedgers will function adequately. If the market were simply composed of hedgers, then who would take on the risk of the hedger? What if a hedger wanted to buy a contract but no other hedgers wanted to take the opposite side and so would not sell at that time? There would be no market. There have been instances of hedgers not being able to trade a market which lead to its demise due to little or no participation by market makers. The orders by hedgers were not enough to keep the market liquid or efficient.

In effect the action of market makers is very important in enhancing the liquidity of a market. Market makers generally have a short-term perspective and may hold a position for only seconds, or much longer positions for weeks or months.

Off-Floor Traders

Off-floor traders provide depth to a market, further enhancing the liquidity of the market. Some off-floor traders can hold huge positions and are able to absorb some of the large orders which hedgers or other floor traders cannot take. Others provide more liquidity simply by their trading.

Off-floor traders generally have a longer term perspective than market makers and often try to position themselves for larger moves.

Most are concerned about fills and liquidity but do not try to buy the bid and sell the offer, but rather attempt to profit from trends in the market or volatility plays in options.

DISTINCTION BETWEEN SPECULATION AND GAMBLING

Speculation and gambling are two entirely different occupations. Speculation is necessary in a capitalist society to take on the risk of the hedgers or provide capital for businesses and government. This action enhances liquidity and makes for more efficient pricing. Speculators make markets in the various commodities and therefore provide an immediate and efficient market for hedgers.

Gambling is a form of entertainment and is not done to take on the risk of hedgers or to provide capital for companies or governments. Gambling is an important part of our society but it does not fulfill the same economic role as speculation.

GAME THEORY

Game theory *is a branch of mathematics which deals with the decision-making process.* Certain rules in game theory help in determining the proper decision to make, given a set of choices. Game theory is not simply a study of games, but a fascinating study of how many different complex problems and situations actually have similar, and sometimes simple solutions.

The business of speculation or trading is highly reliant upon the decision process. Therefore game theory is helpful in understanding some of the decisions required in trading. Another reason game theory is important in trading is that the futures market is a zero-sum game which is one of the games studied in game theory.

ZERO-SUM AND NONZERO-SUM GAMES

A **zero-sum game** *is a game where the amount lost by one or more parties is equally made by one or more parties.* As an example the game of chess is a two person zero-sum game. There can only be one winner and loser, or a draw. The card game of poker is an example of a two or greater person zero-sum game. If there are three poker players then one player can win at the expense of the other two players or two players can win at the expense of one player, but three players can never win because at least one player must lose.

A zero-sum game is not limited to games of fun like chess and poker. Far more serious applications include political elections, wars between countries and marketing a product.

The futures market is a zero-sum game, i.e., an equal amount of money is made and lost. For example, Richard buys a March sugar contract from Sam at 950. If the price of sugar increases to 960 then Richard will make 10 points which is the amount Sam will lose. If the price of sugar drops then Richard will lose what Sam makes. One will make what the other loses if they are on opposite sides of a transaction. When there are more players then the profits and losses may become more magnified. Keep in mind there are not necessarily the same number of winners and losers. If $1,000 is made by one person, ten people might lose $100. The game is actually less than zero-sum because commissions and other expenses must be included.

The stock market is an example of a nonzero-sum game. Assume Richard buys a stock for $100 and a week later sells it to Sam for $110. Sam sells the same stock a week later for $120. Both make $10 on the stock and no other party has lost money. Where did the wealth arise from? The value of the stock or equity in the company has increased creating new wealth. The same wealth creation can yield losses for everyone when stock prices decline. If Richard buys a stock for $100 and sells it to Sam the following week for $90 and Sam sells the stock for $80 a week later, then both parties lose $10. In this example both parties are losers because the value of the stock or equity in the company has decreased.

Is one game better than another? Is a zero-sum game better than a nonzero-sum game? No. Each game is appropriate for the specific situation. A nonzero-sum game is suitable when ownership of an asset occurs whereas a zero-sum game is more apropos for hedging.

DISTINCTIONS BETWEEN FUTURES MARKETS AND STOCK AND BOND MARKETS

The futures markets exist for entirely different, but equally important, economic reasons than the stock and bond markets. The futures markets have come under criticism by unknowing individuals and so-called "experts" who do not understand the distinctions. The function of the stock and bond markets is to raise capital for companies and governments. This is significantly different than the economic purpose of the futures markets, which is to hedge price risk. This is one of the reasons why margins, which we will soon examine, are much lower in futures than in other markets.

One of the most important distinctions, from the perspective of a trader in futures versus all other markets, is that timing is much more critical to success in futures trading. Leverage is much greater in futures trading because margins are much lower. A market move which goes against the trader's position may have more serious consequences than in other markets. Some futures traders have made or lost as much as 50–100% of their capital in one day—an amount which would be significant for an entire year in the stock and bond markets.

THE EFFICIENT MARKET HYPOTHESIS

The efficient market hypothesis is based on the premise that all information relevant to the market is already known so the trader can not hope to make money over time because he has no advantage over any other player. As a result the market is random so it is mathematically impossible to make money consistently. Those who believe in the efficient market point out studies which supposedly prove markets are random. They further contend that those who have made money were lucky or had better access to information than the general public. However, there are some major weaknesses with the efficient market hypothesis:

1. *To prove randomness is mathematically impossible.* A study may suggest either randomness or nonrandomness, but no study can prove randomness with absolute certainty because there may be an order to the system but we are not aware of it. Is the pattern in

FIGURE 2.2
Is the pattern random or is there a hidden pattern to it?

Source: Courtesy the author, Robert P. Rotella, copyright Robert P. Rotella.

Figure 2.2 random or is there an order to it? Furthermore, there may appear to be random patterns in one time frame but very clear nonrandom behavior may exist on shorter or longer time frames. For example, a market may appear to be random with monthly data but not with daily data. It is nearly impossible to quantify every time frame because there are so many.

2. *Assuming all information is available, does that imply every investor will arrive at the same conclusion from the same information?* Does every fundamental analyst have the same predictions for the economy, or is there disagreement amongst them? Will they change their minds even if no new information is disseminated? To assume people have the same feelings about the same information or that they may not

change their minds is to take a rather naive view about human nature.

3. *Markets do trend.* Any efficient market believers who were actually short the stock market for the past 50 years might reconsider their hallowed theory. Of course, it is possible that the strong upward trend in the stock market, or a strong trend in any market, is a "short-term aberration" in a long-term random phase. But 50 years and many dollars later is long enough for me to believe markets trend. The burden of proof is on the efficient market proponents because their key argument of randomness can never be proven.

Finally, we can approach this subject from a different angle with a somewhat philosophical view. Since even an efficient market believer will admit randomness cannot be proven with 100% certainty, let us assume we do not know if the markets are random or not. You now have a choice. Pursue trading and possibly be successful or choose some other endeavor. The choice is yours. We will let the believers in the efficient market debate the nature of life and the state of the market, but we will get on with the business of speculation.

MARGINS

Margin *is the amount of money required to maintain a position in the commodity.* Margins in futures are generally 1–15% of the underlying cash market. Margins in futures markets are lower than in the cash market for two important reasons:

1. Margins are a function of the volatility or absolute movement of the market. They are not dependent on the value of the underlying commodity. Money is not required to buy a commodity because the position never implies ownership of the underlying physical. Instead, margin money is a good faith deposit, put up to cover losses in the event the market should go against the position.

2. The futures markets serve a different economic purpose than the cash markets. Futures markets are needed for price protection, in a way similar to insurance companies' protecting policyholders

from risk. If a policyholder had to pay a premium or margin equal to the amount of protection, few people could afford the insurance. For example, few people would want to put up $30,000 for car insurance on a $30,000 car, even if they would eventually get back all the money. Besides the fact that there would be little need for the insurance, few people would even be able to afford it.

Sometimes as much as 90% or more of the margin requirements for futures can be met with T-Bills. This amount is dependent on the FCM (futures commission merchant) better known as a brokerage firm. Since there is not a significant outlay of cash, much of the interest cost is forgone in buying or selling futures. This will be an important point when determining the price of a futures contract.

THE BASIS

The futures price normally reflects the cash price of the commodity. If the cash price increases the futures price usually increases, and if the cash price decreases the futures price decreases. However the futures price does not have to equal the cash price except at expiration of the contract. *The basis* or **premium** *is the difference between the futures price and the cash price.* The basis is an important concept in futures pricing. One of the best ways to understand the calculation of the basis is to determine how a futures price is determined.

Factors which affect the futures price and the basis are:

1. Cash price of the underlying commodity
2. Prevailing short-term interest rate
3. Holding and storage costs to store the cash commodity
4. Holding period of the contract—expiration date of the futures contract
5. Cash yields—dividends or coupons of the underlying which affect the cost to carry the commodity
6. Volatility of the market
7. Market sentiment
8. Composition of the index

The first five factors are usually the most important and easily measured determinants of the price of a futures contract. Let's calculate the basis for crude oil futures using the first five factors in the following example. Keep in mind the futures price must equal the cash price at expiration of the futures contract.

Example: What should the price be on January 21 of the August crude oil futures contract which expires on July 21?

The cash price for crude oil	= $20.00
Short term interest rate	= 8%
Storage and holding costs	= 2%
Holding time	= 6 months (July 21–January 21)
Yield	= 0%

We will calculate the futures price on a per barrel basis to reduce the number of zeros, but remember the actual cash outlay is on the full value of the contract. If the spot crude oil is purchased on March 15 for $20 and stored till September, the cost to hold the crude oil is:

$$\text{Cost} = \text{Cash price} \cdot \text{time held} \cdot (\text{interest rate} + \text{storage cost})$$
$$= (\$20.00) \cdot (6 \text{ months}/12 \text{ months}) \cdot (.08 + .02)$$
$$= \$1.00$$

If a futures contract on the crude oil is bought most of the margin can be met with treasury bills so no interest is foregone. Therefore the futures price is equal to the cash price plus the cost to hold the commodity:

$$\text{Futures price} = \$20.00 + \$1$$
$$= \$21.00$$

The August crude oil contract should be trading at approximately $21.00 per barrel. Since the basis is the difference between the futures price and the cash price, the basis represents the cost to hold the cash commodity.

$$\text{Basis} = \text{Futures price} - \text{cash price}$$
$$= \$21.00 - \$20.00$$
$$= \$1.00$$

FIGURE 2.3

Spread between the September 1990 S&P500 future and cash

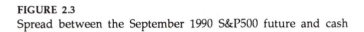

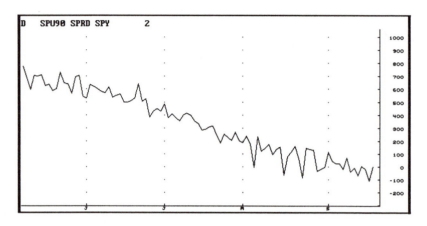

Source: Reprinted with permission, FutureSource, 955 Parkview Blvd., Lombard, IL 60148 (800) 621-2628.

This is the way most futures prices are calculated. The basis normally increases as the life of the contract increases because it is highly dependent on the cost to hold the commodity. Figure 2.3 shows the actual difference between the futures and cash price of the S&P500 as the futures reaches expiration. The basis gradually decreases with time until it eventually reaches zero. If the actual basis fluctuates too much from the theoretical basis, then arbitrageurs will enter the market to bring the basis back into line.

As noted, the futures price must equal the cash price at expiration but each exchange deals with the expiration process differently for each contract. With some contracts such as coffee the buyer can take delivery of the actual product. With other contracts such as stock index futures the futures price must equal the cash price at expiration. This is called a **cash settlement**, and no actual delivery of the physical market occurs. The account is simply debited or credited by the difference in the cash and the entry prices.

We have dealt with the first four elements which affect the futures price because they are easier to quantify. The last four affect the futures price in the following ways:

5. *Cash yields:* Cash yields will lower the cost of carry and therefore reduce the basis. In this example the basis is positive but there are times when the basis can be negative. For example, if the coupon rate is greater than the short term interest rate (T-Bonds), then the basis can be negative. The basis is negative because the cost to carry is negative which means the buyer is paid to own the security. A bond pays a coupon to the holder.

Since crude oil pays no coupons or dividends there was no cash yield to consider in the calculation. Many of the financial futures do have a cash yield or other factors to consider. The stock market pays dividends and the calculation for the basis on stock index futures will be covered in the chapter on the stock market.

6. *Volatility:* The more volatile the market the more the actual futures price will vary with the cash price. This happens because it is harder to arbitrage or keep the markets in line when a market is volatile. Therefore a volatile market can make the basis much greater or smaller than it should be.

7. *Market sentiment:* In a bullish environment the futures price may trade higher than the theoretical price because investors wish to buy the futures. However, there have also been cases where the futures price trades lower than the theoretical price because investors do not believe the market will go higher and sell into the rally. The same holds true in a bearish scenario.

8. *Composition of the index:* If the index is geometric and not arithmetic, the basis is more complex to calculate. The CRB and Dollar indexes are examples of geometric indexes. The basis calculation for the Dollar index will be covered in the chapter on spreading.

NORMAL AND INVERTED MARKETS

For most markets the basis increases the longer the life of the contract because the cost to carry increases with time. *Therefore most futures with a longer time to expiration exhibit higher prices than futures closer to expiration.* This phenomenon is called a **normal market** and is depicted in Figure 2.4. The basis which was calculated previously determines the shape of the line.

FIGURE 2.4
Normal market: Futures that have a longer time to expiration should have a higher price than the ones closer to expiration in a normal market.

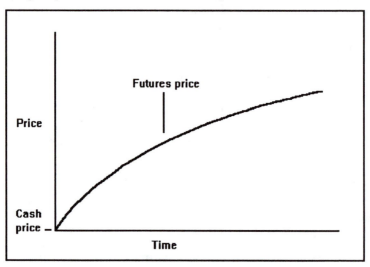

FIGURE 2.5
Inverted market: Futures prices decrease with increasing time to expiration in an inverted market.

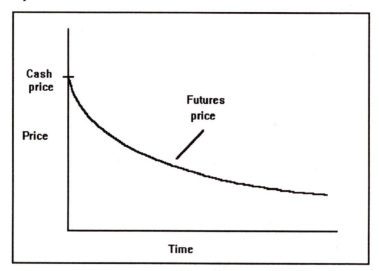

An **inverted market** *happens when the opposite phenomena occurs and the price of the longer term future decreases with time.* Inverted markets may naturally occur in interest rate or currency markets for different reasons but one important reason is always the level of interest rates. Figure 2.5 is an example of an inverted market.

Inverted markets may also occur when a supply and demand imbalance develops in the commodity over different time periods. For example, the short-term supply of copper may be low due to a strike by workers. However the supply in the long term will probably not be affected because the strike may end soon. Therefore the nearby futures price may be much higher than the price of the further out months due to the scarcity in the short term.

ARBITRAGE

In the crude oil example the theoretical price of the futures was determined to be $21.00 but the actual market price can and will deviate from the theoretical price. If the actual futures price is $21.50, traders will seek to make a profit by buying the cash at $20.00 and selling the futures at $21.50. Since the futures price must equal the cash price at expiration the trader will make the difference between the actual basis and the theoretical basis:

1. Profit at expiration from selling the futures and buying cash:

   Actual basis   = Futures price – cash price
                  = $21.50 – $20.00
                  = $1.50

2. Loss from holding the cash till expiration:

   Theoretical basis = Cost to carry which was previously determined to be $1.00

3. Net profit from the transaction:

   Profit = Actual basis – theoretical basis
           = $1.50 – $1.00
           = $0.50

The investor may make $.50 per barrel or $500 per contract without incurring a great amount of risk.

If the actual future price is significantly below the theoretical price, the opposite transaction happens. The investor will buy the future and sell the cash. Assume the future is trading at $20.30 and the cash at $20.00. The investor will forego the $1.00 in interest cost by being short the cash (in other words the investor does not have to pay the cost to carry the cash commodity):

Actual basis   = $20.30 - $20.00

               = $.30

Theoretical basis = $1.00

Profit   = Loss at expiration + interest received

         = - $0.30 + $1.00

         = $0.70

This type of trading is called *arbitrage*. **Arbitrage** *is the simultaneous buying and selling of similar or related instruments or securities to obtain near risk-free profits.* In the above example the arbitrageur is not taking an opinion about the market but instead keeping the futures market in line with the cash market. This is an important function because if the futures and cash markets are out of line with each other then the markets will become inefficient and not serve their intended purpose. Therefore arbitrageurs seek a profit in keeping the markets in line and in the process make the markets more efficient.

WHAT IS A MARKET?

The answer may be obvious, but in fact a market has a myriad of connotations with different people. Markets do not simply move on cold economic data and news reports. Markets are people. Markets change when peoples' perceptions change and stay the same if peoples' feeling about the future remains the same.

Markets exhibit behavior similar to that observed in crowds. In crowd psychology the lowest common denominator may rule. The individual thinker has an edge when this happens and this will be further explored in Part Three, "Psychology and Trading."

CONCLUSION

Free markets are the cornerstone of capitalism and serve many functions in a modern society. The efficient transfer of goods, price discovery, capital and risk transfer, and exchange of ideas are some of the functions markets provide. Risk and the opportunity for reward are always present when prices fluctuate due to changes in supply and demand. The stock and bond markets arose as a means to raise capital. The futures markets evolved to hedge price fluctuations and risk from one group—the hedger—to another group—the speculator. Both participants are required for an efficient market.

CHAPTER 3

Fundamental Analysis

Every individual necessarily labors to render the annual revenue of the society as great as he can. . . . He intends only his own gain, and he is in this, as in many other cases, led by an invisible hand to promote an end which was no part of his intention. . . . By pursuing his own interest he frequently promotes that of the society more effectually than when he really intends to promote it.

Adam Smith, *Wealth of Nations*

Fundamental analysis is the study of various factors which affect the supply and demand situation of a market. The fundamental analyst makes an assessment of important variables that might influence the market to derive the proper price of a good now or in the future. The work is inherently predictive because the analyst makes projections regarding the future supply and demand equation of the market. Fundamental analysis generally deals with broader movements of a longer term nature and is not as concerned with precise market timing. The fundamentalist often looks at the cause and effect of one variable and its impact on the market.

One argument against fundamental analysis is that it is impossible to predict the future, and there is no way to analyze all the myriad factors which influence the market. The argument is true but does not diminish the significance of fundamental analysis. Less time should be spent deriding both technical and fundamental analysis but instead more time should be used to ascertain how they can be of benefit to the trader. Learning the important fundamentals of a market can provide the trader with a deeper understanding of the supply and demand equation of the market. Learning the technical aspects of a market may help a person better time a trade. Knowing fundamental information in conjunction with technical analysis may prove valuable in helping the individual analyze and trade the market more effectively.

SUPPLY AND DEMAND CURVES

A typical supply curve depicted in Figure 3.1 demonstrates that the *supply of a good increases as the price increases*. This is called the **normal supply curve** and is based on the idea that as the price for the good increases more producers are willing to sell their product at the higher prices. For example if the price of oil increases then more oil producers will sell more oil to take in more revenue. If

FIGURE 3.1
Supply curve: The supply increases as the price increases on the normal supply curve.

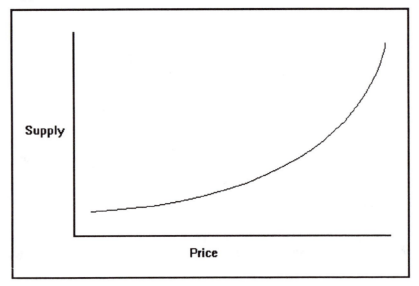

FIGURE 3.2
Demand curve: The demand decreases with increasing price in the normal demand curve.

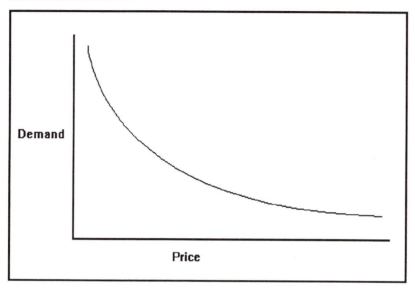

Demand

Price

the price increases for a long enough time producers will increase their efforts to find more oil to satisfy demand.

The normal demand curve depicted in Figure 3.2 shows how the demand for a good increases as the price decreases. This curve is based on the precept that people will often decrease their demand for an item as the price increases. As an example, if the price of meat becomes too high, people will reduce their consumption and look for alternative items. If the price of the good decreases then people will purchase more of the good thereby increasing demand.

You may have noticed that the lines at the extreme ends of the price axis become nearly horizontal or vertical. For example, on the demand curve the line becomes almost vertical at high prices and almost horizontal at low prices. A similar effect is noted on the supply curve where the line becomes almost vertical at high prices and almost horizontal at low prices. *These areas where the price line is almost horizontal or vertical are called* **price inelastic regions.** Price inelasticity occurs where a change in price may slightly alter or not affect the demand or supply in a market. The range between the two extremes is called price elastic because the supply and demand is affected by price. *The supply and demand of a good that is affected by price changes is called* **elastic,** *whereas the supply and demand of a good that is unaffected by price changes is termed* **price inelastic.**

Why does price inelasticity happen? After a certain point for each commodity a price change will not appreciably affect the supply or demand of the good. How could this occur? In the example with meat, if the price increases too much people will not be able to afford meat and there will be virtually no demand. If the price drops too low people will buy more meat but only up to a certain amount because they can only eat so much per day. The same logic applies to producers.

Since demand and supply are both a function of price, let's combine the supply and demand graphs in Figure 3.3. The point

FIGURE 3.3
Supply and demand curves: The combination of the supply and demand curves yields an equilibrium price where supply and price equals demand and price.

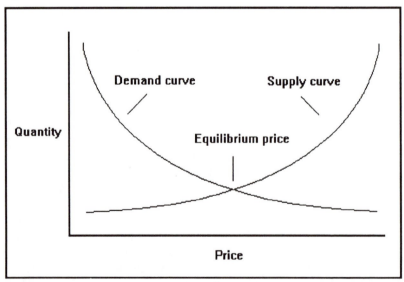

where the supply and demand curves cross is called the equilibrium point and this point determines the fair market price of the good. The fundamental analyst focuses on the equilibrium price to determine what the price of a commodity should be. Analyzing the future supply and demand forces in the market helps the fundamentalist to predict what the price should be in the future.

If the analyst believes the demand for an item will increase and supply will remain constant then the equilibrium price should move higher. If supply increases with demand then the price may not change appreciably.

SUPPLY AND DEMAND IN FUTURES

It is interesting to note how supply and demand can vary with different futures. Both the supply and demand for financial assets may change by large amounts in a relatively quick manner which will result in considerable price moves. An excess supply of stocks or bonds can cause prices to fall whereas strong demand can send prices soaring. In either case supply and demand can be difficult to estimate because both may vary greatly but both are essential to determining the future price.

The supply and demand equation for agricultural products is generally different than for financial futures. Supply may change radically due to weather related incidents or other natural causes such as insect damage. For example, a drought in the cocoa growing regions can destroy 40% of the crop causing prices to rise dramatically. If weather conditions and other factors are beneficial for growing cocoa then an abundant crop might cause prices to fall. In either case the supply of cocoa can greatly affect the market price.

The other side of the equation does not generally change so radically for agricultural products. Demand is relatively constant or usually changes by consistent amounts. For example, people do not usually change their intake of cocoa by large amounts. We do not triple our intake of chocolate one year and eat negative amounts the next. The same reasoning can be applied for other agricultural products such as the grains and the meat complex. Supply is often the more difficult and variable determinant in the price equation.

Demand may change greatly when the supply changes, causing large price changes. People will normally reduce their intake of cocoa when prices become too high. Too low a price will not necessarily increase demand appreciably because people will only eat so much. This is one reason why prices may be raised in tight supply situations but may not always go down by the same amount when supplies become more abundant.

MONEY

What is money? Because it is so frequently used we may tend to forget the important purposes it serves. Money functions in three important ways:

1. *Medium of exchange*: Money may be used as a unit of exchange in the buying and selling of goods or services. Without money the farmer would have to pay for all the things he needs with his crops or livestock. This could become rather tedious in the winter when he has no crop to sell. A lawyer would have to pay for—what *would* a lawyer pay with?
2. *Unit of account or common denominator*: Money provides us with a single measure of value to judge all other goods and services. If every good had a unique but unmeasurable value, we would not be able to judge which one was more or less valuable because there would be no common denominator to judge the worth of the item.
3. *Store of value*: Money allows us to accumulate and store the wealth we possess. Farmers do not have to store soybeans to obtain other goods but instead just store their wealth through money.

Money is integral to capitalism and provides a tremendous efficiency in economic transactions. Money facilitates the process of exchange and therefore improves the well-being of everyone. The amount of money in circulation is a measure of economic prosperity.

Since money is the measure of economic wealth and the medium of exchange it is important in the study of commodities. Investors are constantly deciding whether to exchange money for commodities, or one commodity for another. The flow of money from one commodity to another can easily be seen by the change in prices. If money is flowing into gold and out of Treasury bills, the price of gold is increasing and the price of bills is decreasing. The futures markets provide an interesting panorama of the ebb and flow of money from assets perceived to be overvalued to those perceived to be undervalued.

CONCLUSION

Fundamental analysis is the study of the determinants of supply and demand to see how they affect the price of a market. Fundamental analysis is concerned with how and why the market moves and is normally applied with a long-term perspective. The combination of technical and fundamental analysis may provide to be a powerful tool in trading a market.

CHAPTER 4

Foreign Exchange

I have always played a lone hand. I began that way in the bucket shops and have kept it up. It is the way my mind works. I have to do my own seeing and my own thinking.

Edwin LeFevre, *Reminiscences of a Stock Operator*

The foreign exchange market is the biggest market in the world, with transactions estimated between $50 to $500 billion a day. The exchange of United States dollars for German marks or British pounds for Japanese yen is an example of foreign exchange. Any time you buy a product with foreign parts or tour another country, you have involved yourself in foreign exchange. Foreign exchange trading offers the speculator some of the most liquid and fast moving markets of any futures available.

There are two major markets for foreign exchange:

1. *Cash interbank market*: The transactions that occur in this market are mainly between banks. Trading takes place all over the world, 24 hours a day, except on weekends. The minimum transaction size is around $1,000,000. Most currencies from any country can be traded though some are more liquid than others.

2. *Futures exchanges:* These transactions occur in the United States such as on the IMM futures exchange and are similar to other commodity contracts. Trading mainly takes place during the hours the exchange is open, but "after hours" trading is becoming increasingly popular with many traders. The transaction sizes range from $50,000 to over $100,000, and this is one of the main features which separates this market from the cash interbank market. This market is quite liquid but is limited to a few of the major currencies including:

1. German mark

2. Japanese yen

3. British pound

4. Swiss franc

5. Canadian dollar

6. Australian dollar

7. Dollar index—an index created in 1973 by the Federal Reserve Board which tracks the value of the dollar against ten currencies. The contract trades on the FINEX, a division of the New York Cotton Exchange. The ten currencies and their respective weights in the index are shown in Table 4.1.

TABLE 4.1
Dollar index composition and weight

Currency	Percent Weight
1. German mark	20.8
2. Japanese yen	13.6
3. French franc	13.1
4. British pound	11.9
5. Canadian dollar	9.1
6. Italian lira	9.0
7. Netherlands guilder	8.3
8. Belgian franc	6.4
9. Swedish krona	4.2
10. Swiss franc	3.6

Figures 4.1 through 4.6 are monthly graphs of the German mark, Japanese yen, British pound, Swiss franc, Canadian dollar, and Australian dollar versus the US dollar. Figure 4.7 is a monthly graph of the dollar index.

FIGURE 4.1
German mark versus the US dollar monthly chart

Source: Reprinted with permission, FutureSource, 955 Parkview Blvd., Lombard, IL 60148 (800) 621-2628

FIGURE 4.2
Japanese yen versus the US dollar monthly chart

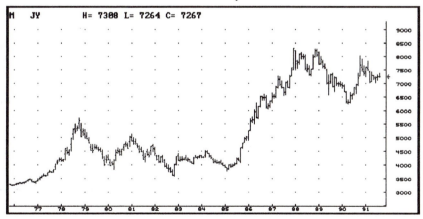

Source: Reprinted with permission, FutureSource, 955 Parkview Blvd., Lombard, IL 60148 (800) 621-2628

FIGURE 4.3
British pound versus the US dollar monthly chart

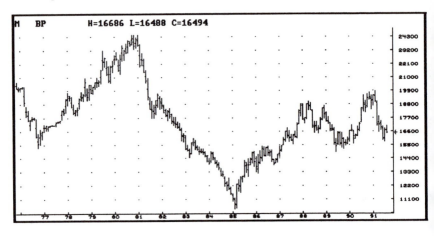

Source: Reprinted with permission, FutureSource, 955 Parkview Blvd., Lombard, IL 60148 (800) 621-2628

FIGURE 4.4
Swiss franc versus the US dollar monthly chart

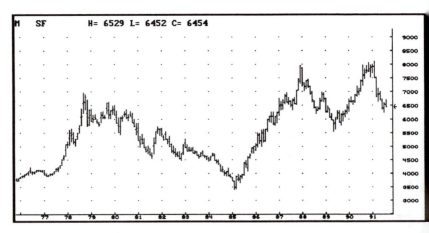

Source: Reprinted with permission, FutureSource, 955 Parkview Blvd., Lombard, IL 60148 (800) 621-2628

FIGURE 4.5
Canadian dollar versus the US dollar monthly chart

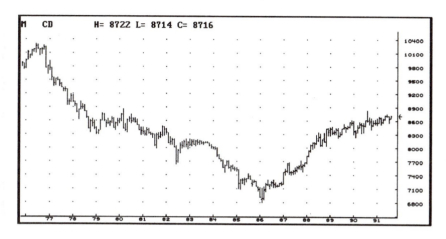

Source: Reprinted with permission, FutureSource, 955 Parkview Blvd., Lombard, IL 60148 (800) 621-2628

FIGURE 4.6
Australian dollar versus the US dollar monthly chart

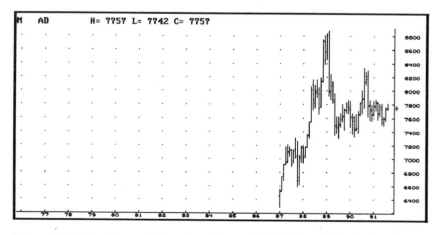

Source: Reprinted with permission, FutureSource, 955 Parkview Blvd., Lombard, IL 60148 (800) 621-2628

FIGURE 4.7
Dollar index monthly chart

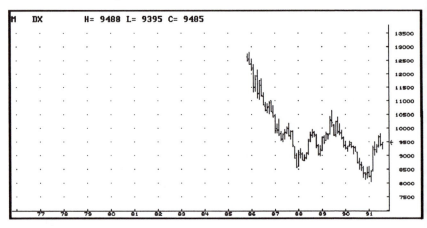

Source: Reprinted with permission, FutureSource, 955 Parkview Blvd., Lombard, IL 60148 (800) 621-2628

FIXED VERSUS FLOATING

Foreign exchange rates are allowed to float or change between each country. After World War II foreign exchange rates were fixed among the countries according to the Bretton Woods agreement. There are still people that argue fixed exchange rates are better for the world economy than floating rates. However, for rates to remain fixed, countries must coordinate their economic policies with other countries and manipulate interest rates and money supply to keep the exchange rate fixed. This can be politically difficult and economically impossible; which was the case, so the governments abandoned the Bretton Woods agreement in the early 1970s.

ECONOMIC NEED FOR HEDGING
IN FOREIGN EXCHANGE MARKETS

The need to hedge foreign exchange has become greater than ever with the burgeoning of world trade. Hedging by import and export companies in the foreign exchange market greatly facilitates world trade. Let's look at an example to see why a company might need to hedge in a foreign currency:

A stereo wholesaler signs an agreement in February to sell audio equipment to a retailer for $1,100,000 in September. She cannot buy the equipment until September when she will receive the money from the retailer. She agrees to purchase the equipment for $1,000,000 payable in yen in September from a Japanese manufacturer. However, if the value of the yen increases by 10% from February to September, the cost will increase to $1,100,000 which would negate the entire profit. If the value of the yen increases greater than 10% then she will begin to lose money on the deal. Of course, if the value of the yen decreases she will make more money on the deal, but her concern is not to speculate on foreign exchange but instead to hedge away the foreign exchange exposure.

She decides to buy $1,000,000 of yen in the futures market to protect the deal and lock in the $100,000 profit. In this case:

Scenario 1: If the value of the yen increases by 10%. The net profit on the goods is:

Cost of goods = $1,100,000
Sales price of good = $1,100,000
Net profit on goods   = $1,100,000 – $1,100,000
                      = $0

The net profit on the futures is:

Futures sales price = $1,100,000
Futures purchase price = $1,000,000
Net profit on futures = $1,100,000 – $1,000,000
                      = $100,000

The net profit on the transaction is:

Net on transaction = Net from goods + net from futures
                   = $0 + $100,000
                   = $100,000

Scenario 2: If the value of the yen decreases by 10%. The net profit on the goods is:

Cost of goods = $900,000
Sales price of goods = $1,100,000

Net profit on goods   = $1,100,000 - $900,000
                      = $200,000

The net profit on the futures is:

Futures sales price = $900,000
Futures purchase price = $1,000,000
Net profit on futures = $900,000 - $1,000,000
                      = -$100,000

The net profit on the transaction is:

Net on transaction = Net from goods + net from futures
                   = $200,000 - $100,000
                   = $100,000

Therefore she is assured of making her profit of $100,000 by hedging away the risk in the futures market.

This example covers an importer of goods but the same idea would apply for exporters. In general exporters need to hedge against a decline in the value of the currency of the country they are exporting to because they will receive less money for their goods.

Another important need for the foreign exchange market is the ability to buy or sell a currency. The ability to buy or sell crude oil or gold should be no different than the ability to buy or sell foreign currencies. Until the IMM opened, it was difficult for a person in the US to sell dollars or buy any other foreign currencies.

DETERMINANTS OF FOREIGN EXCHANGE

Some factors which affect the value of a currency are:

1. *Balance of payments:* The balance of payments of a country is based on the exports and imports of goods and services, and any other types of foreign transactions such as foreign aid or investment. This balance of payments helps to determine the value of the currency of a country. The net of exported goods and services versus the imported goods and services is called the balance of trade, and is often mentioned in determining the value of a currency. Examples of goods could be food supplies such as wheat, mechanical

items such as cars or technical equipment such as computers. Examples of services might be consulting, accounting, medical, or legal services.

2. *Productivity and natural resource allocation:* Goods and products are produced more efficiently when a business has a higher productivity rate. The more natural resources a country has, the more valuable its products are to other countries. Let's look at a simple example to see why certain currencies had more value than others in 1991:

a. *Japan:* The value of the yen was mainly due to the Japanese' technological ability of making excellent products at competitive prices. Japan has few natural resources.

b. *Saudi Arabia:* The value of the riyal was mainly due to the vast reserves of oil and wealth accumulated from these reserves. Unlike Japan, Saudi Arabia does not produce many technological goods but has rich natural resources.

c. *Haiti:* The value of the currency was low because there was little technology and few natural resources. Unfortunately Haiti was a poor country and the currency reflected this fact.

d. *United States:* The value of the dollar was due both to American technology and the abundant variety of natural resources available in the United States. The currency reflected this wealth.

If a country like the United States had both types of wealth, then why did its currency drop relative to other countries from 1985 to 1990? The important thing to remember is that the net amount of goods and services must be considered. The United States exported a large number of goods and services but it also imported a huge amount as well. If imports become too great the value of a currency may still drop even if the country has tremendous wealth. There are many other reasons why a currency may rise or fall which makes the study of foreign exchange both interesting and complex.

3. *Interest rates:* Interest rates are a reflection of the value or cost of money; so generally higher interest rates relative to other foreign interest rates help to strengthen the currency. For example, everything else being equal, if rates are 7% in the United States and 8% in England, investors would tend to put their money in England and receive better returns. Sometimes when a country's

economy is in trouble, interest rates may be extremely high just to keep money from flowing out of the country. In this case the currency may still be very cheap because interest rates alone cannot appreciably change the value of the currency or alleviate the problems of the economy.

4. *Inflation:* The value of a currency erodes with higher inflation so high inflation rates tend to decrease the value of a currency. If inflation rates in the United States and England were 5% and 6% respectively, investors would prefer to keep their money in the United States *ceteris paribus* (all else being equal).

5. *Economic growth:* The strength of a currency may often be linked to the growth prospects of the economy. A country that is growing becomes stronger economically and politically. In the short term the reverse effect may happen. If a country's economy becomes too strong too quickly, then inflation and the balance of payments may become a problem which can weaken the currency.

6. *Money supply:* The amount of money in circulation can affect the value of a currency for the long and short term. If a country prints too much money, the value of the currency should drop because there is too much money in circulation. If a country does not print enough money, the value of the currency should increase because there is not enough money to go around. The long-term implications of too little or too much money in circulation can affect the value of a currency, but the analysis can become rather complex. The velocity of money is another important factor which must be linked with money supply. The velocity of money is a measure of how quickly money is turned over or exchanged from one party to another. If the velocity is too slow as during the great depression then there will be little productive activity and economic growth. If the velocity is too fast then this may be a sign of too much inflation because people do not want to hold onto money for fear it will lose value.

7. *Political conditions*: a stable political situation and a government which fosters economic well-being for the people should tend to have a stronger currency. Political unrest and unresponsive government policies which inhibit business and economic growth such as high taxes and bureaucracies tend to decrease the value of the currency.

8. *Government and central bank manipulation:* A government may want to depress the value of its currency to make exports cheaper. It might go into the open market and sell large quantities of its currency. Another government may want to increase the value of its currency to maintain a parity with other currencies. It might buy large amounts of its currency in the open market in an attempt to raise the value. Political manipulation to increase or depress the value of a currency can change the value for the short term but in the long run the market will eventually determine the fair value of the currency. It is well to keep in mind that the value of a currency is the wealth and well-being of the country, and when the currency drops in value the people are poorer by that amount.

9. *Purchasing power parity:* The cost to purchase one set of goods in one country's currency versus the cost to purchase the same set of goods in another country's currency is called purchasing power parity. If a pound of coffee costs three Australian dollars in Australia but only two United States dollars in the United States, and the current exchange rate is $1 Australian = $1 US, then coffee is cheaper in the United States. A review of many of the basic goods and services between two countries will provide an indication of the purchasing power between the two nations.

10. *Other considerations:* There are other factors which affect the value of a currency. One important factor is investor's expectation about the value of the currency. Investors who are bullish on the currency may tend to bid the price of the currency up and vice versa. Seasonal influences may also affect the currency. Countries whose economies are based on tourism find their currency fluctuates relative to the prospects of foreign travel. Some factors which affect the value of a currency become more or less important with time. For example, in times of severe inflation money supply and inflation may be scrutinized more closely. At other times trade deficit numbers might be a focus of attention if the balance of payments is a problem.

SPOT AND FORWARD PRICING

The **spot market rate** *is the current actual exchange rate.* The spot rate is similar to a rate that a tourist would use to get immediate conversion of one currency for another. *The* **forward market rate** *is the exchange* *rate which can be locked in for a future time.* This rate is based on the spot rate plus the difference in interest rates between the countries. This is the rate which is traded more often because companies and investors are looking to hedge or speculate in the future as opposed to trading for an instant exchange. The forward may be calculated and is similar to the basis calculation for any other future.

CROSS RATES

Whenever any foreign currency transaction occurs the investor must always go long one currency and short another. An investor who buys a German mark contract with dollars has gone long the mark, but has implicitly gone short dollars because marks have been purchased in exchange for dollars.

What if an investor who owns dollars but has no opinion about the dollar wants to go long yen and short marks? The investor may buy $100,000 of yen (or whatever amount is required) and sell $100,000 of marks. The investor has now gone long yen and sold marks with no dollar exposure. This type of trade or exchange rate is called a cross rate. *A* **cross rate** *is simply the rate of exchange between two countries viewed from a third country.* It is a relative concept because a cross rate in the United States would be yen–mark and not dollar–mark. However in Germany a cross rate might be dollar–yen but not yen–mark.

CONCLUSION

The currency markets affect every other market so it is wise to have a good understanding of how they work. Hedging fluctuations in exchange rates can foster trade between countries. Our modern economy is dependent on international trade. Economic and technological progress can be fostered by encouraging international trade. The currencies are the backbone of trading between countries.

CHAPTER 5

Interest Rate Markets

The universe is change; our life is what our thoughts make it.

Marcus Aurelius Antoninus, *Meditations II*

INTEREST RATES

The interest rate market is one of the biggest and most important markets in the world. Much of the futures trading in interest rate vehicles is done on government obligations. *An* **interest rate** *is the cost of borrowing money for a specified period of time.* Interest rates are a good indication of the availability of money for borrowing and lending. If interest rates increase then the cost of money increases and vice versa. In effect interest rates are the cost of money.

TYPES OF INTEREST RATE CONTRACTS

Interest rate contracts are generally categorized into three broad groups:

1. *Short term*: This group would be obligations ranging from three months to a few years and includes treasury bills and eurodollars. Figures 5.1 and 5.2 are monthly graphs of Treasury bills and eurodollars respectively.

FIGURE 5.1
Treasury bill monthly chart

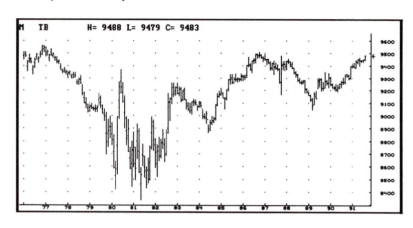

Source: Reprinted with permission, FutureSource, 955 Parkview Blvd., Lombard, IL 60148 (800) 621-2628

FIGURE 5.2
Eurodollar monthly chart

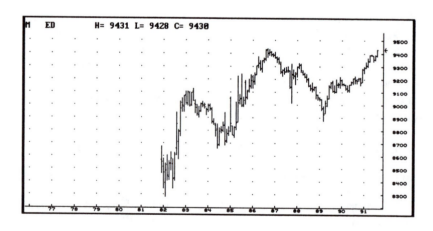

Source: Reprinted with permission, FutureSource, 955 Parkview Blvd., Lombard, IL 60148 (800) 621-2628

FIGURE 5.3
Ten-year note monthly chart

Source: Reprinted with permission, FutureSource, 955 Parkview Blvd., Lombard, IL 60148 (800) 621-2628

FIGURE 5.4
Treasury bond monthly chart

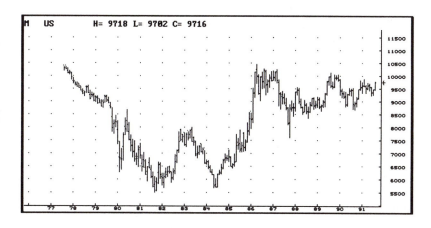

Source: Reprinted with permission, FutureSource, 955 Parkview Blvd., Lombard, IL 60148 (800) 621-2628

2. *Intermediate term*: This group consists of instruments ranging from approximately three years to 10 years and includes 5-year notes and 10-year notes. Figure 5.3 is a monthly graph of 10-year notes. 3. *Long term*: This group consists of obligations greater than 10 years, which include the treasury bond contract. Figure 5.4 is a monthly graph of the treasury bond contract.

The price of an interest rate obligation is inversely proportional to the interest rate. This simply means that if interest rates rise, the price of the contract falls, and if interest rates fall, the price of the contract rises.

Short-term obligations are priced as a function of the percent of the interest rate as shown in the following equation:

Future price = 100% – interest rate

If the T-bill rate is 8% then the T-bill future is equal to:

Future price = 100.00 – 8.00
            = 92.00

Therefore if the interest rate goes to 7%, the price of the T-bill goes up to 93.00 (100.00 – 7.00 = 93.00).

Figure 5.1 is a long-term graph of Treasury bills, and Figure 5.4 is a long-term graph of Treasury bonds. This helps to show the two extreme time frames and how one market may have traded much differently than another. The different interest rate maturities trend in the same direction, but there are times when they move in separate ways depending on economic conditions.

STRUCTURE OF INTEREST RATES

Interest rates have an important relationship with time and generally increase as the term to maturity increases. This phenomenon of increasing yields for longer term instruments is termed the normal yield curve and is depicted in Figure 5.5. The curve is positively sloping and is often measured with government issues.

There is not full agreement as to why long-term interest rates are usually higher than shorter-term rates. Some reasons why there are differences in rates with varying maturities include:

FIGURE 5.5
The normal yield curve, an upward sloping curve where interest rates increase at a decreasing rate.

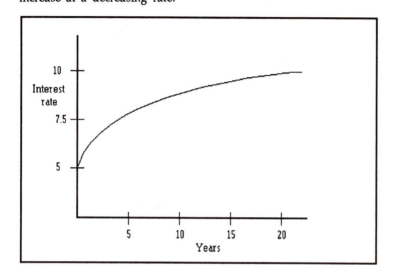

1. *Long-term debt is more risky*: The longer the term to maturity the greater the risk of default, so longer-term obligations should have an extra risk premium attached to the price.

2. *The prices of long-term debt are more volatile for an equal change in interest rates*: Long-term instruments may be more volatile because a change in interest rates affects the price of the long term instrument more than the short-term instrument. However, long-term rates may not change as much as short-term rates so sometimes long-term rates are not as volatile as short-term rates.

3. *There is an extra risk in borrowing short term*: There is an extra risk premium in borrowing short term because an investor who borrows short term and lends long term always faces the risk of losing more than can be gained. The borrower must continually refinance the position when the short-term note comes due. For example, assume long- and short-term rates are equal. If the investor borrows short term at 10% and purchases a bond at 10% interest,

FIGURE 5.6
The spectrum of interest rates may shift to higher or lower levels.

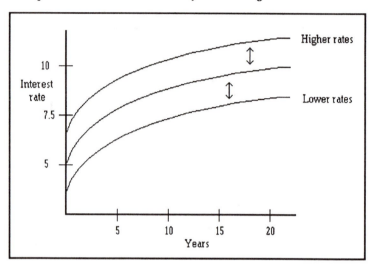

a breakeven will occur. If short-term rates drop a profit will be made up to 10% since rates will not go below zero. If short-term rates rise above 10%, a loss of potentially unlimited magnitude may occur. Therefore a maximum profit of 10% versus a potentially unlimited loss may make borrowing short term and lending long term more risky.

Sometimes the entire spectrum of interest rates shifts causing the yield curve to increase or decrease, as shown in Figure 5.6. A factor such as higher inflation might cause interest rates to shift upward, whereas the opposite effect of lower inflation would tend to shift the curve lower.

The interest rate curve may also change, becoming flat or even negatively sloping. The inverted yield in Figure 5.7 is a negatively sloping curve which occurs when short-term rates are higher than long-term rates. The flat yield curve also in Figure 5.7 will often occur in the transition from normal to inverted and back again.

FIGURE 5.7
Interest rates can shift from the normal yield curve and become flat or inverted.

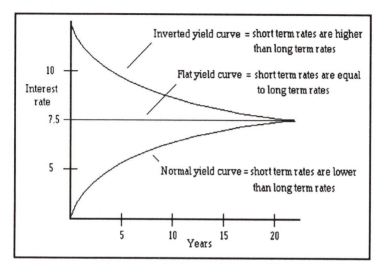

These changes may happen quickly or may take a long period of time to occur.

If long-term interest rates should normally be higher than short-term rates, then why are short-term rates sometimes greater (i.e., why does the inverted yield curve happen)? The yield curve may become flat or inverted in uncertain or unusual economic conditions such as a highly inflationary environment. If the government decides to reduce the money supply to combat inflation, the cost of money (especially in the short term) may increase due to the reduced supply. Lenders, believing inflation will eventually drop, may decide to place their money in long-term obligations to lock in the high rates. Borrowers, also believing rates will drop, will try to continue borrowing short-term to avoid paying high rates on long-term obligations. Both these factors will tend to temporarily keep long-term rates lower than short-term rates.

NOMINAL AND REAL INTEREST RATES

An interest rate is composed of two separate rates which are termed the nominal and real rate. *The* **nominal interest rate** *is the actual or observed interest rate. The* **real interest rate** *is the real cost of borrowing money after adjusting for inflation.* The nominal rate is the one most of us are familiar with because it is the same one we earn interest on or borrow from at the bank. The real rate is the interest rate after inflation and represents the real return or cost to borrow. The real and nominal rate are related by the following equation:

$n = r + i$

where   = nominal interest rate

   r = real interest rate

   i = inflation rate

What is the real cost to borrow if a person borrows money for one year at 10% and the inflation rate is 5% per year? The real cost is:

$r = n - i$

  $= 10\% - 5\%$

  $= 5\%$

Nominal rates must always be positive (otherwise people would be paid to borrow money) but real rates can and have been negative in the past. The inflation rate can be positive or negative since a negative inflation rate would imply a deflationary environment.

The real rate of interest is important in analyzing the economic well-being of the country. For example, if inflation is 20% and interest rates are 10%, the real rate is –10%. Borrowers do well in this environment because they pay back their debt in cheaper dollars. However, lenders will lose money because their real return is negative and will eventually go bankrupt if the situation persists.

In the opposite scenario where inflation is 10% and interest rates are 20%, the real rate is 10%. Lenders can expect to make very good returns but they may never realize them. Borrowers will find the real cost to be burdensome, and may not be able to repay the debt or simply stop borrowing.

There must be a fair medium value for the real rate so that neither borrower nor lender faces undue hardship. There is no conclusive evidence of what the proper real rate should be; however, historical figures indicate a real rate between 2-4% has fostered good economic growth without too great a burden for either group.

PURPOSE OF INTEREST RATE FUTURES

The need to hedge interest rate fluctuations has grown appreciably with the increasing volatility of interest rates. Any institution which borrows or lends may need to hedge its portfolio of interest rate obligations. Let's look at an example:

A bank borrows short term by paying interest in the checking accounts of its depositors. It lends long-term with mortgages to other clients. If short-term rates rise above long-term rates (the inverse yield curve), the bank will be forced to pay rates to the depositors which are higher than the rates they receive on their mortgages. They can help to avoid this predicament by hedging short-term interest rate futures in the market. If short-term rates rise, the amount they lose in paying depositors more money will be offset by the amount they make on the interest rate futures. If short-term rates fall, they will have to pay the depositors less by the amount they lose in the futures market. In this particular example, since the long-term rate is locked they do not have to concern themselves as much with long-term rate fluctuations. Hedging in long-term rates is also quite popular for many reasons.

Interest rate futures may also be used to speculate on the change in interest rates. An investor anticipating a decline in interest rates might purchase T-bond or Treasury bill contracts whereas one anticipating a rise in rates might sell short interest rate futures.

Interest rate futures can be used in the futures market to lock in arbitrages between different months in the same commodity. All the basis calculations for each contract month in the commodity assume a certain interest rate. An arbitrageur may need to hedge an interest rate when trading different commodity contract months to lock in the basis value between contracts. This arbitrage helps to keep markets more efficient and all contracts properly in line with each other.

Another type of speculation often done in interest rates is to buy one maturity and sell another, which is in effect playing the yield curve. Assume the yield curve is inverted (short-term rates higher than long-term rates) but you expect the curve to become normal (short-term rates lower than long-term rates). You might buy short-term obligations such as eurodollars or Treasury bills and sell long-term obligations such as bonds or notes. This type of strategy is often employed because the inverted yield curve invariably returns to normal, though this may take much longer and many more dollars than you initially expected.

Another type of spread is the TED spread which is T-bills over eurodollars. If you feel T-bills will outperform eurodollars then you would buy T-bills and sell eurodollars. This type of spread sometimes reflects a financial panic or flight to quality when investors seek protection and place their money in the least risky vehicles such as T-bills.

CHARACTER OF INTEREST RATES

Since interest rates can vary in many different ways, let's look at some of the factors which affect the level of interest rates:

1. *Inflation:* One of the most important factors affecting interest rates is the rate of inflation. High inflation rates will tend to increase interest rates. Recalling the previous equation of nominal and real rates, if real rates remain constant and the inflation rate increases, the nominal rate must increase. Lenders will need to receive higher interest rates because they are being paid back in cheaper dollars.

2. *Money supply:* Since interest is the cost of money, more available money means cheaper money and lower interest rates. When money is tight interest rates tend to rise because money is scarce. This scenario occurs in normal economic conditions, but the opposite scenario may be observed in unusual times. For example, in highly inflationary conditions, a tight money policy may actually cause interest rates to drop because people believe the government is finally

trying to reduce inflation. Easy money in inflationary times could tend to increase interest rates because people might think inflation will become even worse. The velocity of money can also affect interest rates.

3. *State of the economy:* A growing and healthy economy is usually favorable to interest rates because there is capital to invest and expand. Stagnant or troubled economies generally have higher interest rates because there are few promising ventures for lending money.

4. *Government policy:* Governments have a large impact on interest rates because they are usually the biggest borrowers of money. Governments that tend to keep their financial affairs in order will help to promote lower interest rates and favorable economic conditions.

5. *International rates:* The cost of borrowing must always be considered relative to the cost of borrowing in the international market place. If capital is scarce because economic conditions are bad worldwide (1930s-type depression), real costs to borrow will probably be high. If money is easy then interest rates should be lower.

CONCLUSION

Interest rates are a measure of the cost of money and provide an important indication of the health of the economy. High interest rates usually coincide with a stagnant or declining economy. Low interest rates foster business development and may act as a stimulant for renewed growth. Governments usually have a significant effect on interest rates because they often borrow large amounts of money and also create money. Interest rates can have an important impact on the currency and stock market, and so they are a crucial component of the financial markets.

CHAPTER 6

The Stock Market

Nothing is so firmly believed as what is least known.

Michel de Montaigne

The stock market is one of the best and most important means of raising capital for companies. Many emerging companies cannot issue bonds and do not want to take on too much debt, so they look to the stock market for capital. The trading of stock index futures commenced in 1982 and has become a significant part of stock market activity.

STOCK INDEXES

There are many stock indexes to measure the performance of the stock market. Some of the more popular ones are:

1. *Dow Jones Industrials*: One of the first averages, this is a price weighted average that tracks the performance of 30 blue chip or mature stocks. Figure 6.1 is a long-term graph of the Dow Jones Index.

FIGURE 6.1
Dow Jones Industrials monthly graph

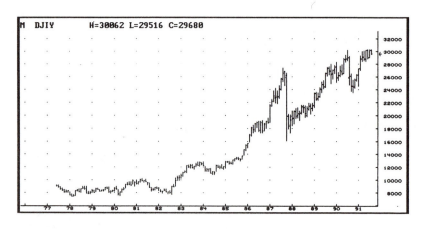

Source: Reprinted with permission, FutureSource, 955 Parkview Blvd., Lombard, IL 60148 (800) 621-2628

FIGURE 6.2
NYSE monthly chart

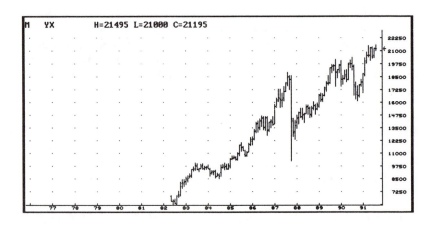

Source: Reprinted with permission, FutureSource, 955 Parkview Blvd., Lombard, IL 60148 (800) 621-2628

2. *S&P500*: A much broader index created by Standard and Poor, this tracks the performance of 500 stocks in many different fields. The index is capitalization weighted, which means it takes into account the price and the number of shares outstanding.

3. *New York Stock Exchange Index*: This broad group of stocks trade on the NYSE. The index is capitalization weighted and shown in Figure 6.2 for comparison.

4. *Value Line Composite*: One of the broadest indices, this comprises stocks on the NYSE, AMEX and over the counter market.

5. *Major Market (XMI) Index*: An index composed of 20 stocks which mimics the Dow.

DETERMINANTS OF THE STOCK MARKET PRICES

Some factors affecting the stock market include:

1. *Economy*: A vibrant and healthy economy provides some of the best conditions for fostering a strong stock market. Companies prosper and grow in good times and this boosts the value of the company, which increases the stock price. The economy prospers, which helps entrepreneurs start and maintain successful businesses, helping to increase stock prices.

2. *Interest rates*: The interest rate market affects the stock market in many ways. The stock and interest rate markets both compete for capital. Investors constantly judge whether to place some of their capital in stocks or interest rates, and the resulting decision greatly affects the stock and bond market. If investors feel stocks are a better buy, they may take money out of bonds or bills and purchase stocks and vice versa.

Interest rates also affect the stock market by affecting the economy. If interest rates are high, growth in the economy may stagnate or even decline, which can be bearish for stocks. An environment of low interest rates and a healthy economy is a powerful force in driving stock prices higher.

SYSTEMATIC VERSUS
UNSYSTEMATIC RISK

The stock market has two kinds of risk:

1. **Systematic risk** *is the risk of the entire market rising or falling.* Anyone who invests in the stock market must face systematic risk. For example, assume you buy the stock of a company with good prospects and a year later it outperforms the market by 10%. You may still lose money because the market may have dropped 30% but your stock only dropped 20%. Even if the company does well and outperforms the rest of the market, your investment may not perform well because of the overall risk of the stock market.

2. **Unsystematic risk** *is the stock-specific risk, or risk inherent in a stock.* Each stock has risk associated with it that is separate from the stock market. No matter how well or badly the market is performing, there will always be stocks which do worse or better than the market. In the previous example, the stock did relatively well but the stock market performed poorly. What about the opposite scenario—where you buy a stock and the stock market soars but unfortunately your stock sinks into oblivion? This is an example of risk associated with a specific stock.

One of the ways of eliminating unsystematic risk is to diversify in a select portfolio of stocks. Some studies indicate investing in as few as ten stocks with low correlations to each other can reduce unsystematic risk to a great degree.

BASIS CALCULATION FOR STOCK
INDEX FUTURES

The basis calculation for stocks is different than for most commodities. Unlike most commodities stocks pay dividends; so the basis calculation is not complete until the dividend yield is included. Let's review an example to obtain the basis on March 15 for the June S&P500 which expires on June 15.

Cash price   = $300.00
Interest rate   = 8%
Dividend yield   = 3%
Time to expiration = 3 months
Storage costs   = 0

Since the dividend yield negates part of the cost to carry the basis calculation for stocks is:

Theoretical basis = cash price · time · (interest rate − dividend yield)
                  = 300.00 · (3/12) · (0.08 − 0.03)
                  = $3.75

Recall the theoretical price for a future is:

Theoretical future price = cash price + theoretical basis

So:

Theoretical future price = $300.00 + $3.75
                         = $303.75

STOCK INDEX ARBITRAGE

In the previous example we determined the theoretical future price to be $303.75. What if the actual market price of the future is 305.00 and the actual cash price is 300.00? An arbitrageur, noticing the markets are out of line, can sell the stock index future and buy the cash. The net result is:

Buy cash   = 300.00
Sell the future   = 305.00
Theoretical basis = Cost to carry the position = $3.75
Actual basis   = 305.00 − 300.00
                  = 5.00

The investor will make $5.00 on the actual basis but lose $3.75 on the theoretical basis, which is the cost to carry the position.

Net profit   = actual basis − theoretical basis
             = 5.00 − 3.75
             = $1.25

The arbitrage of stock index futures against the cash market is called stock index arbitrage and is one kind of program trading. This arbitrage is an example of a buy program. *A buy program occurs when the cash market is bought and the future is sold.* Buy programs are initiated when the actual basis is greater than the theoretical basis. The spread or basis must reach a certain threshold level for a buy program to "kick in." For example an actual basis of 3.80 would not justify a buy program in this example because the brokerage costs and risks involved in executing the transaction would be too great. All program traders have their own threshold levels where they will initiate a buy or sell program.

A **sell program** *occurs when the cash market is sold and the future is bought.* Let's look at a sell program:

The December NYFE is trading at 202 in August when the cash is at 200. Is a sell program possible? We need to calculate the actual and theoretical basis to see if the markets are out of line.

Cash price	= 200.00
Interest rate	= 8%
Dividend yield	= 3%
Time to expiration	= 4 months
Storage costs	= 0
Future price	= 202.00
Theoretical basis	= cash price · time · (interest rate – dividend yield)
	= 200 · 4/12 · (0.08 – 0.03)
	= 3.33
Actual basis	= 202.00 – 200.00
	= 2.00
Net profit	= theoretical basis – actual basis
	= 3.33 – 2.00
	= 1.33

The net profit is $1.33 in buying the future and selling the cash. In the previous example the profit was obtained by subtracting the actual basis from the theoretical basis, but the opposite is done here because the future is bought and the cash sold. If the cash is at 200.00 at expiration the arbitrageur will lose 2.00 when the future settles at 200.00, but will make $3.33 by being short the cash. Institutions which own large quantities of stock can use sell programs and reduce

FIGURE 6.3
June 1992 NYSE future versus the cash

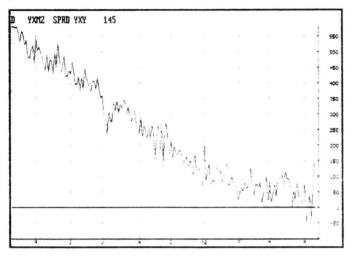

Source: Reprinted with permission, FutureSource, 955 Parkview Blvd., Lombard, IL 60148 (800) 621-2628

or eliminate interest costs by being long the future instead of long the stock. The basis for the June 92 NYSE futures contract versus the cash is shown in Figure 6.3.

These are not risk-free transactions. If interest rates go up or the dividend yield drops, the profit in the buy program could turn into a loss because the cost of carry has increased. However, the sell program would become even more profitable. In the opposite scenario where interest rates decline or the dividend yield increases, the buy program would be more profitable and the sell program less profitable. Transaction costs, slippage, and margin calls are some other factors which add risk to this trade. The programs do not have to be held till expiration and more often are "unwound" or taken off before expiration.

NEED FOR STOCK INDEX FUTURES

Stock index futures serve many important functions:

1. *Stock market hedging.* A portfolio manager who is long stocks but feels the market is due for a temporary sell-off can sell stock index futures against the portfolio of stocks. For example, the manager is long $1 million of stock and decides to sell $1 million of stock index futures against the position. If the market continues to rise the amount made on the stocks will be offset by the amount lost in the futures. However, if the anticipated decline occurs, the amount lost in the stock market will be offset by the amount made in the futures market.

Why not just sell the stocks? Some of the reasons are:

a. Transaction costs are much higher selling and then buying the stocks back again.

b. Tax rules may favor holding the position.

c. The stock index futures provide a quicker and more efficient way of buying or selling a portfolio of stocks.

d. Liquidity of many stocks may make it expensive to trade in and out on a short-term basis.

Stock index futures may be used to hedge a long or short portfolio. A portfolio manager short the market may buy stock index futures to hedge against a market rise. Portfolio insurance is a form of hedging where the investment manager sets price stops at predetermined levels to protect a position.

2. *Eliminate systematic risk:* A portfolio manager believes a group of stocks will outperform the market. The manager can buy the select group and sell the market using stock index futures. If the group of stocks does outperform the market the manager will achieve good performance irrespective of what the stock market does or how much it might drop.

3. *Eliminate unsystematic risk:* A portfolio manager is bullish after spending much time analyzing the market but is not sure which stocks to buy. The manager can buy the entire stock market by buying stock index futures instead of researching numerous stocks to determine which ones are good buys. The manager can devote more time to studying the overall market and the economy instead of particular stocks. This is especially appropriate for those who

look at international stock markets and do not have the time to analyze all the stocks on every exchange. Using stock index futures can eliminate unsystematic risk and the need to trade many different stocks. The very frustrating experience of being right on the market but picking the wrong stocks can now be eliminated using stock index futures.

4. *Individual investor*: The investor who does not have the time or desire to research all the stocks. The investor might feel the market will eventually go up or down and can buy or sell stock index futures and participate in the stock market.

5. *Spreading one index against another*: Spreading a stock index future of one index against another is a way to trade one market average against another. An investor, believing the broader market will outperform the blue chips, decides to buy the NYSE future and sell the Major Market index. This is much easier accomplished using stock index futures instead of buying and selling the individual stocks.

EFFECTS OF STOCK INDEX FUTURES ON THE STOCK MARKET

What are the effects of program trading on the stock market? Whenever the market drops, two repeat arguments (somewhat akin to Chinese water torture) invariably arise. The first argument is the volatility of the stock market has increased to dangerous levels, which may be partly blamed on the program traders. The second argument is the market crash of 1987 and apparently every minor and major market drop since then has supposedly been due to sell programs.

Hedging done in portfolio insurance is also believed to exacerbate market drops. Portfolio insurance and stock index arbitrage are perceived as two of the main causes for both a fall in stock market prices and an increase in stock market volatility. This results in severe losses for the investor and others deciding to flee the market altogether.

Interestingly enough, the criticism against program trading only occurs when the market drops. What happens when the market rises? There seem to be few complaints of the market being too volatile and rising too high and therefore the stockholders making too much money. The market rise is due to "investor enthusiasm" or "savvy money managers" seeking good bargains and is unrelated to program trading. There is little criticism expressed against buy programs and one wonders if they even exist.

The arguments against stock index futures are actually reminiscent of the saying, "Shoot the messenger if the news is bad." Stock index futures are a barometer of the health of the stock market but are not the stock market itself. When a sell program is initiated or portfolio insurance occurs the stock index futures are dropping faster than the cash market. This happens because the futures are much faster and more efficient to trade than a basket of stocks. The stock index futures are not causing the market to drop but are signaling that investors are selling. Market sentiment is more quickly reflected in stock index futures than in the cash market because it is a more compact and efficient market.

Is it fair that people who use stock index futures have faster access to buying or selling the market when the little guy does not? Why allow immediate access to the market when emotions may be running too high? Instead, why not have the players enter in a more relaxed and less hurried fashion so that the prices do not gyrate as much? We could do that. But let's take the argument one step further by eliminating telephones, news wire services, and other technological items which allow us to communicate in a faster way. In essence stock index futures allow faster entry and exit into a market and represent a technological jump in trading the market more quickly. Time is of increasing value to our society and since stock index futures decrease the amount of time to make a transaction this in itself is enough of an argument for their existence.

The stock index futures do not cause the market to drop or volatility to increase but simply mirror the immediate thoughts of the investing public. Stock index futures may cause the market to drop slightly more than if they were not used (but then they would also cause it to go up more too). They may also slightly increase the volatility of the market (though neither point has ever been proven). However, the benefits of stock index futures in regards to hedging needs—more efficient access to the market and reduced transaction costs—far outweigh any possible minor negative effects. Index arbitrage is essential for efficient pricing in the stock market. Portfolio insurance is an excellent way to allow portfolio managers and investors to hedge their positions. Any serious studies of index arbitrage and portfolio insurance conclude that the benefits far outweigh the negatives. Remember that arbitrage between the futures and cash markets is done for every market and not just the stock market.

CONCLUSION

Stocks and bonds are among the most popular forms of investments. The stock market is a good barometer of the state of the economy and is an important measure of the wealth of a nation. Many emerging companies look to the stock market to raise equity for new ventures. The many existing stock markets are the cornerstones of modern-day capitalism.

CHAPTER 7

Natural Resources

There are truths which are not for all men, nor for all times.

Voltaire

THE PETROLEUM MARKET

The petroleum market has grown in 100 years to become one of the most important markets in the world. It is one of the main sources in providing the energy needs for many of the industrialized countries. Products such as plastic and synthetic fibers are derived from petroleum, filling other important needs in our society.

The crude oil market was relatively stable until the development of OPEC. In 1973 OPEC instituted an oil embargo and raised prices. This action changed the crude oil market and created much more volatility in the market. The need to hedge energy prices became apparent, and the New York Mercantile Exchange responded with the creation of a heating oil contract. With the success of the heating oil contract, the exchange followed with a crude oil contract and a gasoline contract afterward.

CRUDE OIL

Crude oil is one of the largest cash markets in the world. There is actually very little use for crude oil in its original state. The products which are derived from crude oil give the oil its value. Refining is a process that extracts different component products from the crude oil. Some of the products include liquefied petroleum gas, gasoline, distillate fuel oil, and heavy fuel oil. Each refined barrel of crude oil yields various percentages of these kinds of products, depending on the type of crude oil and refinery.

The composition of the crude oil is an important determinant in how it is priced. Some grades are more highly valued than others. The place of origin partly determines the chemical composition of the crude oil. Some of the components of crude oil that can affect the price are:

1. *Sweet and sour crude:* Crude oil contains various levels of sulfur. Crude oil with high amounts of sulfur is called *sour,* whereas crude oil with a low sulfur content is called *sweet.* Sweet crude has a higher value than sour crude because high levels of sulfur in the refined oil products such as gasoline or oil can become a serious air and water pollutant.

2. *Light and heavy:* Different grades of crude have different levels of gasoline and oil. The lighter components or less dense products are more valued than the heavier products. *Light* crude has more of the lighter grades of product and therefore has a greater value than *heavy* crude, which has more of the heavier components.

3. *Trace elements:* Other elements and compounds in the crude oil such as trace amounts of metals can affect the price of the crude. Chemical properties such as viscosity and distillation points will further affect the price of the oil.

Crude oil competes with other energy sources such as nuclear, hydroelectric, solar (which is really from nuclear energy) and coal. The crude oil supply is concentrated in various areas such as the Middle East. Demand for crude oil is virtually everywhere but especially in the industrialized nations such as the United States.

The crude oil market tends to go through phases of normal and inverted markets and therefore provides many good spreading opportunities. When the market becomes inverted, a trader may try to sell the near month and buy the distant month in anticipation of the market returning to a normal phase. When the market becomes normal, a trader may buy the near and sell the distant month contract in anticipation of a flat or inverted market. Figure 7.1 is a monthly chart of crude oil prices. Two important products that are refined from crude oil and have futures contracts are heating oil and gasoline.

Heating Oil

The demand for heating oil is greatest in the winter with the colder weather. The price of heating oil can be greatly affected by the price of crude oil and both tend to move in unison with each other. In the summer of 1990 when supplies of crude oil became tight, the price of heating oil also increased, as shown in Figure 7.2. There was not much greater demand for the heating oil but the price increased mainly in response to the crude oil price increase.

The price of heating oil can in turn affect the price of crude oil. When heating oil demand is great due to an unusually cold winter, the price of heating oil can increase which will cause the crude oil price to rise.

Heating oil presents many spreading opportunities. Since the demand is greatest during the winter, the price of heating oil may rise during the winter months and drop during the summer periods. A trader may buy January heating oil and sell July heating oil in anticipation of the potential demand difference. This trade is of course not a sure thing because the weather may be relatively mild or demand may prove less than expected in the winter.

Gasoline

The demand for gasoline is generally greatest in the summer with the increased travel due partly from vacation trips. The price of gasoline can be affected by the price of crude oil in the same way heating oil prices are affected. Gasoline prices also rose during the summer of 1990, as shown in Figure 7.3 mainly due to the tight supplies of crude oil caused by the Iraq-Kuwait war.

FIGURE 7.1
Crude oil monthly chart

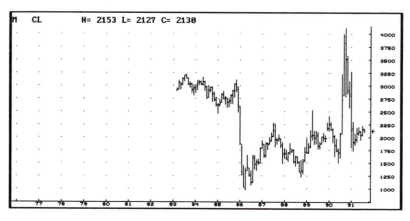

Source: Reprinted with permission, FutureSource, 955 Parkview Blvd., Lombard, IL 60148 (800) 621-2628

FIGURE 7.2
Heating oil monthly chart

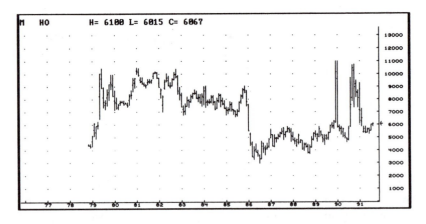

Source: Reprinted with permission, FutureSource, 955 Parkview Blvd., Lombard, IL 60148 (800) 621-2628

FIGURE 7.3
Gasoline monthly chart

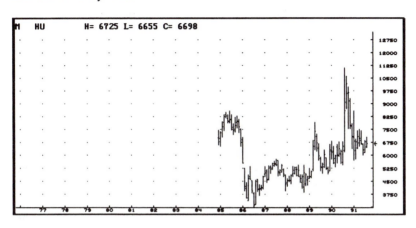

Source: Reprinted with permission, FutureSource, 955 Parkview Blvd., Lombard, IL 60148 (800) 621-2628

   The price of gasoline can also affect the crude oil price. If gasoline demand is high from travel or other reasons, the price of gasoline could increase, causing the crude oil price to rise. Gasoline presents many spreading opportunities. A trader anticipating increased summer demand for gasoline might buy the August contract and sell the February contract. If demand is high, the August might increase relative to February. If demand is less than expected, the August could drop relative to February.
   Gasoline and heating oil indirectly affect the price of each other. If the demand for gasoline is high, then refiners will produce more gasoline to meet demand. However, more gasoline produced will also mean more heating oil on the market. If the demand does not meet the supply of heating oil, then the price may drop relative to gasoline. This situation creates possible spreading opportunities between heating oil and gasoline. If a trader believes gasoline demand will increase in June and feels heating oil demand will be soft, the trader could buy July or August gasoline and sell the July or August heating oil contract.

THE METALS

The metals markets comprise the so-called precious metals—gold, silver, platinum, palladium, and the industrial metal copper. The precious metals are used for investment as well as industrial applications whereas copper is strictly used for industrial purposes.

A Store of Value

The island of Yap is located in the beautiful South Pacific. The natives in this idyllic area base much of their material wealth on certain types of rocks. The people believe the rocks connote wealth so the bigger the rock the greater the wealth. There are times when this can be an inconvenience. These rocks may become quite large and sometimes are bigger than the people. Some may weigh thousands of kilograms (several tons). In other words they do not make great pocket change.

These people are considered "primitive" and it certainly shows in their understanding of money. Why a heavy rock for money? Why not something more convenient like paper money which is what modern civilization uses? Or alternatively why not something with intrinsic value like gold? Anyone who knows anything knows that gold has value. Right?

We in the modern world use gold as a store of value and are therefore much more sophisticated. Or are we? What is the intrinsic value of gold? Some would argue it has value because it is rare. There are many elements which are much rarer but still are valued less than gold. Industrial and technological applications add value to gold, but this does not account for the full price of gold. What makes gold so valuable? *Belief that gold has value has much to do with why gold is considered valuable.*

Gold has intrinsic value because we believe it has value. People often buy gold in times when their paper money is depreciating. People have turned to gold during panics and inflations because they believe gold will retain its value. If people did not believe this, they would not turn to gold as a store of value and own it. What is the difference between us and the natives in the South Pacific? Not much.

Gold

The demand for gold appears most heavily in the jewelry business. Over 50% of gold demand comes from jewelry. After jewelry, the electronics industry accounts for a second important use of gold. Other applications include medical and coinage by countries. South Africa is the largest producer of gold. The United States and Canada follow with other countries affecting supply to a lesser extent.

One of the most important functions of gold is to act as an international currency or substitute for money, as already noted. In times of panic or other unusual situations, many people buy gold and sell their respective currencies because they view gold as a safe haven. This can be especially apparent in the United States if confidence in the dollar is lost. Figure 7.4 is a monthly chart of gold prices.

Gold is perceived as an inflation hedge, but this is again due to the perception of gold as a safe haven in times of economic uncertainty. Many people hoard gold just in case conditions get worse. This will tend to increase the immediate price of gold when hoarding occurs. However, if the panic or economic threat subsides, the hoarding can become a depressing influence on the price of gold if people seek to divest of their holdings.

FIGURE 7.4
Gold monthly chart

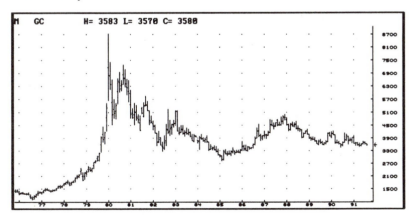

Source: Reprinted with permission, FutureSource, 955 Parkview Blvd., Lombard, IL 60148 (800) 621-2628

Silver, Platinum, and Copper

The demand for silver is related more to industrial applications than as a form of money like gold. Silver has important uses in the photographic industry. The electronics industry is another source for demand in silver followed by the jewelry industry. Silver production is large in Mexico and some South American countries such as Chile and Peru, as well as Canada and the United States. The demand for silver exists throughout the world. Figure 7.5 is a monthly chart of silver prices.

Platinum is similar to gold as a precious metal, but there are more specific industrial applications such as catalytic converters for automobiles. The source of platinum is highly concentrated in South Africa, with other countries like Canada contributing a much smaller proportion. Figure 7.6 is a monthly chart of platinum prices.

Copper, unlike the other metals, is used specifically for industrial applications. The electronics industry is a large user of copper, with the building and machinery industry another important user. There is heavy demand for copper in the industrialized nations, and supply comes from the same areas as silver plus others such as the former USSR and Africa. Figure 7.7 is a monthly chart of copper prices.

FIGURE 7.5
Silver monthly chart

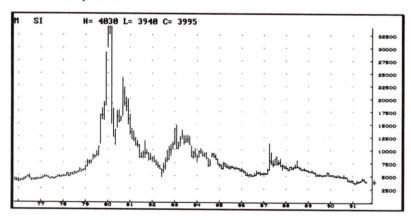

Source: Reprinted with permission, FutureSource, 955 Parkview Blvd., Lombard, IL 60148 (800) 621-2628

FIGURE 7.6
Platinum monthly chart

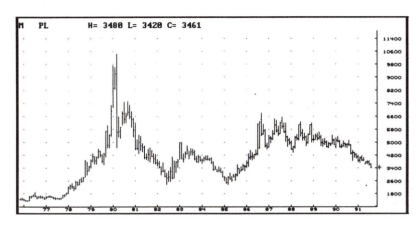

Source: Reprinted with permission, FutureSource, 955 Parkview Blvd., Lombard, IL 60148 (800) 621-2628

FIGURE 7.7
Copper monthly chart

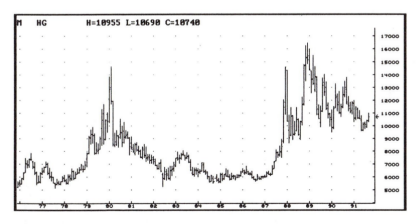

Source: Reprinted with permission, FutureSource, 955 Parkview Blvd., Lombard, IL 60148 (800) 621-2628

Spreads

Most spreads within the metals are more often interest rate plays (except for copper). There may at times be supply problems with any of the metals, but the imbalances do not usually create inverted markets. This is partly due to the amount of hoarding and storage of the precious metals for investment purposes. Copper can exhibit inverted and normal markets due to production and demand imbalances, similar to other commodities like petroleum.

Some spreading is done between markets such as buying gold and selling platinum or vice versa. The silver to gold ratio is sometimes followed to determine if one market is overvalued or undervalued versus the other.

COTTON AND LUMBER

Cotton is grown in many parts of the world and is used mainly in clothing and other types of house and business goods such as towels and sheets. It takes approximately half a year to grow cotton and like many other commodities demand is relatively stable. Large price changes are often due to supply problems such as a drought. Figure 7.8 is a monthly chart of cotton prices.

FIGURE 7.8
Cotton monthly chart

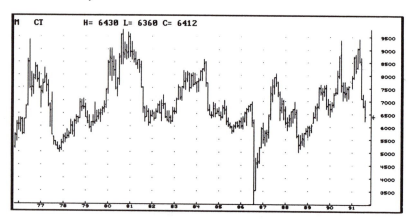

Source: Reprinted with permission, FutureSource, 955 Parkview Blvd., Lombard, IL 60148 (800) 621-2628

FIGURE 7.9
Lumber monthly chart

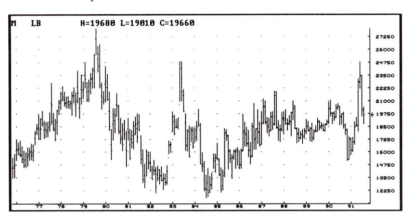

Source: Reprinted with permission, FutureSource, 955 Parkview Blvd., Lombard, IL 60148 (800) 621-2628

Lumber is an important part of the construction industry and the price is often affected by the state of the housing industry. The United States is a large producer and consumer of lumber. Figure 7.9 is a monthly chart of lumber prices.

CONCLUSION

Futures on natural resources are an excellent way to hedge the volatility of oil and metals prices. The petroleum market is one of the largest and most volatile markets so futures are a natural way to reduce risk. Metals and lumber are used in many industrial applications, and cotton is an important component in clothes and household goods.

CHAPTER 8

Food

Nothing is more difficult, and therefore more precious, than to be able to decide.

Napoleon I, *Maxims*

The first commodity trade may have centered around food items such as grains and rice. We will look at the food groups in two ways—plants and meats.

BEANS, GRAINS AND RELATED FOOD PRODUCTS

Corn is a native American plant originally cultivated by the Indians. It is now grown in many parts of the world, but the United States is still both a large producer and consumer of corn. Corn is used for two reasons: feed for farm animals and food for people.

   In its original state corn may be used as feed. People consume it both in the original state, refined into meal and flour, or in oil products such as corn oil. Corn competes with other starches and oils such as wheat and soybeans. Figure 8.1 is a monthly chart of corn prices.

FIGURE 8.1
Corn monthly chart

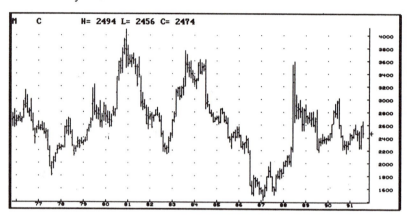

Source: Reprinted with permission, FutureSource, 955 Parkview Blvd., Lombard, IL 60148 (800) 621-2628

FIGURE 8.2
Soybean monthly chart

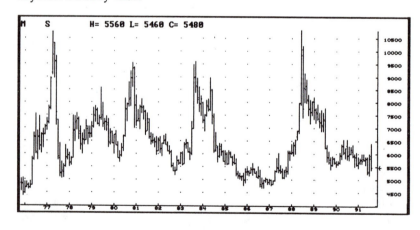

Source: Reprinted with permission, FutureSource, 955 Parkview Blvd., Lombard, IL 60148 (800) 621-2628

FIGURE 8.3
Soybean meal monthly chart

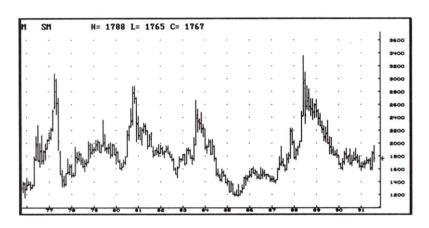

Source: Reprinted with permission, FutureSource, 955 Parkview Blvd., Lombard, IL 60148 (800) 621-2628

Soybeans like crude oil derive much of their value from the important end products. Soybeans are refined or crushed into soybean meal and soybean oil. Figure 8.2 is a monthly chart of soybean prices.

Soybean meal is used as feed for farm animals. It is an important feed item for animals because it contains usable proteins which are essential in the health and maintenance of the animals. Other items which compete with meal are peanuts and fish. Figure 8.3 is a monthly chart of soybean meal prices.

Soybean oil is used in cooking oil and other oil-related products. It is an important part of many peoples' diets because of the amount of unsaturated fats and oils it contains. Bean oil competes with many other oils such as sunflower, cottonseed, palm, peanut, safflower, canola, coconut, and olive oil. Figure 8.4 is a monthly chart of soybean oil prices.

The crush spread is similar in concept to the crack spread in the petroleum markets. It is used in evaluating the refiners' margins in processing soybeans into meal and oil. A bushel of soybeans

FIGURE 8.4
Soybean oil monthly chart

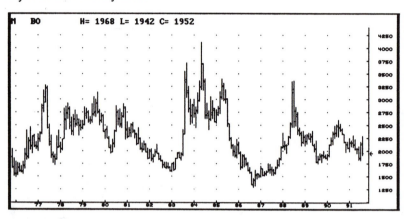

Source: Reprinted with permission, FutureSource, 955 Parkview Blvd., Lombard, IL 60148 (800) 621-2628

FIGURE 8.5
Wheat monthly chart

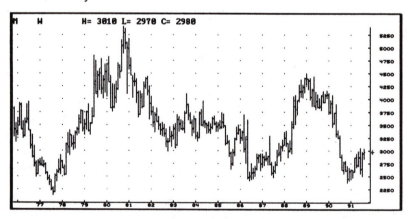

Source: Reprinted with permission, FutureSource, 955 Parkview Blvd., Lombard, IL 60148 (800) 621-2628

yields approximately 48 pounds of meal and 11 pounds of oil. This ratio of meal to oil is slightly less than 5:1.

Wheat is used more often as food for human consumption and to a lesser degree as animal feed. It is most often refined into flour and used in breads and other starch items. Figure 8.5 is a monthly chart of wheat prices.

Soft wheat or spring wheat is planted in the spring and harvested in the late summer. Hard or winter wheat is planted in the fall and harvested in late spring and early summer. The United States is both an important producer and consumer of wheat.

MEATS

Most cattle meat is consumed in the country of origin, partly due to the perishable nature of meat; so prices are highly dependent upon domestic fundamentals. Figure 8.6 is a monthly chart of live cattle prices.

The amount of time required to breed a calf from infancy to eventual readiness for the meat market or human consumption is

FIGURE 8.6
Live cattle monthly chart

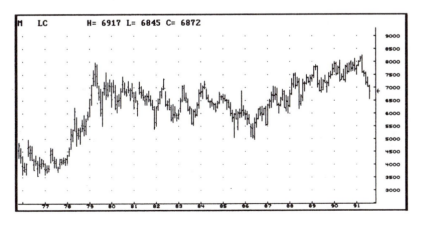

Source: Reprinted with permission, FutureSource, 955 Parkview Blvd., Lombard, IL 60148 (800) 621-2628

FIGURE 8.7
Live hog monthly chart

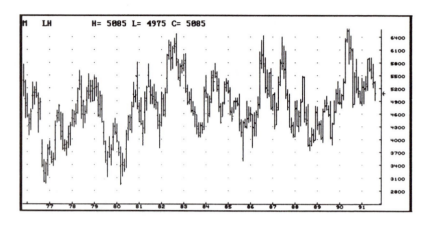

Source: Reprinted with permission, FutureSource, 955 Parkview Blvd., Lombard, IL 60148 (800) 621-2628

FIGURE 8.8
Pork belly monthly chart

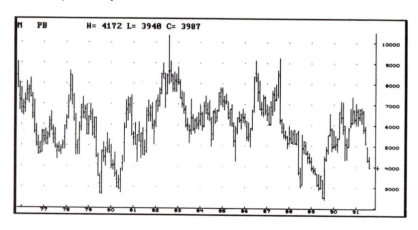

Source: Reprinted with permission, FutureSource, 955 Parkview Blvd., Lombard, IL 60148 (800) 621-2628

approximately 2 1/2 years. This cycle has important implications in the supply and demand equation for meat.

If demand is high and cattle are scarce, then farmers cannot quickly raise cattle to meet demand. High prices cause farmers to raise more cattle, but when the meat eventually comes onto the market the increased supply sometimes causes prices to drop. Low prices cause the farmer to reduce stock, which eventually creates a shortage again. This cycle is repeated with many of the meat products.

Hogs are another important part of the meat complex. Hogs take approximately one year to reach maturity which is less time than cattle. The maturity cycle is similar to the cattle cycle but of a shorter duration. Hogs and cattle are considered competitive with each other. If pork prices are relatively high, many consumers will switch to beef and vice versa. Figure 8.7 is a monthly chart of live hog prices.

Pork bellies are the section of the hog from which bacon is derived. For this reason, the supply and demand equation is similar to that of hogs. Bacon is a meat with relatively stable demand; so the price of bellies often fluctuates due to supply changes. The relevant fundamental information is usually domestic since much of the supply and demand—such as for cattle— occurs in the same country. Figure 8.8 is a monthly chart of pork belly prices.

OTHER FOODS

The rest of the food category includes coffee, cocoa, sugar, and orange juice.

Coffee is one of the largest cash commodities in the world. It is grown all over the tropical and semitropical regions of the world. It is consumed virtually all over the world. There are many different kinds of coffee usually designated by their place of origin, such as Brazilian or Kenyan, and specialty types, such as Hawaiian and Jamaican.

The two main types of coffee are called arabica and robusta. The arabicas are mainly grown in South and Central America and are generally more flavorful and mild. They command higher prices than the robustas. The robustas are grown in Africa and are used more for instant coffee. Figure 8.9 is a monthly chart of New York (arabica) coffee prices.

The futures contract in New York is a contract on the arabicas and the contract in London is for the robustas. Since demand is relatively stable, price changes are more often due to supply problems. Brazil is the predominant producer and any supply problems there can affect the entire market. Drought and frost are two weather problems which can seriously impact the supply of coffee. Coffee is grown on trees and it takes about 2 1/2 years or longer for the tree to reach maturity, partly depending on the type of coffee and its location.

The coffee contract has been one of the most volatile contracts of any food commodity. The dollar value of the future can be substantial so there can be great risk and reward in trading this future.

Cocoa is produced mainly in Africa and South America. Ghana, Brazil, and the Ivory Coast are large producers. Cocoa is consumed all over the world as both a drink and in many people's favorite, chocolate. Cocoa comes from the cocoa tree, which takes at least five years to mature. The supply and demand situation is somewhat similar to coffee. Demand is relatively stable but supply problems can create significant price changes. Figure 8.10 is a monthly chart of cocoa prices.

Sugar is grown in many parts of the world and is derived from two plants: sugarcane and sugar beets. Sugarcane is grown in tropical and subtropical regions whereas sugar beets can be grown in more temperate regions. Sugarcane and beets are both grown in the United States. The difference in plants and harvest times tends to reduce the cyclical swings in the supply of sugar. Demand is relatively stable so price changes are usually a function of supply. Brazil, the United States, Cuba, the former USSR, and India are important producers of sugar. Sugar is consumed virtually all over the world. Figure 8.11 is a monthly chart of sugar prices.

The orange juice market is highly dependent on the major producer which is the state of Florida. Brazil is becoming an important producer as well. The demand for orange juice is relatively stable, but frost problems during the winter in Florida can create violent price changes in the commodity contract. Figure 8.12 is a monthly chart of orange juice prices.

FIGURE 8.9
NY (Arabica) coffee monthly chart

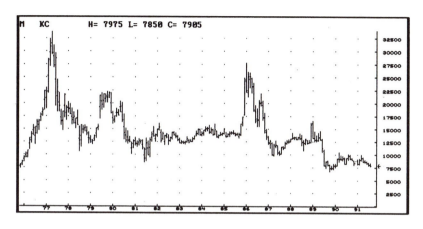

Source: Reprinted with permission, FutureSource, 955 Parkview Blvd., Lombard, IL 60148 (800) 621-2628

FIGURE 8.10
Cocoa monthly chart

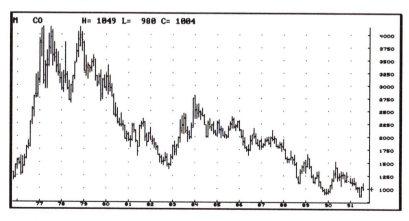

Source: Reprinted with permission, FutureSource, 955 Parkview Blvd., Lombard, IL 60148 (800) 621-2628

FIGURE 8.11
Sugar monthly chart

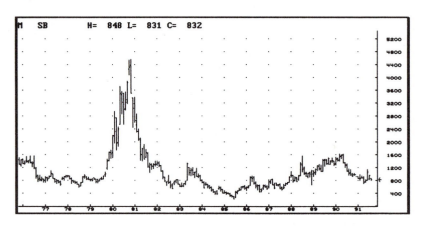

Source: Reprinted with permission, FutureSource, 955 Parkview Blvd., Lombard, IL 60148 (800) 621-2628

FIGURE 8.12
Orange juice monthly chart

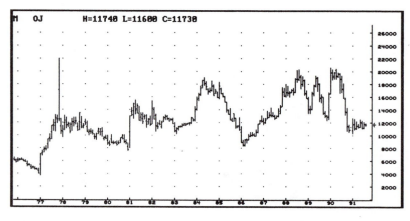

Source: Reprinted with permission, FutureSource, 955 Parkview Blvd., Lombard, IL 60148 (800) 621-2628

CONCLUSION

The food commodities were the first commodities traded and these markets still provide an excellent means to hedge price risk. Huge price variations in food prices are usually the result of supply disruptions—a drought or frost which destroys a crop. Demand is usually more constant than supply or does not change radically from one year to another.

CHAPTER **9**

Technical Analysis

... we have to remember that what we observe is not nature in itself but nature exposed to our method of questioning.

Werner Karl Heisenberg, *Physics and Philosophy*

Technical analysis *is the study of past market behavior to determine the current state or condition of the market.* The technician looks at patterns of market behavior and then observes how the market reacts in these patterns. The technician then waits for a similar pattern to recur to see if the market reacts in a similar way. This enables the technician to determine what may happen to the market in the future. It is not much different than a doctor looking for symptoms or behavior patterns, to check the condition of a patient.

Technical analysis can be used in both a reactive or predictive way to analyze the market. In either case a technical trader observes the behavior of the market to detect its condition. A *reactive* method is one where the person responds to a situation. An example of a reactive system is our reflex system. Upon touching a hot surface we might react by immediately pulling our finger away. A *predictive* method is one where the person tries to anticipate what may happen

101

FIGURE 9.1
The technician reacts to the market by buying or selling at different
price levels.

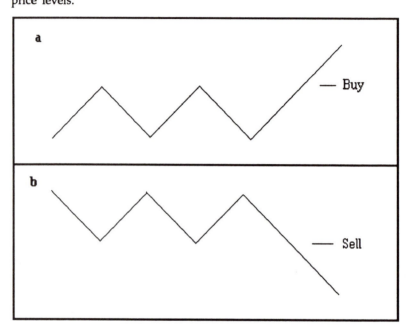

in the future. After knowing a surface is hot, we may predict that
touching it will cause a burn, so we now avoid it.

When technical analysis is used in a reactive way, a trader
watches the market and then responds to it by buying or selling
at the appropriate time. An example of trading in a reactive way
is by buying or selling a breakout from a consolidation formation,
such as a rectangle, as shown in Figure 9.1. A trader may either
buy in Figure 9.1a if the market goes above the previous highs, or
sell in Figure 9.1b if the market goes below the previous lows, but
does not make a trade until then. In this way, the trader is not
always trying to predict the market, but instead, react to it. Again,
this is no different than the doctor recommending a prescription if
the patient should exhibit a certain behavior.

FIGURE 9.2
The technician may sometimes try to predict market movement.

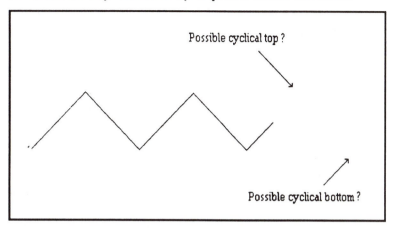

Some technicians employ technical analysis in a predictive manner. The technician will monitor market behavior and then try to predict market action. Figure 9.2 shows an example of using cycle theory to predict a bottom and potential buying opportunity. If the bottoms continue in a similar pattern we have a good indication of where and when the next bottom will appear. The technician, through studying the cycles of a market, is attempting to predict a bottom or top in the market. Various studies in cycle theory and wave analysis are examples of ways of trying to predict market behavior.

DISTINCTIONS BETWEEN TECHNICAL
AND FUNDAMENTAL ANALYSIS

There are constant battles waged by fundamentalists against technicians, and vice versa. It is not the author's intention to state one is better than the other, but rather, to suggest that both methods merit serious study. Technical analysis is often reactive in nature, whereas fundamental analysis is usually predictive in nature. Technical analysis is generally concerned with watching market behavior and then reacting when a move might happen. Fundamental analysis is concerned with why things happen and predicting the outcome of an event. In essence, technical analysis is concerned with the question of when, and fundamental analysis with the question of why.

BASIS FOR TECHNICAL ANALYSIS

Inherent in the study of technical analysis is the belief that recurring patterns in the market have an order, and are not simply random movements. Another important corollary is that market patterns are not just manifestations of economic data and news reports, but also represent the emotion and logic of the people trading the market.

Many people reject the notion that market activity is repeatable or ordered, because they feel whatever pattern occurred before is random or without precedent. They believe present trading conditions are too unlike anything that happened in the past to make any type of valid comparison. The market has no memory and every situation is unique. There is a fallacy in this way of thinking. Every day and market situation is unique, but there are common patterns which may be generalized, just as every person is unique, but generalities exist for all humans. Everyone may not have the same likes and dislikes, but everyone has likes and dislikes.

The technician assumes that different types of market actions will repeat themselves, in the same way a person's actions are repeatable. A person may react to a variety of situations in many different ways, so there is no way to exactly predict how a person will react to a specific situation. But after developing an understanding of a person's character and background, we may be able to determine, with a good degree of accuracy, how a person will react to new circumstances, even if we have not observed them in exactly similar situations before.

The technician looks for repeating patterns, such as the one in Figure 9.3 of the March 90 Australian dollar. Note how the market makes a double top on December 27 and a month later on January 22 at the 7850 level. The top is followed by a waterfall decline, which breaks the first line of support established on January 3 at the 7700 level. Over a year later, the June 91 Australian dollar in Figure 9.4 makes a double top in early April and approximately a

FIGURE 9.3
March 1990 Australian dollar

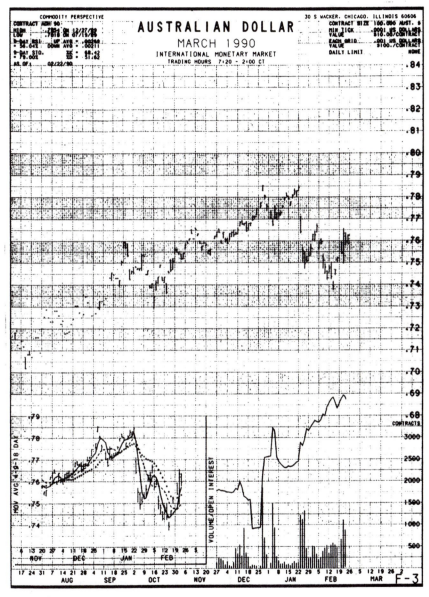

Source: Reprinted with Permission, © 1991 Commodity Perspective, 30 South
Wacker Drive, Suite 1820, Chicago, Illinois 60606

FIGURE 9.4

June 1991 Australian dollar

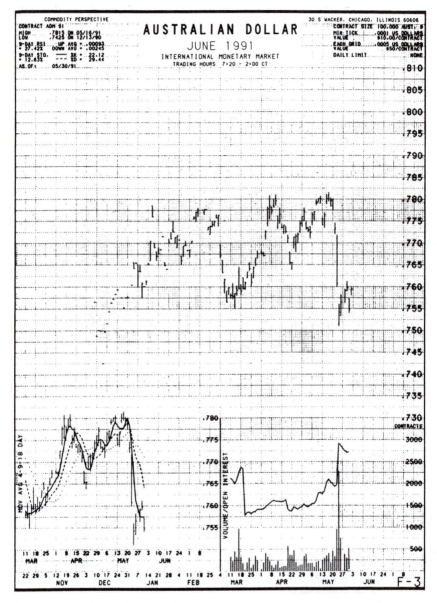

Source: Reprinted with Permission, © 1991 Commodity Perspective, 30 South
Wacker Drive, Suite 1820, Chicago, Illinois 60606

FIGURE 9.5
May 1990 Barley

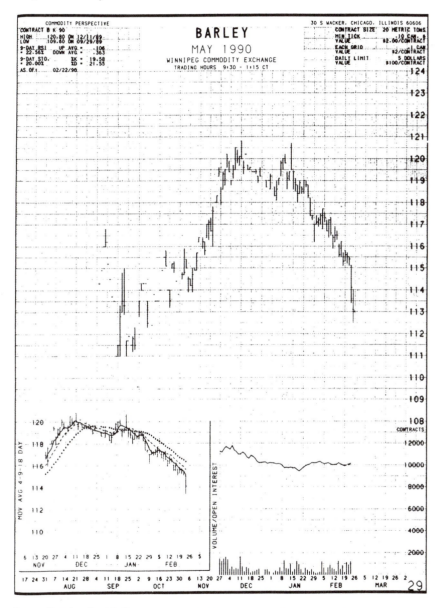

month later another top in mid-May at the 7800 level. The ensuing waterfall decline occurs and breaks the initial support established in mid-April at the 7650 level.

The double tops and subsequent decline are examples of repeating patterns. These patterns repeat in the same market but also occur in related markets, such as the currencies or other unrelated markets, such as the grains. In Figure 9.5 May 90 barley makes a double top in December and January near the 121 level. A swift decline follows, which breaks the support level established in early January near the 118 level.

The premise behind technical analysis is that all factors which directly or indirectly affect the market, such as fundamental information, emotional behavior, or natural laws, are manifest in the price and volume information of the market. A better understanding and feeling of what the market may do under various circumstances may be developed by studying the price and volume behavior of the market. We may not understand, or even care about, the interacting forces which fundamentally drive the market, but simply want to know how the market will react in a given situation.

This basic idea is enticing as well as compelling, because we can never know or understand all the factors, nor how much they will ultimately affect the market. This is partly because there are so many factors which affect the supply and demand equation. There also may be certain parties with vested interests in the market, which either keep secret or actively subvert important information essential to comprehensive evaluation of the market.

Technical analysis is a way of looking at the market from many different perspectives. Markets are not simply the reflections of economic facts and data, but the combination of the hopes, fears, and dreams of all the players. Technical analysis is an attempt at representing all this abstract information in graphic and usually quantifiable form.

A HUMAN ANALOGY FOR TECHNICAL ANALYSIS

Let's look at a human analogy to see why principles in technical analysis might work in the markets.

Mary is the happiest she has ever been in her life. She is at a high point in her life because so many good things have happened to her. Today she receives more good news, and decides to celebrate by throwing a party. The next day she receives some bad news. She takes the news well, treating it more as a minor inconvenience because she still feels elated about her good fortune. If we plotted Mary's emotional highs they would look similar to the graph in Figure 9.6.

Jennifer is sad and the most depressed she has ever been in her life. It seems as though there has only been bad news in the past few months. Today she receives more bad news and drops to an even lower level of despair. The next day she receives some good news. She still feels quite depressed because it is almost inconsequential, relative to the overwhelming bad news she has suffered. Jennifer's emotional lows would look similar to the graph in Figure 9.7.

These two scenarios are no different than what happens to a market when it makes new highs or lows in price. Figure 9.8 illustrates a market in a strong bull trend, similar to Mary's emotional highs. In early 1987, the stock market made a strong upmove, as shown by the March 87 NYSE contract. Any bad news was met with minor sell-offs followed by continued stronger moves to new highs. Figure 9.9 shows the September 88 Swiss franc in a severe bear trend, similar to Jennifer's emotional lows. Any good news was met with continued selling and short-lived rallies.

Ever wonder why bad news in a bull market gets shrugged off as if it doesn't matter, and good news sends the market even higher? Or why does good news in a bear market not seem to matter much, but bad news seems to bring another vicious sell-off? These phenomena happen because the market has an internal strength or weakness just as any person has certain strengths and weaknesses. The market does not move as if everything that happened before is of no consequence. The state of the market (whether it is strong or weak), will have a great deal to do with how it reacts to the present situation.

In essence, technical analysis assumes that markets will exhibit future behavior which is consistent with the past. This behavior is reflective of a combination of many factors, and not just the immediate situation. This assumption is no different than how we expect people

FIGURE 9.6
Mary's emotional highs: Good news is met with even better feelings and bad news is shrugged off.

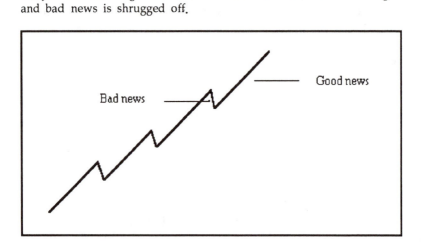

FIGURE 9.7
Jennifer's emotional lows: Good news seems to hardly matter and bad news brings renewed lows.

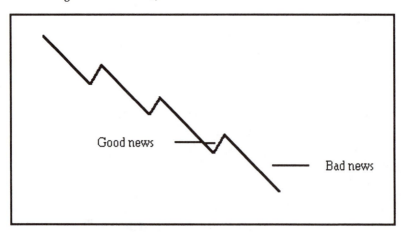

FIGURE 9.8
March 1987 NYSE composite index

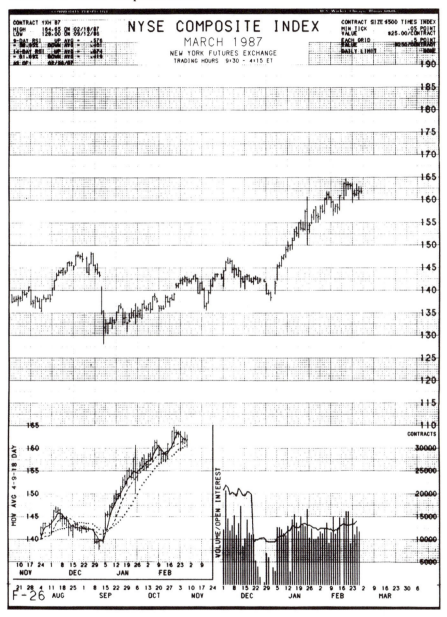

Source: Reprinted with Permission, © 1991 Commodity Perspective, 30 South Wacker Drive, Suite 1820, Chicago, Illinois 60606

FIGURE 9.9
September 1988 Swiss franc

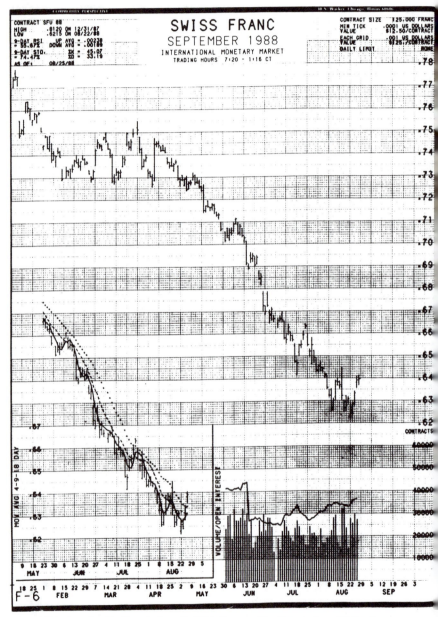

Source: Reprinted with Permission, © 1991 Commodity Perspective, 30 South Wacker Drive, Suite 1820, Chicago, Illinois 60606

to act. Most people are predictable, and one can usually expect certain actions from people we are familiar with. This is because people have a basic personality that is not easily changed. In fact, when people exhibit extremely erratic and totally unpredictable behavior, unfortunately, they are often not well. Technical analysis is an attempt to measure the strengths and weaknesses of the market in a variety of ways. Past patterns which have exhibited bullish or bearish behavior often repeat in the future. The idea of trading is not to exactly predict an outcome, but instead to have a reasonable idea or probability of an outcome. Technical analysis will never provide a completely accurate way of trading the market, but it will provide an excellent framework to analyze the market.

STARTING POINT

The starting point of most technical studies is a price chart of the market. The majority of price charts, called *bar charts*, plot price versus time, and some include volume and open interest on the horizontal axis. Japanese candlestick charts are similar in nature to bar charts, but look slightly different. Some charts, such as point and figure charts, plot price versus movement and are more concerned with how the market moves through various price levels. Some of the various types of charts include:

Bar charts

Japanese candlestick charts

Point and figure charts

Market profile

Swing charts

Bar Charts

Bar charts are the most commonly used method of charting the market. The June 91 S&P500 in Figure 9.10 is an example of a bar chart with open, high, low, and last price information, which also includes the volume and open interest of the future. Any time

FIGURE 9.10

June 1991 S&P500

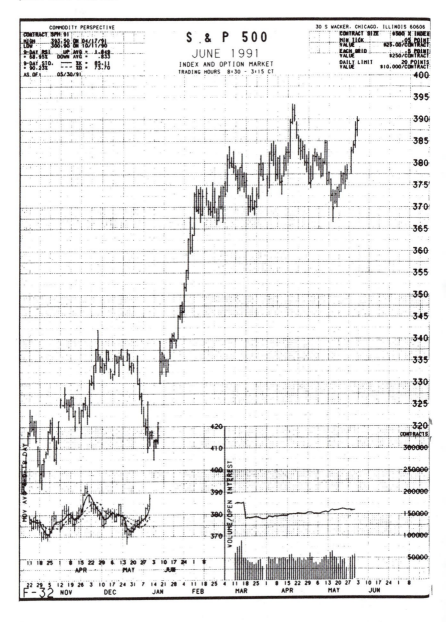

Source: Reprinted with Permission, © 1991 Commodity Perspective, 30 South Wacker Drive, Suite 1820, Chicago, Illinois 60606

frame such as a daily, weekly, or hourly period may be used in a bar chart, but the daily time frame is the most popular. Bar charts depict price information with vertical bars. Volume is represented by a vertical bar drawn at the bottom of the chart. Open interest is usually depicted as a continuous line drawn above the volume. The vertical price bar contains the following information:

1. *Open:* The open is the first price recorded, or the opening range for the period. The point on the left side of the bar is the open.

2. *High:* The high for the day is the highest point on the bar.

3. *Low:* The low for the day is the lowest point on the bar.

4. *Close:* The close, or settlement price, is the last price or closing range for the day. The point on the right side of the bar is the closing price.

Japanese Candlestick Charts

Japanese candlesticks are an oriental variation of the western bar chart (or perhaps it is more correct to say bar charts are a variation on candlesticks, because candlesticks may have a longer history). The construction of candlesticks will be done in this section, and some of the trading patterns will be covered in the pattern recognition section. Candlesticks may be used just like bar charts and may also represent any time frame. Figure 9.11 shows two common candlestick patterns, called the spinning top and doji pattern, in candlestick and bar chart form.

The top and bottom of the candlestick represent the high and low for the day, just as in regular bar charts. Where the candlestick varies is in the representation of the close and open. The wider part of the candlestick, called the *real body,* is the difference between the close and open for the day. If the body is white, the close is higher than the open; so the close is the top of the rectangle and the open is the bottom of the rectangle. If the body is black, the close is lower than the open; so the bottom of the rectangle becomes the close and the top of the rectangle signifies the open. A single horizontal line would imply the close is equal to the open, which is the same for bar charts. Any trading outside of the wider body is intraday activity, represented by the thin vertical line outside

FIGURE 9.11
The spinning top and doji are shown in a candlestick and bar chart formation for comparison.

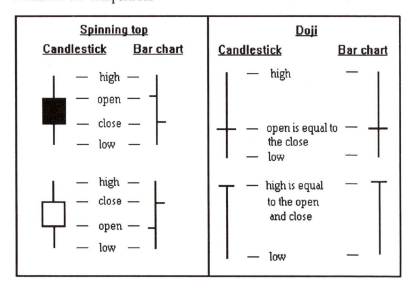

FIGURE 9.12
March 1991 Treasury bond chart

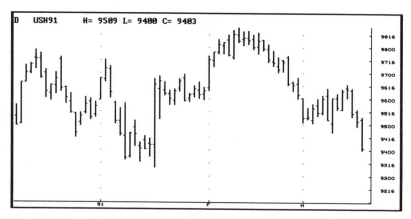

Source: Reprinted with permission, FutureSource, 955 Parkview Blvd., Lombard, IL 60148 (800) 621-2628

FIGURE 9.13
March 1991 Treasury bond candlestick chart

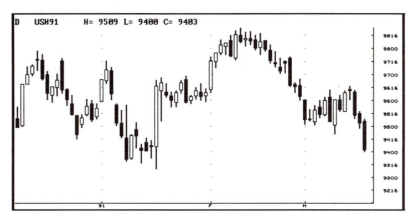

Source: Reprinted with permission, FutureSource, 955 Parkview Blvd., Lombard, IL 60148 (800) 621-2628

both the closing and opening range. The top thin vertical line is called the upper shadow, and the bottom thin vertical line is called the lower shadow. Figure 9.12 shows a vertical bar chart of March 91 Treasury bonds, and Figure 9.13 shows the corresponding candlestick chart.

Point and Figure Charts

A point and figure chart depicts price versus movement, and is an excellent means to study how the market moves through different price levels. Figure 9.14 is a point and figure graph of the NYSE (New York Stock Exchange Index) during 1983.

A point and figure chart is calculated in the following way.

1. *Determine the size of a box.* A box may contain either an X, which represents a price moving up, or an O, which represents a price moving down. The smallest box would be the minimum price change possible for the future, which is one tick. For example, one tick in the NYSE future is 5 points, therefore the minimum increment is 5 points or some multiple of 5, such as 10, 15, and so on. If the

FIGURE 9.14
NYSE point and figure chart

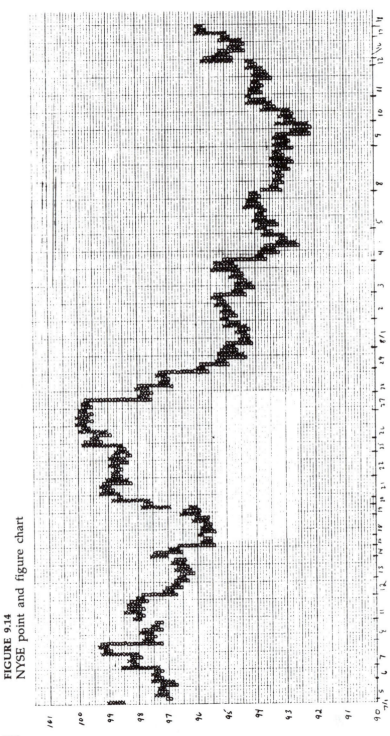

German mark were used, the minimum tick would be 1 and any integral number could be used such as 2, 3, or 13. Determining the size of the box is similar to determining the time frame in a bar chart, such as a minute, daily, or weekly. A smaller box size, such as ten, in the NYSE will show more movement but also a lot more noise in the market, and not be appropriate for long-term trading. A larger box size will show the more significant moves, but does not show many of the short-term support and resistance points helpful for short-term trading.

2. *Determine the minimum price reversal for the market.* The minimum price reversal is the number of boxes required to change the vertical column from an X to an O, or vice versa. The commonly accepted number is a three box reversal, but other forms may be used too. If a three box reversal is used, and the box size is five, the minimum reversal must be 15 (three boxes times five).

3. *The chart is started by recording the first minimum reversal move up or down.* An upward move by the minimum reversal size is denoted by an X, and a downward move by the minimum reversal size is denoted by an O. A move that continues in the same direction is recorded with an X or an O until a minimum reversal occurs. The reversals are recorded independently of time.

The minimum box size in Figure 9.14 is a 10-point move (0.10 on the graph), and the minimum reversal is 30 points (0.30 on the graph), or three boxes. One tick, or the minimum movement on the NYSE contract, is five points, so a 2-tick move is necessary for a box. This would be an example of a short-term chart similar to a 30- to 60-minute bar chart. Let's determine how some of the reversals are drawn at the beginning of the point and figure chart in Figure 9.14, with the help of Table 9.1.

The chart is drawn as follows:

The market opens at 98.50 and rallies to 98.80 which is a .30 move so 3 X's are recorded. The market then drops from 98.80 to 98.60 but this is not enough for a minimum reversal. It rallies to 98.90 and then to a high of 99.05 so X's are drawn to 99.00 to show the continuation of the move up. No X is drawn at 99.10 because the market must actually trade at 99.10 to record an X.

TABLE 9.1
Sample price moves to construct a point and figure chart

Price	X	O	0.30 point movement for a price change
98.50			begin
98.70			no
98.50			no
98.80	X		yes: 98.50 to 98.80
98.60			no
98.90	X		yes: continuation from 98.50
99.05	X		yes: continuation from 98.50
97.00		O	yes: 99.05 - 97.00
96.85		O	yes: continuation from 99.05
97.10			no
96.95			no
97.20	X		yes: 96.90 - 97.20

On the next day, the market opens down at 97.00 and sells off to 96.85, so an O is recorded at 97.00 and 96.90. Again, the market must trade to 96.80 to record an O at 98.80. It then rallies to 97.10, and finally reaches 97.20, which is enough for a minimum reversal of 0.30 points so three X's are drawn to 97.20.

Point and figure chart formations can be traded just like time charts. Each market will have various box sizes, depending on the volatility of the market and the time frame of the trader. The more volatile the market and the longer the time frame of the trader, the larger the box size.

Market Profile

The Market Logic technique is a method developed by Peter Steidlmayer for looking at the market in a unique price and time basis. The trader must be cognizant of where buyers and sellers agree or disagree on price. This is determined by how often a price will occur during a time period. The time periods are usually half-hour bracket periods, signified by a letter. The A bracket period might

FIGURE 9.15

September 1991 S&P Market Profile

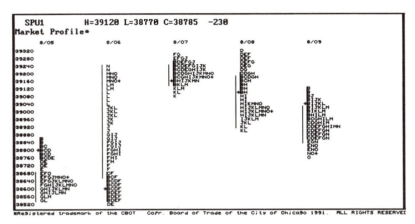

Source: Reprinted with permission, FutureSource, 955 Parkview Blvd., Lombard, IL 60148 (800) 621-2628

refer to the 8:00 AM to 8:30 AM time period. The B period would then refer to the 8:30 AM to 9:00 AM time interval. A bracket period is a distinct time period, often designated by the exchange, but the user may employ any period.

A market frequently trading in a time period would imply a level where buyers and sellers agree on price. Price levels in which the market does not trade are often not areas where buyers and sellers agree on price. A profile of the September 91 S&P500 in Figure 9.15 shows how the market finds congestion areas, or places where buyers and sellers agree on price, and other areas where prices readily trend. The bibliography contains more references on market profile techniques.

Swing Charts

Swing charts are constructed in a similar fashion to point and figure charts, in that the price movement, as opposed to time, is the *x* axis. Any movement greater than a certain amount is plotted on the chart. Trading patterns are similar to point and figure charts. An example of a swing chart is presented in Figure 9.16

FIGURE 9.16
A swing chart of price movement

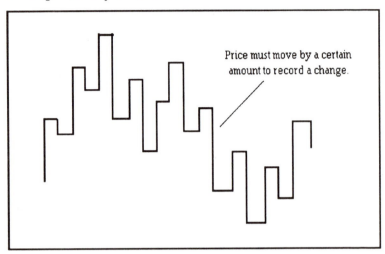

Price must move by a certain amount to record a change.

WHICH CHART TO USE?

Which chart is the best, or which one gives the best signals? Bar charts or candlesticks are best used when time is the most important consideration in the trading method. Japanese candlestick charts are similar to bar charts and the choice of which one to use is simply a question of preference. Different types of patterns evident in candlesticks can also be discerned in bar charts, and vice versa.

Other traders rely on point and figure and swing charts, because they provide a good indication of the action and reaction of market movements. Point and figure charts display excellent interaction of supply and demand by showing how the market moves through different price levels. The charts give good indications of support and resistance, but, unfortunately, do not represent time well.

The question of which chart to use is more a question of which method of charting the trader feels more comfortable with. Different charts do not necessarily provide better or truer signals but instead should be used depending on the time frame and needs of the trader.

WHICH TIME FRAME TO USE?

The tick chart shown in figure 9.17 of September 91 Treasury bonds is the shortest time frame available for analysis. The tick chart is helpful in determining possible fills, and places of high slippage or short-term resistance and support levels.

The 30-minute bar chart in Figure 9.18 of September 91 Treasury bonds is the next longer time frame after tick charts. Minute bar charts can be varied usually from 1 to 60 minutes for each period. They are one of the most frequently used charts for day traders, and provide a good indication of the short-term trend.

The daily bar chart of September 91 Treasury bonds in Figure 9.19 is the most popular time frame. It is in between the short-term tick and minute charts, and long-term weekly and monthly charts. The daily chart might be used to actually provide buy and sell signals, and also provide the intermediate trend of the market.

The weekly bar chart in Figure 9.20 and monthly bar chart in Figure 9.21 of the Treasury bond market yield a good indication of the long-term trend of the market. A trader viewing the market from a longer-term perspective might use a monthly, weekly, and

FIGURE 9.17
September 1991 Treasury bond tick chart

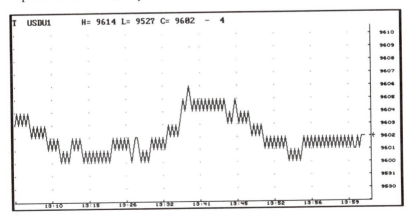

Source: Reprinted with permission, FutureSource, 955 Parkview Blvd., Lombard, IL 60148 (800) 621-2628

124   Chapter 9

FIGURE 9.18
September 1991 Treasury bond 30-minute bar chart

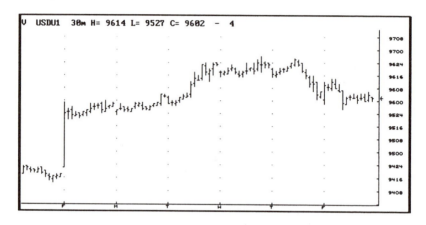

Source: Reprinted with permission, FutureSource, 955 Parkview Blvd., Lombard, IL 60148 (800) 621-2628

FIGURE 9.19
September 1991 Treasury bond daily bar chart

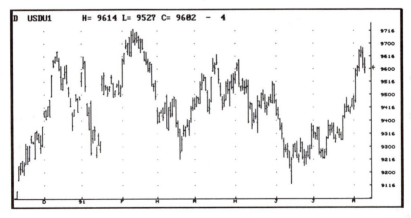

Source: Reprinted with permission, FutureSource, 955 Parkview Blvd., Lombard, IL 60148 (800) 621-2628

FIGURE 9.20
September 1991 Treasury bond weekly bar chart

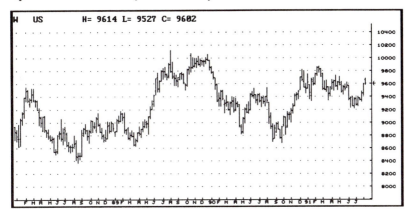

Source: Reprinted with permission, FutureSource, 955 Parkview Blvd., Lombard, IL 60148 (800) 621-2628

FIGURE 9.21
September 1991 Treasury bond monthly bar chart

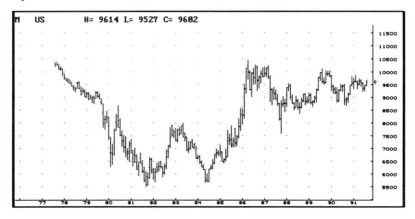

Source: Reprinted with permission, FutureSource, 955 Parkview Blvd., Lombard, IL 60148 (800) 621-2628

daily chart for trading. Weekly and monthly futures charts are continuation charts and will be discussed further in the next section. Which is better, a daily chart, or a 30-minute intraday chart? The question is best answered by determining how long you plan to hold onto a trade. A good rule of thumb for trading is to use a chart one size smaller than your intended holding period. If you plan on day trading, a minute bar chart in the range of 5-60 minutes and a daily bar chart might be used. A monthly or weekly chart is of little value to the active day trader except in knowing the major trend of the market. If you plan on holding onto a trade for a week or longer, consider a daily and weekly bar chart. In this case, the short-term intraday chart will not normally provide information that is relevant for longer-term trading.

Many good traders actually look at more than one time frame to get an indication of the long, intermediate-, and short-term trend of the market. The daily bar chart is a good start in any trading program, because it is a midpoint between the extremes of short- and long-term trading. No chart is superior to another, so you should choose one depending on your needs and trading time frame. Most traders have a favorite chart they stay with, depending on what has worked best for them in the past.

CONTINUATION CHARTS

Any charts, such as weekly or monthly, which do not have the same contract for every time period, run into the problem of continuity. In futures, the most active contract month is the one in which the greatest volume of trading occurs. However, the most actively traded contract constantly changes from one contract month to another, depending on the time. The different contract months often have different prices, so when the contract month changes or expires there is a problem in deciding how to continue the price activity.

On February 22, the March 91 S&P500 future in Figure 9.22 closed near 366.50, while the June 91 S&P500 future in Figure 9.23 closed higher at 370.00. The continuous weekly or monthly futures chart uses the most recent futures contract. The near term (March) is priced lower than the farther out month (June), so how should

FIGURE 9.22
March 1991 S&P500

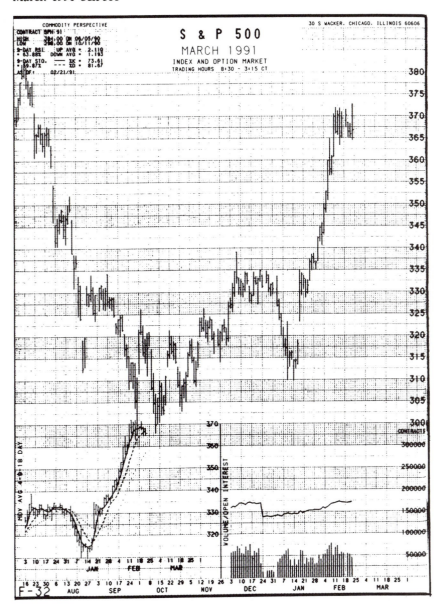

Source: Reprinted with Permission, © 1991 Commodity Perspective, 30 South
Wacker Drive, Suite 1820, Chicago, Illinois 60606

FIGURE 9.23
June 1991 S&P500

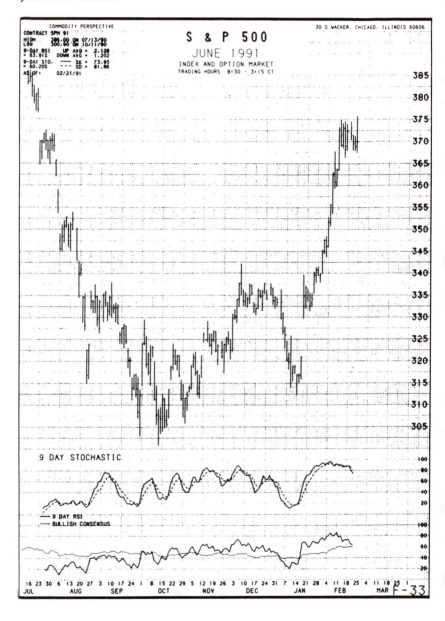

Source: Reprinted with Permission, © 1991 Commodity Perspective, 30 South Wacker Drive, Suite 1820, Chicago, Illinois 60606

the chart be continued when the March contract stops trading and June becomes the active month? If we want to make a continuous daily chart of the futures, how should this price discrepancy be reconciled?

The problem becomes more apparent in commodities where the front months may not be related to the pricing in the back months, such as the meats or grains. August 90 pork bellies in Figure 9.24 closed near the 44 level on July 20. The next trading month after August is the February 91 contract in Figure 9.25 which closed at 52 on July 20. The February contract closed approximately 8 cents higher than the August contract. Furthermore, the February contract declined nearly 14 cents from the June highs to the July lows, whereas the August contract dropped over 25 cents in the same period. The bottom of Figure 9.25 shows the weekly continuation chart for pork bellies.

Imbalances in the supply and demand for a commodity can cause one contract month to change differently than another contract month during the same time of the year. The supply and demand fundamentals for February pork bellies may be quite different than for the August contract, which can cause pricing discrepancies. Markets may become inverted where the near-term future is priced higher than the back months. This occurred in the pork belly market during June, when the August contract was trading above the February contract. Note, on June 11 the August contract closed above 67, but the February contract closed near 63. The August contract subsequently dropped below the price of the February contract. Normal markets occur when the short-term future is cheaper than the long-term months, such as the example in the S&P500 futures.

Each charting service has its own way of dealing with the dilemma. Some simply wait till the lead month expires and use the next one, ignoring the price gap. Others average the contracts together to get a continuous or perpetual contract. There are other methods to deal with the problem, but there is no right answer. Each way leads to a series of compromises, but the problem should not be too severe unless the trader intends to study precise long-term patterns.

FIGURE 9.24
August 1990 pork bellies

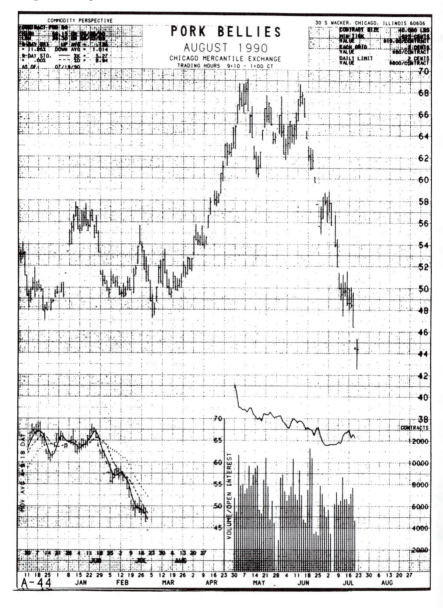

130

FIGURE 9.25

February 1991 pork bellies

Source: Reprinted with Permission, © 1991 Commodity Perspective, 30 South Wacker Drive, Suite 1820, Chicago, Illinois 60606

131

PRICE, VOLUME, AND OPEN INTEREST

Price, volume, and open interest provide important information about the market for the technical analyst, and are used in many technical studies. Most charts show the open, high, low and close or settlement price. For day charts, the open and close represent the price at a particular time of the day. The low and high represent the lowest and highest prices recorded during the day, independent of time. They are a good indication of short-term support and resistance.

The **volume** *is the number of contracts which trade during the time period. The* **open interest** *is the number of contracts outstanding at the end of the time period.* The total number of outstanding long positions must always equal the total number of outstanding short positions. Let's look at an example to help clarify the difference between volume and open interest.

Day	Volume	Open Interest
1. Teresa buys 1 contract from Joe	1	1
2. Diane sells 2 contracts to Rose	2	3
3. Teresa sells 1 contract to Diane	1	2

On day one, when Teresa buys one contract from Joe, the volume is one contract and the number of contracts outstanding is one. On day two, when Diane sells two contracts to Rose, the volume is two, but now there are three contracts outstanding. On day three, Teresa sells the contract she bought and Diane buys back the contract she sold, so the volume is one but the number of contracts outstanding is reduced to two.

THREE PHASES OF A MARKET

Markets continually exhibit three distinct phases of congestion, trending, or random behavior.

1. *Congestion*: Market is at an equilibrium level and buyers and sellers agree on price.

2. *Trending*: Perceptions and fundamentals change and the market moves higher or lower.

3. *Random*: Market is in disarray with no discernible congestion range or trend.

Markets trend when fundamental factors cause significant variations in supply and demand, or when people's perceptions change. These changes cause the market to trend higher or lower. Markets go through congestion phases when both supply and demand forces are in equilibrium, and prices consequently become mired in a trading range. Markets manifest random behavior when there is great uncertainty, and no clear supply or demand force materializes. *One of the most important objectives of a trader is to determine the current state or phase of the market.*

Congestion markets have fairly well defined equilibrium levels, which the technician terms support and resistance levels. Note, in Figure 9.26, how July 87 silver trades within the congestion range of 5500 to 6000 level from December to March. Buyers and sellers have a range where silver is considered fairly valued, so the market does not stray too far from this level. Congestion areas are also termed consolidation areas.

Trending markets are characterized by strong price moves which break out from previous congestion ranges. In late March, silver breaks out from the tight trading range and changes from a congestion pattern to a strong upward trending phase. The market has changed and buyers now dominate, so that the price moves higher. The opposite effect of trending to consolidation occurs in Figure 9.27, where the June 87 S&P500 is in a strong upward trend. It tops out in March and begins a congestion phase.

Random markets are different than congestion or trending markets, because there appears to be no order to a random market. Figure 9.28 shows April 91 gold in a random phase. In October, it breaks below the low at 390, set in September, but does not continue lower but instead reverses and breaks out in late December at 400, above the highs previously set in November. It does not follow through, and reverses trend again by breaking below the lows of October. There is no clearly defined congestion range and even less of any significant trend. Although the author flatly rejects the efficient

FIGURE 9.26

July 1987 Comex silver

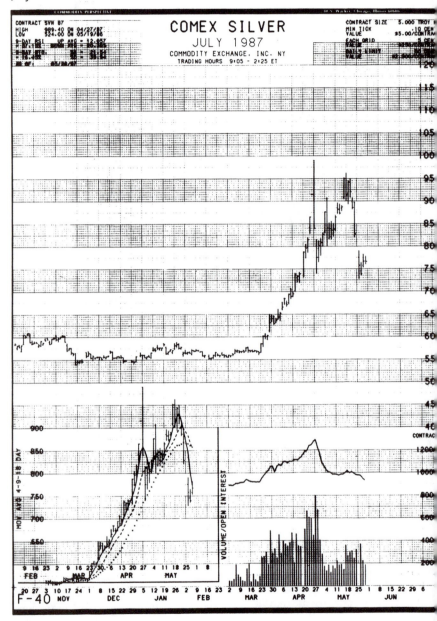

Source: Reprinted with Permission, © 1991 Commodity Perspective, 30 South Wacker Drive, Suite 1820, Chicago, Illinois 60606

FIGURE 9.27
June 1987 S&P500 index

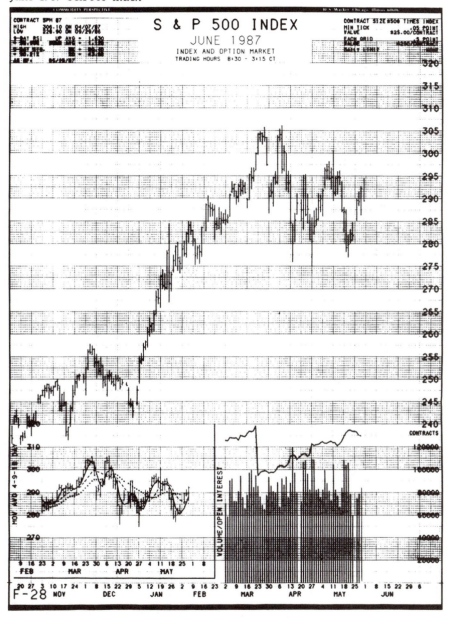

FIGURE 9.28

April 1991 Comex gold

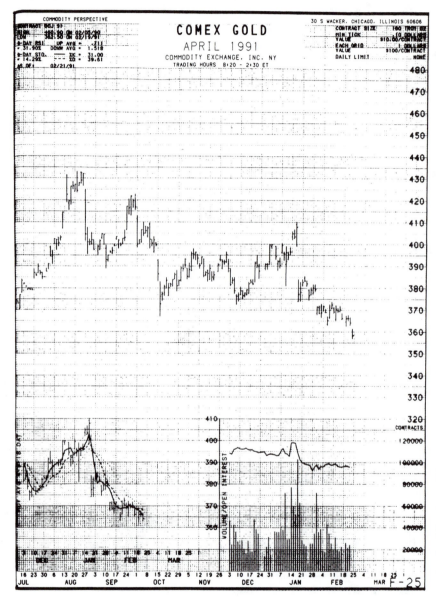

Source: Reprinted with Permission, © 1991 Commodity Perspective, 30 South Wacker Drive, Suite 1820, Chicago, Illinois 60606

FIGURE 9.29

December 1990 Japanese yen

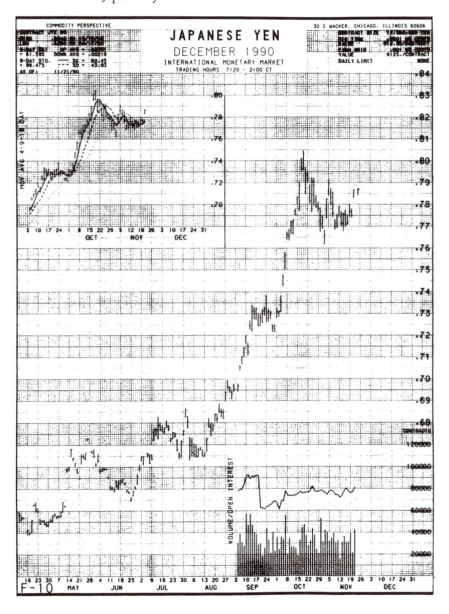

137

FIGURE 9.30

March 1991 cocoa

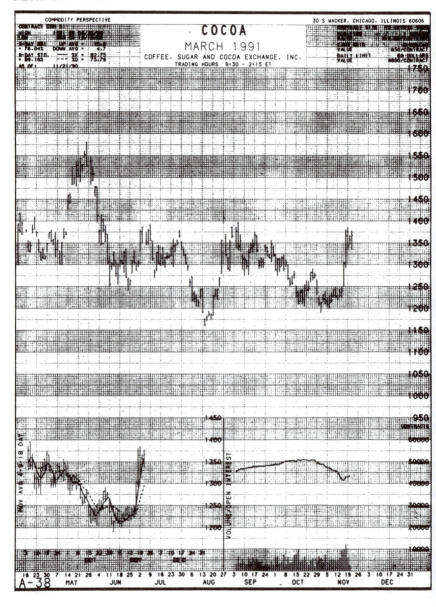

138

market hypothesis, he is painfully aware from real trading experiences of the sometimes random character of the market.

The reason every trader must determine the state of the market is that it is theoretically possible to make money in the first two phases but mathematically impossible in the third phase. For example if the market is in a congestion phase, selling the tops and buying the bottoms should result in profitable trades (easier said than done!). If the market is trending, buying in a bull trend or selling in a bear trend should result in profitable trading. However, if the market is in a random phase, there is no clear technique to employ, since either following or fading a trend will not necessarily yield winning trades. In fact, the only known way to effectively deal with random markets is to stop trading for a while and take a long vacation! One of the purposes of technical analysis is to identify these different states.

There is a common perception that markets are in the congestion or random phases as much as 80% of the time (more in some markets and less in others). This is not easy to measure quantitatively and verify; nevertheless, certain markets such as the currencies have historically manifested much broader and longer-lasting trends. The December 90 Japanese yen in Figure 9.29 is in a very clear uptrend, whereas March 91 cocoa in Figure 9.30 cannot decide whether to go up or down.

DOW THEORY AND THE THREE TRENDS AND PHASES OF THE MARKET

Charles Dow is credited with the idea that market averages discount all information, and are better indicators of the overall trend of the market than individual stocks. Dow believed there were three trends to the market, which he called the primary, secondary and minor trends, and used the analogy of the tide, the wave, and the ripple. *The* **primary move** *was considered the major move in the market, with the* **secondary** *and* **minor trends** *the actions or reactions of the major move.* An important consequence of this idea is that the trader should always be aware of the major move, and try to trade in the direction of the major trend. The three trends are shown in Figure 9.31.

FIGURE 9.31
The three Dow trends of primary or main trend, intermediate or
secondary trend, and minor or short-term trend.

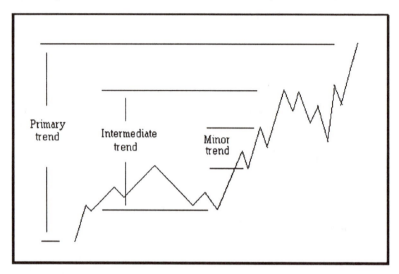

The major trend exhibits three phases called the accumulation,
markup, and distribution. *The* **accumulation phase** *occurs when the
market is trading near its lows and public interest is minimal.* Knowledgeable
players begin accumulating the contracts or shares from a disinterested
public. *The* **markup phase** *occurs when the market starts to move higher
and public interest and participation begins to increase. The* **distribution
phase** *occurs when the market has reached higher levels and is now fairly
valued or overvalued.* Public participation and awareness is now at
the highest level, but the more knowledgeable players are distributing
their holdings to the public. The three phases are noted in Figure
9.32.

*If the major trend of the market is up, the primary move and the
markup in prices is called a* **bull market.** *If the major trend is down,
then the primary move and the mark down in prices is called a* **bear
market.**

Using the ideas in the Dow Theory, it is often convenient to
break the market into three separate time frames of long, intermediate,
and short term. The size of the time frames may vary among traders

FIGURE 9.32
The three phases of accumulation where smart interests buy and the
public is disinterested, mark up where the public develops an interest,
and distribution where the smart interests sell but the public is most
enthusiastic.

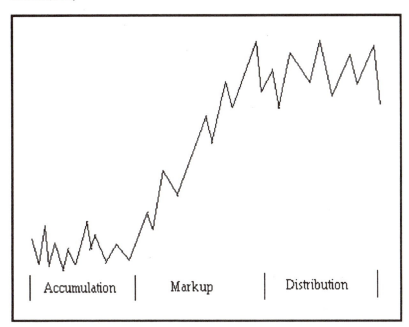

depending on their holding period and price objectives. A good
starting point for time frames is to consider the long term one or
more years, the intermediate term between three to twelve months,
and the short term less than three months. For some day traders
the long term could conceivably be one week, the intermediate term
one day, and the short term five minutes. Long-term position traders
would have much different time frames. An exact definition is not
really important. It is often helpful to think in terms of relative but
distinct time frames and trends, and always try to trade with the
major trend.

The monthly chart of the S&P500 futures in Figure 9.33 clearly shows the market in a long-term bull trend. The weekly chart in Figure 9.34 shows the intermediate trend to be sideways, with a bias to the upside. The daily chart in Figure 9.35 depicts the short-term trend to be sideways.

FIGURE 9.33
S&P500 futures long-term chart

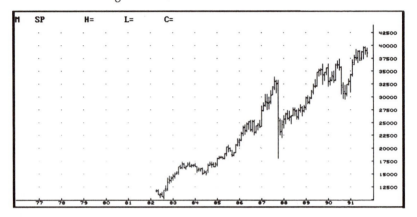

Source: Reprinted with permission, FutureSource, 955 Parkview Blvd., Lombard, IL 60148 (800) 621-2628

FIGURE 9.34
S&P500 futures weekly chart

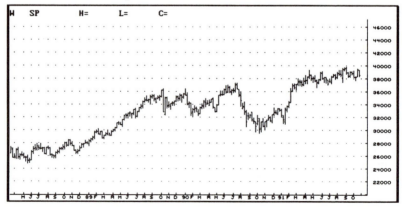

Source: Reprinted with permission, FutureSource, 955 Parkview Blvd., Lombard, IL 60148 (800) 621-2628

FIGURE 9.35
September 91 S&P500 futures daily chart

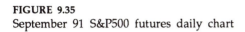
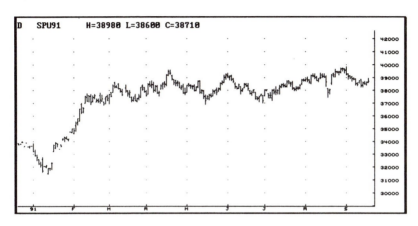

Source: Reprinted with permission, FutureSource, 955 Parkview Blvd., Lombard, IL 60148 (800) 621-2628

TREND FOLLOWING METHODS

Most of the trading rules and studies in technical analysis have been devised to detect and catch trending markets. One of the trend follower's goals is to trade markets that have better than average potential to trend, and try to stay out of markets which are in the congestion or especially the random phase. Trend following methods have been developed using trading rules based on moving averages, chart patterns, and many other kinds of technical studies.

Many trend following rules were created in the 1970's and early 1980's, which was an era when many markets exhibited large and long-lasting trends. The monthly gold chart in Figure 9.36 depicts how the volatility and trending behavior of the market has changed with time. Note that the large trends in the late 1970's and early 1980's were followed by less volatile and trending markets in the mid and late 80's. Inflation was much greater in the late 1970's and early 80's, and this fostered many of the huge price moves in commodities. As inflation abated during the 1980's, the commodity markets did not trend as greatly as before.

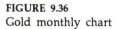

FIGURE 9.36
Gold monthly chart

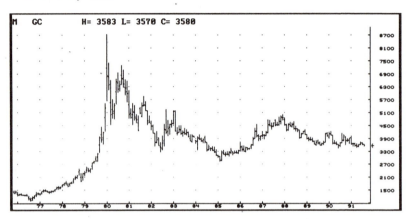

Source: Reprinted with permission, FutureSource, 955 Parkview Blvd., Lombard, IL 60148 (800) 621-2628

The same trend following rules that were hugely successful during this time period did not always work as well in the ensuing period of the mid-and late 80's. The latter markets were less trendy and not as volatile, and became more congested or random. More studies are now being developed to trade congestion markets, since they have become more common. The theory of chaos, which is a branch of mathematics and science, is now being investigated for possible use in trading.

Since markets and times change, historical trading rules or "time-tested methods" should be used as flexible guideposts for further study. You should include personal experiences and your own creativity in developing a set of trading rules, instead of considering the standard technical rules as inviolate laws. The ultimate trading rule is more a figment of one's imagination than a reality.

Markets are the reflections of people's hopes and dreams. Certain aspects of markets, like greed and fear, do not appear to change because people always seem to have these kinds of timeless traits. Other aspects of markets, like trends and volatility, do change because people have other kinds of traits and beliefs which change in time.

TIMING

Proper market timing is important in any type of trading, but is absolutely critical to successful futures trading. The leverage in futures is much greater than in other markets, so the profits and losses tend to get magnified more quickly. It is not enough to know whether the market is going up or down. An investor who is correct about market direction may still consistently lose money because the entry and exit points of trades may not be timed correctly. *It is equally and sometimes more important to know when the market may go up or down.*

The importance of timing brings up one of the main distinctions between technical and fundamental analysis. Fundamental analysis is essential to understanding the economics and driving forces which affect the market. This knowledge may help the investor to make better informed trading decisions. Fundamental analysis does not always provide the best time to initiate or exit a trade, because the analysis is often broad and general in scope. For example, after studying the fundamentals of the coffee market in early May, an investor expects a decline in prices. When should the investor enter the market, and where should protective stops be placed to limit risk in Figure 9.37 of December 89 coffee? The investor is considering selling in the middle of May, but hesitates, because there are rumors of a frost or drought which could cause the market to rally. However, if the investor waits and the market drops precipitously, the entire move will be missed. The investor goes short at 120, but watches the market rise in late May to 125. When the market drops in early June, the investor decides to cover at 120 and break even on the trade, but unfortunately, misses the ensuing downmove. Has this ever happened to you or someone you know?

In many cases, the fundamental analysis may have been excellent, and the market *eventually* went in the direction anticipated. But, an investor who has the correct fundamental perception of a market may not necessarily make money trading because the timing may be off. The trade may be entered too early, too late, or not at all in order to take advantage of the fundamental information.

Inherent in the study of technical analysis is a means and study of the timing of entry and exit points for every trade. The studies in technical

FIGURE 9.37

December 1989 coffee

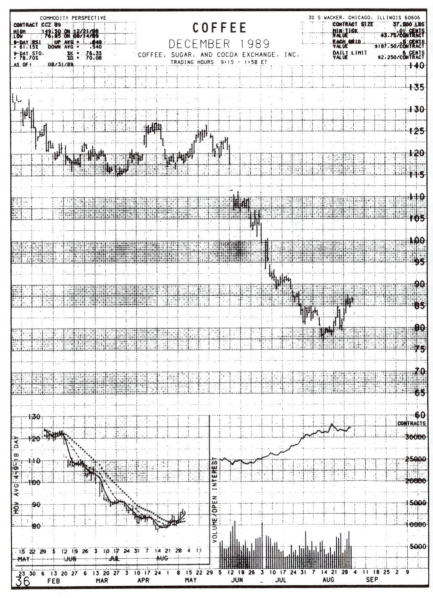

Source: Reprinted with Permission, © 1991 Commodity Perspective, 30 South Wacker Drive, Suite 1820, Chicago, Illinois 60606

analysis provide a framework in developing trading methods that are based on entering and exiting the market at specific times. Most technical studies do not address the question of why things happen, or the fundamental aspects of the market. Instead, they are more concerned with analyzing different market patterns, to assess the best risk/reward characteristics and the timeliness for a trade.

The preceding discussion is not meant to suggest that technical analysis will always provide the best entry and exit point for a trade. Anyone who has used technical analysis is familiar with the phrase "false breakout" or other terms synonymous with being whipsawed or losing money in a trade. However, technical analysis employed effectively can assist the trader in the decision process of improving entry and exit points in any trade.

Successful trading is a combination of correct assessment of market direction and proper timing of entry and exit. One of the main benefits of technical analysis is that it provides a means of timing entry and exit points for trading.

SUBJECTIVE AND OBJECTIVE ANALYSIS

Virtually all forms of technical analysis fall under the broad description of pattern recognition. **Pattern recognition** *is the study of recurring formations or patterns.* These patterns may be as simple as a gap formation, or as complex as a head and shoulders or Elliott Wave formation. The patterns may be generated from price or volume information which is directly related to the market, or from data such as astrological or weather information not directly related to the market. A "narrower" view of pattern recognition falls under the extensive study of artificial intelligence, which will be covered in the objective section.

The various types of technical analysis can be separated into the two broad categories of *subjective* and *objective* analysis:

I. **Subjective analysis** *refers to studies that are subject to interpretation and therefore not easily verified using statistical methods.* An example of a subjective pattern would be a head and shoulders pattern, because the actual formation is not always mutually agreed upon by all technicians.

2. **Objective analysis** *refers to studies that can be analyzed, and the results verified, using statistics or other mathematical methods.* An example of an objective pattern is a moving average, because there is a specific mathematical definition for a moving average.

Technicians may use both kinds of analysis in arriving at a trading decision.

The study of technical analysis will be separated into two different categories for the following reason. Fast and powerful computers now allow the trader to test objective technical studies to see how they perform historically. This allows the trader to decide which studies yield better results with specific markets over certain times. Of course, this does not imply that past performance will be similar to future performance, but the trader now has a reference frame to work from.

Subjective studies are inherently more difficult to analyze in a rigorous manner like objective studies. Although some work on subjective studies is being done in the field of artificial intelligence, there is still a long way to go. This by no means weakens the value of subjective analysis, but simply implies that the studies must be viewed from a different perspective. A technician may use an objective study in a subjective way, and in fact many traders do employ objective studies this way. For example, moving averages are sometimes used in a similar way as trendlines to detect support or resistance points.

CONCLUSION

Technical analysis is the study of market behavior to determine the present condition of the market. Technical analysis may be dichotomized into subjective studies, which cannot be statistically verified, and objective studies which may be statistically verified. Technical analysis provides valuable insight into assessing the condition of the market, and helping in the timing of a trade.

CHAPTER 10

Subjective Analysis

The most beautiful thing we can experience is the mysterious. It is the source of all true art and science.

Albert Einstein, *What I Believe*

Subjective analysis *refers to studies that are subject to interpretation and therefore may not be easily verified using mathematical methods.* Price patterns, such as a triangle or the Elliot Wave theory, are subjective because the pattern and resultant outcome may be interpreted differently by different technicians.

SUPPORT AND RESISTANCE POINTS

A **support point** *is a place where buying overcomes selling and, consequently, the market tends to rise.* Figure 10.1a depicts idealized examples of support points in a market. These support points develop quite often, and indicate places where traders believe the market is oversold, or a good buy.

A **resistance point** *is a place where selling overcomes buying, and therefore, the market drops.* Figure 10.1b shows idealized examples of

FIGURE 10.1
Support points are places where buying overcomes selling and the market rises. Resistance points occur where selling overcomes buying and the market drops.

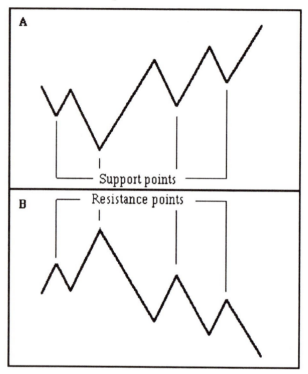

resistance points in a market. These resistance points recur often, but indicate areas where traders believe the market is overbought, or a good sale.

The September 90 municipal bond contract in Figure 10.2 provides many examples of support and resistance points. Two important support points occur near the 87 level around April 30 and the 90 level around June 25. Two resistance points develop, at the 93 level around July 30 and between the 91 and 92 level around August 13.

Support and resistance are important concepts in understanding many of the studies employed in technical analysis. These support and resistance

FIGURE 10.2

September 1990 muni-bond index

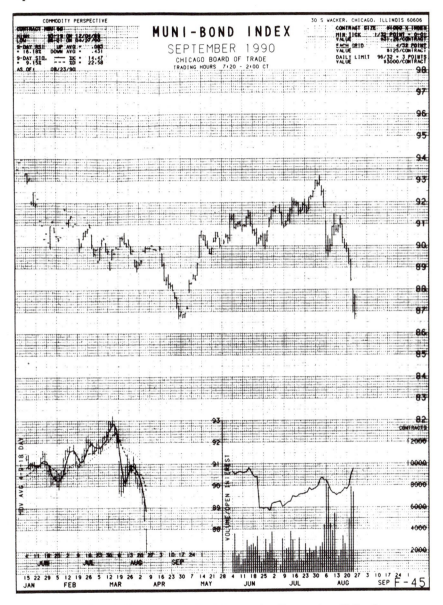

Source: Reprinted with Permission, © 1991 Commodity Perspective, 30 South Wacker Drive, Suite 1820, Chicago, IL 60606.

points constantly recur on a short-, intermediate-, and long-term level, and become the basis for making trading decisions. The points are reference frames providing possible areas to enter the market, and equally important areas for exiting the market. This will be investigated further when we look at trendlines.

Many people find support and resistance frustrating to work with because the levels are ranges, as opposed to exact numbers or levels. Some believe these levels do not really signify anything, especially when markets violate these levels. For example, the previously mentioned 90 support level in June is broken on August 6 and decisively penetrated on August 21. However, these levels cannot be predicted with 100% accuracy, like an experiment in physics. *The trader must realize we are really studying the actions of people, and not merely precise economic data. Therefore, we are working in probabilities, not certainties.*

Once a support point is broken, the level becomes a resistance point. The converse is true where a resistance point which is broken, becomes a support point. The transformations of support to resistance, and of resistance to support, are depicted in Figure 10.3.

FIGURE 10.3
Once broken, the support level becomes a resistance level and the resistance level becomes a support level.

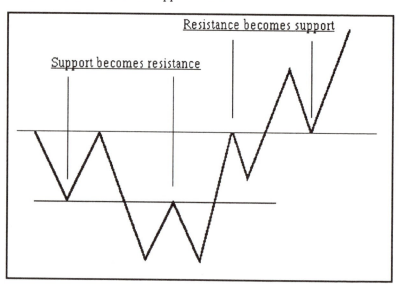

FIGURE 10.4

September 1989 NYSE composite

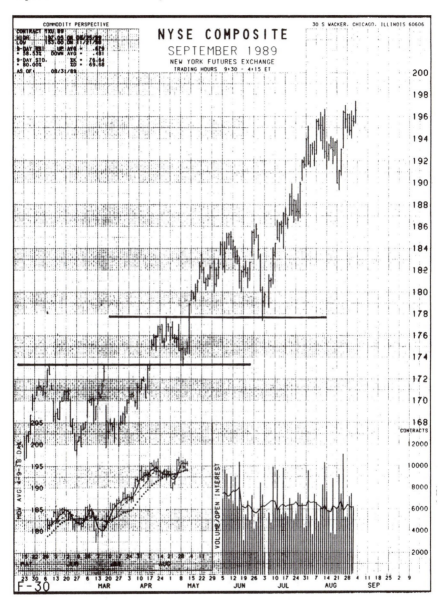

FIGURE 10.5

February 1990 live hogs

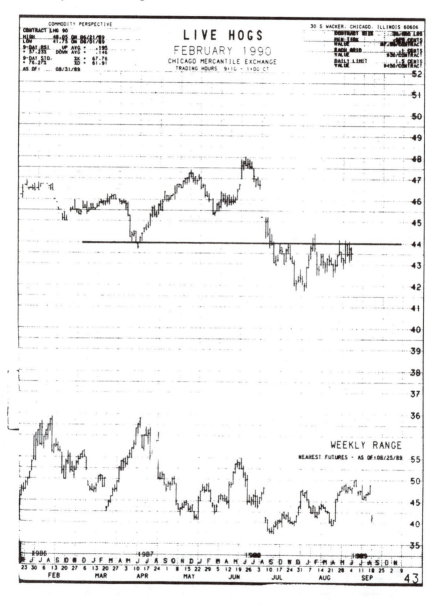

Source: Reprinted with Permission, © 1991 Commodity Perspective, 30 South Wacker Drive, Suite 1820, Chicago, IL 60606.

Why does this happen? Support and resistance points indicate levels where significant buying and selling occur. If a support point is broken, the traders who were long will now tend to become sellers at the same place in order to break even on the trade. Whenever a trader begins to lose money, one of the first impulses is to get out at the original point of entry, in order to break even. This is one of the most important reasons why support points become resistance points, and vice versa. The selling at the old support point will now provide resistance in the market. The same reasoning applies for resistance levels.

Another reason for this transfiguration is that support and resistance points may represent important fundamental price levels. Buyers and sellers converge at these points, so the levels become areas of inertia, where price moves may be slowed in either direction.

Figure 10.4 of the September 89 NYSE contract is an example of resistance becoming support. The resistance level of 173, established in February and March, is taken out decisively in April, and becomes support when the market retraces in May. The high between 177 and 178 in April is broken through in May, and becomes support in late June and early July.

The chart of February 90 live hogs in Figure 10.5 is a good example of a support level becoming a resistance area. The support level of 44, established in April, is broken in July, and then becomes a heavy resistance area in July, August, and September.

SUPPORT AND RESISTANCE LINES

Support and resistance lines are the next step in determining support and resistance levels on a chart. A support line is obtained by drawing a line through two support points, while a resistance line is drawn through two resistance points. The two kinds of support and resistance lines which serve two different purposes are:

1. Horizontal support and resistance lines identify important price levels in the market. Figure 10.6a is an example of a horizontal support line drawn through support points, and Figure 10.6b is an example of a resistance line drawn through resistance points.

FIGURE 10.6

(2) Horizontal support line; (b) horizontal resistance line; (c) diagonal support line; (d) diagonal resistance line. Horizontal support and resistance lines indicate important price levels; diagonal support and resistance lines help to portray the trend.

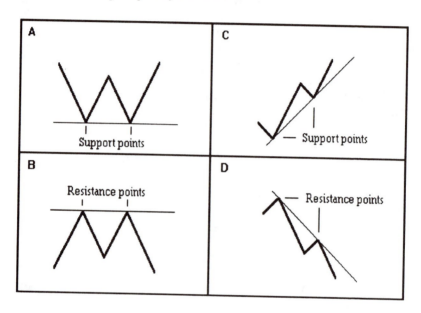

2. Diagonal support and resistance lines are drawn to portray the trend of the market. Figure 10.6c shows an example of a diagonal support line drawn through two support points, and Figure 10.6d is an example of a resistance line drawn through two resistance points.

HORIZONTAL SUPPORT AND RESISTANCE LINES

Horizontal support and resistance lines are drawn to identify important price levels of resistance and support in the market. These lines help the trader anticipate where support or resistance levels may develop in the future. The Dow 3000 level in Figure 10.7 is a good example of a resistance level. The lower weekly chart shows how the market

FIGURE 10.7
Dow Jones Industrials daily chart

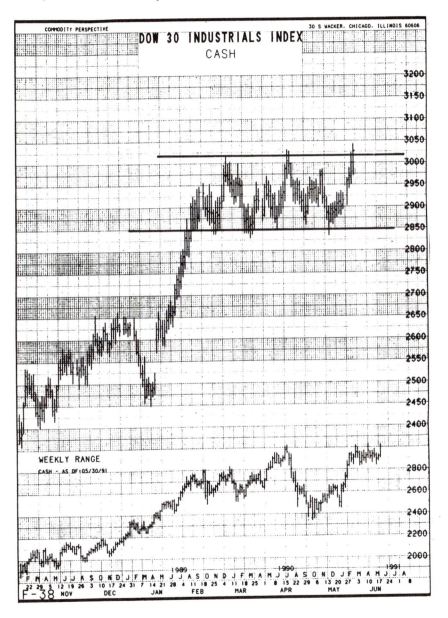

Source: Reprinted with Permission, © 1991 Commodity Perspective, 30 South Wacker Drive, Suite 1820, Chicago, IL 60606.

develops resistance at the 3000 level in July 1990, and then sells off until the beginning of 1991. In the upper daily graph, the market rallies strongly in February, but hits a "brick wall" at the 3000 level again in March and April.

The 2850 level on the Dow is an example of a significant support level. The market finds continuous strong support at this level in February, March, April, and May. Strong buying emerges at the 2850 level because it may represent an area where investors view stocks as being cheap, relative to alternative investments such as bonds or cash. Heavy selling occurred in the 3000 level as investors became cautious, believing the market was overvalued at this level.

In between the most significant horizontal trendlines of long term highs and lows are many intermediate levels of support and resistance. For example, the price of crude oil tended to gravitate in the 1980's to OPEC's benchmark level of $18.00 a barrel. If oil was trading around $20.00 a barrel, the $18.00 level was considered support, and might stop or slow any initial price decline. If oil was trading around $16.00 a barrel, the $18.00 level was considered resistance, and might impede any initial price rise.

Figure 10.8 shows May 89 crude oil rise in December and January, and then find resistance from "out of the blue" in the middle of January at the $18.00 level. The October 90 contract in Figure 10.9 finds important support in the $18.00 level in late November, early December, and again in June.

Some horizontal support and resistance lines may often identify significant fundamental price levels in the commodity. For example, a horizontal support line may represent an important fundamental price level, such as the cost of production of the commodity. A long-term horizontal resistance line for a commodity may be a price level where cheaper alternative commodities will begin to replace the higher priced commodity. The Dow 3000 level might have been considered a fundamental area, where investors felt stocks were too expensive versus other investments. The $18.00 level in crude oil might represent an area where suppliers increase or decrease supply, or where consumer demand increases or decreases, depending on the level of the market.

FIGURE 10.8
May 1989 light crude oil

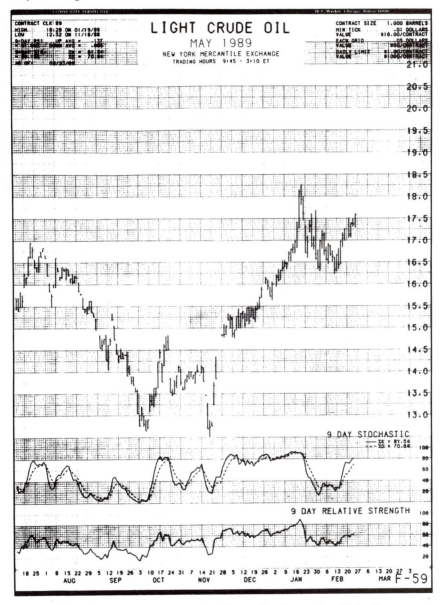

Source: Reprinted with Permission, © 1991 Commodity Perspective, 30 South Wacker Drive, Suite 1820, Chicago, IL 60606.

FIGURE 10.9

October 1990 light crude oil

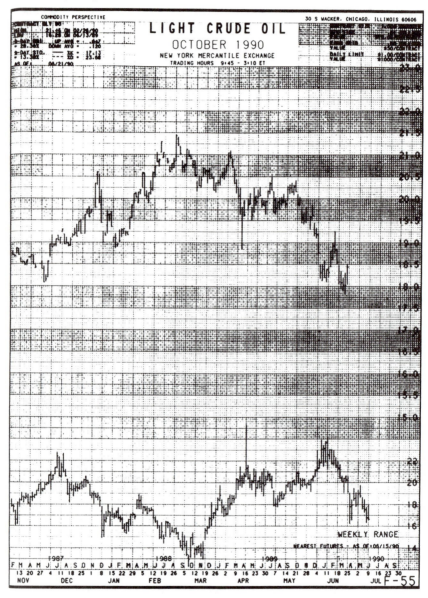

Source: Reprinted with Permission, © 1991 Commodity Perspective, 30 South Wacker Drive, Suite 1820, Chicago, IL 60606.

TRENDLINES

Diagonal trendlines are drawn to both portray and project the trend of the market, and also help to indicate the possible end of a trend. Diagonal trendlines help the trader anticipate where support or resistance may develop in a trend in the future. Figure 10.10 of October 90 cotton is an example of a diagonal support line. The line is drawn from the two support points near 65.50 on March 28 and 66.50 on April 9. Notice how the sell-offs, in the weeks of May 14 and 21, at 69.50 and 70.50, are contained by the support line. The major sell-off in July is again supported at the 74.00 level, but the August decline finally breaks the line. The diagonal support lines first portray the trend as going up, and then project where support may materialize. The lines show where the bullish trend is ending and, possibly, the beginning of a congestion phase or bear trend.

Figure 10.11 of March 91 sugar is an example of a diagonal resistance line. The line is drawn from the two resistance tops in early and late May, near 15.25 and 14.25. The market rallies in July and finds a first area of resistance from the line. The resistance lines portray the downtrend and project where resistance may occur. They show where the bearish trend is ending, and the beginning of a congestion phase, or possible bull trend.

Does a horizontal line have to be exactly 180°, or when is a horizontal line a diagonal trendline? A better question is, does it matter? Technicians and traders often get caught up in trying to make an exact science out of an abstract art. These subjective studies are not rigid definitions, but should be used as guidelines for trading. The trader should use the studies as an aid in trading, not as inviolable rules which must be followed.

Support and resistance lines may be used with support and resistance points. Both may provide excellent reference levels for entry and exit points in trading.

CHANNELS

The technician will often draw a line parallel to a trendline to depict the trading range of the market. *The trading range between the trendline*

FIGURE 10.10
October 1990 cotton

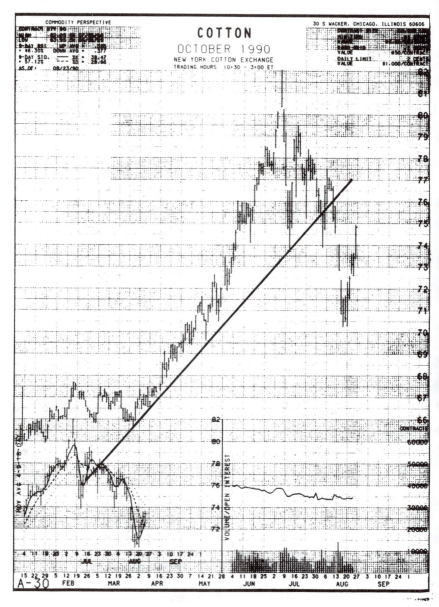

Source: Reprinted with Permission, © 1991 Commodity Perspective, 30 South
Wacker Drive, Suite 1820, Chicago, IL 60606.

162

FIGURE 10.11
March 1991 sugar

Source: Reprinted with Permission, © 1991 Commodity Perspective, 30 South
Wacker Drive, Suite 1820, Chicago, IL 60606.

FIGURE 10.12
Channel lines drawn from horizontal and diagonal support and resistance lines to define the possible trading range of the market.

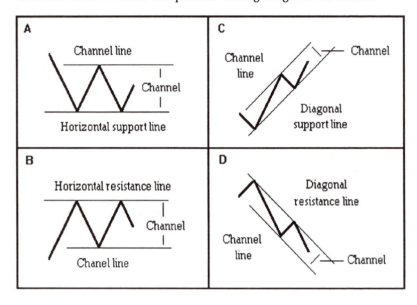

and the line parallel to it is called a channel. A channel helps to define the trading range of the market. Examples of channel lines drawn from horizontal and diagonal support and resistance lines are shown in Figure 10.12.

Channels can be drawn in the following manner. In Figure 10.13 of March 91 eurodollars, a diagonal support line is drawn through the lows in late August near 91.60 and September near 91.80. A parallel resistance line is obtained by drawing a parallel line through the high, between the two lows, which define the diagonal trendline. Referring to Figure 10.13 again, the parallel resistance line is drawn parallel to the trendline, through the high at 92.10 in September. The parallel line drawn from a support line becomes a resistance line, and helps to define the uptrend by projecting where resistance may develop in the uptrend. Notice how the market finds resistance at this line in October and December.

FIGURE 10.13
March 1991 Eurodollars

Source: Reprinted with Permission, © 1991 Commodity Perspective, 30 South Wacker Drive, Suite 1820, Chicago, IL 60606.

FIGURE 10.14

March 1991 soybean meal

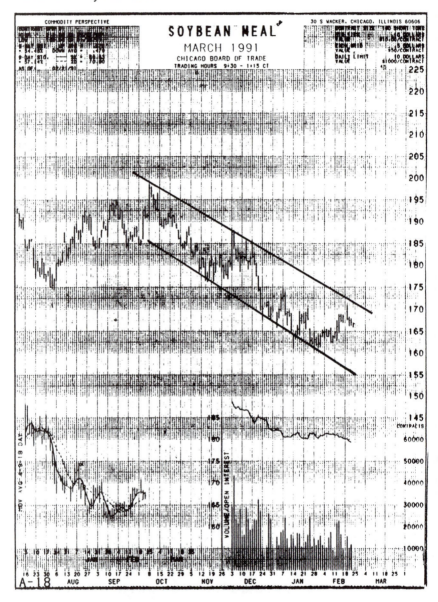

Source: Reprinted with Permission, © 1991 Commodity Perspective, 30 South Wacker Drive, Suite 1820, Chicago, IL 60606.

FIGURE 10.15

October 1990 live cattle

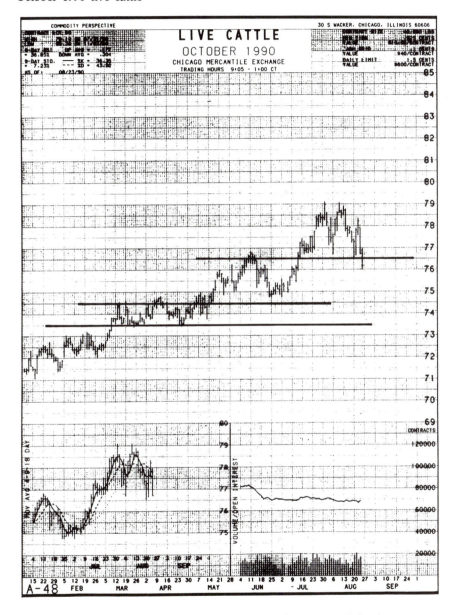

A parallel support line drawn from a resistance line would emanate from the first immediate bottom or support point, and define the first channel. A resistance line may be drawn in Figure 10.14 of March 91 soybean meal, from the top near 198 in October to the second top near 188 in December. A parallel support line may be drawn parallel to the resistance line and through the low between the two tops near 176 in November. A parallel line drawn from a resistance line becomes a support line and helps to identify where support may develop in the downtrend. Notice how the market finds support in December and January between the 161 and 168 area.

Parallel horizontal support and resistance lines may be drawn just like parallel diagonal lines. A series of horizontal lines can be drawn in Figure 10.15 on October 90 live cattle. The 7350 level is a support area, and a parallel resistance line drawn off the first top in March at 7450 becomes an important resistance level. Once 7450 is broken in May, it becomes an important support area in July. The 7650 line becomes the next important resistance level and, once broken, turns into an important support level in August.

Channel lines provide the technician with an indication of the possible trading range of the market. This helps the trader obtain a better idea of where support and resistance areas might appear.

COMBINING SUPPORT AND RESISTANCE LINES

The breaking of a support or resistance line provides an initial indication that a new trend may arise. Figure 10.16 of November 90 lumber provides an example of using both diagonal and horizontal support lines to analyze the market. A diagonal support line can be drawn from the support points at 194 during the week of April 23, and 196 on May 23. A horizontal resistance line, which began in February at the 200 level, becomes a support line on June 19 and 27. The diagonal and horizontal support lines are slightly penetrated on July 5 for a potential sale, and decisively broken on July 9 below the 200 level. The market collapses and finds initial support at the 191 level, which is a previous support point from March 2.

FIGURE 10.16

November 1990 lumber

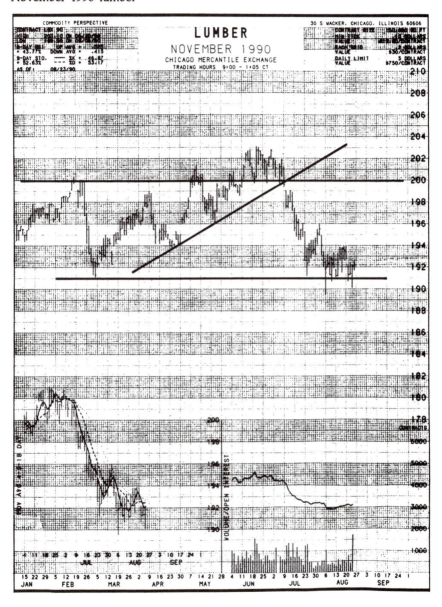

Source: Reprinted with Permission, © 1991 Commodity Perspective, 30 South Wacker Drive, Suite 1820, Chicago, IL 60606.

A trader might consider a sale near the 200 level on July 5, with a protective buy stop in the 202–204 area. Why place a sell order at 200 and a buy stop above the 202 area? The 200 area represents an important break of a diagonal and horizontal support area. The 203 level is a horizontal resistance level which was clearly carved out in June. If the market breaks through the 200 level, a decline should occur, but if the market breaks 200 and retraces above 203, a bull trend may ensue. Where should the exact sale and concomitant buy stop be placed? The determination of an exact entry and exit point in any trade is an essential aspect of successful trading, and will be addressed more thoroughly in the money management section.

ROBERT EDWARDS AND JOHN MAGEE

Chart patterns are one of the most popular forms of subjective analysis. Two of the first technicians to categorize and document the different chart formations were Robert Edwards and John Magee in their book, *Technical Analysis of Stock Trends*. Figures 10.17 through 10.29 show idealized and actual examples of some of the patterns traders look for in a market. The breaking of support or resistance levels in these patterns provides an indication that a change in trend may occur. The support and resistance levels are also helpful in providing possible entry and exit points for trading.

The idea behind trading market patterns is to identify formations which have exhibited bullish or bearish behavior in the past. The technician looks for these same formations with current market data for possible trading opportunities. The patterns are generally traded by buying or selling the breakouts which occur above or below the support or resistance points determined from the charts. The following patterns are some of the more commonly found patterns in trading.

Figure 10.17 is an idealized example of a triangle formation. The triangle is formed by the resistance line off the two tops and the support line off the two bottoms. Possible buy points include the breaking of the resistance line, or the lower or higher top. Possible sell points include the breaking of the support line, or the higher or lower bottom. If a buy point is reached first, then the original

FIGURE 10.17
Triangle: This formation occurs when a higher top is followed by a
lower top and a lower bottom is followed by a higher bottom.

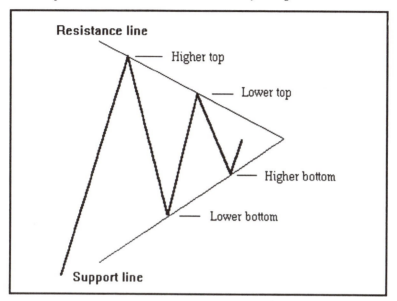

sell points can be used as protective stops for a long position. The
reverse holds true if a sell level is hit first.

Figure 10.18 of the December 90 S&P500 is an example of a
triangle formation. The top of the triangle occurs in early October
near the 326 level, and the lower top develops in mid-October near
the 321 level. The bottom of the triangle begins in mid-October near
the 298 level, and the higher bottom occurs in late October at the 303
level. The market initially breaks through the resistance line in early
November at the 317 level, and rallies higher into December. This
was a difficult triangle pattern to trade because each time a resistance
level was broken the market did not follow through immediately.

Figure 10.19 is an example of a rectangle formation. A rectangle
develops when a resistance line is drawn from two or more similar
highs, and a support line is drawn from two or more similar lows.
A possible buy point is the breaking of the resistance line. A possible
sell point is the breaking of the support line. As with the triangle,

FIGURE 10.18

December 90 S&P500 future triangle formation

Source: Reprinted with permission, FutureSource, 955 Parkview Blvd., Lombard, IL 60148 (800) 621-2628

FIGURE 10.19

Rectangle: This is defined by two similar highs and lows.

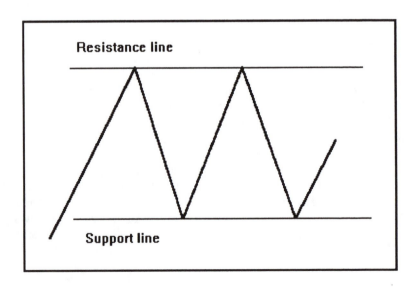

FIGURE 10.20
June 1987 Treasury notes

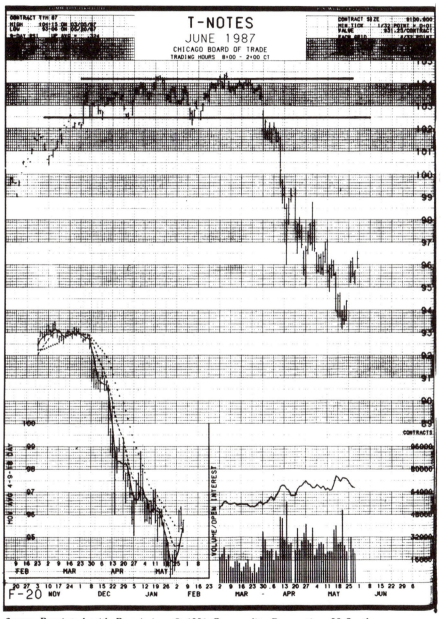

if a sell point is reached first, the buy level can become the area to place a protective buy stop, and vice versa.

June 87 ten-year notes in Figure 10.20 develop a rectangle formation in January, February, and March in the 102–104 area. The market collapsed through the rectangle at the 102 level in late March and early April. A sell order might be placed at the 101 area, with a protective stop in the 103 or 104 area.

The popular head and shoulders formation is depicted in Figure 10.21. The left and right shoulder are defined by similar highs and lows. The center top or head is higher than either shoulder. A sale may be initiated when the neckline is broken. An inverse head and shoulders would yield a possible buy at the neckline. A head and shoulders pattern may be a continuation pattern, so it is usually best to wait for a breakout from the neckline. Once the neckline is broken, and a sell initiated, the shoulders may be used as the protective buy stop level. In an inverse head and shoulders formation, a protective sell stop could be placed at the shoulders if a buy occurs at the neckline.

FIGURE 10.21
Head and shoulders: This formation develops when a left top is followed by a higher center top and a lower right top with similar bottoms.

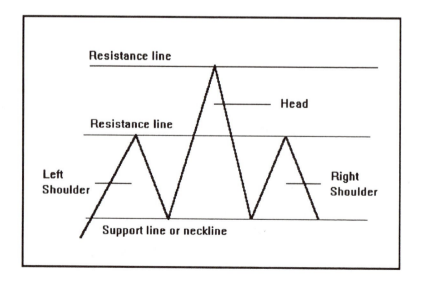

FIGURE 10.22
March 1987 British pound

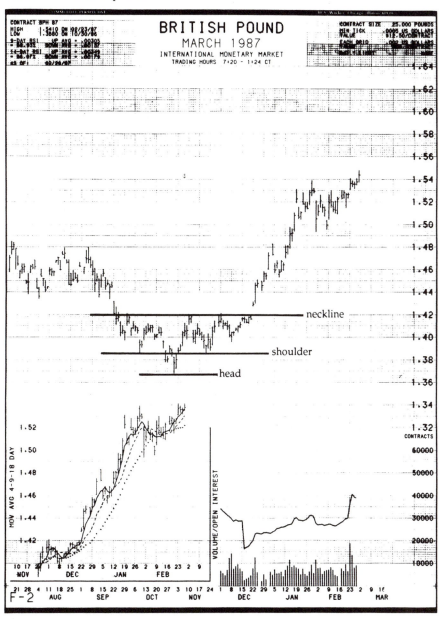

The March 87 British pound in Figure 10.22 is an example of an inverted head and shoulders pattern. The two shoulders occur in the 1.39 area in October and November, with the head in the 1.37 area in late October. A strong upmove develops after the 1.42 level is broken in December. A trader may consider buying at this level, with a protective stop placed at the 1.39 or 1.37 levels.

The V bottom or top is a common pattern shown in Figure 10.23. This pattern is difficult to trade because no prior support or resistance level is established before the top or bottom. The December 90 Canadian dollar in Figure 10.24 exhibits many V bottoms and tops in August, September, and October. Where would you go long or short the market in this pattern, or where should a protective stop be placed? There is only one reference point of support in a bottom and resistance in a top; so it is hard to determine good entry or exit points.

FIGURE 10.23
(a) Single bottom (left): There is only one low and the market reverses direction. (b) Single top (right): This has only one high and the market reverses direction.

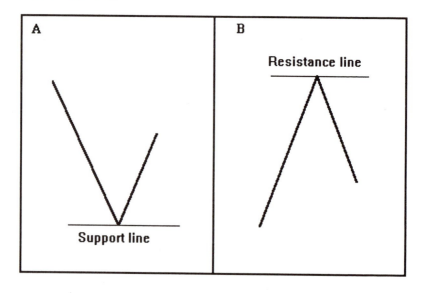

FIGURE 10.24
December 1987 Canadian dollar

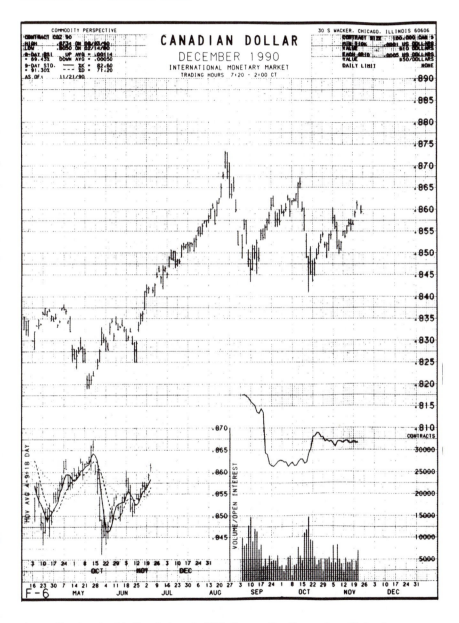

Source: Reprinted with Permission, © 1991 Commodity Perspective, 30 South Wacker Drive, Suite 1820, Chicago, IL 60606.

FIGURE 10.25

(a) Double top (left): The left and right tops are approximately equal.
(b) Double bottom (right): The left and right bottoms are nearly equal.

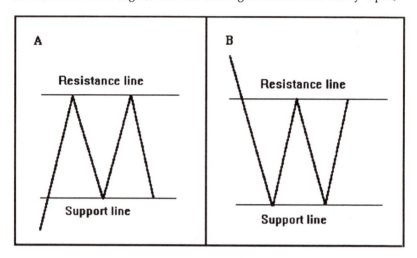

A double top and bottom are shown in Figure 10.25. The line drawn off the two highs of a double top provides a strong resistance level. The low between the two tops is an important support level, so a break below this level may indicate lower prices. A protective buy stop may be placed at the resistance line. The reverse holds true for a double bottom. The line drawn off the two lows on a double bottom indicates a good support level. The high between the two lows is an important resistance level, so a break above this area may indicate higher prices. A protective sell stop may be placed at the support line.

March 91 Treasury bonds in Figure 10.26 exhibit a classic double bottom in August and September, between the 86 and 87 level. The market breaks through the middle resistance top above 89 in October for a possible buy. A pull back to the 88 area retraces about 50% of the move, but the market resumes the uptrend in late October.

The broadening triangle in Figure 10.27 is a reverse triangle because the support and resistance lines diverge, instead of converge, with time. The broadening triangle is a particularly dangerous for-

FIGURE 10.26
March 1991 Treasury bond

FIGURE 10.27
Broadening triangle: The formation is characterized by higher highs and lower lows.

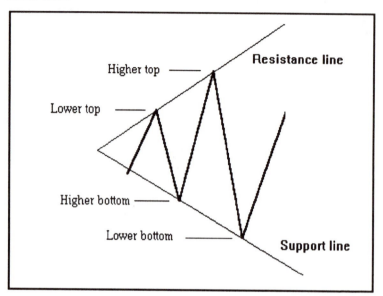

mation to trade, because any breakout from the resistance or support lines entails more risk than a regular triangle. For example, if a buy occurs from a breakout from the resistance line, a protective stop placed at the support line will be more risky, because a larger dollar loss may occur, as shown in Figure 10.27.

May 91 coffee in Figure 10.28 shows an example of a broadening triangle. The highs near 9900 in mid-February and 10,000 in the beginning of March, establish the resistance line. The lows near 9500 at the end of February, and the slightly lower low in mid-March, determine the support line. Both lines are breached within three days at the end of March, giving buy and sell signals. Anyone trading this market would have lost money going in either direction.

The pennant, flag, and wedge in Figure 10.29 are all variations on the triangle and rectangle formations. These patterns develop when the market is trending and then goes into a consolidation

FIGURE 10.28

May 1991 coffee broadening triangle

Source: Reprinted with permission, FutureSource, 955 Parkview Blvd., Lombard, IL 60148 (800) 621-2628

phase. They are usually considered continuation patterns because the market may often resume the previous trend after the consolidation phase is broken.

There are many other types of patterns, but they are often variations on the previously mentioned ones. Some technicians believe certain patterns have predictive value, while others trade most patterns as consolidation phases, where the market is waiting to break out on one side or the other.

When trading, it is often much easier to look for simple consolidation patterns than to search for exact formations which are more often an idea than a reality. Even when the exact pattern is found, there is still no guarantee the market will trade in the way it is "supposed to." You are far better off trying to understand the dynamics behind a pattern than memorizing the exact rules of a formation and being able to see one clearly in hindsight.

The previous examples showed some common formations and resulting profitable trades. Many traders become frustrated in using chart patterns because the signals do not always yield profitable trades. No chart formations will always provide winning trades, but the trader should not be searching for patterns which work

FIGURE 10.29

(a) Pennant; (b) flag; (c) wedge; (d) ascending triangle. The pennant, flag, wedge. and ascending triangle are often considered continuation patterns because the market may usually resume the trend; the patterns are shown for a rising market but the same ideas apply in a bear trend.

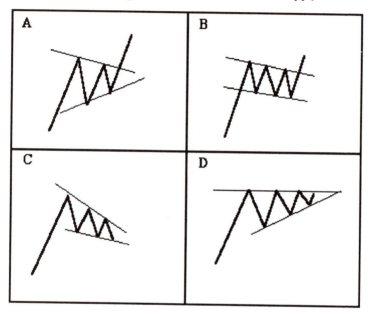

100% of the time. A more realistic goal of the trader is to find patterns that have a reasonable chance of yielding profitable trades.

Many technicians have somewhat precise and specific rules about trading each pattern. However, the patterns are inherently subjective, so it is better to know the fundamental ideas of why a pattern might work. Then the trader can observe the standard patterns, and create new ones which will help in developing more insight into trading them.

RICHARD WYCKOFF

Richard Wyckoff traded the stock market in the early and mid-1900's, and developed an extensive course for analyzing the market. Although developed for the stock market, the course is an excellent guide in learning how to view and trade any market. Many of the ideas are universal and may be applied in analyzing any market. He used a combination of price, wave, and point and figure charts in his analysis. He looked at relatively simple formations and developed his own terminology, such as a spring or shakeout. Price objectives could be obtained from different charts through measuring the horizontal length of a price pattern.

Wyckoff analyzed the market to determine where risk and reward were optimal for trading. He emphasized the placement of stops and the importance of controlling the risk of any particular trade. The interested reader can view the bibliography to obtain more information.

W. D. GANN

W. D. Gann researched the markets and devised all kinds of technical studies during the early and mid-1900's. Some of his ideas were grounded in empirical studies, while others were more mystical in nature. Irrespective of one's opinions about his work, he was clearly one of the most creative and thorough technicians who also wrote extensively about his work. He contended that certain laws governed not only the markets, but nature as well, and were therefore universal in scope.

One of his most important contributions was the concept of combining price and time. Gann believed crucial price movements happened when price and time converged. These points usually indicated important changes in trend. However, if price and time were not synchronized or did not converge, time always held priority over price. Therefore, time was the ultimate indicator because all of nature was governed by time.

Gann believed the bottom, designated 0, and the top, designated 100, of any major move, provided valuable clues in analyzing the market. He postulated that 0 and 100 represented important price levels to many people. Halfway between the major high and low is the 50% level, which signified the next important range for support and resistance in the market. The next important level would be the 25% and 75% level because these were halfway between the 50% and 0% and 100% level, respectively. Another significant division is the 33% and 67% level.

The weekly chart of corn in Figure 10.30 provides an example using some of his ideas:

1. In the summer of 1989 corn hit a low of 220 and rallied to a high of 300 in the summer of 1990, for an 80 point move.

2. It dropped back to 220 retracing 100% of the 80 point move in November 1990.

3. It then rallied 40 points, or 50%, of the 80 point move to 260 in March 1991.

4. It declined to 240 losing 20 points, or 50%, of the 40 point move in May 1991.

These percentages may also be applied in measuring time, with a full year (100%), 1/2 year (50%), and 1/4 year (25%) representing important times of the year. A market might make a significant retracement or change of trend during these times. Returning to Figure 10.30, the high in corn at 300 in July 1990 is approximately one year from the important low near 220 in July 1989. The low in September 1990 is nearly 1/4 of the year from the high in July 1990, and the low in December is almost 1/2 year from the high in July 1990.

Gann also applied his techniques to angles using 360° as the full circle, 180° which is 1/2 of 360°, and 90° which is 1/2 of 180°, and so on, as important angles. Gann angles can be drawn on a bar chart to show the relationship between price and time. A line drawn from an angle might provide support if the market is trading above the line. A line would provide resistance if the market is trading below the line. A possible change in trend also might be indicated with the angles. Figure 10.31 of the Dow Jones Industrials provides an example of Gann angles and lines.

The squaring of price and time was another one of his innovative ideas. This concept dealt with placing price levels on a square or other geometric shape. The diagonal, horizontal, and vertical lines resulting from the square were considered important support and resistance points. Gann would create these squares with hexagons

FIGURE 10.30
1989–1991 corn weekly chart

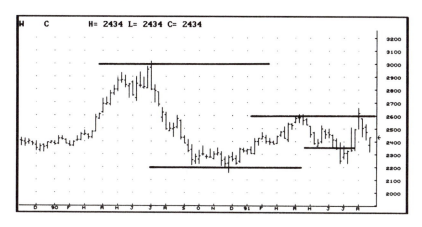

Source: Reprinted with permission, FutureSource, 955 Parkview Blvd., Lombard, IL 60148 (800) 621-2628

FIGURE 10.31
Dow Jones Industrials—Gann angles and lines

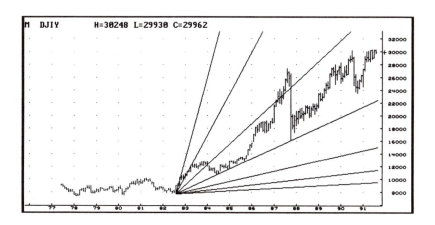

Source: Reprinted with permission, FutureSource, 955 Parkview Blvd., Lombard, IL 60148 (800) 621-2628

FIGURE 10.32
The squaring of price and time; the horizontal, vertical, and diagonals all contain prices that may provide support or resistance in a move.

114	113	112	111	110	109	108	107	106	— Diagonal
115	86	85	84	83	82	81	80	105	
116	87	66	65	64	63	62	79	104	
117	88	67	54	53	52	61	78	103	
118	89	68	55	50	51	60	77	102	— Horizontal
119	90	69	56	57	58	59	76	101	
120	91	70	71	72	73	74	75	100	
121	92	93	94	95	96	97	98	99	
122	123	124	125	126	127	128	129	130	— Diagonal

— Vertical

and other kinds of geometric figures, and apply the same principles. An example of the squaring of price and time appears in Figure 10.32.

These are but a few of his many ideas. Since he was a prolific writer, the interested reader is advised to check the bibliography.

LEONARDO FIBONACCI

Leonardo Fibonacci was a brilliant Italian mathematician who lived during the late 1100's and early 1200's. He introduced or discovered many important new ideas, but one of his most famous is a natural mathematical series. The *Fibonacci series* is the sum of the two previous numbers. Starting with one and two, the next number in the series is the sum of one and two:

1 + 2 = 3

The next number is the sum of 2 plus 3:

2 + 3 = 5

The series continues:

3 + 5 = 8
5 + 8 = 13

and so on and is written as:

1, 2, 3, 5, 8, 13, 21, 34, 55, . . .

and continues indefinitely.

Fibonacci believed the numbers in the series had special importance. He visited the great pyramid of Gizeh in Egypt, and noted many of the dimensions. He believed the ancient cultures may have maintained a significance with this series of numbers because certain dimensions in the great pyramid corresponded with the series.

The ratio of two consecutive numbers in the Fibonacci series approaches 0.618 as shown in the following calculations:

1/2   = 0.5
2/3   = 0.667
3/5   = 0.6
5/8   = 0.625
8/13 = 0.615

The ratio 0.618 is called the *golden mean* and had special significance with the ancient Greek and Egyptian cultures. They believed the number had important implications in many areas of science and art. Many buildings, including the pyramid, were built with this dimension in mind. The golden mean has been, and still is, an important reference level in the arts, such as painting.

Many occurrences in nature seem to exhibit either the Fibonacci series or the golden mean. For example, certain flowers such as daisies increase the number of their petals in a Fibonacci sequence. Certain animal shapes and dimensions in galaxies exhibit the golden mean. Figure 10.33 is an example of using Fibonacci lines in the market to determine potential support and resistance levels.

FIGURE 10.33
September 91 coffee

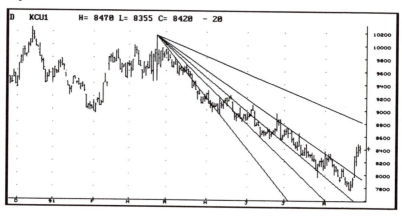

The Fibonacci series is an interesting mathematical idea, but what does it have to do with trading? Many studies, such as the Elliott Wave theory, are based on some of the concepts of the Fibonacci series.

WAVE THEORY—ELLIOTT WAVE

Wave theory revolves around the idea that markets are cyclical and exhibit waves of pessimism and optimism. Some believe the markets are governed by powerful waves of nature which affect us in many unknown ways. Theorists view wave analysis as important in understanding the movement in the market. Wave theory is also a branch of cycle theory, which will be covered in the objective analysis chapter.

R. N. Elliott believed markets had well-defined waves that could be used to predict market direction. The Elliot Wave theory is a unique way of viewing patterns in the market. Elliott believed the market moved in five distinct waves on the upside and three distinct waves on the downside. The basic shape of the wave is shown in Figure 10.34, with waves one, three, and five representing the "impulse," or minor upwaves in the major bull move. Waves two and four represent the "corrective," or minor downwaves in the major

FIGURE 10.34

Elliot Wave pattern: The Elliot Wave is comprised of five waves in the upmove and three waves in the down move.

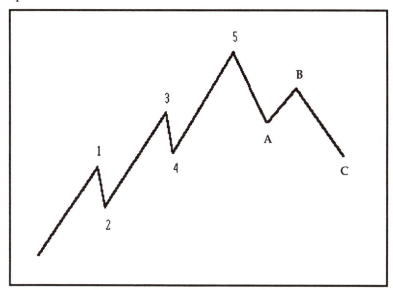

bull move. The waves lettered A and C represent the minor downwaves in the major bear move. Wave B represents the one upwave in the major bear move. This pattern is the basic form and rhythm of the market according to Elliott Wave theory.

Elliott postulated that the waves existed at many distinct levels, which meant there were waves within waves. Figure 10.35 is an example of a wave within a wave. Each minor wave in the Elliott Wave was composed of another series of waves in the same form as the Elliott Wave. He gave the waves names in descending size:

1. Grand Supercycle
2. Supercycle
3. Cycle
4. Primary
5. Intermediate
6. Minor

FIGURE 10.35
Wave within a wave: Elliot Wave theory states that each wave may be
further broken down into smaller Elliot Wave patterns.

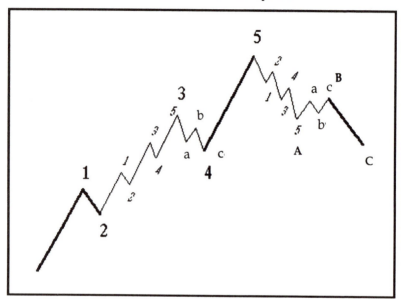

7. Minute
8. Minuette
9. Sub-Minuette

The major waves determined the major trend of the market. Minor
waves within the major waves determined the minor trend of the
market. The idea is somewhat similar to the Dow Theory of a primary
and secondary trend. There is a major trend, and within this trend
are smaller bull and bear trends. Elliott also had various extensions
or variations on the main wave which appeared in the market.

Elliott attached great importance to the Fibonacci series and
considered it a natural and universal mathematical series. He also
believed the Elliott Wave pattern was a naturally occurring pattern
in nature. The number of waves in a bull move was five and the
number of waves in a downmove was three—both numbers in the

Fibonacci series. Elliott placed particular importance on the golden mean, or 0.618, as a significant percentage for retracements in the market. The idea behind trading the Elliott Wave patterns is simple. The trader identifies the main wave or supercycle, and then works to progressively smaller waves to the specific time interval of interest. Although the idea is appealingly simple, the execution is usually more difficult because the trader must make assumptions as to whether various extensions apply, and what cycle the market is in. The trader may then predict the direction of the market, after determining where the market is currently trading in the overall Elliott Wave pattern. The Wave interpretation is subjective, which would account for predictions not always being correct, or why one Wave follower might have a different projection than another.

This is a brief outline of the Wave, but anyone desiring more information should review any of the works by Robert Prechter or Elliott, mentioned in the bibliography.

PERCENTAGE RETRACEMENTS

Percentage retracements refer to the market reacting from a high or low by a certain percentage. The more popular retracements include the 25%, 33%, 38%, and 50% retracement levels which are derived from the importance of the common fractions 1/4, 1/3, 3/8, and 1/2. The 3/8 is an important fraction because of its relationship with the golden mean. Recall from the Fibonacci section the golden mean 0.62 is considered an important number. The 38% retracement is derived by subtracting 1 from the golden mean or 1 − 0.62 = .38.

These percentage levels, when measured from the high of a move, should act as a support level when the market retraces from the high. The percentage levels, when measured from the low of a move, should act as a resistance level when the market retraces from the low. Figure 10.36 is an idealized representation of a market retracing 25%, 33%, 38%, and 50% of a move. Figure 10.37 is an actual example of the April 90 crude oil market making two 50% retracements. The market moves from 17.50 in August to 19.75 in

FIGURE 10.36
Percentage retracements: Some important retracement levels in the
market include the 25%, 33%, and 50% levels.

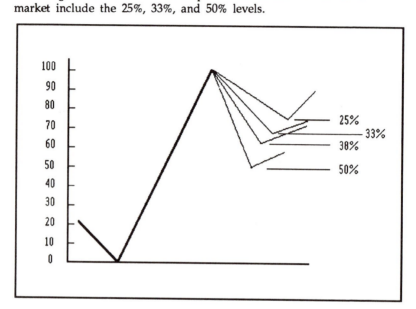

October, and retraces 50% of the move in November to the 20.80
level. It rallies again from 18.50 in November to 22.50, and retraces
50% of this move in mid-January at 20.50.

CONTRARY OPINION

When market opinion becomes one sided, and most of the public
is either bullish or bearish, an important change of trend may be
developing. The reasoning is simple. If everyone is long, and therefore
bullish on the prospects of the market, there is no one left to buy.
The market can only go lower as some investors begin to sell. The
same holds true on the downside, but in this case everyone is either
short or out of the market. Since there is no selling left in the
market, the market can only go up. There were few bears in the
stock market in 1929 before the great crash, and perhaps even fewer
bulls in 1932 before the extended bull market.

FIGURE 10.37
April 1990 light crude oil

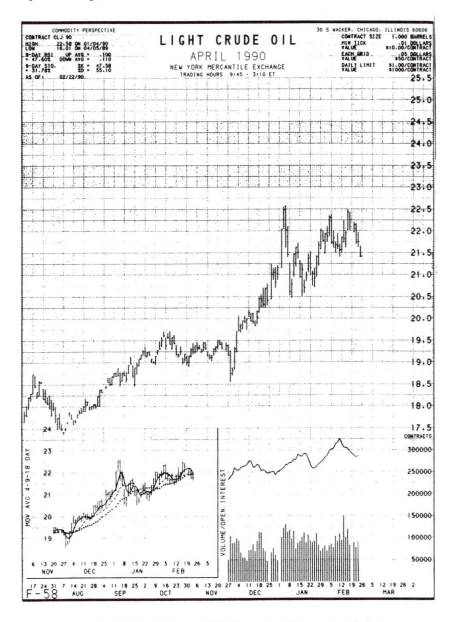

Source: Reprinted with Permission, © 1991 Commodity Perspective, 30 South Wacker Drive, Suite 1820, Chicago, IL 60606.

Some astute traders use sentiment indicators to monitor the prevailing opinions of market participants. These sentiment indicators may be the opinions of market players or recommendations of analysts and market services. A consensus opinion in either direction is often considered a prelude to a change in trend of the market. The stronger the opinions and sentiment indicators in one direction, the greater the reversals in trend in the other direction.

ASTROLOGY

Most people are quite happy to pass up any information linking astrology and trading. But keep in mind that forces in the universe affect all of us in many ways, and most likely some in which we are not even aware of. For a down-to-earth example, the moon has a very real and strong effect on the tides in the oceans. The sun has a tremendous effect on our weather patterns, which directly affect certain commodities such as the agricultural products. The amount of light in the winter versus the summer may have a large effect on certain people's moods, leading to happiness and depression. The sun and moon have an obvious impact on our lives, but what about the other planets? For the most part, we do not know how, or if, other bodies in the universe affect us.

Some studies have mentioned that certain commodities may move in conjunction with the phases of the moon. Even the sunspots may have a great effect on our weather patterns, which we are just beginning to understand. The study of astrology is unjustly neglected in market analysis. Part of the reason for this is that it can be hard to do some of the studies on a frequent basis. For example, some analysts look for special occurrences, such as when certain planets line up with each other, like Jupiter with Saturn. These occurrences may happen infrequently, so it may be hard to get statistically valid results related to the market with such little data.

Another reason it is difficult to quantify astrological results is that it is hard to isolate one factor when so many other factors may affect the market. For example, Jupiter and Saturn may influence the market, but other bodies such as the moon and sun may also be affecting the market. It may be very difficult, or impossible, to separate many of the other influences from the specific one being studied. Nevertheless, the study of astronomy and astrology merits more attention in relation to how it may affect the markets and people.

A SOUND APPROACH?

I have wondered whether listening to the frequency of prices may somehow provide signals in trading the market. Some scientific evidence indicates that approximately 90% of a person's sensory input comes from seeing. Most people rely more strongly on visual, as opposed to auditory or other types of sensory stimuli. However, there are some people, such as musicians or the blind, who may rely on auditory stimuli much more than visual stimuli. Certain music has rhythms and patterns which some people are more attuned to than others. Listening to music is quite a different experience, and generally more enjoyable than reading the sheet music. Could the same be said for a trader trying to *hear* the patterns of sound rather than see them?

All of the published research in market patterns has been on the visual level. But is it possible that certain people might better understand the market patterns by listening to them? Is it possible that certain patterns are more easily identified in an audible, rather than a visual way?

The work to set market prices to sound began as a practical attempt to allow a blind cousin, interested in trading, to hear the markets. This idea might allow him to study past market data by listening to it. A computer program was written to set each different price level to a specific sound frequency. For example, the German mark at the 0.5000 level would be set to a frequency of 1000 hertz, and the next tick up, or 0.5001, would be set to the 1001 hertz level. For those who disbelieve, keep in mind the same thing is done for visual market data, but the frequencies are at the visual level versus the auditory level.

The results are still being reviewed, but some of the work holds promise. The problem with this kind of work is that I do not know how to offer any kind of observable results. We are still in the testing stage and have not done any real time trading with the patterns. Any rhythm or pattern discerned by one person would, of course, be highly subjective and therefore learning the pattern may not necessarily be duplicated by another individual. We did not hear anything approaching the music of Bach, Beethoven, or Copland, but wonder if some of the more modern composers may have derived some of their inspiration from listening to the sounds of the market!

NEBULOUS PATTERNS

Most of the previously mentioned patterns have no clearly delineated form, and some may even appear unrecognizable or undefinable. In fact some of the typical arguments used to discredit technical analysis are the following:

1. Price patterns are not obvious, or only obvious after the fact.
2. No definitive patterns work all the time.
3. All technicians do not agree on the same pattern.

These are some of the arguments lodged against technical analysis. However, if we use this narrow-minded reasoning, we would also have to discredit all art, since people arrive at differing conclusions regarding the same art piece. All *technical and fundamental* analysts are never in agreement because the essence of trading is having disparate views about the prospects of a market. Those looking for precision and constancy are best advised to seek another occupation. We are fortunate when people come to differing conclusions, otherwise it would be quite a boring world indeed.

CONCLUSION

Some analysts have devised elaborate rules for identifying all types of subjective patterns. However, the patterns and rules are all subject to interpretation and therefore cannot be verified statistically. This does not imply that chart patterns are "magic," or any less reliable than objective methods. Instead, their study should also include the trader's own valuable experience in analyzing and trading the myriad formations of the market.

CHAPTER 11

Objective Analysis

In theory there is nothing to hinder our following what we are taught; but in life there are many things to draw us aside.

Epictetus, *Discourses*

Objective analysis *refers to studies that can be analyzed and the results verified, using statistics or other mathematical methods.* Moving averages and oscillator calculations are examples of this form of study. We can develop clear and specific trading rules, then test the trading rules to determine if a trading method has made or lost money in the past, with an objective study. Of course, this does not necessarily imply that future results will be similar to the past, but proper testing does provide a solid foundation for discovering potentially promising trading methods.

We have a means to test a trading hypothesis or idea, and observe the historical results to see how it compares with other trading strategies. After selecting a promising trading method, we can trade the system real time to see how *it and we* perform in the real world. This allows us to test our testing system, test and improve our trading system, and test ourselves.

DATA PRESENTATION

Time Series

A **time series** *is a mathematical term referring to a series of equally spaced data points arranged over time.* For example, a time series in trading might be the closing prices of a futures contract on a daily basis. Time series are frequently used in all kinds of trading studies. A daily bar chart is an example of a time series because there is an open, high, low, and closing price associated with each day.

X and Y Axes

When graphing a relationship such as time and price, we need to know what each line or axis represents. With most price charts, the time line or horizontal line is called the X axis, while the price line or vertical line is called the Y axis.

Figure 11.1, December 91 soybean oil, depicts many different relationships versus time. The price chart on the top shows how prices vary with time. Sometimes we need to see how another factor or dimension changes with time. The figure also shows how the volatility, 9-day stochastic, and 9-day RSI (Relative Strength Index) study, and bullish consensus vary with time.

The graphs portray a relationship of how one variable changes against another variable. The variable on the X axis is usually considered the *independent* variable because it changes independently and is not affected by any other variable. The variable on the Y axis is called the *dependent* variable because it changes depending on how the independent variable on the X axis varies.

The X axis, which usually represents time, is considered the independent variable. The Y axis, which often represents price, is considered the dependent variable because the price of the future is dependent on the time. Time is not a function or dependent of price but instead moves independently of price. What about the relationship of volatility and price? Which one is the dependent or independent variable? Sometimes it is not always easy to know which variable is dependent or independent, or if there is a well-defined relationship. Some might argue that volatility is a function of price while others might feel volatility is independent of price.

FIGURE 11.1

December 1991 soybean oil

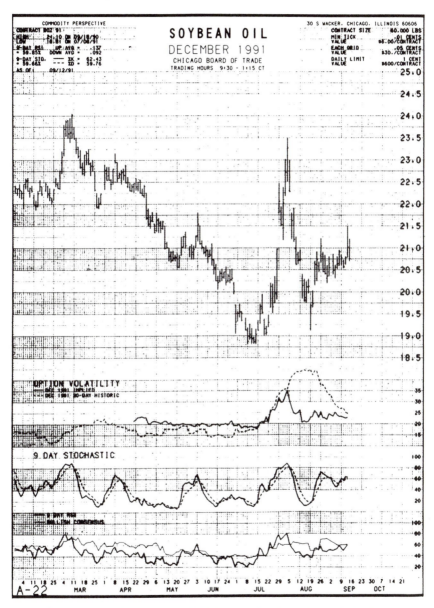

Source: Reprinted with Permission, © 1991 Commodity Perspective, 30 South
Wacker Drive, Suite 1820, Chicago, Illinois 60606.

FILTERING

Filtering *is the process of selecting data which meets certain criteria, and eliminating data which does not.* We are bombarded by all types of stimuli which must be filtered all the time. Selective filtering makes us conscious of certain stimuli and unaware or unconscious of other types. For example, what does your sense of touch tell you? If you thought about your hands or fingers pressing on the book, then you selectively focused on one part of the body, but eliminated another part like your foot or leg. Because there is so much to see, we must filter a large amount of data with our eyes by selectively focusing on specific objects.

Filtering is an important process in many technical studies, both in the subjective and objective areas. For example, a trader may wait until the market closes below the neckline on a head and shoulders pattern. The trader is filtering price data and is selecting only closing prices as a significant signal, and ignoring any intraday market information.

Any trading study will invariably use some type of filtering process. When reviewing these methods it will be helpful to consider different ways of filtering the information. Filtering is a very important concept in pattern recognition, where it will be discussed in more detail.

MOVING AVERAGE

Simple Moving Averages

A **simple moving average** *is the average of a series of prices during a specified period.* Moving averages, or variations, on a theme are some of the most widely used technical trading studies, and therefore, deserve a good understanding of their construction and use.

The general formula for a simple moving average is:

$$M_n = \frac{\sum_{i=1}^{n} P_i}{n}$$

where i = specific period
P = price at period i
n = total number of periods

Table 11.1 displays a series of prices and the corresponding four-day moving average.

Let's use the simple moving average formula to see how to calculate the four-day average:

$$M_4 = (P_1 + P_2 + P_3 + P_4)/4 \text{ days}$$
$$= (100 + 105 + 110 + 105)/4$$
$$= 420/4 = 105$$

The moving average value for period four is 105. The next period in the moving average would be calculated in the same manner.

A moving average can be calculated on any time period such as a daily, weekly, or minute basis. One reason for using a moving average is to reduce some of the noise inherent in the shorter-term movements, and better depict the major trend of the market. This process, called smoothing the data, is often done in statistics to allow for easier analysis of all types of data.

TABLE 11.1

Day	Price	Four-Day Moving Average
1	100	
2	105	
3	110	
4	105	105
5	120	110
6	115	113

Four- and twenty-day moving averages are overlaid on the daily price chart of July 91 orange juice in Figure 11.2. Note how the 4-day moving average reacts much more quickly than the 20-day average to changes in the market price. The longer the number of days in the moving average, the smoother the moving average line. However, there is a danger in smoothing too much data over too long a time frame because many important short-term price fluctuations, such as seasonal patterns, may be lost in the smoothing process.

FIGURE 11.2
July 1991 orange juice daily price chart

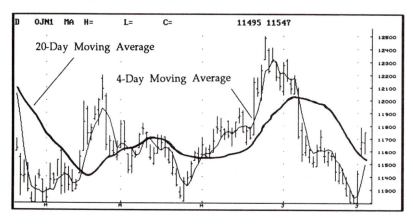

Source: Reprinted with permission, FutureSource, 955 Parkview Blvd., Lombard, IL 60148 (800) 621-2628

As one can see from Figure 11.1, a moving average greater than one day (a one-day moving average is the same as the daily price activity) will move less quickly than the daily price. Later we will see how this phenomena is the curse and blessing of using moving averages for trading. Moving averages always seem to be either too fast or too slow. All kinds of periods may be used, but one of the most popular combinations is the 4-, 9-, and 18-day moving average.

Weighted and Exponential Moving Averages

There are many variations on a theme with moving averages which allow for a faster or slower reaction to market moves. One of the ways to have a faster moving average is to use less days in the calculation, such as a 5-day instead of a 20-day. Using the same logic, a 20-day moving average might be preferred over a 5-day moving average if a slower average is required.

Another way to make the average react more quickly or slowly to market movement is by weighting the time periods of the average.

A **weighted** *moving average places weights on each time period of the moving average.* In the previous example, the simple four-day moving average weighted each period equally by dividing each day by four. The simple moving average is actually a weighted moving average, but the weights are equal for each period.

A weighted moving average can be designed to place more emphasis on certain time periods. For example, if a trader desires an average which reacts more quickly to market movement, then an average could be constructed to place emphasis on the more recent time periods.

The calculation for the weighted moving average is:

$$M_n = \sum_{i=1}^{n} w_i \cdot P_i$$

where n = number of periods

P_i = price in period i

i = specific period

w_i = weight of period i

We can develop values for the weighted moving average by using the prices in the previous example, and arbitrarily weighting the periods in the following manner:

$w_1 = 0.15$

$w_2 = 0.15$

$w_3 = 0.3$

$w_4 = 0.4$

The following values result:

M_4 = $0.15 \cdot 100 + 0.15 \cdot 105 + 0.3 \cdot 110 + 0.4 \cdot 105$

= $15 + 16 + 33 + 42$

= 106

The weighted value is 106 for period four. The trader may weight any time period any amount, and is not restricted to weighting the more recent data more heavily.

The **exponential** moving average is another variation on a moving average, but is calculated differently. The exponential moving average uses all the price data and does not drop off older price data, like the simple and weighted moving average. However, the recent price

FIGURE 11.3
March 1991 Treasury bonds

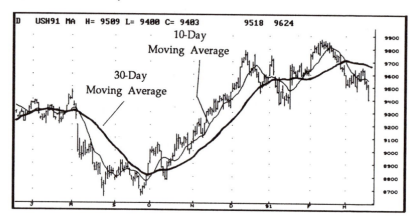

Source: Reprinted with permission, FutureSource, 955 Parkview Blvd., Lombard, IL 60148 (800) 621-2628

action is weighted more heavily than the earlier prices. The calculation for the exponential moving average is:

$$E_n = E_{i-1} + [r \cdot (P_i - E_{i-1})]$$

where P = price in period i
i = specific period
r = constant for smoothing
n = number of periods
E_{i-1} = exponential moving average value in the previous period

Let's calculate an exponential moving average. Assume the previous exponential average was 105, the current price is 110, and the constant is 0.2, then the current exponential moving average is:

$$E_n = 105 + (0.2 \cdot (110 - 105))$$
$$= 105 + 1 = 106$$

As may be seen by the calculations, an exponential moving average is actually easier to calculate than a simple moving average. You may be wondering—how do you arrive at the first exponential

FIGURE 11.4
March 1991 Treasury bonds

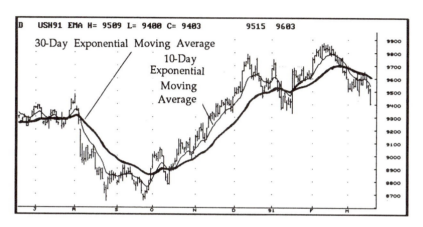

Source: Reprinted with permission, FutureSource, 955 Parkview Blvd., Lombard, IL 60148 (800) 621-2628

moving average value? Simply substitute the market price in the first period as the first exponential value, and then begin calculating the exponential average for period two as already described. The smoothing constant will change the weighting of the data.

A 10- and 30-day simple moving average is overlaid on the March 91 Treasury bonds in Figure 11.3. A 10- and 30-day exponential moving average is overlaid on the same contract in Figure 11.4 for comparison. The averages are similar, but there are some notable differences, such as in mid-October and January. The trading rules for an exponential moving average are the same as for a simple moving average,and will be discussed in the following section.

TRADING WITH MOVING AVERAGES

Trading systems designed with moving averages are generally trend-following systems. Trend-following trading systems are designed to catch a trend in the market, so the methods often generate buy

FIGURE 11.5
March 1991 copper

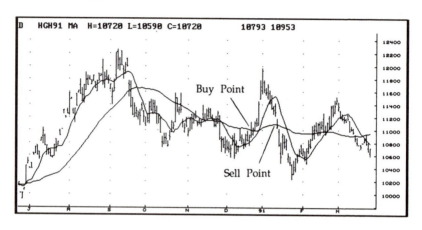

Source: Reprinted with permission, FutureSource, 955 Parkview Blvd., Lombard, IL 60148 (800) 621-2628

signals when the market is going up, and sell signals when the market is going down. This is called buying the market on strength, and selling the market on weakness. Three of the more commonly known rules for moving averages are:

1. Buy when the market closes above the moving average or combination of averages. Sell when the market closes below the moving average or combination of averages.

These rules are perhaps the simplest of the three, and usually provide the best entry and exit prices on profitable trades. Figure 11.5 shows March 91 copper with a 10- and 40-day moving average. One buy signal that is generated occurs when the market closes above both moving averages in late December near the 11,000 level. A sell signal occurs in mid-January when the market closes below the 11,000 level.

These rules usually provide the greatest number of whipsaws, which can be especially apparent in congestion type markets when even a small move will generate a signal. Therefore, the better entry and exit levels come with a tradeoff of more false signals and losing trades.

2. Buy when the short-term moving average crosses above the long-term moving average. Sell when the short-term moving average crosses below the long-term moving average.

These rules usually do not generate as many trades and, therefore, may promise fewer false breakouts. However, the entry and exit levels will usually be worse than in the first set of rules. Referring to March 91 copper again, a buy signal is not generated until the end of December near the 11,500 level. A sell signal is not generated until later in January near the 10,600 level.

3. Buy when the short- and long-term moving averages both point up. Sell when the short- and long-term moving averages point down.

These rules are similar to the second set and the same ideas apply.

You may notice the above rules would have a position in the market all the time. Such trading systems are called stop and reversal systems because the position is stopped out and reversed, leaving the trader always in the market. The rationale behind this type of system is that the trader is always in a position to catch a big move.

Should a trader have a position in the market all the time? The answer to this question is clear to some and uncertain to others. Some people adamantly believe it is necessary to always maintain a position in the market to be certain of catching a major move. Other traders wait for times and markets they believe to be optimal for their type of trading.

Do not be deceived into thinking you will catch every move if you always have a position in the market. You may have a position, but it could be on the wrong side and may prove quite costly. For example, being long July 91 platinum in May, in Figure 11.6, proved to be costly when the market opened lower near the 370 level near the end of May. Going short at that point did not help much either as the market rallied from the 370 level. Sometimes it is best to simply sit on the sidelines when trading, because markets do not always trend and can be quite random or trendless at times.

FIGURE 11.6
July 1991 platinum

Source: Reprinted with permission, FutureSource, 955 Parkview Blvd., Lombard,
IL 60148 (800) 621-2628

WHICH MOVING AVERAGE IS BEST?

There are trade-offs in trading for most situations, and moving averages
offer some of the best examples of them. Some studies have suggested
that the simple moving averages have actually outperformed the
more complex weighted, or exponential moving averages. The evidence
is by no means conclusive because changing certain parameters, markets, and times can vastly affect the results of the different averages.
The trader is better off testing systems which are designed around
the markets of interest, and the trading style of the person, instead
of searching for the "ultimate" trading method.

Referring to the three moving average rules in the previous
section, the trader may want to consider the following questions.
What might be the trading results when rule one is combined with
rule two? Or when rules one, two, and three are combined? Or
perhaps, a 5-and 20-day moving average is used instead of a 4-,
9-, and 18-day moving average? As one might guess, the number
of possibilities is infinite, but this type of questioning may partly
be answered with the aid of computers. Many traders now use

computers to test or optimize different trading systems, and see how they perform on a historical basis. We will investigate optimization further in developing a trading plan in the money management section.

Longer-term moving averages will generate fewer signals, but will normally not generate as many false breakouts. Shorter-term moving averages will generate more trades with usually better entry and exit levels, but also a greater number of losing trades or false breakouts.

Numerous studies have been made on trading systems, but the results must be reviewed with great caution. Even trading methods that have been tested for statistical accuracy and rigorously studied will not necessarily guarantee any future profits. The rules are not rigid laws which must be followed to the letter, but should instead provoke thought and ideas in creating rules, in conjunction with the trader's own experience.

ENVELOPES AND BANDS

Many traders think of the market as being either in a state of equilibrium or disequilibrium. A market that trades within a narrow range similar to the congestion patterns discussed earlier might be considered a market in a state of equilibrium. From a fundamental perspective the supply and demand forces are balanced.

A market breaking out of a range, or envelope, and developing a trend would be one in a state of disequilibrium, or out of balance. A market out of balance searches for a new equilibrium level by probing new highs or lows. August 90 feeder cattle in Figure 11.7 is in a congestion pattern, or state of equilibrium, in January and February in the 80 to 81 level. It breaks out of the trading range in early March and finds a new equilibrium level between 81 and 83. The market breaks out of the congestion pattern in early May and begins another search for a new equilibrium level. From a fundamental perspective, the supply and demand forces are not balanced, so the market is driven up by demand or down by supply.

Bands or envelopes may be placed above and below the highs and lows in the market to delineate the equilibrium levels. Any

FIGURE 11.7

August 1990 feeder cattle

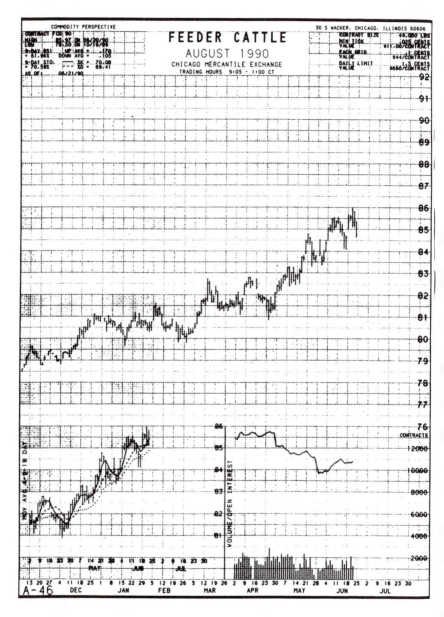

FIGURE 11.8
July 1991 wheat

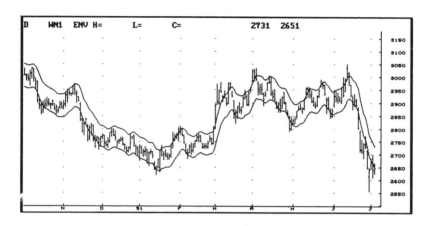

Source: Reprinted with permission, FutureSource, 955 Parkview Blvd., Lombard, IL 60148 (800) 621-2628

significant penetration above or below the bands would be construed as a break of the equilibrium level, which would generate a buy or sell signal.

There are many ways to construct these bands. One way to create the bands is by using a moving average of the highs and lows as shown in Figure 11.8 of July 91 wheat. A buy signal would be generated in late February when the market penetrates the high band. A sell signal would occur when the market penetrates the low band in late June.

In general, the tighter the band the more frequent the signals and possible whipsaws. The wider the band the less frequent the signals, but a greater part of the move is missed. Many of the trade-offs mentioned in the moving average section, such as shorter and longer time frames, would apply equally well with envelopes.

These methods are normally used as a trend following system, but they may also be used in countertrend trading. In this case a break above the band would be construed as a sell signal, and a break below the band would be a buy signal.

OSCILLATORS

Oscillators cover a broad class of indicators which measure movement about an equilibrium level, usually designated as zero. An oscillator is often used to identify overbought and oversold conditions. Another use for oscillators is to establish confirmations and nonconfirmations of market movements. Some use oscillators in trend following methods similar to moving average systems.

When oscillators are employed in counter trend trading, many of the trading rules may yield signals opposite to those developed for moving averages or trend following methods. Since oscillators and moving averages can be mathematically similar, the trader is free to use either study in any way deemed appropriate. There are certainly plenty of traders who wish they had employed the "standard methods" the opposite way, after losing money the old fashioned way.

Moving Average Oscillators

One of the most common types of oscillators measures the difference between two moving averages. Figure 11.9 is a graph of five- and ten-day moving averages overlaid on the price chart of March 91 Treasury bonds. Figure 11.10 shows a five- and ten-day oscillator of the bonds, which displays the difference between the two moving averages. The oscillator has the largest value near 108 in October, when the two moving averages are furthest apart, and the short-term average is above the long-term average. The oscillator has the lowest value near –124 in August, when the moving averages are further apart, but now the short-term average is below the long-term average. The oscillator becomes zero when the two moving averages cross, such as the beginning of November.

Some of the trading rules or uses for oscillators are:

1. Buy when the oscillator crosses the zero line, changing from a negative to a positive value. Sell when the oscillator crosses the zero line, changing from a positive to a negative value. These rules are the same as buying or selling when the moving averages cross, so the results are similar.

2. Buy when the oscillator becomes oversold. Sell when the oscillator becomes overbought. A market is considered overbought when the oscillator value reaches extremely high levels, such as 108

FIGURE 11.9
March 1991 Treasury bonds 5- and 10-day moving averages

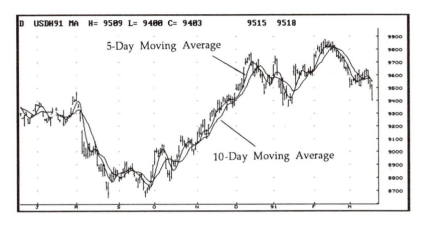

Source: Reprinted with permission, FutureSource, 955 Parkview Blvd., Lombard, IL 60148 (800) 621-2628

FIGURE 11.10
March 1991 Treasury bonds 5- and 10-day oscillator

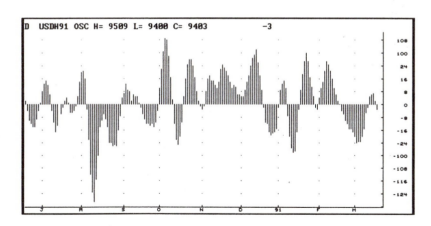

Source: Reprinted with permission, FutureSource, 955 Parkview Blvd., Lombard, IL 60148 (800) 621-2628

in this example. A market is considered oversold when the oscillator value reaches extremely low levels, such as –124.

How high must the oscillator be for an overbought reading, and how low for an oversold reading? An oscillator measures absolute amounts, so 100 may be overbought in the Treasury bond market, but may be insignificant in another market. Each market will have different values, depending on the price and volatility of the commodity. The trader must determine what values constitute overbought and oversold by reviewing the oscillator for the particular market. The same market may have a large variation in oscillator values over time. Some traders may use 100, and others may use 75, while others may use 50 or lower as an overbought condition.

This type of method is called counter trend trading because buying occurs on market weakness, and selling on market strength. This type of trading works well when markets are congested, but is less than a pleasurable experience when markets trend.

3. Oscillators may also be used to confirm or not confirm a trend. A divergence occurs when the market makes new highs but the oscillator does not or the market makes new lows but the oscillator does not. For example the oscillator drops below -124 in the beginning of August and makes a higher low near -24 at the end of August. The bonds make a low in early August below 90 and then resume the downtrend bottoming out below 87 during the same interval in August. The oscillator does not make new lows during the same time and therefore does not confirm this new price low. This is an example of a bullish divergence. This might suggest the market is developing internal strength and may be ready for a rally. A bearish divergence would occur when the market rallies and makes new highs but the oscillator does not make new highs suggesting possible internal weakness.

An oscillator confirms a move when the market makes new highs (lows) and the oscillator makes new highs (lows). For example in the middle of December the oscillator reaches a high of 100 and then makes a lower high in the beginning of January around 16. The market makes a high the same time in December near 98 and then makes a lower high near 97. The oscillator confirms the lower high suggesting the market may possibly head lower.

FIGURE 11.11
March 1991 Treasury bonds 5- and 10-day line oscillator

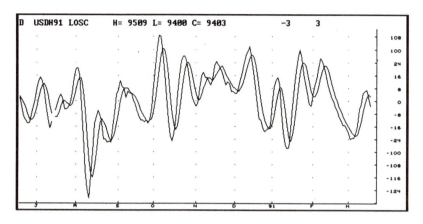

Source: Reprinted with permission, FutureSource, 955 Parkview Blvd., Lombard, IL 60148 (800) 621-2628

FIGURE 11.12
March 1991 Treasury bonds 5- and 10-day moving average convergence divergence

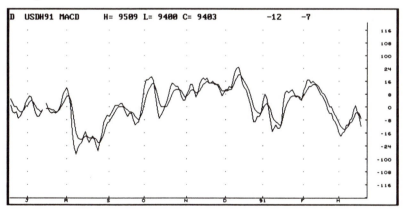

Source: Reprinted with permission, FutureSource, 955 Parkview Blvd., Lombard, IL 60148 (800) 621-2628

Line Oscillators and the Moving Average Convergence Divergence (MACD)

A **line oscillator** *is a simple moving average of the moving average oscillator values (ie. a moving average of an oscillator).* Moving averages are used to smooth data, as mentioned in the moving average section. A line oscillator smoothes the data to a greater degree, since it is a moving average of the difference of two moving averages. A line oscillator can be employed in a similar fashion as the moving average oscillator. A five- and ten-day line oscillator of March 91 treasury bonds is shown in Figure 11.11.

The moving average convergence divergence (MACD), is similar to the line oscillator, but is calculated with an exponential moving average instead of a simple moving average. A five- and 10-day MACD of March 91 Treasury bonds is shown in Figure 11.12 for comparison.

MOMENTUM

Momentum *measures the change in price with time.* Momentum is calculated by taking the difference in price of the two time periods, as shown in the formula:

Momentum $_i = P_i - P_{i-t}$

where P = price of future

i = specific time period

t = number of time periods in the past

The momentum value is used in a similar way as other oscillators. Momentum can identify oversold and overbought areas, and can also be employed as an indicator to go long or short the market when the value crosses the zero line.

The momentum value provides an indication of the rate of change in the market. A large positive change in the momentum value means the market is rapidly moving higher, which may imply there is good internal strength to the market. A large negative change in the momentum value means the market is rapidly moving lower, which may imply there is much internal weakness in the market.

The March 91 Canadian dollar and the corresponding momentum chart are shown in Figures 11.13 and 11.14, respectively. The strong

FIGURE 11.13
March 1991 Canadian dollar

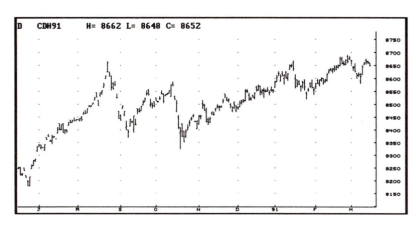

Source: Reprinted with permission, FutureSource, 955 Parkview Blvd., Lombard, IL 60148 (800) 621-2628

FIGURE 11.14
March 1991 Canadian dollar momentum chart

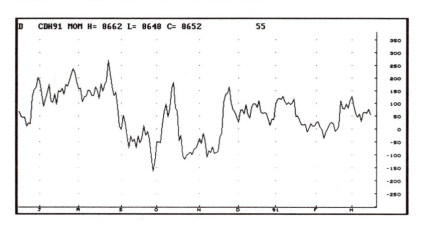

Source: Reprinted with permission, FutureSource, 955 Parkview Blvd., Lombard, IL 60148 (800) 621-2628

upmove in July and August is confirmed by the high momentum readings. The market takes a swift drop in late August and September, which is reflected in the momentum values. A slower move higher develops in November and December, so the momentum values take on less extreme values.

RATE OF CHANGE

Whereas the momentum indicator is an absolute measure of price change, the rate of change is a relative measure of price change. The rate of change is calculated by dividing the present price by the price in a previous period.

Rate of change = $P_i \ / \ P_{i-t}$
where P = price
i = specific time period
t = number of time periods in the past

Rate of change may be used in a similar way as the momentum indicator. Figure 11.15 is a graph of the rate of change of the March 91 Canadian dollar, which may be compared with Figures 11.13

FIGURE 11.15
March 1991 Canadian dollar, rate of change

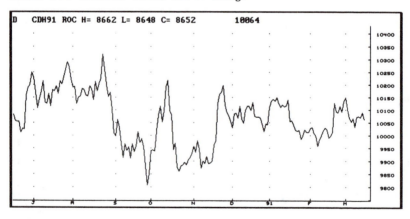

Source: Reprinted with permission, FutureSource, 955 Parkview Blvd., Lombard, IL 60148 (800) 621-2628

and 11.14. The rate of change value is multiplied by 10,000 in the graph, but any value may be used.

STOCHASTICS

Stochastics are another type of oscillator widely used by many technicians, and developed by George Lane. They are a form of oscillator which place significance on where the closing price is, relative to the high and low for the period. The theory behind stochastics is simple. Rising prices are often accompanied by closes near the highs of the range, while falling prices are often accompanied by closes near the lows of the range. Prices which close near the middle of the range suggest a listless or trendless market.

One stochastic value is called the %K value and is calculated as follows:

$$\%K = \frac{C_i - L_n}{H_n - L_n} \cdot 100$$

where C_i = closing price in current period
L_n = lowest low during the n time periods
H_n = highest high during the n time periods
i = specific time period
n = number of periods

The %D value is simply the moving average of the %K value. The moving average can be calculated in any way such as the simple or exponential calculation. The equation for the simple moving average calculation is:

$$\%D = \frac{\sum_{i=1}^{n} \%K_i}{n}$$

where i = specific time period
n = total number of periods
$\%K_i$ = the %K value for period i

The %K value reacts more quickly, or is "faster", than the %D value, because the %D value is a moving average of the %K value. The stochastics can be varied to give faster or slower signals just like a moving average.

Figure 11.16 of June 91 Treasury bills, and Figure 11.17 of the corresponding stochastic show some possible trading signals. Stochastic

FIGURE 11.16
June 1991 Treasury bills

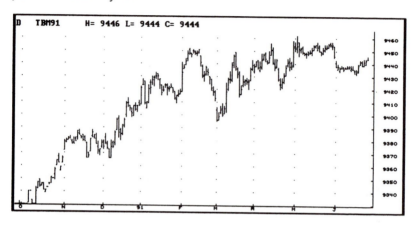

Source: Reprinted with permission, FutureSource, 955 Parkview Blvd., Lombard, IL 60148 (800) 621-2628

FIGURE 11.17
June 1991 Treasury bills stochastic

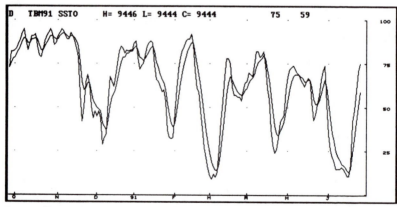

Source: Reprinted with permission, FutureSource, 955 Parkview Blvd., Lombard, IL 60148 (800) 621-2628

values below 30% suggest the market is oversold, whereas values above 70% imply the market is overbought. Many types of rules can be developed to trade with stochastics. For example, one rule is to sell when the fast (%K) crosses the slow (%D), and both are pointing down but above the 70% level. A buy signal would be generated when the fast crosses the slow, and both point up but are below the 30% level. These rules did not provide many good sell signals in 1990 because the market was in a strong uptrend, but a good sale could have been made in February. A good buy signal was generated in early March. Another type of signal occurs when the stochastic confirms, or diverges, from a price move similar to the moving average oscillator rules.

An even slower version of the %K and %D values can be calculated with the slow stochastic. In this version the original fast %K is not used and is replaced by the old %D value. A moving average of the new %K becomes the new %D value. In essence, the new %K value is the old %D value, and the new %D value is a moving average of the new %K. Many traders like to use the slow stochastic because it does not give as many signals and whipsaws as the regular stochastic. The stochastic in Figure 11.17 is a slow stochastic.

WILLIAMS %R

Larry Williams is credited with developing the %R oscillator. This is similar to the stochastic as the calculation shows:

$$\%R = \frac{H - C}{H - L}$$

where H = highest high of the period
C = close of the current period
L = lowest low of the period

The %R may be calculated under any number of time periods, but one of the most common is a ten-day period. The signals for the %R are similar to those for stochastics and moving average oscillators. September 91 silver is shown in Figure 11.18, and the corresponding %R oscillator is depicted in Figure 11.19.

FIGURE 11.18
September 1991 silver

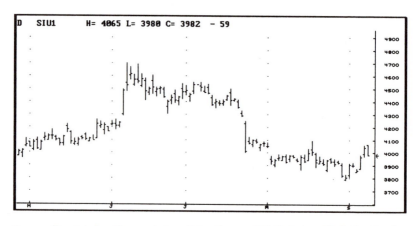

Source: Reprinted with permission, FutureSource, 955 Parkview Blvd., Lombard, IL 60148 (800) 621-2628

FIGURE 11.19
September 1991 silver %R oscillator

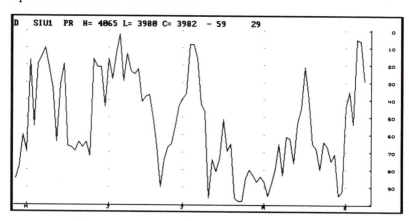

Source: Reprinted with permission, FutureSource, 955 Parkview Blvd., Lombard, IL 60148 (800) 621-2628

WILDER'S RELATIVE STRENGTH INDEX

The Relative Strength Index, developed by Wells Wilder, is used in a similar way as the other oscillators. The calculation is:

RSI = 100 − 100/(1+R)
where R = U/D
      U = average of the days closing higher during the interval
      D = average of the days closing lower during the interval

A 14-day interval is frequently used, but any number of days can be used for the interval. The oversold and overbought areas are usually considered in the 30% or 70% area, respectively, but again you are encouraged to experiment with different levels and intervals. November 91 soybeans are shown in Figure 11.20. The RSI in Figure 11.21 provided an excellent buy signal, around 25 in early July, when soybeans were trading in the 530 and 540 area. The RSI also yielded a good sell signal at 70 in early August, but the trade would have been made in the 580 area.

FIGURE 11.20
November 1991 soybeans

Source: Reprinted with permission, FutureSource, 955 Parkview Blvd., Lombard, IL 60148 (800) 621-2628

FIGURE 11.21
November 1991 soybeans RSI

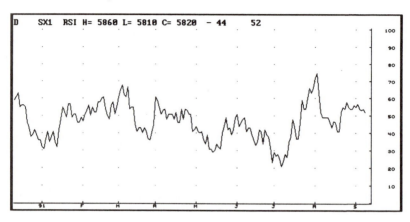

Source: Reprinted with permission, FutureSource, 955 Parkview Blvd., Lombard, IL 60148 (800) 621-2628

VOLATILITY SYSTEMS

Volatility and time are some of the most commonly used measurements in trading. However, volatility, like time, is not always well understood. Volatility will also be studied in the money management and options chapters, but for now, we will concern ourselves in applying it to trading systems. There are many ways to calculate volatility, but in this section we will use the percentage price change of the market. Therefore, if the market moves from 100 to 110, the volatility or percentage change is 10% [(110 − 100)/100 = 0.10].

Volatility trading systems are based on the following premise. If the market moves a certain percentage from a previous price level, it has broken out of a trading range and is a buy or sale. This type of system is called a *volatility breakout system*. There are many variations on this, but the general idea is to catch a move which breaks out above or below a band or envelope of prices.

How are the bands or breakout ranges determined? One way of calculating the bands is to use the moving averages of the highs and lows of the market, as discussed previously. Another type of band which may be created is a volatility band around the price data. A buy or sell signal occurs when the market moves beyond a certain percentage amount or volatility from the previous level.

Let's look at a way to use a simple system. Assume the market price is 100, and a volatility or percentage level is 5%. The lower range of the price band becomes 95 (100 · 0.95 = 95), and the upper range of the price band becomes 105 (100 · 1.05 = 105). A buy signal is generated if the market moves above 105, and a sell signal occurs, if the market moves below 95. The market must hit one of these bands within a certain time frame or the trade is canceled.

How are the percentage levels chosen? The market volatility is a good start because it tells what percentage moves have occurred in the past. Any increase above the normal volatility level of a market may signal a strong change in trend. The dramatic increase in volatility in September 91 cocoa signaled higher prices, and the breaking of volatility bands in Figure 11.22.

The concept of a volatility breakout system may have partly originated from options trading. Many options traders have positions which need to be hedged if the market goes above or below certain levels. A typical position might be a straddle where a call and put

FIGURE 11.22
September 1991 cocoa

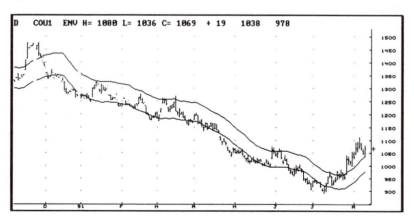

Source: Reprinted with permission, FutureSource, 955 Parkview Blvd., Lombard, IL 60148 (800) 621-2628

are sold. Some of the bigger traders automatically buy above and sell below the market at predetermined levels to decrease part of the risk of their positions. The effect of this buying or selling at specific price levels may cause the market to go even higher or lower if there are many orders bunched at the same price levels.

VELOCITY AND ACCELERATION

The **velocity** *is a measure of how quickly the market moves from one point to another.* The formula for velocity is:

Velocity = d/t

where d = distance moved

t = time of move

In trading, the distance is measured by price, so a market that moved from 100 to 105 in one day would have a velocity of:

Velocity = 5/1

= 5 points/day

Velocity is similar to the momentum calculation. The December 89 NYSE in Figure 11.23 goes through many different changes in velocity, especially in October.

The acceleration is a measure of how quickly the velocity changes. The formula for acceleration is:

Acceleration = v/t

where v = change in velocity

t = time

In the previous example, the market moved from 105 to 113 the next day, so the acceleration is:

$Velocity_2$ = (113 − 105)/1 = 8

The change in velocity = $v_2 - v_1$ = 8 − 5 = 3

The acceleration = 3/1 = 3

Table 11.2 shows the velocity and acceleration calculation for 8 days.

FIGURE 11.23

December 1989 NYSE composite

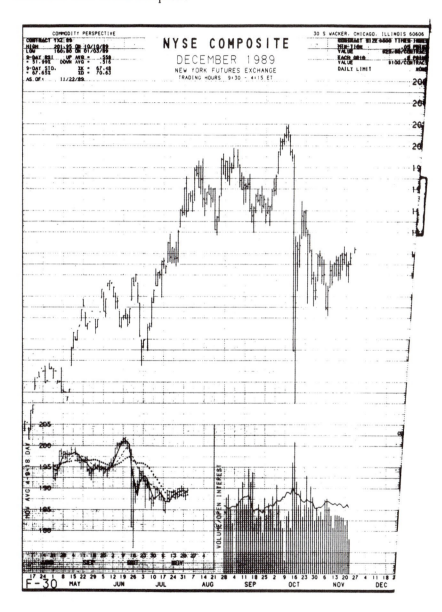

227

TABLE 11.2
Velocity and acceleration calculations

				Days				
	1	2	3	4	5	6	7	8
Price move	100	105	113	115	115	109	103	110
Velocity		5	8	2	0	–6	–6	7
Acceleration			3	–6	–2	–6	0	13

The velocity, acceleration, and volatility calculations are ways of measuring market movement. The velocity and acceleration measurements provide an indication of how fast the market moves. The volatility calculation shows the likelihood of market movement within a certain time or provides a measure of price movement in the past.

In calculus, velocity is the first derivative of distance, or the slope of the line, and acceleration is the second derivative of distance. A derivative is the change of one variable with respect to another variable, so velocity is a measure of the change in distance with respect to time. Acceleration is the change in velocity with respect to time.

VOLUME AND OPEN INTEREST

Volume and open interest can be used with price data to confirm a market move. The general rules are:

Price	Volume	Open Interest	Significance
Up	Up	Up	Bullish
Up	Down	Down	Bearish
Down	Up	Up	Bearish
Down	Down	Down	Bullish

These rules are based on the belief that volume drives the market. If the market is moving in a certain direction, high volume and open interest confirm strong momentum in the direction the market is moving. In the opposite case, movement without much volume and open interest suggests a lack of interest, or substance to the move.

The idea is interesting but volume and open interest data can be tricky to actually use. The trader must decide whether to use the total contract amount or the individual contract amount. The total contract amount includes all the contracts traded, whereas the individual contract amount is the amount for each single contract month. Volume and open interest for a specific contract can shift dramatically in one day, because some markets change the active trading month on one day. Front and back months (near- and long-term expirations) are often related by interest rate levels. In these cases, it is usually better to use total volume and open interest figures.

Other markets change the volume and open interest amounts gradually. Some back months exhibit behavior unlike the front months, so figures for one contract month are not related to another contract month. In this case, it is better to use the individual figures for each month.

COMMITMENT OF TRADERS REPORT

The Commitment of Traders report, issued by the Commodity Futures Trading Commission (CFTC), is a good source to determine the types of traders holding positions in the market. The report indicates whether hedgers or speculators are long or short the market. Some studies have noted that certain groups, such as hedgers and large speculators, may trade more successfully than other groups, such as the small speculator. Figure 11.24 is an example of a report.

FIGURE 11.24
Sample commitment of traders report

```
                        COFFEE C - COFFEE, SUGAR & COCOA EXCHANGE
        COMMITMENTS OF TRADERS IN ALL FUTURES COMBINED AND INDICATED FUTURES, JUNE 28, 1991
--------                                                                                    -----
        :  TOTAL  :                    REPORTABLE POSITIONS                                 :
  F     :--------:-------------------------------------------------------------------------: NONREPORTAULE
  U     :        :           NON-COMMERCIAL                   :             :               : POSITIONS
  T     :        :---------------------------------:          :             :
  U     :  OPEN  : LONG OR SHORT: LONG AND SHORT: COMMERCIAL  :    TOTAL    :
  R     : INTEREST:   ONLY     : (SPREADING)   :             :             :
  E     :        :---------------------------------------------------------------------------
  S     :        :   LONG : SHORT:  LONG : SHORT:  LONG : SHORT:  LONG : SHORT:   LONG : SHORT
------------------------------------------------------------------------------------------------
        :        :                     (CONTRACTS OF 37,500 POUNDS)                          :
  ALL   : 41,395:  5,496   6,017    444     444  23,559  27,587  29,499  34,048: 11,896   7,347
  OLD   : 29,554:  3,985   5,103     67      67  18,189  19,365  22,241  24,535:  7,313   5,019
  OTHER : 11,841:  1,888   1,291      0       0   5,370   8,222   7,258   9,513:  4,583   2,328
        :        :             CHANGES IN COMMITMENTS FROM JUNE 14, 1991                     :
  ALL   : -4,565: -1,504     120   -523    -523    -997  -2,267  -3,024  -2,670: -1,541  -1,895
        :        :PERCENT OF OPEN INTEREST REPRESENTED BY EACH CATEGORY OF TRADERS:
  ALL   : 100.0%:   13.3    14.5    1.1     1.1    56.9    66.6    71.3    82.3:   28.7    17.7
  OLD   : 100.0%:   13.5    17.3    0.2     0.2    61.5    65.5    75.3    83.0:   24.7    17.0
  OTHER : 100.0%:   15.9    10.9    0.0     0.0    45.4    69.4    61.3    80.3:   38.7    19.7
        :NUMBER OF:
        :TRADERS :                 NUMBER OF TRADERS IN EACH CATEGORY                         :
        :---------:
  ALL   :  141   :     29      28      3       3      62      41      94      69:
  OLD   :  133   :     29      26      1       1      53      33      83      59:
  OTHER :   56   :      8       5      0       0      32      22      40      27:
        :------------------------------------------------------------------------------------
        :                             CONCENTRATION RATIOS
        :       PERCENT OF OPEN INTEREST HELD BY THE INDICATED NUMBER OF LARGEST TRADERS
        :------------------------------------------------------------------------------------
        :            BY GROSS POSITION              :              BY NET POSITION
        :------------------------------------------------------------------------------------
        :  4 OR LESS TRADERS   : 8 OR LESS TRADERS  : 4 OR LESS TRADERS  : 8 OR LESS TRADERS
        :----------------------------------------------------------------------------------
        :  LONG  :   SHORT   :   LONG  :   SHORT   :   LONG  :   SHORT   :   LONG  :   SHORT
  ALL   :  25.8      38.0       36.1      50.8       19.0      30.9       26.9      41.6
  OLD   :  31.2      44.7       42.2      55.8       27.5      38.9       36.1      50.0
  OTHER :  22.6      43.5       33.6      60.7       20.3      40.7       28.9      53.6
```

ON BALANCE VOLUME

Joseph Granville developed the On Balance Volume (OBV) Indicator for the stock market, but it has been applied to futures trading. The OBV attempts to measure the influence of both price and volume on the market. It is calculated by adding the volume of the day if the price change for the day is positive, and subtracting volume of the day if the price change is negative. A cumulative total of the volume is kept and plotted against the price. If the OBV is rising, then this confirms an upmove, but if it is dropping, a potential downmove is possible. Figure 11.25 is an example of an On Balance Tick Volume chart, with the corresponding five-minute bar chart of the September 91 NYSE index in Figure 11.26.

FIGURE 11.25
September 1991 NYSE on balance tick volume chart

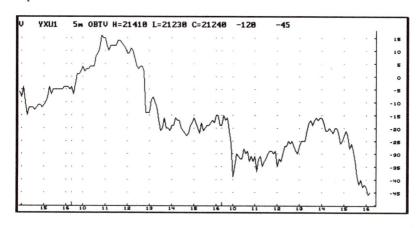

Source: Reprinted with permission, FutureSource, 955 Parkview Blvd., Lombard, IL 60148 (800) 621-2628

FIGURE 11.26
September 1991 NYSE 5-minute bar chart

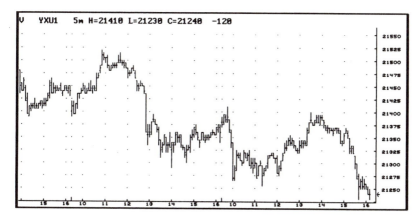

Source: Reprinted with permission, FutureSource, 955 Parkview Blvd., Lombard, IL 60148 (800) 621-2628

DONCHIAN METHOD

Richard Donchian developed a simple, but effective trading method called the four-week rule:

1. Buy when the market makes new highs over the past four weeks.
2. Sell when the market makes new lows over the past four weeks.

This system is a trend following method and works very well in trending markets. However, the results, like any other trend following method, can be less than comforting in choppy and random markets. The time frame can be varied to a smaller or greater amount such as two weeks or six weeks.

CHAOS THEORY

Chaos theory *is a branch in both mathematics and science, which deals with the fascinating study of random behavior.* Through the study of chaos theory, many scientists are beginning to wonder if there may be certain types of "order" to random behavior. Benoit Mandelbrot was a pioneer in this field, developing some of the equations and theories of the science of chaos. The beautiful and intricate patterns in fractal geometry are created using some of the ideas of chaos theory.

The appeal to the trader should be clear. If markets are random part of the time, then employing certain studies in chaos may unlock some of the mysteries, or even profit opportunities in the markets. Some research has been performed in studying various markets to observe if some of the laws of chaos apply. The work has just begun in this area and it is intriguing.

CONCLUSION

Technical studies in objective analysis can be mathematically tested to determine their performance in the past. This can be quite beneficial in deciding which trading methods to employ. The results provide a framework for developing a trading style, but you must always remember—past performance is no guarantee of future results.

CHAPTER 12

Cycles

To everything there is a season, and a time to every purpose under the heaven.

Ecclesiates 3:1-8

Each thing is of like form from everlasting and comes round again in its cycle.

Marcus Aurelius Antoninus, *Meditations II*

The study of cycles encompasses many broad topics such as seasonal indicators, time cycles, and wave analysis. Skeptics abound when it comes to cycle theory. But consider this. What would people think if they were told 200 years ago that light and sound were actually cycles and waves? They would probably react by laughing and considering the person mad who would suggest such a preposterous idea. Cycles are very real phenomena which affect us in various ways, some of which we are probably not even aware of.

Some people might concede that cycles do affect certain commodities, since the change in weather from one season to another can have a great impact on agricultural and livestock prices. But what kind of cycle phenomena could impact bond prices or the stock market? How about the quarterly refunding by the Treasury, or the cyclical dividend payouts and quarterly movement of money management funds? These events are timely and cyclical when they occur, and may have a substantial impact on the financial markets.

DEFINITIONS

A **cycle** *is a series of recurring patterns which are spaced over a number of approximately equal time intervals.* One of the most important cycles which affects everyone is the earth revolving around the sun. Another equally important cycle is the rotation of the earth on its axis every 24 hours. Figure 12.1 depicts the earth revolving around the sun in a circle. It is often convenient to depict a circle as a wave, so the earth revolving around the sun is shown as a cycle in Figure 12.2. Drawing the circle as a wave allows each point on the Y axis to have a unique point on the X axis.

Detecting cyclical patterns in a market may help a person better analyze and trade a market. For example, buying the market at a time when a cyclical bottom is expected, or selling when a cyclical top is anticipated, may offer a good trading opportunity. For most cycle analysis, we will be looking at price versus time, and will use this assumption in the rest of the chapter.

FIGURE 12.1
The earth revolving around the sun is an example of a very important cycle.

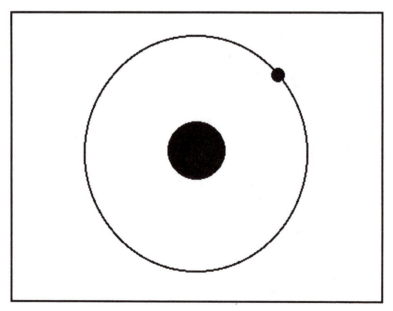

FIGURE 12.2
The revolution of the earth around the sun may also be depicted as a cycle on an *x* and *y* axis.

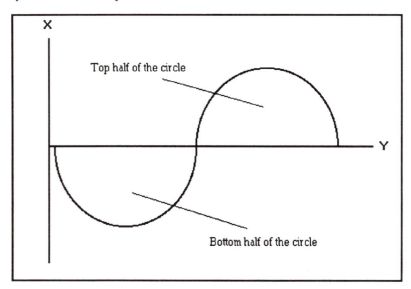

Some terms helpful to know in cycle analysis, and depicted in Figure 12.3 are:

1. *The* **peak** *or* **crest** *is the top of a cycle, or highest price.* The peak is 70 in the example.

2. *The* **trough** *is the bottom of a cycle, or lowest price.* The trough is 50 in the example.

3. *The* **amplitude** *is the height of a cycle, and is measured from the center of the wave, or X axis, to the bottom or top of the wave.* Some books measure from the top to the bottom of the wave, but we will use the standard conventions of math or physics. In trading, the units for measuring amplitude will normally be in dollars. In the example, the amplitude of the cycle is 10.

4. *The* **period** *is the length of time for a full cycle to repeat and is normally measured from one bottom to another.* For trading, the period

FIGURE 12.3
The peak is the top of the wave; the trough is the bottom of the wave;
the amplitude is the magnitude of the wave measured from the x axis
to the top or bottom of the wave; and the period is the length of time
of a full cycle.

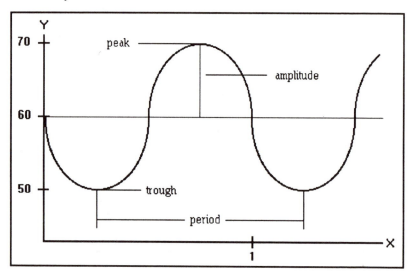

is usually measured in units of time. The period of the cycle in
the example is one day.

5. *The* **frequency** *is the number of times a full cycle occurs for a
given time.* The frequency is simply the inverse of the period, or
1/period. Since the period is one day, the frequency is 1/1 or one.

What might the cycle in Figure 12.3 represent? Possibly the
temperature in New York City on a spring day.

This type of movement is called simple harmonic motion. The
frequency is independent of the amplitude with simple harmonic
motion. This means the amplitude may change, but the frequency
is not necessarily affected by it. For example, the amplitude may
be increased to 20, but the frequency and period will remain the
same. To see how this can occur, assume the temperature rises to
80 and falls to 45 on the following day, as shown in Figure 12.4.

FIGURE 12.4
The temperature represents a cycle that may change each day.

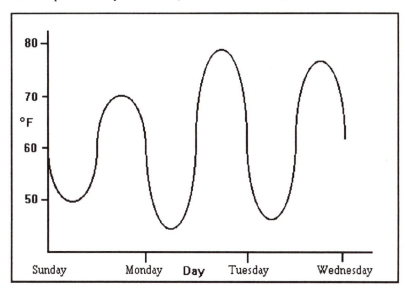

FIGURE 12.5
The projection of an eliptical pattern like the earth revolving round the sun will look similar to the cycle pattern on the left.

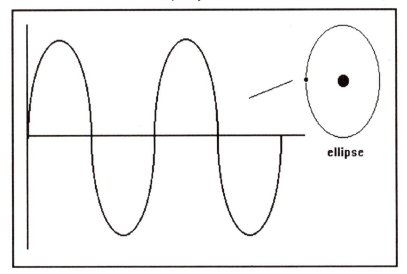

ellipse

In this case, the amplitude has increased, but the length of the day, or frequency, and period are the same.

A circle was projected as a wave in the first example, but many types of figures may also be depicted as a cycle. The projection of an ellipse to a cycle will appear as in Figure 12.5. The ellipse is much closer to the actual orbit of the earth around the sun, which cycles us back to the beginning of the chapter!

TWO OR MORE CYCLES

The temperature was observed on a daily basis in the previous example, but any time period, such as a week, may be used. The amount of rain each day is another cycle which could have been

FIGURE 12.6
The cycles are out of phase by 180° in A and 0°, or in phase in B.

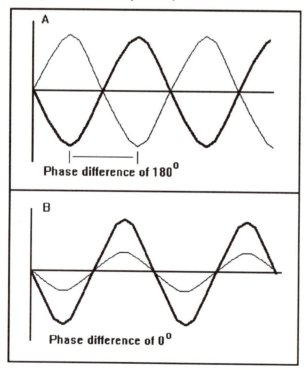

observed. In this case we would be looking at more than one cycle to analyze. When working with more than one cycle there are other terms which are helpful to know:

1. *The* **phase** *is the difference in time between two cycles.* The phase is usually measured in degrees from 0° to 360° with 0° and 360° representing waves in phase, and 180° representing waves totally out of phase, as shown in Figure 12.6. For trading, it is convenient to measure the phase from the bottom of the two cycles in units of time. The cycles are in phase in Figure 12.6a, and out of phase by 180°, or five hours, in Figure 12.6b.

FIGURE 12.7
The first harmonic is also called the fundamental harmonic; the second and third harmonic are overtones of the first harmonic.

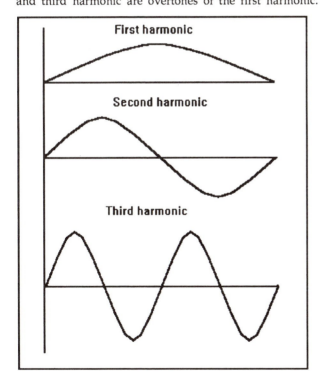

First harmonic

Second harmonic

Third harmonic

2. *The* **harmonic** *is a division of a larger cycle into two or more equally spaced cycles.* The first or fundamental harmonic is the major cycle which cannot be broken down any further into equally divisible cycles. Any integral multiple of the fundamental harmonic is called a harmonic, or overtone, as depicted in Figure 12.7. Therefore, the second harmonic is the first harmonic multiplied by two, the third harmonic is the first harmonic multiplied by three, and so on. Anyone musically inclined is probably familiar with harmonics and harmonies.

3. **Synchronicity** *is the tendency for cycles to bottom or top at the same time.* The cycles in Figure 12.8a do not show synchronicity, or are not in "sync," because the bottoms and tops do not coincide. The cycles in Figure 12.8b exhibit synchronicity because the bottoms coincide.

FIGURE 12.8
(a) Cycles out of sync; (b) cycles in sync. The cycles in (a) do not show synchronous behaviour because the tops and bottoms do not coincide; the cycles in (b) exhibit synchronous behaviour because some of the bottoms coincide with each other.

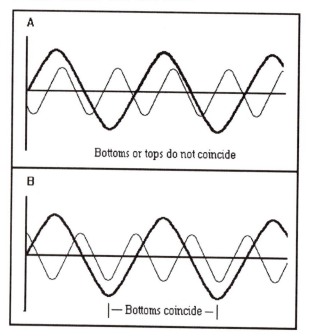

Synchronicity occurs when two or more cycles meet at the same time. For example, an eclipse of the sun does not occur all the time, but only at certain times, when the moon and sun are in a specific position, or in synchronicity. When we are in sync and feeling well, we seem to be able to accomplish much more than when we are out of sync, and can't seem to get anything done.

We live in an environment with many different kinds of cycles, some of which may be observed. For instance, many people have a job part of the day, and must catch a train or car another time, and must eat at still other times. When these cycles are in synchronicity, or in sync, everything is okay, but when they are out of sync, problems often arise. If the person has to work late, the train may be missed which causes a bunch of other cycles to be skipped or missed such as dinner. Therefore, we attempt to synchronize all the different cycles in our life in order to live more harmoniously.

ADDING AND SUBTRACTING CYCLES

One important area of cycle analysis is concerned with adding and subtracting many different cycles to form one cycle, or the breaking down of one cycle into its component parts. Many observed cycles are actually the combinations of many other cycles. For example, the current weather condition is affected by the earth's rotation about its axis, revolving around the sun, and many other kinds of cyclical phenomena.

Figure 12.9 shows an example of adding together two separate cycles with equal periods and amplitudes to form a new cycle. The amplitudes for the same time period are simply summed together and a new cycle is formed. A new cycle with twice the amplitude but the same period is created when the two component cycles are added together in this example.

In the previous example both cycles were in sync with each other, but what if the two cycles are out of sync (i.e., the phase does not equal zero)? Figure 12.10 shows an example of the same two component cycles out of sync by 1/2, which, added together, cancel out each other. The net effect is a cycle with 0 amplitude or no apparent cycle.

FIGURE 12.9

The addition of waves A and B which have the same amplitude and period and are in phase, creates wave C which has twice the amplitude but the same period.

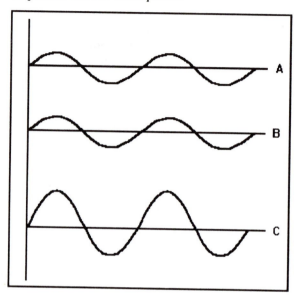

FIGURE 12.10

The addition of waves A and B which have the same amplitude but are out of phase by one-half cancels their effect as shown in C.

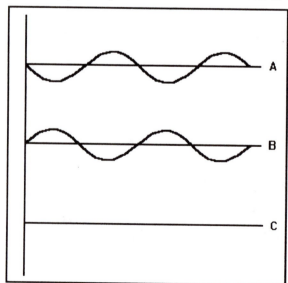

FIGURE 12.11

The addition of cycles A and B yields the cycle in C which is the more commonly known head and shoulders pattern.

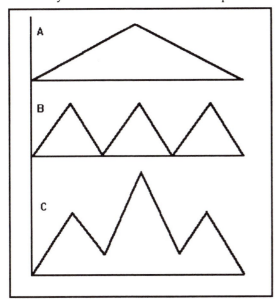

FIGURE 12.12

The addition of waves A and B creates wave C which is similar to the Dow theory of a primary and secondary trend.

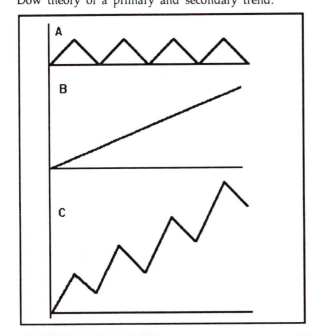

The addition of cycles with different amplitudes and periods can yield some interesting patterns. For example, the combination of cycles one and two in Figure 12.11 to form the third cycle, is the familiar head and shoulders pattern. Another combination such as the Dow Theory, which is a major upward trend followed by the minor secondary trend, is shown in Figure 12.12. These examples show how separate cycles can tend to exaggerate and weaken the major and minor cycles, which may have important applications in trading.

CYCLE THEORY APPLIED TO THE MARKETS

We can also think of the market as having different cycles. Any graph of a market may be considered a representation of the major cycle. Each major cycle is composed of many minor cycles of varying importance on the major cycle. For example, the wheat market is affected by major long-term weather patterns lasting ten years or more, and by shorter-term, seasonal weather patterns which may affect the supply of wheat. Some of the cycles in a market are understood much better than other ones.

The stock market has many cycles which affect it, such as tax selling at year end, dividend cycles, and economic cycles. Each one of these cycles has a different period and amplitude, which affects the stock market in varying ways at different times. When the cycles in any market are in synchronicity, a pronounced bottom or top, such as the Great Crash of 1929, may happen. When the market is out of sync, there may be no significant trend, and the cycles may be harder to define. Any market has a number of complex and often conflicting cycles which makes cycle study interesting but equally challenging.

Sometimes we expect a cycle top or bottom to occur and the exact opposite occurs. This is a very familiar problem with the trader who uses cycle analysis. For example, a trader might notice a market tends to bottom approximately every fifth day; so on the tenth day he decides to go long the market expecting a cyclical bottom. However, the market makes a top on the tenth day and drops to even lower levels, eventually bottoming out on the fifteenth day. This phenomenon is called a cycle inversion and is depicted in Figure 12.13. *A* **cycle**

FIGURE 12.13
A cycle inversion occurs when a top is expected and a bottom
occurs, or when a bottom is expected and a top occurs.

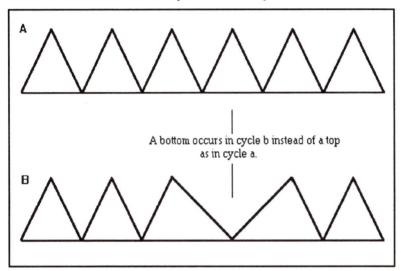

A bottom occurs in cycle b instead of a top
as in cycle a.

inversion *occurs when an expected bottom in a cycle becomes a top, or
an expected top becomes a bottom.* We can see from the addition and
subtraction of certain cycles in the previous examples why this can
happen. Another component cycle which has not been observed
eventually manifests itself and changes the major cycle of the market.

DETRENDING CYCLES

We have looked at ways to combine minor cycles into major cycles,
but can a major cycle be broken down into minor cycles? Much of
cycle analysis in trading involves breaking the major cycle, which
is the actual market price, into its component cycles, since the market
is the major cycle. If the component cycles can be discerned, we
may be able to know what affect these cycles will have on the
market, and possibly predict the direction of the market.

   Detrending *a cycle is the process of breaking a cycle down into
its respective component cycles.* It is generally easier to add component
cycles to form a new one than to reduce an entire cycle into all

its component cycles. This is certainly true for market cycles, because there may be many distinct minor cycles which comprise the whole market cycle, as well as noise or random behavior which makes detrending even harder.

There are many ways to detrend cycles, and some are more complex and mathematically involved than others. The Box Jenkins approach, Fourier analysis, and spectral analysis are some of the more complex methods available. We will   investigate a simpler way, which most of us should be familiar with by now. The method requires the calculation of moving averages.

The method of ratio to moving average is an easy-to-use and readily available means of detrending time series or market data. The idea is to smooth the data with a moving average, and isolate the different cyclical components which form the main trend. The moving average effectively becomes the main or important trend.

Let's look at a moving average and the corresponding price chart to see how this process works. October 91 sugar is overlaid with a 20-day moving average in Figure 12.14. Note how the last moving average value is placed at the last price, which is how a moving average is normally depicted on a price chart.

The first step when detrending a market is to center the moving average, by placing the last moving average value exactly between the middle of the time periods which were averaged. For example, the same 20-day moving average of October 91 sugar is shifted to the left by 10 days to place it at the center of the prices, as shown in Figure 12.15. If a 40 day moving average were used, we would shift the average by 20 days to the left. Note how the centered moving average moves more closely with the price data.

The next step is to calculate the differences between the moving average and the respective daily data points to arrive at the detrended data. These differences above and below the moving average show the noise, or smaller-term cycles affecting the longer-term cycle. Some of the differences are plotted in Figure 12.16 to show the detrended market data.

The next step is to look through a series of different moving averages, such as a 10-day or 18-day, to see which ones more closely follow the market cycles. The moving averages with the best fit may be considered the component cycles of the market.

FIGURE 12.14
October 1991 sugar 20-day moving average

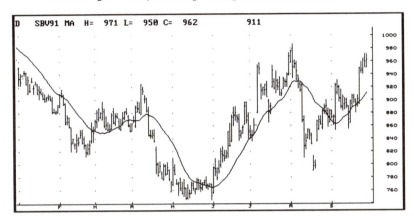

Source: Reprinted with permission, FutureSource, 955 Parkview Blvd., Lombard, IL 60148 (800) 621-2628

FIGURE 12.15
October 1991 sugar with a centered 20-day moving average

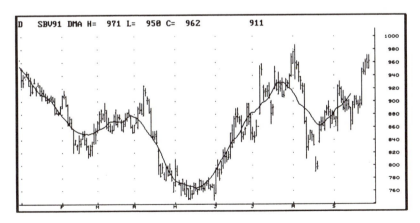

Source: Reprinted with permission, FutureSource, 955 Parkview Blvd., Lombard, IL 60148 (800) 621-2628

FIGURE 12.16
October 1991 sugar detrended

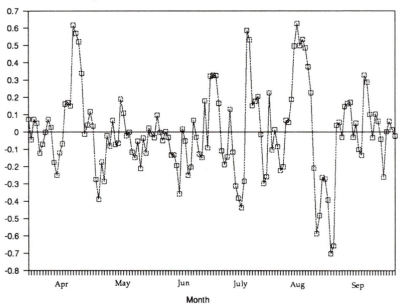

BUSINESS AND TRADING CYCLES

When detrending or adding cycles, it is helpful to know the different components which may affect the overall business or economic cycle. Some of the components are depicted in Figure 12.17 and include:

1. *The* **main trend component,** *which is the major cycle.* This to a large extent determines if the market is in a bull or bear move, or in a congestion or random phase. It may last three to four years or longer.

2. *The* **yearly** *or* **cyclical component,** *which lasts approximately one year.* It describes the intermediate fluctuations of the market.

FIGURE 12.17
(a) Main trend; (b) cyclical component; (c) seasonal component;
(d) irregular component. Many trading and economic cycles are
composed of four separate cycles which include the main trend which
lasts over a year, the cyclical component lasting about a year,
the seasonal component lasting approximately three months, and the
irregular lasting less than two months.

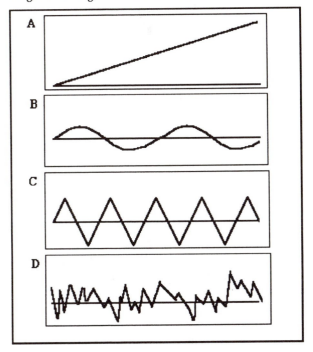

3. The **seasonal component**, *which reflects how the market changes during
   the year.* It may be computed on a quarterly basis.

4. The **irregular component**, *which reflects the minor variations which
   may occur throughout the year, lasting less than two months.*

The interaction of these cycles may have a profound effect on
the economy. The idea of distinct time cycles can be applied in
markets, as well as the economy, to discern various trading cycles
for a particular market. For example, in Figure 12.18 the main trend

FIGURE 12.18

Dow Jones Industrials monthly chart

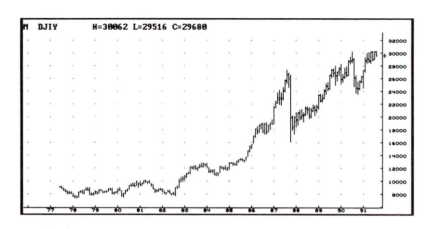

Source: Reprinted with permission, FutureSource, 955 Parkview Blvd., Lombard, IL 60148 (800) 621-2628

in the stock market during the 1980's was a long-term bull trend which lasted over ten years. Examples of cyclical bear trends include 1981-82 and 1987, and examples of cyclical bull trends include 1982-83 and 1985-86. Seasonal and irregular trends may be seen, which last less than six months.

The object of detrending is to discern these component cycles, for two reasons. The first reason is that the component cycles may be easier to predict than the overall cycle. The second reason is that even if the component cycle is difficult to predict, it is still helpful to know the different cycles that compose, and ultimately determine the major movement.

Some analysts use different time frames for each component, such as six months for the seasonal component. The choice is up to the trader and dependent on the market, because there are many different cycles to choose from. This method of detrending is a way of identifying some of the more prominent cycles. Detrending will not necessarily separate all of the component cycles; there may be some cycles which appear, disappear, and then reappear, making them especially difficult to detect.

SOME OBSERVED CYCLES

Kondratieff Cycle

The Kondratieff cycle is named for the Russian economist Nikolai Kondratieff who worked in the early 1900's studying various cycles in economics. He noted that capitalist societies went through boom and bust periods of approximately 50–60 years in duration. The average cycle is considered to be 54 years, but it is by no means an exact number. Kondratieff was sent to Siberia for his impressive work and ideas because Stalin did not appreciate his conclusions, and considered them anticommunist propaganda. Figure 12.19 depicts the Kondratieff cycle over the past 200 years.

Kondratieff looked at commodity prices, interest rates, production levels, and a variety of other economic data to arrive at his conclusions. One of the most interesting aspects of his work is that Kondratieff tried to link social and human reasons to these cycles. He believed

FIGURE 12.19
Kondratieff's long wave: annual averages, ratio scale

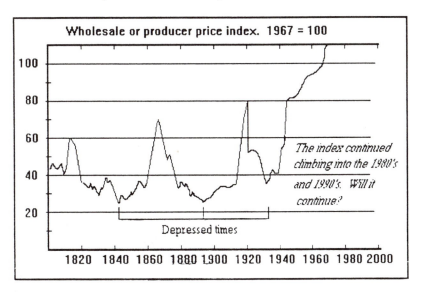

the cycles were partly based on human nature and not just a result of economic fundamentals.

He observed that great social upheavals occurred when the cycle was in an uptrend. He also believed intermediate cycles interacted with the major cycle to exaggerate or weaken the effect of the major cycle. Some proponents of his work feel the cycle was linked to the average life span of a person at that time and therefore represented a changing of the guard of one generation of people and ideas to another. He and others speculated that innovation and technology had much to do with these cycles.

Some of the conclusions of the wave cycle are broad and far reaching. The depression and ensuing recovery were all part of the normal process of capitalism. Technological innovations were also partly the cause of these cycles. When a new industry replaced an existing one (i.e., automobiles replacing horse and carriage), the workers in the old industry would be displaced and would not always find other jobs easily. These economic dislocations were partly the cause of recessions and depressions. Workers who lost jobs from sunset industries (those industries on the decline), were not always able to find jobs, which contributed to more unemployment and stagnation.

Business Cycle

Economists Joseph Schumpeter and Jay Forrester have both noted the effects of many different kinds of cycles on the economy. One of the more noticeable of these is the business cycle, which lasts approximately four to five years. Some have speculated that this cycle is partly due to the tendency of many business planners to make longer-term decisions within this time frame. Others believe the cycle is a result of the presidential election cycle.

It is clear that there are different business cycles, but it is not always clear how or why they occur and disappear. Part of the problem stems from the difficulty in measuring the state of the economy. For example, our economy is much more service oriented, and less production oriented, versus 100 years ago. How do we compare our economy now versus then, or can we even make an accurate comparison? How should technological improvements be accounted for in measuring the progress of the economy? These are difficult questions which may not have easy answers.

CIRCADIAN TIMING CYCLES

The previously mentioned cycles are external forces which affect us and our world in many ways. There are also internal cycles we all must live by, like the internal clock which awakens us in the morning and puts us to sleep at night. The *circadian rhythm cycle* is the scientific study of the various internal clocks which, we have only begun to realize, have a profound impact on our lives. Our sleep and wake cycle, our complex hormonal cycles, and our hunger cycle are just a few of the many circadian cycles which affect us.

One of the classic studies in circadian rhythms was an experiment in which a plant was placed in total darkness over an extended period of time. Many plants will open their leaves during the day and fold or close them during the night. At the time, scientists believed the opening and closing of the leaves was caused by a reaction to light during the day and darkness at night. Would the plant still open its leaves during the day and close them at night if there were no light cue of day and night? To the surprise of many, the plant continued to open its leaves during the day and close them at night, even though it was totally cut off from any light. Equally amazing was the observation that the plant regularly opened and closed its leaves about every 24 hours. The plant appeared to have its own internal clock which ran independently of light and darkness.

Similar studies have been done with animals and people, and confirm the existence of an internal clock in most, but not all, living things. Many of the internal clocks seem to run at approximately a 24-hour interval. Is it possible this interval is due to evolutionary development on earth, or a natural rhythm or cycle of the universe? More immediately for our purposes is it possible the market has its own internal clock which governs highs and lows at certain times? If markets are the manifestation of people's emotions and thoughts, it certainly is conceivable the market has an internal clock. The study of cycles is one possible way of watching this clock.

Cycles are a fascinating way of looking at the market because many of the ideas are related to other natural phenomena in math, physics, biology, and a host of other subjects.

CONCLUSION

Cycles within and without us affect our lives in diverse ways. There are definite market cycles, but some or many may be difficult to isolate and identify. The study of cycles in trading is relatively new, but a better understanding of cycles in the market should provide a decided edge in trading.

CHAPTER **13**

Pattern Recognition

Facts which at first seem improbable will, even on scant explanation, drop the cloak which has hidden them and stand forth in naked and simple beauty.

Galileo Galilei, *Dialogues Concerning Two New Sciences*

Pattern recognition *is the study of recurring formations or patterns.* These patterns may be quite simple or intricately complex. Pattern recognition is not limited to trading; it is also studied in such diverse fields as psychology, engineering, artificial intelligence, and art.

We actually begin pattern recognition sometime when we are born by trying to identify or make sense out of our surroundings. We learn to distinguish patterns such as lines, colors, sounds, and textures, and then classify them into various objects or things. Figure 13.1 is a pattern of only a circle, a line, and two dots and yet we can immediately recognize it as a face. Pattern recognition may be an unfamiliar term, but it is in fact something we experience and do our entire lives.

All of the topics covered in subjective or objective analysis could easily be placed under pattern recognition. One person's perception of a chart may be quite different from another person's, even though they both view the same chart. Neither is right or

FIGURE 13.1
Recognize the pattern?

wrong since this difference of opinion is what makes a market. Furthermore, it is not essential to perceive each market pattern in the same way as everyone else, but instead to trade the pattern in an effective manner. Most traders are trying to successfully trade a market—not agree on works of art.

The first step is to recognize recurring patterns in the market to see if they are predictive. The next step is to look for patterns which are relatively easy to identify and measure. This will allow possible further study with powerful computer programs to determine if these patterns are predictive and profitable. A simple pattern might be selling a market if it gaps higher, or buying the market if it gaps lower.

There is a distinction between patterns in this section and ones in the subjective section, like a head and shoulders formation. The patterns covered in this chapter can be objectively measured and tested to see how they have performed in the past. Pattern recognition is not limited to objective methods, but it is more difficult to study subjective patterns with a computer.

WHAT TO LOOK FOR IN PATTERNS

Patterns need to be identified by at least one or more variables. One of the most important variables in trading is price. Price must be set relative to another variable to develop a pattern. For instance, you cannot simply look for a price which goes higher, but must place the movement relative to either time or price or some other variable. Therefore, the price may go higher by a certain time, or the price may increase by a certain amount, or the price may increase within a certain time by a certain amount.

Let's look at some of the more common combinations:

1. *Price*: Point and figure charts are a good example of a pattern which only contains price. Price is plotted against change in direction of the price. Many simple types of patterns may be observed in point and figure charts, such as the rectangle pattern in Figure 13.2.

FIGURE 13.2
The common rectangle formation in a point and figure chart is one type of pattern.

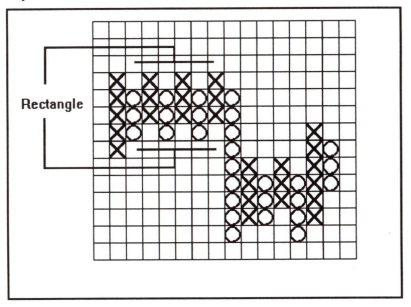

FIGURE 13.3
April 1991 live cattle

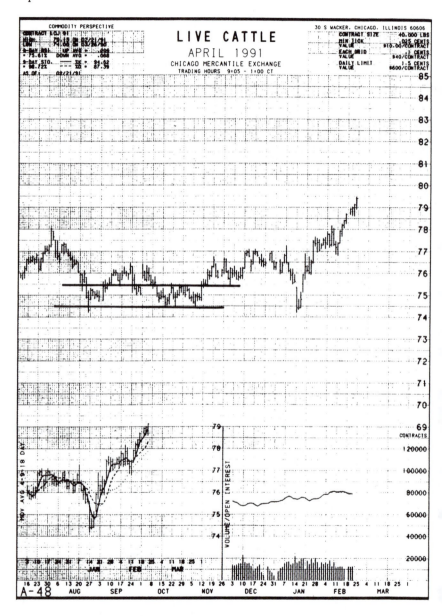

Source: Reprinted with Permission, © 1991 Commodity Perspective, 30 South Wacker Drive, Suite 1820, Chicago, Illinois 60606.

Some of the more complex patterns include the Elliott Wave, cycle patterns, and head and shoulders configurations. A swing chart is another type of price versus price movement chart.

2. *Price and time*: The combination of price and time is the most popular kind of pattern to observe. Virtually all of the price patterns covered so far in the objective and subjective section can be included in this category. April 91 live cattle in Figure 13.3 has many well-defined rectangles, such as the 7450 to 7550 level in late October and early November.

3. *Price, time, and volume and open interest*: The combination of price and time with volume and open interest can yield other types of patterns. One typical study is the On Balance Volume Indicator (OBV). This type of study is not done as much in futures as in stocks because the exact volume and open interest figures may take as much as a day longer to get than price information.

PRICE PATTERNS

Point and figure charts are a good start for looking at price patterns. One of the simplest formations is the rectangle, which was previously shown in Figure 13.2. Trading rules may be developed, such as buying on the breakout or selling on the breakdown. More complex configurations can be tested to see what type of results they yield. The trading rules can be varied to see how the results change.

The formations can become increasingly complex when viewing actual charts. Simple formations and rules may be combined to create new patterns and sets of trading rules. The results can always be arrived at by hand but a powerful computer will greatly facilitate the testing process. A swing chart can be used like a point and figure chart to analyze the patterns.

PRICE AND TIME PATTERNS

Price and time patterns are the most common charting methods used for evaluating markets. Most of the rules in pattern recognition are based on price and time together. We can combine rules for both price and time to look at some possible trading strategies. For example, the January effect suggests that if the stock market is higher at the end of January, the market will probably be up for the rest of the year. The price has to be at a certain place within a certain time, so this would be an example of using both price and time in our trading system. If the market is up in January then a buy signal would occur on February first.

The rules can be varied in pattern recognition when testing a formation. In the January effect example we can also sell the market on February first instead of buying if the market is higher at the end of January. The rules could be further changed by buying or selling in the middle of February to see how the results change again. We can make a rule and do the exact opposite, or add nuances to the rules and see the results.

There are an infinite number of these patterns, but here is a glimpse of a few:

1. *Weekly pattern:* If the market closes down Monday, Tuesday, and Wednesday, sell the market on Thursday and cover on Friday. If it closes up three days in a row, buy the market on Thursday and cover the position on Friday.

2. *Daily pattern:* If the market opens higher after three days of higher prices, buy the open and sell on the close. If the market opens lower after three days of lower prices, sell the open and buy on the close.

3. *Hourly pattern:* If the market opens higher and is higher in the third hour of trading than where it initially opened, buy and cover at the close. The reverse can be done if the market opens lower.

We can vary the periods and look at the market at any time frame, such as a 30-minute interval or much longer monthly interval, using the same rules. Each one of these patterns can lead to an infinite number of trading possibilities, so the rules need to be specific to narrow down the possibilities. For example, in the weekly pattern a buy or sell could occur on Wednesday instead of Thursday or the position might be covered on Monday of the next week.

PRICE, TIME, AND VOLUME

These patterns can become even more complex because now the three variables of price, time, and volume create a pattern. The OBV study described in the objective analysis section is one type of indicator which may be used for this type of pattern recognition. Other relationships, such as buying the market if the price and volume increase, or selling the market if price decreases and volume increases, may be studied.

IDENTIFYING PATTERNS

We often seek to simplify or generalize more complex patterns when using pattern recognition. We do this for two reasons:

1. *Look for some common elements to generalize a formation.* This generalization process may be better understood with the following analogy. How would a child identify his mother? Does the child look at his mother from head to toe and identify every physical feature and piece of clothing to be certain this is his mother? Of course not. The child will look for simple cues such as the eyes or lips and realize without further identification—this is Mom! This is one of the ways we learn. We recognize most of the things we sense by looking for common features and then identify the rest of the pattern which, in fact, may be extremely complex.

We are looking for some of the most basic patterns which then allow us to identify more complex ones. A triangle is an example of a simple pattern which can be identified in many more complex formations, as shown in March 91 silver in Figure 13.4. Two common elements in the formation of a triangle are a high followed by a lower high, and a low followed by a higher low. The silver triangle, which begins in the middle of December and ends in the middle of January, is formed from the high at 440 and low at 400, with the lower high at 435 and higher low near 410. This simple pattern is part of an overall pattern which defines the move in silver.

FIGURE 13.4

March 1991 COMEX silver

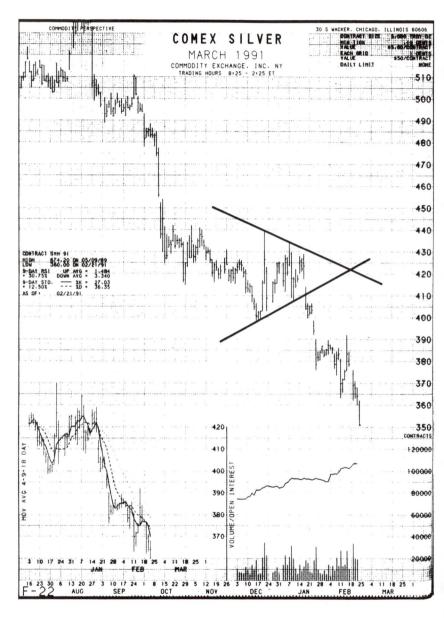

Source: Reprinted with Permission, © 1991 Commodity Perspective, 30 South Wacker Drive, Suite 1820, Chicago, Illinois 60606.

2. *Look for recurring patterns.* The more complex the trading pattern the less the likelihood of seeing it again. It is not always helpful to identify an extremely complex formation since the chances of seeing the same one again might be virtually zero. Even if we do find a pattern, which only occurs every 50 years, it will be impractical, inconvenient, and maybe even impossible to trade. An infrequently occurring pattern would also be hard to test for statistical significance.

It is also not advisable to go to the other extreme and look for the simplest patterns because they may just be random behavior and have no predictive value. For example, one of the simplest patterns is one close followed by a higher or lower close, but this happens most of the time and may not signify anything. We must look for more detail such as three or more higher closes to obtain a pattern which may have some significance.

We seek to generalize or simplify the more complex patterns and look for more complexity in the simple patterns. *In essence, the more complex the pattern the more we seek to generalize it; the more simple the pattern, the more we seek complexity in it.*

A trader should have some concept of why a formation might be predictive when devising rules for pattern identification. For example, if the market closes strong on Monday, Tuesday and Wednesday, what is the chance it will close strong on Thursday and Friday? Perhaps the momentum of the past three days will spill over into Thursday and Friday? Or possibly selling the close on Wednesday is a good strategy because the market may tend to reverse trend in the middle of the week? There is an underlying feeling or logic behind why the pattern might show promising results, which might merit testing.

Of course, we can look at any kind of pattern without serious consideration and sometimes find promising results. But remember, an infinite number of patterns would take approximately an infinite amount of time (give or take a few years) to analyze. We are trying to eliminate as many random patterns and false leads as possible to arrive at a few promising ones that are predictive and tradable. The use of computers will definitely ease the workload but a judicious choice of which patterns to analyze will be equally beneficial.

TESTING A PATTERN

Testing patterns can be more tricky than one might think because there are many considerations in the entire process. Let's look at the weekly price and time pattern to better understand the testing process.

Weekly Trending Pattern

Buy signal: If the market is up on Monday, buy on the open of Tuesday and exit the position on Wednesday's close.

Sell signal: If the market is down on Monday, sell on the open of Tuesday and exit on Wednesday's close.

There are already some problems with this system. These trading rules will almost always have a position in the market. Unless Monday's close equals Friday's close, there will always be a position taken that week. Do we always want to be in the market? This is an example of a pattern which is probably too simple to derive any nonrandom or trending characteristics. We need to filter out the random behavior and develop more selective trading rules. Let's modify the rules:

Buy signal: If the market is up on Monday, Tuesday, and Wednesday, buy the open on Thursday and sell the close on Friday.

Sell signal: If the market is down on Monday, Tuesday, and Wednesday, sell the open on Thursday and buy the close on Friday.

This type of pattern may be more suggestive of nonrandom behavior because a trend may be developing. However, there are still many considerations such as:

1. What if Wednesday closes unchanged or up just slightly, but Monday and Tuesday close down? Should the signal be modified to account for this minor difference? Or perhaps a percentage change should be used instead of number of closes up or down. An unchanged Monday and Tuesday close followed by a 5% move up on Wednesday may be more significant than three slightly higher closes in a row.

2. Maybe a countertrend method should be used to sell on Thursday if the market closes higher on the first three days. Countertrend trading systems are being increasingly developed because a market may exhibit choppy behavior more often than trending movement.

3. Perhaps the position should be entered on the close of Wednesday instead of the open on Thursday. The rules for entry and exit can be changed in many ways.

4. Should a stop be placed above or below a certain point to limit the amount of loss or profit to a specific amount? This is one of the most important questions whenever trading and will be covered in the money management section. For now, consider limiting losses to a certain amount. You may also want to limit profits by getting out at certain price objectives, but the limiting of losses is generally much more important. We do not want to hold onto a trade if it goes badly against us.

ANALYZING RESULTS

Two different kinds of results are normally observed after going through the testing process:

1. *Breakeven*: The patterns do not show any bias and yield profits similar to the amount of losses. Most of the results will turn out this way. Many of the patterns will not yield results which are highly profitable. This happens because markets exhibit random behavior and the patterns tested do not really suggest any large bias in the market. The best solution is the same as a trade. Try again.

2. *High profits or losses*: A method may yield extremely good or bad results. There are usually three reasons for this:

    a. The test was not statistically significant, therefore the results are not reliable. More back-testing is required to see how the method performs on a longer-term basis. If the initial results were for six months or a year, three to six years might be tested next to obtain more results. Another market may also be chosen to see how the method performed under different conditions. However, some traders believe each market is unique, and rules which apply for one do not always apply for another.

b. The market made an extremely large move once, and the pattern was able to catch it. This type of result may be more a stroke of luck or coincidence than a predictive pattern. Markets will always make a large move at certain times, and the pattern may have just occurred randomly before the move began. However, if the same pattern seems to recur in similar large moves, it may deserve further analysis. The pattern which preceded the stock market crash in the December 87 S&P500 in Figure 13.5 may not necessarily be indicative of another crash.

c. The pattern actually may suggest nonrandom and significant behavior. In other words, it works! Unfortunately this is least often the case. But, when it does occur, the eventual trading possibilities may make up for much of the work in finding it. Assuming the first two criteria of statistical significance and unusual market activity may have been met, further tests are warranted. What happens when slippage is included? What about commissions? We will look at this in the money management section.

TESTING FOR NONRANDOM BEHAVIOR IN PATTERNS

The theory of runs will be covered in the money management section, but for now think of it as a way to determine the chance of a certain event occurring repeatedly. If an event occurs more frequently than chance would suggest then there is a probability the event is nonrandom. For example, if a coin is flipped 10 times, there is a likelihood heads may appear every time. If the coin is flipped 100 times and heads still appears every time, one may begin to wonder if the coin is not fair. The theory of runs is a way to calculate the probability of a series of events occurring, such as heads appearing 10 times in a row, or any other combination.

FIGURE 13.5
December 1987 S&P500 index

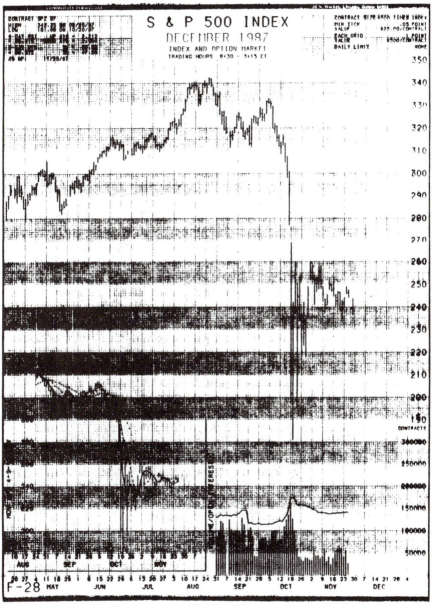

Source: Reprinted with Permission, © 1991 Commodity Perspective, 30 South
Wacker Drive, Suite 1820, Chicago, Illinois 60606.

The theory of runs is a powerful tool in pattern recognition to test whether certain patterns are random or nonrandom. The patterns which are nonrandom may be separated from all the others to possibly yield good trading methods.

Another consideration when testing rules is that the best and worst results usually merit the most attention. For example, most traders would be wildly enthusiastic about a pattern which exhibited consistently profitable results. However, a pattern which exhibited consistently bad results may also be worth noting. If it is possible to apply the opposite set of rules on the pattern then the new results may become consistently profitable. This is not always the case because the rules may not be exactly transferable. For example, a simple strategy which cuts losses and lets profits run may lead to margin calls and other problems if reversed, by cutting profits and letting losses run.

Good or bad results are not as important as consistent results. We are looking for nonrandom behavior which may be predictive and tradable, and try to always avoid random behavior in the market. When a pattern elicits consistently good or bad results, this suggests the possibility of nonrandom behavior. In essence we may have a good pattern to trade.

SOME PATTERNS TO CONSIDER

Gaps

Gaps seem to hold some kind of fascination with many traders. Some traders believe gaps must always be filled, but they may have to wait the rest of their lives (and perhaps longer) and face a total loss of capital to celebrate the occasion. Perhaps they somehow feel the market is incomplete until the gap is filled. Gaps may be categorized into four types:

1. The *general or common gap* is the one which occurs most frequently and may be seen in many different market configurations. There are many common gaps in Figure 13.6 of the March 91 Japanese yen, such as the one on January 2 when the price gapped to 7440 on the open from the previous close near 7380.

FIGURE 13.6
March 1991 Japanese yen

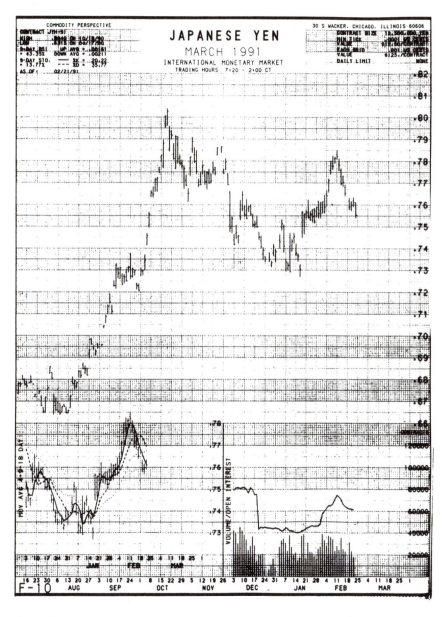

2. A *breakaway gap* may occur after a congestion phase. The market gaps above or below a congestion area and maintains a trend. A breakaway gap occurs on November 29 when the yen breaks out of the congestion range at the 7650 level.

3. A *runaway gap* may occur when a market is trending. The market gaps to even higher or lower levels. There are a series of runaway gaps from August to October in the yen, such as October 4 at 7420 and 7510 the next day.

4. An *exhaustion gap* may occur after a strong trend. It may signify the possible end of the trend. The yen makes an exhaustion gap on October 17 when it opens at the 8000 level and tops out.

Be careful when analyzing gaps. Some markets gap more than others, such as the currencies, because they are actively traded 24 hours a day. Other markets, like the stock market, do not gap as readily because the markets may only be open at certain times of the day.

We can test for all of these gaps, but for simplicity, let's look at common gaps to develop a general case for all gaps. Some analysts would object and say gaps must be analyzed individually or by category. This is certainly a valid argument, but the testing process becomes much harder and will not be dealt with here. Here are some possible rules for testing gaps:

1. Sell if the market gaps open 1% above the previous close, and close out the position at the end of the day.

2. Buy if the market gaps open 1% below the previous close, and close out the position at the end of the day.

For those who prefer trending methods, the rules can always be changed to buy if the market gaps higher and sell if the market gaps lower.

Inside Day

An inside day occurs when the high and low of the most recent period are contained by the high and low of the previous period. Therefore, the high of the recent day is less than the high of the previous day, and the low of the recent day is greater than the low of the previous day. On January 28, May 91 cotton had an inside day which was well contained from the previous day's high of 77.50 and 76.20 as shown in Figure 13.7. The market pushed higher on January 29 and made a series of new highs afterwards.

Some traders believe an inside day represents an equilibrium point from which the market will make an important move. A breakout above the previous high or below the previous low will provide a possible answer to the eventual direction of the market. Trending rules are often used with the inside day method:

Buy if the market trades above the previous day's high.

Sell if the market trades below the previous day's low.

Some variations on a theme include buying above the inside day's high or selling below the inside day's low.

Key Reversal Day

A key reversal day pattern may provide the initial indication of a change in trend. A sell signal is generated when the high of the current day is above the high of the previous day, and the close of the current day is below the close of the previous day. A buy signal occurs when the low of the current day is below the low of the previous day, and the current day close is above the close of the previous day. June 89 Sterling in Figure 13.8 yields several key reversal signals on March 20, April 20, 21, and 28.

There can be many variations of this rule, such as requiring the open and the low of the current day to be below the low of the previous day, for a valid buy signal. A sell signal might require the open and high of the current day to be above the high of the previous day. Another sell rule might require the close of the current day to be below the low of the previous day. The corresponding buy rule would require the close of the current day to be above the high of the previous day.

FIGURE 13.7
May 1991 cotton

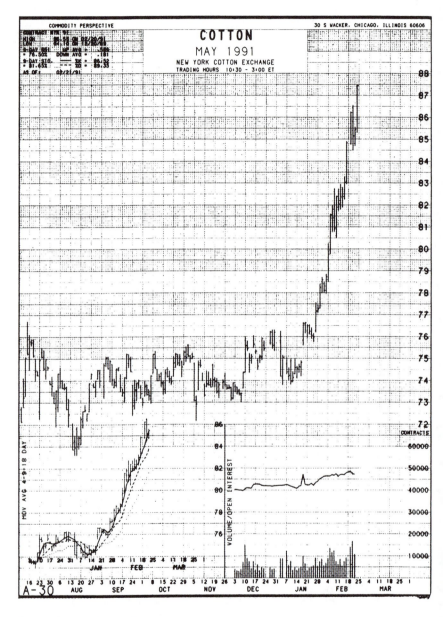

Source: Reprinted with Permission, © 1991 Commodity Perspective, 30 South
Wacker Drive, Suite 1820, Chicago, Illinois 60606.

FIGURE 13.8
June 1989 short sterling

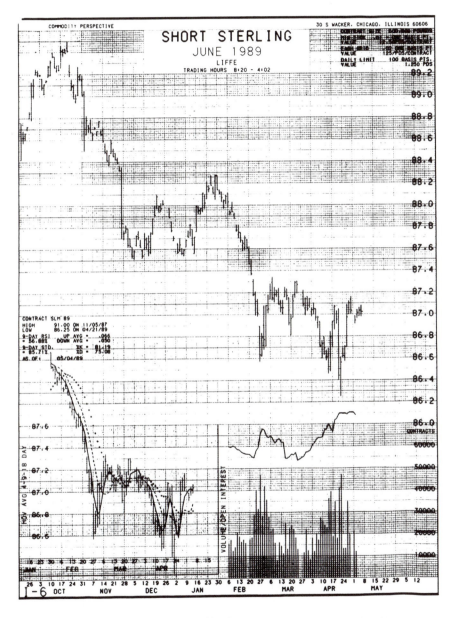

Source: Reprinted with Permission, © 1991 Commodity Perspective, 30 South Wacker Drive, Suite 1820, Chicago, Illinois 60606.

Island Reversals

An island reversal occurs when a market gaps above previous highs and gaps down on the next or subsequent days, leaving an island formation. The opposite downside island would occur when a market gaps below previous lows and gaps up on the next or subsequent days. The three-day island reversal on January 14 in June 91 gold, seen in Figure 13.9, signaled the end of the upmove and beginning of the bear market. The formation suggests a reversal in trend.

Some possible rules might be:

Sell if the market gaps below an island.

Buy if the market gaps above an island.

Consecutive Closes

Another pattern we will consider is buying or selling if the market closes higher or lower a specific number of times. This type of action may suggest the beginning of a trend, and therefore, a trading opportunity.

Buy market on close if the market closes higher three days in a row, and close out the position at the close of the fifth day.

Sell market on close if the market closes lower three days in a row, and close out the position at the close of the fifth day.

This type of trading system has hints of a moving average system but does not have the lag time of longer-term moving averages. The patterns can be varied to trade on the fourth day, wait for a down day to buy or an up day to sell, and so on. The three-day consecutive close pattern yielded a short-term sale near 212.50 on February 20 in the July CRB future in Figure 13.10. The buy signal at the 213.00 level on February 27 proved to be an even better trade. Another buy signal on April 2 near 220.50 was not as fortuitous, but the trader must realize no system or method will always yield profitable trades.

FIGURE 13.9
June 1991 COMEX gold

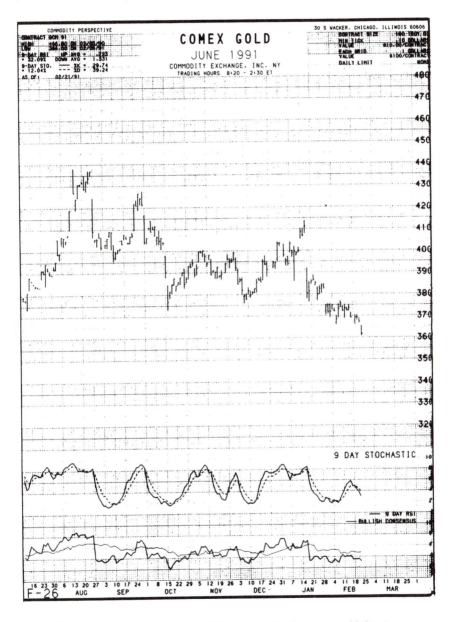

Source: Reprinted with Permission, © 1991 Commodity Perspective, 30 South
Wacker Drive, Suite 1820, Chicago, Illinois 60606.

FIGURE 13.10
July 1991 CRB index

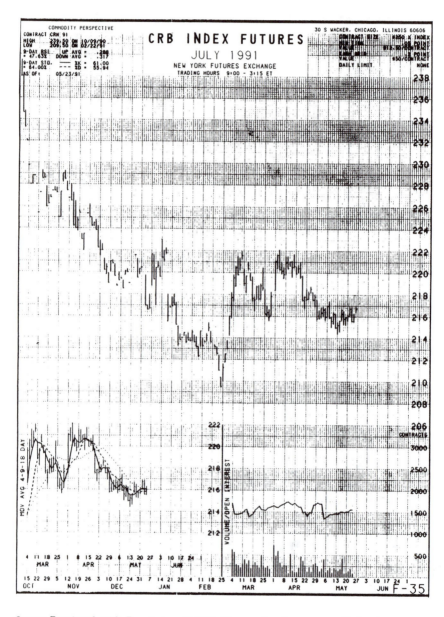

Source: Reprinted with Permission, © 1991 Commodity Perspective, 30 South Wacker Drive, Suite 1820, Chicago, Illinois 60606.

FIGURE 13.11
September 1991 S&P500 futures 30-minute bar chart

Source: Reprinted with permission, FutureSource, 955 Parkview Blvd., Lombard, IL 60148 (800) 621-2628

Intraday Breakout

Another pattern which some intraday traders watch is a breakout from a specified range, such as the first hour of trading. The 30-minute bar chart of the September 91 S&P500 future in Figure 13.11 yields a winning trade on Friday marked point A after the first hour range is broken near 389.00 on the third bar (second hour of trading). The second day also provides a winning sale near 388.00 on Monday denoted as point B. Tuesday yields a frustrating sale below 386.00 at point C with a subsequent strong rally in the third hour. Changing the breakout range to the first half-hour or second hour might greatly affect results for better or worse, so the trader must experiment with different rules.

COMPLEX PATTERN RECOGNITION

At this point you might be thinking the patterns and rules just discussed are rather simple. What about considering more complex patterns, such as a head and shoulders or Elliott Wave formation, for testing? Slightly more complex patterns such as a rectangle or triangle are actually more complex than might first appear. *Even simple patterns have an infinite number of possibilities or variations.* The process of finding a simple pattern such as a rectangle actually requires a lot of rules to make sure every nuance is caught. Figure 13.10 shows different patterns, but which ones are rectangles and which ones are not? We have advanced to a much higher level in learning and often take for granted the complexity of many patterns. The learning process is partly the combination of learning simple skills and then combining them into more complex tasks. We take for granted that the simplest skills actually require tremendous amounts of information and rules to carry out. We are only trying to identify them now and have not yet even considered ways of trading them.

One of the reasons for developing a series of simple rule systems is to eventually combine many of them into a rather sophisticated rule system, which recognizes more complex patterns. We may then have a powerful method of analyzing market patterns. It may be much easier to study more complex patterns by breaking them down into much simpler ones, similar to the process of detrending in cycle analysis.

JAPANESE CANDLESTICK CHART PATTERNS

Some of the trading rules for Japanese candlestick charts are actually good examples of simple time and price pattern recognition. Traders look for different patterns which may portend bullish or bearish behavior. There are many types of patterns and some of the more common formations include:

1. The *hammer* is characterized by a large sell-off and then a close above 50% of the range for the day, as shown in Figure 13.12. The hammer occurs after a downmove and may signal a reversal in trend and higher prices.

2. The *hanging man* in Figure 13.12 is similar to the hammer but occurs after a rally, and indicates lower prices may be imminent.

3. *Engulfing pattern*: The real body of the current period must engulf the real body of the previous period. The color of the current period should be different than the color of the previous period,

FIGURE 13.12
The hammer, the hanging man, and engulfing patterns are all examples of patterns that may signal a change in trend.

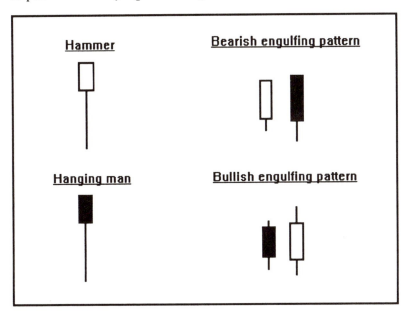

so if the previous period is white, the current period should be black. The engulfing patterns are similar to the key reversal days previously discussed. If the market is in an uptrend and the engulfing pattern occurs, as in the top right corner of Figure 13.12, a possible change of trend may occur. The bullish engulfing pattern in the lower right corner of Figure 13.12, occurring after a downmove, might signal higher prices.

4. *Dark cloud cover*: The market opens above the highs of the previous day and closes within the real body of the previous day, as shown in Figure 13.13. A possible downmove may now occur.

5. *Piercing pattern*: The market opens below the lows of the previous day but closes within the real body of the previous day,

FIGURE 13.13
The dark cloud cover, piercing pattern, harami, and morning star are all
patterns that may signal a change in trend.

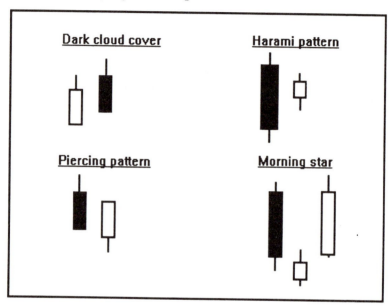

as depicted in Figure 13.13. This is the opposite pattern of the dark
cloud cover and signifies a possible upmove.

6. *Harami pattern*: The candlestick equivalent of an inside day,
and shown in Figure 13.13.

7. *Morning star*: A three-day pattern comprised of a black body
representing a downmove on the first day. The small real body on
the second day gaps lower, which is followed by a white real body
on the third day which closes strongly higher. The morning star is
depicted in Figure 13.13 and may denote the beginning of an uptrend.
The evening star is the opposite of a morning star and may indicate
a possible downtrend.

The March 91 Japanese yen in Figure 13.14 shows some of
the candlestick formations and resulting moves.

FIGURE 13.14

March 1991 Japanese yen candlestick chart

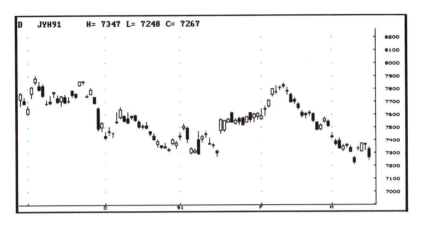

Source: Reprinted with permission, FutureSource, 955 Parkview Blvd., Lombard, IL 60148 (800) 621-2628

MATHEMATICS, REASON, EMOTION
AND THE MARKETS

The patterns reviewed were objective and easy to quantify, but any quantitative study, no matter how complex or rigorous, cannot include or measure all the factors that affect the market. This is because some of the factors are not rational, but emotional in nature and therefore beyond easy measurement. Most mathematical studies assume rationality, which may rule in many cases, but certainly not in all.

There will eventually be more studies dealing with irrational and emotional behaviors and how they affect the market. We need to learn more about how feelings such as fear and hope affect the interactions of the market on many different levels. But as long as the markets are traded by people, we will never fully comprehend them because we can never fully understand ourselves and others.

Does this mean that mathematical modeling is incomplete and not effective? Yes and no. Mathematical modeling can never encompass all the variables which affect the market; so it can never completely predict or account for all market action. But it can help in developing and analyzing the past performance of different kinds of trading rules. The goal of the trader is not to predict every market move with absolute certainty, but instead to be on the right side of the probabilities, like an insurance company or casino. It is in this realm where mathematics and statistics may be of great value if used in an appropriate and practical way.

ANOTHER THOUGHT ON PATTERN RECOGNITION

Working with pattern recognition and artificial intelligence demonstrates there is actually a tremendous amount of thought and decision required, even for the simplest pattern or trade. There are an immense number of thoughts and feelings that go into making each trading decision. What makes the decision even harder is that we may not even be aware of all the different interactions and feelings that go through our minds in making the final decision to buy or sell.

The beauty and frustration of artificial intelligence and pattern recognition analysis is that it is a way to learn how we learn. There is clearly much to be learned in this area.

CONCLUSION

Many impatient traders wish to dispense with learning the various kinds of indicators, and simply want to know the "best" way to trade, or the one that works all or most of the time. The answer to their question will be as simple as the answer to the meaning of life.

The rich diversity of studies in technical analysis provides a good start in developing trading methods for the market. The methods may be used independently or in conjunction with other methods. The same method may be used in exactly opposite ways and still provide winning or losing trades for both market participants. The ultimate judge of any trading system is not the theoretical argument behind it, but whether it helps the trader make money. Some successful traders swear by methods others find useless.

No ultimate trading methods will always make money, although some seem to consistently lose money! The trader must realize there are compromises in every method. The trader must give up something in order to get something else. A faster moving average will usually get the trader in the market more quickly, and more often at better prices than a slower moving average. But the faster moving average will also get the trader into trouble more often by sometimes signaling more losing trades and being whipsawed more frequently.

There are an infinite number of technical studies and this review has only covered some of the more salient kinds of technical analysis. For a more comprehensive look, see the bibliography. The number of technical studies is limited only by the imagination.

CHAPTER 14

Option Basics

Far better it is to dare mighty things, to win glorious triumphs, even though checkered by failure, than to take rank with those poor spirits who neither enjoy much nor suffer much, because they live in the gray twilight that knows not victory nor defeat.

Theodore Roosevelt

Options provide a rich variety of ways to speculate or hedge in the market. The risk and reward characteristics of options are much different than buying or selling outright (i.e., naked long or short position). The investor should thoroughly understand these characteristics of options before trading them.

Traders find options appealing because they feel options offer unlimited profit potential with limited risk. Others believe options are less risky because their loss is limited when buying them. In reality, options are just as risky as trading outright positions, but the risk is of a different nature.

DEFINITIONS

Options *are the right, but not the obligation, to buy or sell the underlying future at a specific price for a predetermined time.* There are two kinds of options:

1. *A* **call** *is an option to buy a future or security at a specific price for a predetermined time.* For example, on January 31 Robert decides to buy a call which allows him to buy a future at the specific price of 100. The option ceases trading on the predetermined time of December 15. The future is currently trading at 98. He will have the right, but will not be obligated, to purchase the future at 100 until December 15.

2. *A* **put** *is an option to sell a future or security at a specific price for a predetermined time.* For example, on June 21 Susan decides to buy a put which allows her to sell a future at the specific price of 100. The option will cease trading on the predetermined time of December 29. The future is currently trading at 98. She will have the right, but will not be obligated, to sell the future at 100 until December 29.

The specific price and predetermined time for a call and a put have special terms:

The **strike** *or* **exercise price** *is the specific price where the investor may buy or sell the option.* In both examples the call and put are options with a 100 strike price. Robert has the right to purchase the future at 100, whereas Susan has the right to sell the future at 100.

The **expiration date** *of the option is the date the option will stop trading. The* **time to expiration** *is the predetermined time, or amount of time left that the option may trade till the expiration date.* The expiration date for Robert's option is the day the option expires, which is December 15. The time to expiration is approximately 11 months (December 15—January 31). The expiration date for Susan's option is the day the option expires, which is December 29. The time to expiration for Susan's option is approximately 6 months (December 29—June 21).

Now that you are familiar with basic option terms, let's investigate more option terminology:

An option is **exercised** *when the person converts the option into a long or short future position.* For example, if Robert exercised his option he would become long the future at 100. If Susan exercised her option she would become short the future at 100.

An option may be **assigned** *to a person who is short a call or put.* When someone exercises an option another person automatically gets assigned. For example, if Robert exercises his call and becomes long the future, someone else who is short the call must get assigned and now become short the future. If Susan exercises her put, she will become short the future, and someone else who is short the put will get assigned and become long the future. The number of long positions must always balance the number of short positions.

An option may be **in the money, at the money,** *or* **out of the money,** *depending on the strike price, the future price, and whether the option is a call or put.*

1. *In the money option*: A call is in the money if the underlying future is trading above the strike price. A put is in the money if the underlying future is trading below the strike price. Susan's put is in the money because the future is below the strike price.

2. *At or near the money option*: A call or put is at the money if the underlying future is trading close to the strike price of the option. If the future trades at 100, both Robert's and Susan's options will be at the money.

3. *Out of the money option*: A call is out of the money when the future is trading below the strike price. A put is out of the money when the future is trading above the strike price. Robert's call is out of the money because the strike price is above where the future is trading.

Figure 14.1 shows the three kinds of options and how they relate to the price of the security. Assume the market is currently trading in the 100 range. A call or a put with a 100 strike would be considered an at the money option because the future is trading at the strike price.

Calls above the 100 level would be considered out of the money options because the future is trading below the level where the calls may be exercised. Exercising the calls would make the owner long the market above the level it is currently trading—an unwise and unprofitable situation. Puts above the 100 level would be considered in the money options because the owner of the puts could exercise or sell the future above the level the market is currently trading.

FIGURE 14.1
The distinction between in the money, at the money, and out of the money options.

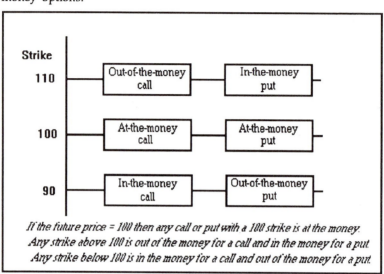

Strike

110 — Out-of-the-money call — In-the-money put

100 — At-the-money call — At-the-money put

90 — In-the-money call — Out-of-the-money put

If the future price = 100 then any call or put with a 100 strike is at the money.
Any strike above 100 is out of the money for a call and in the money for a put.
Any strike below 100 is in the money for a call and out of the money for a put.

Calls below the 100 level would be considered in the money options because the owner could exercise or buy the future below the level the market is currently trading. Puts below the 100 level would be called out of the money options because the future is trading above where the put may be exercised. Exercising the put would make the owner short the market, below the level it is currently trading—another unwise and unprofitable situation.

The **intrinsic value** *of an option is the portion of the price of the option attributable to being in the money.* The amount the option is in the money is therefore equal to the intrinsic value, as shown by the following formulas:

Intrinsic value for a call = future price – strike price
Intrinsic value for a put = strike price – future price

The intrinsic value of Robert's call is:

Intrinsic value of call = 98 – 100
                         = –2 or no intrinsic value

If an option has a negative or zero intrinsic value, we usually say it has no intrinsic value. The intrinsic value of Susan's put is:

Intrinsic value of put = 100 – 98
= 2

The **extrinsic value** *is the portion of the price of the option which is not dependent on being in the money.* The extrinsic value for a call or put is:

Extrinsic value = price of the option – intrinsic value

Assume Robert paid $3 for his call and Susan paid $4 for her put. The extrinsic value for Robert's call is:

Extrinsic value = $3 – 0
= $3

The extrinsic value of Susan's put is:

Extrinsic value = $4 – $2
= $2

The extrinsic value may be positive, negative, or zero. Most options usually have a positive extrinsic value. Some deep in the money options may have a negative extrinsic value, partly because it is often more efficient to buy or sell the future than the option. In the money options near expiration may often have an extrinsic value near zero because they are somewhat of a proxy for the future. The extrinsic value is a function of various factors, such as the volatility of the underlying contract and the time to expiration of the option.

To **write** *an option is the same as to sell it.* The seller of an option is granting the rights of the option to the buyer. The seller receives a premium or the price of the option for these rights.

An **American option** *allows the buyer to exercise it any time during the life of the option.* If the future is trading at 105 and the 100 call is trading at 5 with a few days to expiration, Robert may choose to exercise the option. A person might want to exercise an option before the expiration date for various reasons, such as owning a stock which is about to pay a dividend. The owner of the option does not receive a dividend, so exercising the option will allow ownership of the stock which will allow the dividends to be received.

A **European option** *can only be exercised at the expiration of the option.* An American option may be valued somewhat differently than a European option because there is a slight benefit in being able to exercise an option at any time before expiration.

Looking at the prior examples will help us to understand the option terms:

Call Example. Before Robert purchased the 100 call, he looked at the 95 call which was in the money, the 100 call which was at the money, and the 105 call which was out of the money. After buying the 100 call the market went up to 110 and Robert decided to exercise the call, which meant he was long the future at 100.

Put example. Before Susan purchased the 100 put, she looked at the 105 put which was in the money, the 100 put which was at the money, and the 95 put which was out of the money. After buying the 100 put the market rallied and closed at 105 on December 29. Susan had the right to exercise the put which would give her the ability to sell the future at 100, but there would be no reason to do this. Since she can sell the future at the market at 105, she would not choose to exercise the put and sell the market at the lower price of 100.

To better understand options and some of the advantages and disadvantages of trading them, look at the following example. Robert and Susan still hold divergent opinions about the market. Let's see how three different market scenarios affect their profits and losses when trading options. In these examples both intend to hold the option until it expires:

1. Robert is bullish on the market which is currently trading at 100, and he believes the future may appreciate to 120 in the next five months. He does not wish to purchase the future outright, partly because if the market drops instead of rallies he is concerned he will lose too much money. He decides to purchase a 105 call for $3 which expires in six months. The call allows him to buy the future at 105 anytime in the next six months. He would not choose to buy the future now at 105 since it is presently trading at 100.

He may sell the call before it expires but feels it is better to hold on for the long term.

   2. Susan is bearish on the same market but is not certain how far it might drop. She decides to sell the same 105 call at $3. If the market should rally above 105 at expiration, she will have to sell the future at 105.

   Scenario 1: Market rises to 120. If Robert bought the call, how much money did he make? He exercises the call, which enables him to buy the future at 105 and simultaneously sell the future at 120. The profit is 120 – 105 = 15. But remember he paid $3 for the call so he must subtract $15 – $3 = $12. His profit is $12.

   If Susan sold the call then the reverse holds true. She will be assigned the future and become short at 105. She must buy the future back at 120 to cover her sale at 105. She received $3 for the sale of the call so her total loss is $12.

   Scenario 2: Market ends unchanged at 100. Robert is long the call but he would not want to exercise the option. If he exercised the option, he would effectively buy the future at 105, which would be senseless since he can buy it at the market at 100. Therefore, the call expires worthless and he loses $3 or the original price of the call.

   If Susan sold the call the reverse holds true. She will make $3 for the amount received from the call sale, and it would be highly unlikely that she would be assigned the call.

   Scenario 3: Market drops to 80. The same results in scenario two would apply in this scenario because the call would not be exercised at 105. If both traders decide to hold onto the option until expiration, the market would have to go above 108 for Robert to make money and Susan to lose money.

   This example points out the reasons why investors buy or sell options. If the market goes strongly in your favor, as it did for Robert in scenario 1, you will make a good profit on a small outlay of cash. However, if a good move never occurs you will most likely end up losing money. Robert and Susan held the options till expiration, but what if they had decided to exit the position before then, as many traders do? The question is not always easily answered because of the various factors which affect the pricing of options, but will be addressed in the following sections and chapters on options.

RISK AND REWARD CHARACTERISTICS OF BUYING
AND SELLING A FUTURE

One of the best ways to see why options are used is to view a graph of the profit and loss potential of options versus outrights.

Figure 14.2 depicts the profit and loss potential of an outright future. The horizontal, or x axis, is the price of the future and the vertical, or y axis, is the profit or loss of the position. The positively sloping 45° line represents the profit and loss potential in buying the future, and the negatively sloped 45° line represents the profit and loss potential of selling the future. For every dollar the future moves the position will make or lose one dollar.

Outright positions are the simplest and usually most popular form of trading. The profit and loss situation is straightforward and simply a function of the price of the future.

FIGURE 14.2
Outright long or short position: The positively sloped diagonal line represents an outright long position; the negatively sloped diagonal line represents an outright short position.

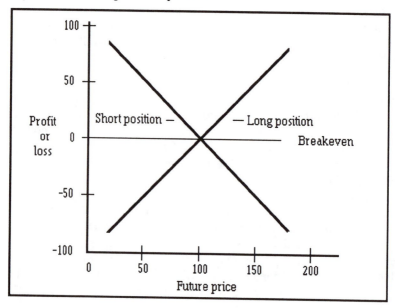

RISK AND REWARD CHARACTERISTICS
OF BUYING A CALL

Figure 14.3 shows the profit and loss potential at the expiration of a January 100 call which was initially purchased for $5. The call allows the holder to buy the future at 100, so it will generally not be exercised if the market is below 100. Three scenarios develop at expiration:

1. If the market is below 100 the call will probably not be exercised because the holder can buy the future at a lower price in the open market. The maximum loss is $5, which is the original purchase price of the option and is shown by the horizontal line when the future is below 100.

2. If the market is at 100 the call may or may not be exercised since the owner can buy the future in the open market at 100. The loss is still $5 as in 1.

FIGURE 14.3
Long a call: The profit and loss potential at expiration of buying a January 100 call for $5 as a function of the underlying price of the future.

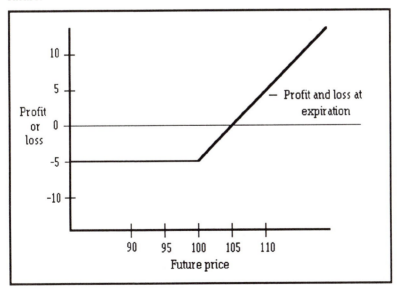

3. If the market is above 100 the call should, and probably will, be exercised because the holder will own the future at 100, which is below where the market is trading. Assume the market is trading at 105. The call is exercised so the holder is long the future at 100 and can immediately sell the future at 105 for a profit of $5. However, the $5 profit is negated by the original purchase price of $5 so the holder will breakeven on the trade.

The call does not have the downside risk associated with buying the outright as in Figure 14.2 because the maximum loss is limited by $5. However, the call closely resembles the 45° line and profit potential of an outright long position initiated at 105, if the market rises above 100. Breakeven for the option occurs when the market reaches 105, which is the same breakeven point if the future were purchased at 105.

The next graph in Figure 14.4 shows the approximate profit and loss potential in the present, and at expiration of purchasing

FIGURE 14.4
Long a call: The profit and loss potential in the present and at expiration of buying a January 100 call for $5 as a function of the price of the underlying future.

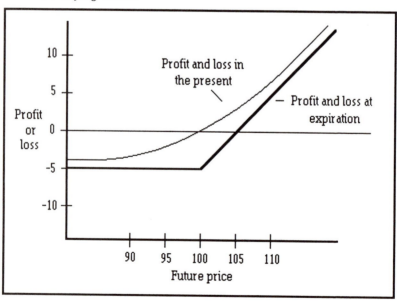

the January 100 call. The price of the call option is relatively insensitive to the price of the underlying future below the 80 price level. The price of the call option will change by approximately 0 to 1/2 point for every 1-point change in the price of the underlying future between 80 and 100. After the 100 level the call option will move approximately 1/2 to 1 point for a corresponding 1-point move in the underlying future. After 110 the call will move about the same amount as the future. As time passes the potential profit and loss line in the present will eventually move closer to the profit and loss line at expiration. The potential profit and loss line in the present is approximate and may vary greatly because it is a function of factors, such as the volatility of the future and time to expiration of the option.

RISK AND REWARD CHARACTERISTICS
OF BUYING A PUT

Figure 14.5 shows the profit and loss potential at expiration of buying a February 100 put for $5. The put allows the holder to sell the future at 100, so it will generally not be exercised if the market is above 100. The three scenarios outlined with the call expiration entail the opposite results:

1. If the market is below 100, the put should, and probably will, be exercised because the holder can sell the future at 100, which is above the level the market is trading. Assume the market is trading at 90 at expiration. The put is exercised so the holder is short the market at 100 and can immediately buy the future at 90 for a $10 profit. The $5 price of the put is subtracted against the $10 profit to arrive at a total profit of $5, as shown on the graph. If the future were trading at 95 then the holder would breakeven.

2. If the future is at 100, the put may or may not be exercised since the owner can sell the future in the open market at 100. The maximum loss is $5 or the price of the put, as shown in Figure 14.5.

3. If the future is above 100 the put should not be exercised and the maximum loss is $5 as shown in Figure 14.5.

FIGURE 14.5
Long a put: The profit and loss potential at expiration of buying a put
as a function of the underlying future price.

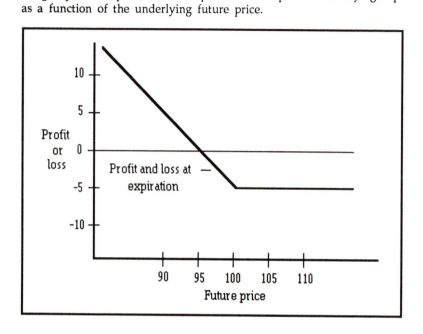

The put does not have the upside risk associated with selling
the outright as in Figure 14.2 because the maximum loss is limited
to $5. The put closely resembles the 45° line and same profit potential
of selling short the future at 95 if the market is below 100.

Figure 14.6 shows the approximate profit and loss potential in
the present and at expiration of buying the February 100 put. The
price of the put will move about the same amount as the future
if the future is below 80. The price of the put will move from
approximately 1/2 to 1 point for each 1-point move in the future
between 80 and 100. The price of the put will move from 0 to 1/2
for each 1-point move in the future between 100 and 120. The potential
profit and loss line in the present will vary greatly and approach
the profit and loss line at expiration, as in the call example, due
to the same reasons.

FIGURE 14.6
Long a put: The profit and loss potential in the present and at
expiration of buying a put as a function of the underlying future price.

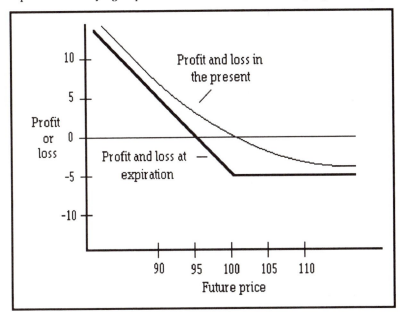

From the preceding scenarios we see the loss is limited in
purchasing an option but the reward is not limited for calls. The
profit potential in buying a put is limited to the underlying dropping
to zero, and therefore is not the same profit potential as buying a
call. The idea of limited risk and nearly unlimited profit potential
is one of the most alluring reasons why investors choose to buy
options. For every purchase there is a sale, so let's review the other
side of option trading in the next section.

RISK AND REWARD CHARACTERISTICS
OF SELLING A CALL

Selling versus buying options is a less familiar concept to many
investors. However, because option trading is a zero-sum game there
is just as much money made or lost selling options as buying them,

so investors should become more knowledgeable in selling options, too.

Figure 14.7 presents the profit and loss potential in the present and at expiration of selling a March 100 call for $5. Many of the characteristics of selling options are opposite to the ones of buying them. For example, the profit potential is limited but the loss potential is not limited and similar to being short the future. The profit and loss potential at expiration is the same as being short the future at 105 when the future is above 105. The most the call writer can make is $5 no matter how low the future drops, whereas the short seller can profit substantially if the market drops significantly.

The three possible scenarios for selling options are:

1. If the market is below 100 the future will probably not be assigned, so the call seller should expect to make $5 from the premium received, as shown in Figure 14.7.

FIGURE 14.7
Selling a call: The profit and loss potential in the present and at expiration of selling a March 100 call for $5 as a function of the underlying price of the future.

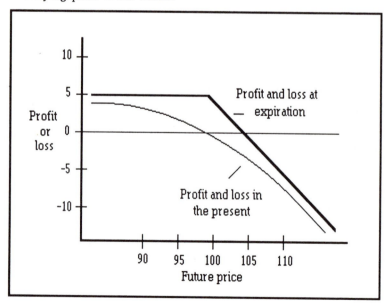

2. If the market is at 100, the future may be assigned, which would make the seller short the future at 100. If assigned the future, the seller can buy the future back at 100 and breakeven on the trade, but still receive the $5 premium from selling the call.

3. If the market rises to 105, the call seller will be assigned the future, which would mean being short the future at 100. The trader would purchase the future at 105 in the open market and lose $5 to close out the trade ($100 – $105 = –$5). However, the $5 premium received from selling the call would offset the loss incurred in buying back the future, so the call seller would breakeven at 105. If the market rises above 105 the call seller will lose the same amount as being short the future at 105.

The call writer will make a profit as long as the future is below 105 at expiration, but may begin to lose substantial amounts if the market rallies sharply. The price of the call exhibits the same sensitivity to a price change in the future as described previously in buying a call.

RISK AND REWARD CHARACTERISTICS
OF SELLING A PUT

Figure 14.8 depicts the profit and loss potential in the present and at expiration of selling an April 100 put for $5. The profit potential is limited, but the loss potential is not limited and similar to being long the future at 95. The most the put seller can make is $5 but the loss is limited to the future dropping to 0, but still much greater than the potential gain.

The three scenarios at expiration are:

1. When the future is above 100, the put seller will probably not be assigned the future; so a profit of $5 will be made from the premium received in selling the put.

2. If the future is at 100, assignment may occur which would make the put seller long at 100. The future can be sold at 100 in

FIGURE 14.8

Selling a put: The profit and loss potential in the present and at
expiration of selling an April 100 put for $5 as a function of the price
of the underlying future.

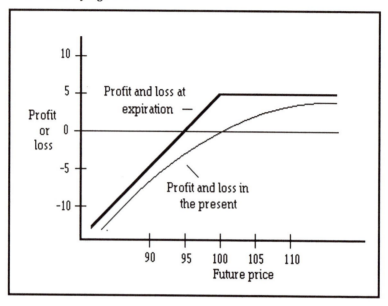

the open market to scratch the long position. The put seller will
still make $5 from the premium received in selling the put.

3. If the future is at 95, the put seller will be assigned and
long the future at 100. Selling the future in the market at 95 will
incur a loss of $5 ($95 − $100 = −$5) but this will be negated by
the $5 premium received from selling the put for a breakeven trade.
Below 95 the put seller will lose just as much as if being long the
future at 95.

The put writer will make a profit as long as the future is
above 95 at expiration, but may begin to lose substantial amounts
if the market drops precipitously. The price of the put exhibits the
same sensitivity to a price change in the future as described previously.

TO BUY OR SELL?

Many people find selling options unsettling because of the limited profit opportunity and unlimited loss potential. Why risk so much to make so little? The same people find purchasing options attractive for the same reasons. Why not risk a little to make a lot? There are very good reasons to buy and sell options. When markets become less volatile option writers will probably achieve better results than option buyers. When markets become more volatile, option buyers will probably do better than option writers. There is a time to buy and a time to sell options, just as in outright position trading, where it is better to go long in a bull market and short in a bear market.

The option writer can generally do better than the option buyer in dull or congested markets, which may occur more often than strongly trending markets. For example, the put buyer and seller will profit in the previous examples if the market remains between 95 and 105, whereas the option buyer may lose money.

When buying or selling options the trader must be concerned with the fair value or proper price of the option. There are many ways to evaluate the price of an option by using option valuation models, which we will explore in later chapters.

The graphs in this chapter form the basis for understanding all the complex strategies in combining options and futures, which will be covered next. Virtually any other strategy such as a straddle, time spread, or butterfly are simply combinations of these graphs. To summarize, the six possibilities are:

1. Buying the outright.

2. Selling the outright.

3. Buying the call.

4. Buying the put.

5. Selling the call.

6. Selling the put.

CONCLUSION

Options provide a way to trade both market direction and volatility. They allow more flexibility in hedging and speculating in a market, and may better meet the needs of traders seeking more complex strategies. They are no more or less risky than outright futures, but the risk is of a different nature because it can be quantified by the premium or price of the option.

CHAPTER 15

Option Combinations

Things without all remedy
Should be without regard. What's done is done.

William Shakespeare, *Macbeth*

There are many ways to combine options and outrights into more complex trading vehicles. Virtually every option strategy, no matter how complex, is really a combination of the basic ones described in Chapter 14.

STRADDLES

Buying a straddle *is the simultaneous purchase of a call and a put of the same strike and expiration.* An example of buying a straddle is the purchase of the May 100 call for $5 and the May 100 put for $5. Figure 15.1 shows the profit potential in the present and at expiration of buying a straddle. The figure is simply the combination of the graphs previously shown in Chapter 14 where purchasing a call and a put was discussed.

FIGURE 15.1
Buying a straddle: The profit and loss potential in the present
and at expiration of buying a May 100 straddle for $10 as a
function of the price of the future.

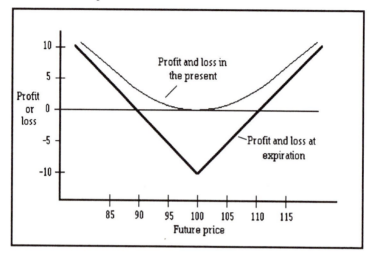

Recall the call and put buyer will each lose $5 if the future
closes at 100 on expiration day. Therefore, the straddle buyer will
lose $10 ($5 + $5) if the future settles at 100 at expiration. However,
the straddle buyer will incur a profit if the future is below 90 or
above 110 at expiration. Anyone buying a straddle expects the market
to move either up or down by a large amount but will lose money
if the market remains at the same price level.

Selling a straddle *is the simultaneous sale of a call and a put of
the same strike and expiration.* Selling the June 100 call for $5 and
the June 100 put for $5 is an example of selling a straddle. Figure
15.2 shows the profit potential in the present and at expiration of
selling a straddle. The figure is the combination of the graphs previously
shown in Chapter 14 where selling a call and a put was discussed.

The call and put seller will each make $5 if the future settles
at 100 on expiration day, so the straddle seller will collect $10 if
the future closes at 100 on expiration. The straddle seller will lose
money if the market drops below 90 or rises above 110. Anyone
selling a straddle expects the market to remain within a relatively

FIGURE 15.2
Selling a straddle: The profit and loss potential in the present and at expiration of selling a June 100 straddle for $10 as a function of the price of the future.

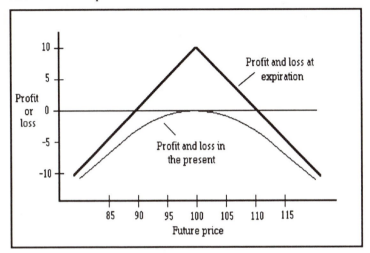

narrow or well defined trading range but will lose money if the market moves considerably in either direction.

STRANGLES AND GUTS

Buying a strangle *consists of the simultaneous purchase of a higher strike call and a lower strike put with the same expiration but different strikes.* An example of purchasing a strangle is buying the July 105 call for $3 and buying the July 95 put for $3. The profit and loss potential in the present and at expiration is depicted in Figure 15.3.

The following scenarios may develop at expiration:

1. If the future is above 105 the call will be in the money and the position will be long one future at 105. Since the total outlay of cash is $6 ($3 + $3) the position will become profitable above 111.

FIGURE 15.3

Buying a strangle: The profit and loss potential in the present and at expiration of buying a July 95 put – 105 call strangle for $6 as a function of the price of the future.

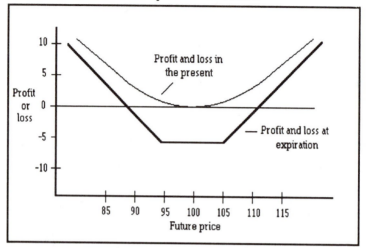

2. If the future is between 95 and 105 the call and put will expire worthless, and a loss of $6 will be incurred which is the price paid for the strangle.

3. If the future is below 95 the put will be in the money and the position will be short one future at 95. The position will become profitable below 89.

A strangle is somewhat similar to a straddle in that the purchaser expects the market to make a large move in one direction or the other. The cash outlay is less for a strangle than a straddle if the straddle is between the 2 strikes of the strangle. For example, the 95 put and 105 call strangle should always be cheaper than the 100 straddle with the same expiration, no matter where the future is trading. This occurs because the straddle will always yield more potential reward than the strangle. The straddle will always have more intrinsic value, except when the future is at 100. If the future closes at 105 on expiration, the straddle will be worth $5 but the strangle will be worthless. The future must move a greater amount for a strangle than a straddle to become profitable.

The **sale of a strangle** *is the simultaneous sale of a higher strike call and lower strike put with the same expiration but different strikes.* The sale of the August 105 call for $3 and the August 95 put for $3 is an example of selling a strangle. Figure 15.4 shows the profit and loss potential in the present and at expiration of selling a strangle. In this case the investor will profit if the market is between 89 and 111 at expiration. Below 89 the position is similar to being long the future at 89 and above 111 the position is similar to being short the future at 111. The strategy for selling a strangle is similar to selling a straddle because in both scenarios the investor believes the market will remain within a relatively narrow, or well defined, trading range.

The **purchase of a gut** *is the simultaneous purchase of a lower strike call and a higher strike put,* such as the August 95 call and August 105 put. **The sale of a gut** *is the simultaneous sale of a lower strike call and higher strike put.* A gut has similar profit and loss characteristics as a strangle, but the trader may need to be concerned about early exercise with a gut because both options may be in the money at the same time.

FIGURE 15.4
Selling a strangle: The profit and loss potential in the present and at expiration of selling an August 95 put – 105 call strangle for $6 as a function of the price of the future.

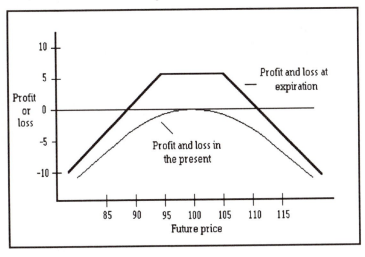

VERTICAL CALL AND PUT SPREADS

A **vertical call spread** *is the buying of one or more calls (puts) and selling of one or more calls (puts) of a different strike but the same expiration.* Buying one September 100 call for $5 and selling one September 105 call for $3 is an example of a vertical call spread. Figure 15.5 shows the profit and loss possibilities in the present and at expiration in purchasing this call spread. The total cash outlay is $2 (called a $2 debit) which is the difference between the 100 and 105 call ($5 − $3 = $2), so the most which can be lost is $2, as shown in Figure 15.5. The maximum possible profit is $3 which is the difference between the two strikes minus the purchase price of the spread ($5 − $2 = $3).

A **vertical put spread** *is the buying of one or more puts and selling of one or more puts of a different strike but same expiration.* An example of buying a put spread is buying the October 100 put for $5 and selling the October 95 put for $2, for a $3 debit. Figure 15.6 depicts the profit and loss possibilities in buying this put spread. The put spread has some characteristics similar to a call spread in that the profit and loss potential is limited, but now the investor anticipates the market will decline. The maximum possible loss for this spread is the $3 purchase price, whereas the maximum possible profit is $2 ($5 − $3 = $2), as shown in Figure 15.6.

Selling a vertical call spread *is the sale of a lower strike call against the purchase of a higher strike call with the same expiration.* The sale of the November 100 call for $5 and the purchase of the November 105 call for $3 is an example of selling a call spread for $2. Figure 15.7 displays the profit and loss potential in the present and at expiration of selling this call spread.

The figure is similar to buying a put spread, but there are important distinctions. For example, at expiration a profit is realized if the market is below 102 when selling the call spread but a profit is not realized until the market is below 97 when buying the put spread. The purchase of a put spread or sale of a call spread are examples of bear spreads because the investor expects the market to decline.

Selling a vertical put spread *is the sale of a higher strike put against the purchase of a lower strike put with the same expiration.* The purchase of the December 95 put for $2 and sale of the December

FIGURE 15.5
Buying a call spread: The profit and loss potential in the present and at expiration of buying the September 100–105 call spread for $2 as a function of the price of the future.

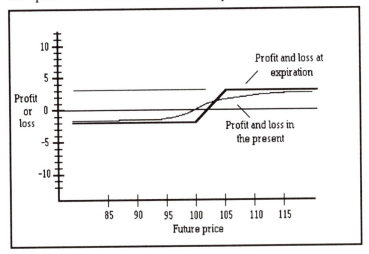

FIGURE 15.6
Buying a put spread: The profit and loss potential in the present and at expiration of buying the October 95–100 put spread for $3 as a function of the price of the future.

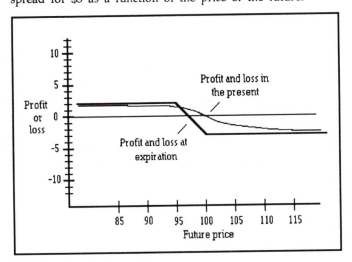

310

FIGURE 15.7
Selling a call spread: The profit and loss potential in the present and at expiration of selling the November 100–105 call spread for a $2 credit as a function of the future price.

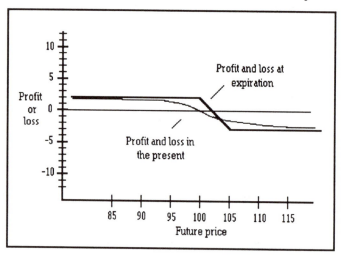

100 put for $5 is an example of selling a put spread for a $3 credit. Figure 15.8 depicts the profit and loss potential in the present and at expiration of selling this put spread.

This figure is similar to buying the call spread, but again there are distinctions. At expiration a profit is realized if the market is above 97 when selling the put spread, but a profit is not realized until the market is above the 102 level when buying the September call spread for $2. The purchase of a call spread or sale of a put spread are examples of bull spreads because the investor will profit if the market rises.

"Vertical" call and put spreads are usually termed just call or put spreads. Profits and losses are limited in buying or selling a call spread, which makes them appealing to many investors. If you are bullish, which is the better choice—buying the call spread or selling the put spread? If you are bearish which is better—buying the put spread or selling the call spread? The answer to this question is partly a function of the proper valuation of the options, which will be investigated in Chapter 16.

FIGURE 15.8
Selling a put spread: The profit and loss potential in the
present and at expiration of selling the December 95–100
put spread for a $3 credit as a function of the price
of the future.

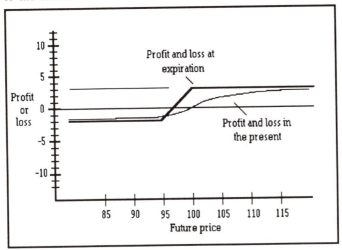

DEBIT AND CREDIT

A **debit transaction** *occurs when money is laid out or a net premium
is paid.* For example, buying the May 100 call and May 100 put
straddle required a net outlay of cash of $10. Buying the September
100 call for $5 and selling the September 105 call for $3, for a net
outlay of $2, is the same as buying the call spread for a $2 debit.

A **credit transaction** *occurs when money is received or a net premium
is taken in.* For example, the seller of the May 100 call and May
100 put straddle will receive a $10 credit. The seller of the September
100–105 call spread (selling the September 100 call and buying the
September 105 call) will receive a $2 credit.

Trades should not be done based on whether you can receive
a credit or cheap debit, but instead on proper theoretical values of
the options. This will be explored further in the options valuation
section.

RATIO SPREADS

A **ratio call spread** *is similar to a call spread but more calls are sold than bought.* For example, the purchase of one January 100 call for $5 and the sale of 2 January 105 calls for $3 is a 1 by 2 ratio call spread. This ratio is termed a 1 by 2 call spread because 1 call is bought for every 2 calls sold. Ratios may be done in any proportion such as 1 by 3 or 2 by 3. In this example, the buyer receives $1 for each spread because $6 is received from the 2 calls sold for each $5 paid for the 1 call bought ($6 – $5 = $1). These spreads may be done for debits or credits.

Figure 15.9 depicts the profit and loss potential at expiration of this spread. The profit and loss potential in the present will not be shown for the remaining spreads because it is highly dependent on the volatility and time to expiration of the options. For example, assume the market is trading at 95 and suddenly moves to 105. Ratios with options of a long-term expiration will probably lose money because the volatility increase may make the 105 calls increase in value much more than the 100 calls. However, ratios with options that expire in a week will probably become profitable because the 100 calls will more likely increase in value much more than the 105 calls.

An investor buying a ratio may expect the market to remain where it is, or rally slightly. Unlike the previous spreads, the profit is limited, but the loss is potentially unlimited if the market rises sharply. A person employing this strategy is accepting the unlimited risk on the upside, for the possibility of making more money than a 1 by 1 call spread if the market closes at the 100 strike. The downside risk is not as great with a ratio spread as with a 1 by 1 call spread, and if the spread is done for a credit the trader may make money if the market falls.

A **ratio put spread** *is similar to a put spread but more puts are sold than bought.* Buying 1 February 100 put for $5 and selling 2 February 95 puts for $2 is an example of a 1 by 2 ratio put spread. This spread is done for a $1 debit because only $4 from the 2 February 95 puts is received for the $5 paid for each February 100 put. Figure 15.10 depicts the profit and loss potential at expiration of this spread.

FIGURE 15.9
Ratio call spread: The profit and loss potential at expiration of the January 100–105 1 by 2 ratio call spread purchased for a $1 credit as a function of the future price.

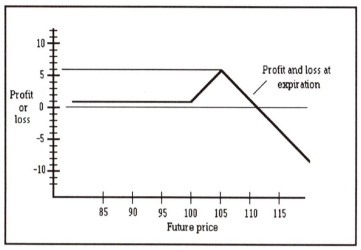

FIGURE 15.10
Ratio put spread: The profit and loss potential at expiration of the February 100–95 1 by 2 ratio put spread purchased for a $1 debit as a function of the future price.

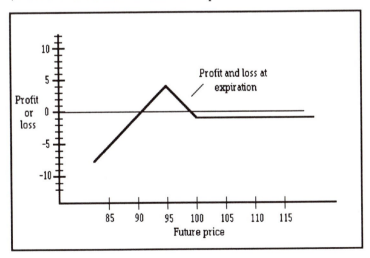

Ratio put spreads are purchased for exactly the opposite reason the ratio call spread is bought. The investor expects the market to drop, but in a relatively stable manner. Any violent or precipitous drop in the market would not be profitable for the spread as can be seen in Figure 15.10. Since this spread is done for a debit, the investor will lose money if the market rallies.

A christmas tree is another variation of ratio call and put spreads. A christmas tree is the buying of one call, selling one call at the next higher strike, and selling one call at the next higher strike. Buying one December 100 call, selling one December 105 call, and selling one December 110 call is an example of buying a christmas tree. The profit and loss profile is somewhat similar to a 1 by 1 1/2 ratio spread, depending on how far apart the strikes are and how close to expiration the trade is done. The strategy for purchasing a christmas tree would be similar as for any ratio spread—a steady move upward or the market staying in the same area. Selling a christmas tree would involve buying the two higher strikes and selling the lowest strike. Christmas trees may be done with puts too.

BACKSPREADS

A **backspread** *is the opposite of a ratio, so that more options of the same expiration are bought than sold.* The purchase of two March 105 calls for $3, and the sale of one March 100 call for $5, is an example of a 2 by 1 call backspread done for a $1 debit. Figure 15.11 shows the profit and loss potential at expiration of this backspread. Backspreads may be done in any ratio such as 3 by 2 or 3 by 1.

The investor must not only be bullish on the market, but also expect the market to move sharply higher as well. The investor will actually lose money if the market creeps upward and stays near the 105 level at expiration, as shown in Figure 15.11. The loss potential is limited but the profit potential is unlimited with these spreads.

A **put backspread** *is similar to a call backspread but more puts of the same expiration are bought than sold.* The purchase of 2 April 95 puts for $2, and the sale of 1 April 100 put for $5, is an example of a 2 by 1 put back spread done for a $1 credit. Figure 15.12 shows the profit and loss potential at expiration of this backspread.

FIGURE 15.11
Call backspread: The profit and loss potential of the March
105 – 100 2 by 1 call backspread at expiration done for
a $1 debit as a function of the future price.

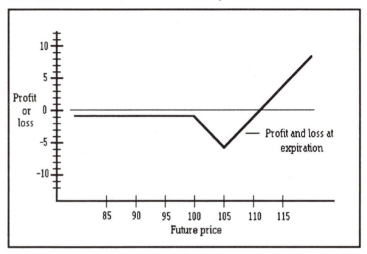

FIGURE 15.12
Put backspread: The profit and loss potential at expiration
of the April 95 – 100 2 by 1 put backspread purchased
for a $1 credit as a function of the future price.

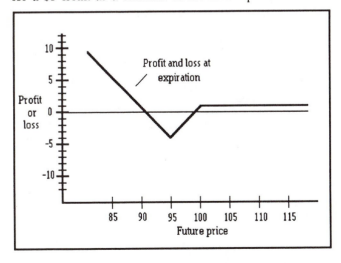

The investor expects the market to drop sharply, but since the spread is done for a credit a profit will be made if the market is above 99 at expiration.

BUTTERFLIES

A **butterfly** *is the purchase of one option on one strike, the sale of two options on the next strike, and the purchase of one option on the next strike, all of the same expiration.* For example, the purchase of 1 May 95 call for $8, the sale of 2 May 100 calls for $5, and the purchase of 1 May 105 call for $3, is an example of buying a call butterfly for a $1 debit ($8 – (2 · $5) + $3 = $1). The purchase of 1 May 95 put for $2, 1 May 105 put for $9, and sale of 2 May 100 puts for $5 each, is an example of buying a put butterfly for a $1 debit ($2 – (2 · $5) + $9 = $1). The profit and loss of the May put or call butterfly is depicted in Figure 15.13.

The most which can be lost is the debit price or cost of the spread which, in this example, is $1. The maximum profit is $4 which is obtained by taking 1/2 the difference between the two strikes minus the price of the spread [(105 – 95)/2 – 1 = $4]. The

FIGURE 15.13
Buying a butterfly: The profit and loss potential at expiration of the May 95, 100, 105 call or put butterfly purchased for a $1 debit as a function of the price of the future.

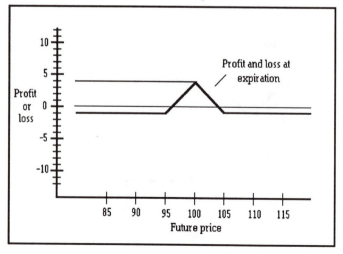

FIGURE 15.14
Selling a butterfly: The profit and loss potential at expiration
of the June 95, 100, 105 call or put butterfly sold for a
$1 credit as a function of the price of the future.

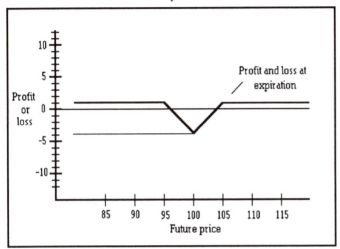

investor expects the market to stay within a certain range when
purchasing a butterfly. Buying a butterfly has some profit characteristics
similar to selling a straddle, without the unlimited risk associated
with selling the straddle.

An example of selling a butterfly is the sale of the June 95
call for $8, the purchase of 2 June 100 calls for $5 each, and the
sale of the June 105 call for $3, for a $1 credit. The puts would
follow in the same order. Figure 15.14 shows the profit and loss
potential of selling the June 95,100, 105 butterfly for a $1 credit.

The most that can be made is $1, which is the amount received
for selling the spread. The most that can be lost is $4 if the market
settles at 100 at expiration. Therefore, the profit and loss potential
is limited when buying or selling a butterfly. The seller of a butterfly
expects the market to move away from the center strike.

FENCES

A **fence** *is the purchase of one option and sale of a different option with
a different strike.* The purchase of 1 July 105 call for $3, and the sale

FIGURE 15.15
Bull fence: The profit and loss potential at expiration of buying the July
105 call and selling the July 95 put fence for even money as a function of
the future price.

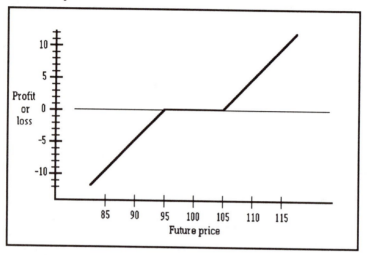

FIGURE 15.16
Bear fence: The profit and loss potential at expiration of
buying the August 95 put and selling the August 105 call bear
fence for even money as a function of the future price.

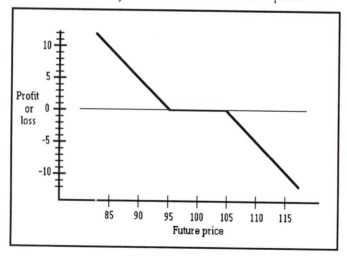

of 1 July 95 put for $3 is an example of buying a bull fence for even money. The profit and loss potential at expiration is depicted in Figure 15.15.

An example of a bear fence is the purchase of the August 95 put for $2 and sale of the August 105 call for $2, for even money. Figure 15.16 shows the profit and loss potential at expiration of the purchase of a bear fence.

The fence has characteristics similar to an outright purchase or sale, outside the extremes of the strike prices of 95 and 105. Fences are often traded by hedgers or speculators who need to automatically buy or sell at certain price levels.

SPREADS WITH DIFFERENT EXPIRATIONS

Another realm of option trading is buying or selling of one or more options, and the simultaneous selling of one or more options with a different expiration. These spreads can be more difficult to analyze because volatility and time considerations become crucial for proper evaluation. The relationship between the months of the futures contracts such as the possibility of a normal or inverted market, also becomes critical for correct evaluation.

HORIZONTAL OR TIME SPREADS

A **time spread** *is the purchase of one or more calls (puts) and sale of one or more calls (puts) of the same strike but different expiration.* Time spreads are also called horizontal or calendar spreads. The purchase of the June 100 call for $5 and sale of the March 100 call for $3 is an example of buying a call time spread for a $2 debit. The purchase of a June 100 put and sale of the March 100 put is an example of buying the put time spread. Figure 15.17 shows the profit and loss potential at expiration of this strategy.

The most that can be made occurs when the March 100 call or put expires worthless, and the future is at 100 so the June call or put still has value. Although not always the case, usually the most that can be lost is the purchase price of the spread, which in

FIGURE 15.17

Buying a time spread: The profit and loss potential at expiration of buying the June-March 100 call or put time spread for a $2 debit as a function of the future price.

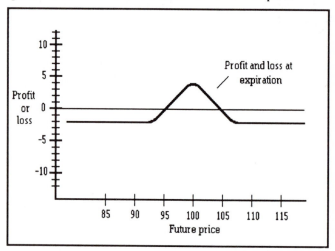

FIGURE 15.18

Selling a time spread: The profit and loss potential at expiration of selling the September-December 100 call or put time spread for a $2 credit as a function of the future price.

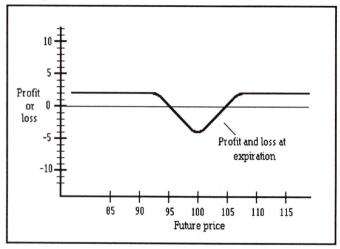

this example is $2. The profitability of time spreads is highly dependent on the implied volatilities of the 2 options and the spread relationship between the 2 months. In fact, it is possible to lose money on buying a time spread, even if the future is at the strike at expiration, if the call or put is cheaper than the price paid for the spread. For example, the June 100 call may be trading at $1 with the June future trading at 100 when the March 100 call expires worthless. Since $2 was paid for the spread, a net loss of $1 is incurred in this case. However, if the June 100 call were trading anywhere above $2 and the March 100 call expired worthless, a profit would be made. Assuming the future is at 100, the pricing of the June 100 call will be highly dependent on the volatility and time to expiration of the option.

The sale of the December 100 put or call and purchase of the September 100 put or call is an example of selling the time spread. The profit and loss potential at expiration is depicted in Figure 15.18. In this scenario the investor expects the market to move either higher or lower than the 100 level.

DIAGONALS

The purchase of one or more options and sale of one or more options with a different strike and expiration is called a **diagonal spread.** Buying 2 February 100 calls and selling 1 January 90 call is an example of a 2 by 1 diagonal call spread. The profit and loss potential of this type of spread is somewhat similar to the backspread in Figure 15.10, but not exactly the same.

It is difficult to analyze these spreads so it is not easy to graph the profit and loss potential of a diagonal. For example, buying the 2 by 1 call diagonal should be profitable if the market goes up in a strong move. However, the January future might rally much more than the February future due to an inverted market, which would cause the January 90 call to gain more than the February 100 call. In this case an investor could lose money even if the market moves much higher. If the market creeps up slowly the January 90 call may increase in value, but the February 100 calls may stay the same price or even drop in value. Even if no inversion occurs, a trader could lose money in a diagonal spread if the market slowly rises because the January 90 call might move more than the February 100 call.

Diagonal spreads can become rather complex to analyze, especially if the underlying futures market changes from a normal market to an inverted market. Any diagonal must be understood with a thorough knowledge of the volatility of the market *and* the spread differentials between the two different expirations.

SYNTHETIC POSITIONS

A **synthetic position** *is the combination of one or more options and outrights to simulate an equivalent position.* Options allow the trader to simulate various outright and option positions and therefore allow more possibilities in trading.

SYNTHETIC LONG OR SHORT POSITIONS

A **synthetic long or short position** *may be created using options of the same strike and expiration.* For example, the simultaneous purchase of a September 100 call for $5 and sale of a September 100 put for $5 will create a synthetic long position, as depicted in Figure 15.19. A synthetic short position can be created by the purchase of the October 100 put and sale of the October 100 call. These positions exhibit the same profit and loss possibilities as being long or short the future.

SYNTHETIC CALLS AND PUTS

Buying a future and selling a call is known as **covered call writing.** For example, the profit and loss potential in the present and at expiration of buying the future and selling the November 100 call is depicted in Figure 15.20. The reward is limited by the sale of the call, but the risk may be much larger due to the long future position. What position does this strategy simulate? It is exactly the same as in Figure 14.8 of selling a put.

FIGURE 15.19
The profit and loss potential of a synthetic long or short position is the same as outright long or short position in the underlying future.

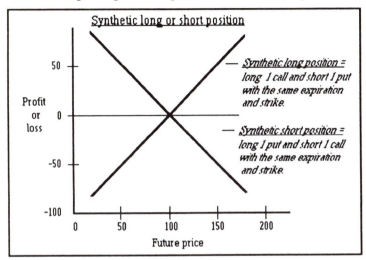

FIGURE 15.20
Selling a call and buying a future: The potential profit or loss of selling the November 100 call and buying the future in the present and at expiration as a function of the future price.

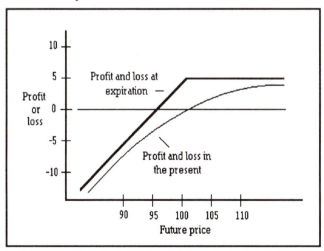

FIGURE 15.21
Buying a future and buying a put: The profit and
loss potential in the present and at expiration of buying
the future for 100 and buying the put for $3 as a function
of the future price.

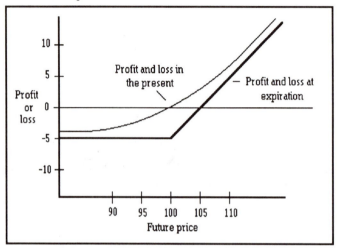

The supposedly conservative covered call writer is in fact selling
puts. The logic for using this strategy follows. The call protected
the owner of the stock or future from a slight drop in price. If the
market went up, the writer received the call premium and the stock
or future covered the short call. This type of strategy was widely
used before the great stock market crash of 1987 when "conservative"
investors wrote covered calls. However, when the stock market collapsed, the "conservative" investors found out the hard way that
they were actually selling puts and lost substantial sums of money.

To this day there are people who swear they would not sell
options naked because of the obvious risk, but are quite comfortable
writing covered calls. This is perhaps one of the best examples of
why options should be thoroughly understood before using them.

A synthetic short call position may be established by selling
a put and selling the future short. The profit and loss potential is
identical to selling a naked call, which was depicted in Figure 14.7.

Buying a future and buying a put is an example of buying a
synthetic call. The purchase of the December 100 put for $3 and

the purchase of the future at 100 is the same as buying the December 100 call for $3. The profit and loss potential in the present and at expiration is shown in Figure 15.21, and is exactly the same as buying a call, which was shown in Figure 14.3. Selling short the future and buying the call is the same as buying a put, which was shown in Figure 14.6.

REVERSALS AND CONVERSIONS

A **conversion** *is the combination of a long future position and short synthetic position.* The person is long the underlying future, long the put, and short the call. A reversal is the opposite position which is short the future, long the call, and short the put.

These types of trades are a form of arbitrage and are usually done by market makers or other participants with low commissions and margins. The trades are usually done for small profits to take advantage of minor price discrepancies in the market. For example, assume the future is trading at 100 and the January 100 call is $5, and the January 100 put is $4. The market maker would buy the future at 100, buy the put for $4, and sell the call for $5, and receive $1. The synthetic short position is equivalent to being short at 101 due to the $1 received from buying the put and selling the call. Since the future is purchased at 100, a profit of $1 is made through the arbitrage.

WHEN SHOULD THESE TRADES BE DONE?

When should a ratio or backspread be done, and what is the proper ratio of options for these spreads? Anyone trading these spreads should have some idea of where the market will be trading in the future. For example, buying a call spread is a bullish strategy, whereas selling a call spread is a bearish strategy, but selling a straddle may be neither, and is instead, a volatility play.

Anyone wanting to seriously trade options should have an idea of *delta neutral* option trading. This will be discussed in Chapter 16. Ratios or backspreads should not be done simply for credits, or because they require less cash outlay than a 1 by 1 spread.

Backspreads may be highly profitable when markets become volatile and trend strongly, which is exactly when ratios become unprofitable. If markets are quiet or trend slowly, backspreads become unprofitable and ratios become profitable. Neither spread is better but the profit and loss potential under varying times to expiration and volatilities should be thoroughly understood before trading them.

Many option spreads do not trade market direction, but instead market volatility. For example, buying a straddle should be profitable in a market which becomes highly volatile, irrespective of whether the market goes higher or lower. A ratio spread may make money in a calm market, irrespective of whether the market drifts higher or lower within a certain range.

ADVANTAGES AND DISADVANTAGES OF OPTIONS

The possibility of infinite profits and limited risk in buying options is immediately appealing to many investors. The appeal is deceiving and unwarranted since the probability of infinite profits is zero. The potential of finite profits and infinite risk in selling options is shunned by many investors. The investor should understand that having a bias towards buying or selling options, is similar to having a bias in being long or short outrights. Being a bull in a bear market or a bear in a bull market can prove disastrous. Buying options is usually most advantageous when the volatility is increasing, and selling options is usually most advantageous when the volatility is decreasing. The decision to buy or sell options is a function of the time and market.

Why sell options when there is so much to lose and so little to gain? Isn't this exactly the opposite of all the hallowed advice about cut your losses short and let your profits run, or go for the big hit in commodities. Yes, but people do sell options, and some make considerable sums of money in relatively low-risk conditions. This glaringly points out why most of the axioms in futures are best buried.

Much is written about how options offer unlimited reward and limited risk. Remember, no investment offers unlimited reward because nothing can go up or down forever. Options do offer limited risk but this must be paid for in the price of the option, and therefore, the price of the option becomes a risk of loss in itself. Buying and selling options should be looked at from a rational perspective, of each being a correct trade at the right time. A groundless fear of selling options is no different than not being able to sell futures outright. There are countless stories of forlorn investors selling options and losing fortunes when the market went severely against them. Be assured, there are just as many stories of people loading up on options and losing just as much money, but the process is usually dragged out in a more tortuous fashion on hoped for moves that never materialize. In either case, options offer essential alternatives to the trading spectrum and are excellent vehicles for hedging and speculation.

HEDGING WITH OPTIONS

Remember the farmer who hedged his soybean crop and the refiner who hedged her gasoline sales? Let's look to see how options could enhance their hedging strategies. The farmer was concerned about soybeans dropping below $7 a bushel. When using futures he could lock in his price and protect himself from a price decline, but could not benefit if the market rallied. Options will allow him to participate in upside moves.

Instead of selling futures he can buy puts to protect a downside move. Assume the farmer purchases for $1, the August 7.00 soybean put, which expires when he plans to sell his crop. What are the possible outcomes of this strategy?

Scenario 1: The price declines to $5. At expiration the farmer will sell his put for $2, which is the intrinsic value of the option.

1. Profit from put = Sale price − purchase price
                    = $2.00 − $1.00
                    = $1.00

2. Loss from soybeans = $5.00 − $7.00
                       = −$2.00
                Net = $1.00 − $2.00
                     = −$1.00

The put will effectively allow him to sell the soybeans at $6. If the farmer wanted to protect his position from dropping below $7, as in the futures example, he could purchase a higher strike put such as the 8.00 or 9.00 strike. The price of these puts would be more but they would offer more downside protection. For example, assume the 8.00 strike put was trading at $1.50 and the 9.00 strike put was trading at $2.25. The 8.00 and 9.00 strike put would effectively make him short at $6.50 and $6.75, respectively.

Scenario 2: The price rises to $10. The farmer will now be able to participate in any upward price move, unlike the outright futures. If soybeans rally to $10 he will be able to sell his soybeans for $10, but the puts will expire worthless. For example:

1. Loss from buying put = purchase price of put

    = –$1.00

2. Profit from soybeans = $10.00 – $7.00

    = $3.00

    Net = $3.00 – $1.00

    = $2.00

The farmer will be able to make an extra profit of $2. In fact, he will be able to participate in any upmove greater than the purchase price of the put. If soybeans should go even higher to $12 he will make an extra $4.

Scenario 3: The price remains at $7. The farmer will lose $1 on the put which will expire worthless, and sell his soybeans at $7. He will lose $1 in this case.

Options expand his hedging possibilities considerably. Using spreads will provide even greater flexibility. For example, the fence is a popular hedging vehicle. Recall, that the fence is buying a call and selling a put with different strikes (or selling a call and buying a put with different strikes). Let's see how Rose can use a fence to enhance her hedging possibilities.

Rose was concerned that the current price of gasoline which was at $0.45 might rise above $0.50 a gallon in December. She will make a $0.05 profit if the price is $0.45 a gallon, but breakeven if the price is $0.50 a gallon. She could buy calls to protect herself against a price rise. She could also buy the December 50 call–40 put fence.

1. Assume the December 50 call and 40 put are both trading at $0.01.
2. Assume the December 48 call is trading at $0.02.

Rose could buy the December 48 call for $0.02 which would effectively protect her from any price rise above $0.50.

Scenario 1: The price rises to $0.50.

1. Breakeven on the call = $0.02 − $0.02

    = $0.00

2. Breakeven on the gasoline = $0.50 − $0.50

    = $0.00

She will breakeven on the transaction if gasoline rises anywhere above $0.48 a gallon. For example, if gasoline rises to $0.48 a gallon she will lose $0.02 on the call, and make $0.02 on selling the gasoline for $0.50 a gallon.

Scenario 2: The price drops to $0.40.

1. Loss on the call = purchase price = −$0.02
2. Profit on the gasoline = $0.50 − $0.40

    = $0.10

She will do considerably better and make $0.08 a gallon instead of her originally expected profit of $0.05.

Scenario 3: The price remains the same.

1. Loss on the call = −$0.02
2. Profit on the gasoline = $0.50 − $0.45

    = $0.05

She will make $0.03 a gallon which is less than anticipated, but remember, she is now protected from any price increase. She has in essence paid an insurance premium or the price of the option for this protection.

How would a fence change her profit and loss opportunities? Assume she bought the December 50 call for $0.01 and sold the December 40 put for $0.01. She would be buying the fence for even money. Her profit and loss possibilities follow:

Scenario 1: The price rises to $0.50.

1. Lose $0.01 on the call, but make $0.01 on the put so she will breakeven on the fence.
2. Breakeven on the gasoline.

She will breakeven above $0.50 a gallon.

Scenario 2: The price falls to $0.40.

1. Breakeven on the fence again.
2. Profit from the gasoline = $0.50 − $0.40

    = $0.10

She will make a $0.10 profit on the transaction.

Scenario 3: The price remains the same.

1. Breakeven on the fence again.
2. Profit from the gasoline = $0.50 − $0.45

    = $0.05

She will make a $0.05 profit on the transaction.

Notice how the fence has enhanced her profit opportunities versus buying the call outright. However, if the price of gasoline drops below $0.38, the outright purchase of the call would prove more profitable.

These are a few of the many strategies which can be employed when hedging with options. There are many other strategies which are particular to the market and hedger. As in speculating there is no good or bad strategy with options, but instead, a set of opportunities which should enhance the profit possibilities of the intelligent hedger.

no good or bad strategy with options, but instead, a set of opportunities which should enhance the profit possibilities of the intelligent hedger.

CONCLUSION

Option strategies can become quite complex but even the most sophisticated ones are based on the simple concept of buying or selling one or more options against another option or outright. These combinations are used by many traders and also form the basis of theoretical option trading where options are bought and sold based on their theoretical value versus trading on market direction. Some option combinations such as straddles and ratios may be traded on volatility considerations of the market versus a strong conviction on market direction.

Options offer many ways to trade a market. Option combinations increase this variety by offering profit and loss combinations not available in any other trading method. Option spreads may at first seem difficult to understand but their use enhances the tools of the speculator and hedger.

CHAPTER **16**

Option Pricing

Life can only be understood backwards, but it must be lived forwards.

Soren Kierkegaard, *Life*

Chapters 14 and 15 presented different kinds of option strategies and trading possibilities, but how is the correct price of an option determined? The question is difficult and becomes even more complicated when option combinations such as spreads are evaluated. The question of option valuation is best answered by considering factors which affect the price of an option.

The next five factors are crucial to determining the price of an option and are depicted in Figure 16.1.

1. Strike price: The more the option is in the money, the more intrinsic value it should have, which will result in a higher price. Options which are in the money are worth at least their intrinsic value less any other opportunity costs, such as interest rates. For calls, the higher the strike price the cheaper the option, for puts, the lower the strike price the cheaper the option.

FIGURE 16.1
The five important factors that affect the price of an option—the underlying future price, strike price, time to expiration, interest rates, and volatility.

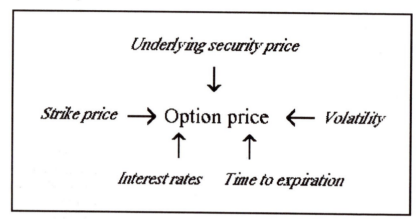

2. *Underlying security price*: The reasoning is the same as for the strike price. The underlying future and strike price have a direct impact on the price of an option.

3. *Time to expiration*: The greater the number of days to expiration the more expensive the option. A future has a greater chance of going into the money with an option which has a longer expiration date, therefore, an option buyer should be willing to pay more for a longer term option. An option writer will incur more risk with longer term options and will consequently need to collect more premium for selling options which have a longer expiration.

4. *Volatility*: The volatility of the market is one of the most important factors affecting the price of an option. There are many different ways to calculate the volatility of a market. The volatility of a market is a measure of how the price changes on a relative or percentage basis. Markets which move 50% in one year are more volatile than ones which only move 25% in the same time period.

Markets which are more volatile have a greater chance of reaching a strike price and going into the money. Options in markets with a higher volatility should have bigger premiums than options in less volatile markets. An option seller will want more premium to sell an option in a highly volatile market because the risk is greater. An option buyer should expect to pay more for an option in a market with a higher volatility.

5. *Interest rates*: In the money options can be a proxy for buying or selling the outright. Certain underlying instruments such as stocks pay dividends, which reduces their carrying cost. This will also affect the pricing of the option.

Of the five variables volatility is the most crucial in evaluating the price of an option. The first three factors—strike price, underlying security price, and time to expiration—are easily known when evaluating an option. The fifth factor—interest rates—can become significant if rates are volatile and make large moves, as in the early 1980s. Interest rates do not generally change so radically and a range can be predicted with a reasonable degree of accuracy. The fourth factor—volatility—can be hard to predict and may change quite rapidly, greatly affecting the price of an option. Furthermore, volatility is measured in various ways by different people, making it more difficult to quantify.

THE BLACK SCHOLES MODEL

The previously mentioned variables can be combined in an equation to arrive at a theoretical price for an option. Various models have been created to determine the price of an option. Fisher Black and Myron Scholes made a great contribution to the understanding of options when they developed the Black Scholes theoretical equation to evaluate option prices. Before their work in the 1970's, traders had little information and few models to use in determining the theoretical price of an option.

The basic option model for a call is:

Call value $= e^{-rt} [pN(x) - sN (x - v\sqrt{t})]$

Put value $= e^{-rt} [sN(v\sqrt{t} - x) - pN(-x)]$

where p = price of the security

   s = strike price

   t = time to expiration expressed as a percent of the year

   r = risk free interest rate

   v = volatility of the security measured as the annual standard deviation

$$x = \frac{\ln(p/s) + (v^2 t)/2}{v\sqrt{t}}$$

$N(x)$ = normal distribution curve

Different models are used to evaluate different kinds of options. For example, a model may be used for calls and another variation of the model for puts. Different markets may require separate models. For instance, stock option models may need to include a dividend for a stock, whereas futures do not pay dividends. The bibliography suggests references for further study in this area.

Much work is being done to create a better model but do not be mislead into thinking a slightly more accurate model will predict the proper price of an option. The *difficult work of option evaluation is determining the proper input variables and specifically the future volatility of the underlying security price.* Anyone trading with a crude evaluation model, but correct volatility estimates, will probably achieve better results than another person trading with a more accurate and sophisticated model, but incorrect volatility estimates.

More sophisticated models have been developed in the ensuing years to compensate for various shortfalls in the Black Scholes model, but it is still one of the most widely used models for option evaluation. Any shortfalls in the model are relatively minor and do not affect the theoretical option prices substantially. This is especially true when you compare how uncertain the input variable volatility is and how large an effect it has on option pricing.

DELTA

The **delta** *is a measure of how the option price changes for a 1-point price change in the underlying future.*

$$\text{Delta} = \frac{\text{change of price in the option}}{\text{change in price of the future}}$$

Figure 16.2 shows how to determine the delta of a call option. The delta of an option is simply the slope of the line which depicts the price of the option as a function of the price of the future. The delta changes as the price of the future changes, as can be observed from the graph. The graphs are similar to the ones shown in the two previous chapters depicting the profit and loss possibilities of the options. The delta for a call will always be positive and range from 0 to 1. The delta of a call is positive because an increase in the price of the future will result in an increase in the price of the call, but a drop in the price of the future will result in a decrease in the price of the call.

When the future is at 100, the December 100 call will move approximately 1/2 point for a 1 point move in the future. The delta is calculated:

Delta = change in price of the option / change in price of the future
     = 1/2

FIGURE 16.2
The delta is the slope of the option price line and measures how the price of the option changes for a specific change in price of the future. The delta of a call is positive because the slope of the line is positive.

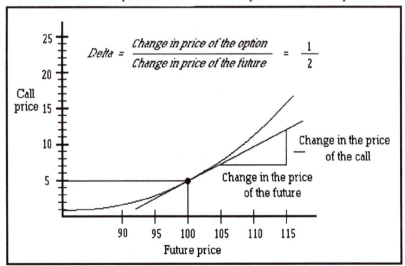

FIGURE 16.3
The delta of a put is negative because the slope of the price line
is negative. A decrease (increase) in the price of the future will
result in an increase (decrease) in the price of the put.

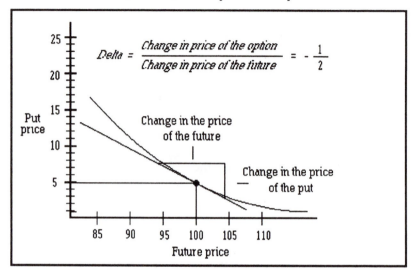

Figure 16.3 shows how to determine the delta for a put option.
The delta for a put will always be negative and range from –1 to
0. The delta of a put is negative because an increase in the price
of the future will cause the price of the put to drop, whereas a
decrease in the price of the future will cause the put value to increase.
The delta is –1/2 at the 100 strike in this example because a 2-point
decline in the future will cause the put to increase by approximately
1. If we use calculus, the delta is the first derivative in the Black
Scholes equation.

The delta of an option indicates how many options approximate
one future. For example a call which has a delta of 1/2 should
move about 1/2 point for a 1-point move in the future. Therefore
2 calls will approximately equal the movement of 1 future when
the delta is 1/2. From the previous option graphs we can see that
the delta of a call or put is usually 1/2 when the future is at the
strike price. The trader must remember the delta changes as the
future price changes which introduces the next idea—the gamma.

GAMMA

The **gamma** *is the amount the delta changes with respect to a change in price of the underlying security.*

$$\text{Gamma} = \frac{\text{change in the delta of the option}}{\text{change in the price of the security}}$$

The delta constantly changes as the price of the security changes. The trader must also monitor the gamma to determine how the delta changes so that the position does not become too long or short. Figure 16.4 depicts how the gamma changes with a March 100 call as the security price changes. The delta changes the most when the future is at the strike price and changes less the further the underlying is from the strike price. Therefore the gamma is greatest at the strike price. The gamma provides the trader with an indication of how long or short a position may become as the underlying future price changes. The delta and gamma are dynamic and usually measured by a 1-point move on the future.

FIGURE 16.4
The gamma is the greatest when the future is near the strike price and declines as the future moves away from the strike price.

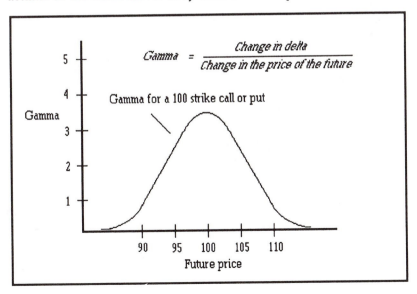

FIGURE 16.5
The delta increases as the market rises and decreases as the market declines when long a straddle; this is an example of a positive gamma position.

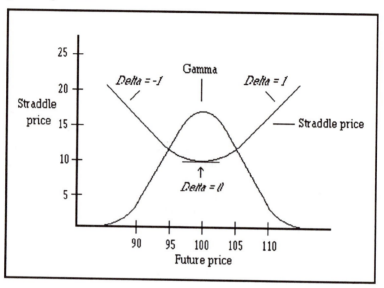

Any position that is long options will have a positive gamma irrespective of whether the options are calls or puts. For example, assume you are long the January 100 straddle, which means being long 1 January 100 call and long 1 January 100 put and the market is currently trading at 100. The net delta of this position is 0 because the call delta is 1/2 and the put delta is –1/2 (recall, if the future is trading at the strike price the delta of a call is approximately 1/2 and the delta of a put is approximately –1/2). If the market rallies, the delta of the position will become more positive and increase from 0 and rise to as high as 1. If the market drops, the delta of the position will become more negative and decrease from 0 to as low as –1. This position will always become longer as the market rises and shorter as the market drops. Figure 16.5 is an example of a positive gamma position and shows how the gamma changes as the future price changes.

Any position that is short options will have a negative gamma irrespective of whether the options are calls or puts. Assume the opposite strategy and you are now short 1 February 100 call and short 1 February 100 put and the market is trading at 100. The net delta of the position is 0 as before. If the market increases, the delta will decrease and become negative so the position will become increasingly short up to –1. If the market drops, the delta will increase and become more positive so the position will become longer up to 1. This position will always become shorter as the market rallies and longer as the market drops.

Most novice traders are easily enticed by the benefits of a positive gamma which automatically allows the trader to get longer or shorter as the market goes up or down. A positive gamma is somewhat similar to pyramiding a position as it goes in your favor. A negative gamma is similar to pyramiding a position as it goes against you. However, the gamma must be evaluated with another important factor—the theta.

THETA

*The **theta** measures the change in the option price with respect to a change in time.*

$$\text{Theta} = \frac{\text{change in the option price}}{\text{change in time}}$$

The theta value is a measure of the effect time has on the option price. The value of the option premium should decrease with time when all other variables are held constant, so the theta is always negative. However, this change is not linear but becomes much greater as the option nears expiration as shown in Figure 16.6. The theta is greatest near expiration and becomes less pronounced the further the option is to expiration. For example, if the future and volatility do not change, the time decay in one day will be much greater for an option with one day versus one year to expiration. The change in price of the option with time is also partly a function of whether the option is at the money or away from it.

FIGURE 16.6

The option price decreases at an increasing rate as it nears expiration. Theta is a measure of the change in price of the option over time.

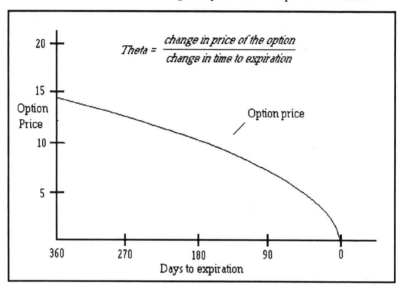

The theta is related to the gamma because positions with a positive gamma will have a negative theta. This simply means the price of the option will erode due to time decay. The position will incur a loss if there is no significant movement in time. For example, a trader holding a positive gamma position such as a straddle will lose money with time if the market does not move. The premium of the options will decay with time. However, the trader with a negative gamma such as short the straddle will make money if the market does not move.

A positive gamma is always offset by negative theta, as shown in Figure 16.7. A negative gamma is helped by time decay. The option trader must always realize there is a constant trade-off between being long options and watching them decay, or being short options and concerned about a significant price move. It is always necessary to understand the relationship of gamma and theta.

FIGURE 16.7
Gamma and theta: A positive gamma position will be subject to time decay, whereas a negative gamma positon will have the benefit of time decay.

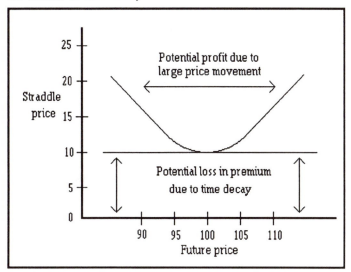

VEGA

*The **vega** is the change in price of an option with respect to a change in volatility of the underlying security.*

$$\text{Vega} = \frac{\text{change in the price of the option}}{\text{change in the volatility}}$$

Figure 16.8 shows how the option price changes as the volatility changes. The absolute change is most pronounced with at the money options and becomes less of a factor with in or out of the money options. However, out of the money options may exhibit a much greater percentage change in price due to their lower absolute price.

Figure 16.9 shows how the vega is highly sensitive to time to expiration of the option. The vega is greater the longer the time to expiration. In essence, a change in volatility will affect the price of a longer-term option much more than an option which is closer to expiration. Options very close to expiration will not appreciably be

FIGURE 16.8

The vega is normally greatest near the strike price and measures the change in the option price with a change in volatility.

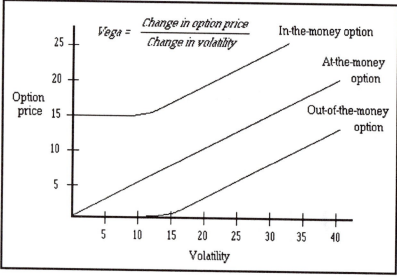

FIGURE 16.9

The vega increases with longer term options so options with longer times to expiration are affected more by changes in volatility.

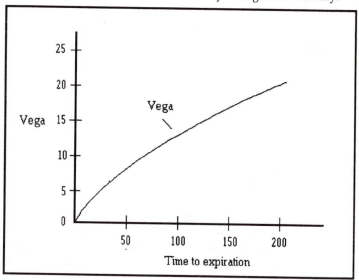

affected by changes in volatility unless the volatility change is extremely large. The vega is an important measure to know, especially when doing option spreading and delta neutral trading. The vega, theta, gamma, and delta are all interrelated and affect the price of an option. Any comprehensive option strategy must account for all these factors and how each factor relates to the other.

RHO

The rho *is the change in the price of an option with respect to a change in interest rates.*

$$\text{Rho} = \frac{\text{change in the price of the option}}{\text{change in interest rates}}$$

Unless interest rates change drastically, the change in volatility, future price, and time to expiration are usually a much greater determinant on option pricing than a change in interest rates.

DELTA NEUTRAL TRADING

The delta of an option may be used in the following way for trading options. Robert used the Black Scholes model to determine the theoretical price of a call to be $5 and the delta to be 1/2 but the actual market price is $4. The option is cheap according to his calculations, but if he buys the naked call (buying or selling an option alone) and the market drops the call will become even cheaper. He can neutralize the position by buying two calls, which is approximately equivalent to one future, and sell one future outright. In this way if the market drops the calls will lose approximately the same amount as the future gains. If the market rises the calls will make approximately what is lost from the future rising. He hopes the market will eventually revalue the call to the higher price so he can sell the call at $5 for a $1 profit and breakeven on the future.

The process of buying or selling options and buying or selling corresponding futures against the options is called **delta neutral trading**. This is often done in options trading to buy what are considered cheap options, or sell what are considered to be expensive options. Delta neutral trading is dynamic because the delta changes as the future price changes and as the volatility and time change.

Determination of the delta is also helpful in deciding how many options to buy or sell in various spreads. For example, if you want to buy the January 100–105 call backspread how many options should be bought and how many should be sold? If the delta on the January 105 call is 0.25 and the delta on the January 100 call is 0.5, then buying two January 105 calls for each January 100 call will delta neutralize the position.

WHY USE THE OPTION MODELS?

In Chapter 15 many kinds of option trading strategies were discussed. How do you know which method to use and if the options are priced correctly? For example, if you are bullish on a market should you buy a call, sell a put, buy a call spread, sell a put spread, buy a straddle, etc.? The option valuation models will help in determining which options are undervalued, fairly valued, and overvalued. The models are a valuable resource in determining which options are correctly priced which will help in implementing a strategy.

If you are bullish and options are underpriced then buying calls outright, straddles, or backspreads may be appropriate trading strategies. If options are expensive then selling puts, buying call spreads, or selling put spreads may be the better way to trade the market. If options are fairly valued then any method is equally appropriate.

Theoretical models allow us to determine the value of spreads and more sophisticated strategies quite easily that would otherwise be difficult to evaluate. Theoretical models also help in estimating the delta, gamma, theta, vega, and rho of an option. These important concepts are actually derived from the option valuation models.

SPECULATING IN OPTIONS—WHY TRADE OPTIONS?

Although options are often used to trade the direction of the market, perhaps one of the main differences between an option and an outright is in the view of the trader. *Options are ideal for trading the volatility of the market whereas outright positions are ideal for trading market direction.*

Some traders have made considerable sums of money trading the volatility of the market with options even though they have not had any strong opinion about the direction of the market. Other traders who have had a correct opinion about the market have lost money in options because they did not understand the implications of how volatility affects the pricing of options.

Options can be traded with a strong view about volatility, but not necessarily a strong view about market direction. However, the converse is not true. Options should not be traded on market direction without an understanding or feeling for the volatility of the market.

The trader who uses options to trade market direction must also have some concept of the time of the move, as well as how volatile it will be. Otherwise the trader may be right about the direction, but lose money in the option because of volatility and time considerations. How could this happen?

Don is bullish on the market trading at 100. He buys a 105 call at 5. The market eventually rises to 105 at expiration, but the call expires worthless. The market went up but not high enough to yield a profit in the option. He was correct about the market going higher but incorrect about how volatile the market would be.

A trader who is correct about volatility but wrong about direction can still make money. How could this happen?

Joseph is bearish on the market which is currently at 100 and he believes it will drop to 95. He also feels it will not move appreciably so he sells a 105 call for 5. The market does not sell off but instead settles at 100 on expiration so the call expires worthless. He makes 5 on the call because the market was not volatile and did not move in any significant direction. He was incorrect about market direction but correct about his assumption on the volatility of the market and was still able to profit.

Between these two extremes are traders who are not trying to predict market direction but have a sense of volatility. For example, Barney has no opinion on market direction but believes it will move in a strong manner soon. He buys a 100 straddle for 10 points and will make a profit if the market goes below 90 or above 110. If he feels the market will settle down and not move greatly he may sell the same straddle and the profit and loss potential would be reversed. In either case, he does not have a strong feel for market direction but does have an opinion about volatility.

Some option traders can simply trade market volatility and always remain delta neutral, thereby not taking outright positions in the market. The option trader who has a reasonable feel for the market and a good understanding of volatility will have a far greater advantage than a person who only has an opinion about market direction. The trader must understand how the price of an option is derived and the factors which affect the value of an option, and then decide the best strategy to employ when using options.

Many people find options appealing because they feel options offer "unlimited" profit potential with limited risk. This feeling is partly true but remember, the limited risk and tremendous profit potential come at a cost in the option premium. Buying an option provides a means to participate in a move in the market without the corresponding risk of the market moving severely against you. Selling options allows the investor to profit if the volatility of the market drops.

Options are another way to change the risk reward characteristics of a trading strategy. They are also a means to trade the market in different ways, and so, offer the trader more strategies and possibilities. Options are perhaps best viewed as another type of important trading method. Just as there is a time to go long and short the market with outrights, there are also appropriate times to buy or sell options. Options provide many more options to the intelligent trader.

CONCLUSION

The advent of option pricing models which was led by the Black Scholes model opened up the field of option trading by quantum leaps. Options can now be evaluated to determine appropriate theoretical values. These models allow trading based on theoretical valuation as well as market direction, opening up entirely new arenas of trading.

The models provide a framework for option evaluation. An options trader cannot blindly use the models and watch money pour in. A "cheap" option according to the models may remain cheap or even get a lot cheaper. The models are guides—not answers. The ultimate judge of value is the market price.

CHAPTER 17

Volatility

Nothing endures but change.

Heraclitus

There are many ways to measure volatility but there is no definitive calculation which applies for all situations. Though volatility is an idea we are somewhat familiar with and have experienced, it is not always an easy concept to mathematically measure. Much work has been done on measuring and attempting to predict the volatility of the market.

The first, and simplest way, is to look at the absolute change in price. This is a way many people look at volatility. A market trading at 100 moves to 105. The absolute change is 5.

The second way is to look at the percentage change in price. In the previous example, the move from 100 to 105 would be a 5% change.

The next way is one of the most common methods used to determine volatility for option valuation. Volatility for option evaluation is the standard deviation of price changes. The standard deviation is normally calculated using the closing prices and is shown in the following equations and steps:

1. We first need to know the mean of the prices:

$$\text{Mean} = \frac{1}{n} \sum_{i=1}^{n} P_i$$

where n = number of time periods
         i = specific time period
         P = price at specific time period i

2. The second step is to calculate the variance:

$$\text{Variance} = \frac{1}{(n-1)} \sum_{i=1}^{n} (P_i - m)^2$$

where m = mean

3. The third step is to calculate the standard deviation:

$$\text{Volatility} = \text{standard deviation} = \sqrt{variance}$$

To get an annualized volatility when daily prices are used, the standard deviation must be multiplied by the square root of the number of trading days. Since there are approximately 250 trading days in a year the square root of 250 is approximately 16. If weekly prices are used, the square root of 52 is used (approximately 7.2). Closing prices are normally used in the calculation but highs, lows and opens are equally acceptable.

Table 17.1 presents a sample calculation of volatility.

TABLE 17.1
Calculation of Volatility

Day	Price
1	90
2	100
3	95

1. The mean = $(90 + 100 + 95)/3 = 95$
2. The variance = $\{(90 - 95)^2 + (100 - 95)^2 + (95 - 95)^2\}/(3 - 1)$
                 $= \{25 + 25 + 0\}/2 = 25$
3. The volatility = $\sqrt{25} = 5$

The 3-day volatility is 5%.

Since daily prices are used, the annualized volatility is obtained by multiplying the three-day volatility by 16. Therefore, the annualized volatility is equal to $5 \cdot 16 = 80\%$.

Volatility numbers should not be intimidating, and, in fact are quite easy to use. Since they are based on percentages they are similar to measuring market change on a percentage basis. For example, if the market is currently at 100 and the annualized volatility is 25%, the market can be expected to trade up to 125 or down to 75 about 68% of the time during the year. This is obtained by:

1. Dollar move $= 100 \cdot 0.25$

                  $= 25$

2. Potential upside move $= 100 + 25$

                           $= 125$

3. Potential downside move $= 100 - 25$

                           $= 75$

Where did the 68% come from in the previous example? In statistics the standard deviation is a range about the mean which can be estimated by certain percentages:

1. A 1-standard deviation move includes approximately 68% of all possible moves.

2. A 2-standard deviation move includes approximately 95% of all possible moves.

3. A 3-standard deviation move includes almost 100% of all possible moves.

In this example 1-standard deviation is equal to 25. A 2-standard deviation or 50 point move would account for almost 95% of all occurrences.

Volatility calculations are integral in evaluating the theoretical value of options. The Black Scholes model, discussed in Chapter 16, was a pioneering breakthrough in determining option prices and employed volatility calculations like these.

TYPICAL VOLATILITY DISTRIBUTIONS

It is often convenient to look at a volatility distribution of prices. This can provide us with a graphic indication of where prices might be in the future. The normal bell curve in Figure 17.1 is called the standard normal distribution in statistics. This curve is sometimes used to represent the distribution of prices in any market. The y axis is the chance of the price occurring and the x axis is the price of the future. This distribution shows there is a 30–40% chance of the future price being around 50. There is an equally small chance of less than 5% of seeing the future price at 90 or 10.

A much wider distribution of prices is shown in Figure 17.2. This wider distribution suggests there is a greater chance the market will make more extreme price moves than the distribution in Figure 17.1. The second distribution is more volatile because there is greater percentage price movement. This means there is a greater chance of observing a wider range of prices in more volatile markets than in less volatile markets. Note how there is a better than 5% chance

FIGURE 17.1
Standard normal price distribution: shows the chances of a price occurring over various price levels.

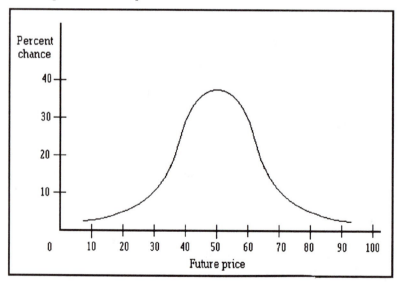

FIGURE 17.2
A wider price distribution: The distribution of prices is much wider than in Figure 17.1, which means there is a better chance the market may make more extreme moves.

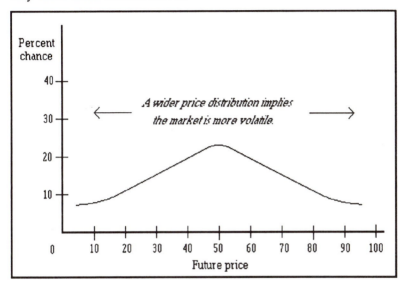

of seeing the price of 10 or 90 with the more volatile market. These graphs of the standard deviations give us an indication of the volatility of the market. A comparison of three different volatilities is shown in Figure 17.3.

The lognormal distribution in Figure 17.4 is another type of price distribution. The lognormal distribution has a characteristic skew which allows for greater price movement on the upside than the normal distribution. This type of distribution is generally more representative of a market for various reasons. For example, some markets have exhibited a historical bullish bias such as the stock market, so there may be a greater probability for the stock market to go higher than lower. Another reason is that some commodities, such as coffee or oil, have manifest large explosive upmoves in the past which have been much greater than the downside moves. There are floor prices to many commodities which are not always apparent on the upside.

FIGURE 17.3
Markets that exhibit wide price fluctuations are highly volatile, and markets which exhibit small price fluctuations less volatile.

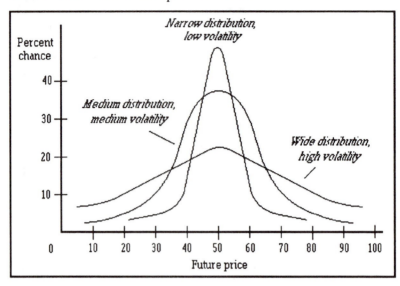

FIGURE 17.4
Lognormal price distribution: This formation is more skewed to the upside and less skewed to the downside than the standard normal distribution.

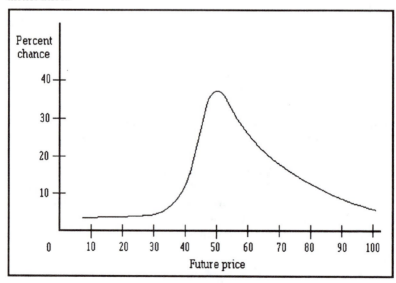

FIGURE 17.5
Lognormal distribution allows for greater price movement on the
upside than the standard normal distribution.

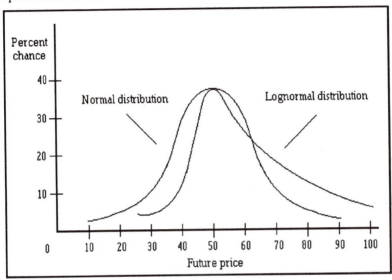

A comparison of the lognormal and standard normal distribution
is made in Figure 17.5. Much work has been done in determining
the proper distribution of prices. A better understanding of the distribution of prices will allow a more accurate evaluation of volatility,
which is critical to better option pricing.

A SECOND LOOK AT VOLATILITY

Since volatility plays such an important role in trading and evaluating
options it will be helpful to look at the different kinds of volatility:

1. *Historical volatility*: The actual volatility that the market has traded
   in the past. This is the easiest to determine, although the historical
   can vary greatly depending on the time frame used.

2. *Seasonal volatility*: Many commodities sometimes exhibit seasonal tendencies, becoming more volatile at certain times and less volatile at other times of the year.

3. *Implied volatility*: The volatility derived from the option price and the Black Scholes or equivalent model. This is the actual market volatility of the option. Some traders consider the implied volatility to be a good estimate of future market volatility or the best estimate of current volatility.

4. *Predicted volatility*: The volatility the trader believes the market will trade in the future. This is not the same as the implied but is the volatility a trader will use in the options evaluation model.

5. *Future volatility*: This is the volatility the market will actually trade at in the future and is not only the most important, but also the hardest to know.

HISTORICAL VOLATILITY

The historical volatility is calculated using past price data for a specific time period. The number is sometimes smoothed using moving averages or other mathematical methods. The historical volatility furnishes one of the best indications of what the volatility of the market may be in the future, because it provides a reference frame on what the volatility of the market was in the past.

A 10-day volatility refers to the volatility of the market over a 10-day period. The 20- and 50-day volatility for December 1991 coffee is shown in Figures 17.6 and 17.7, respectively. The volatility of a market may change depending on the time frame measured. Some markets may be more volatile in the short term than the long term, and vice versa. Notice how the short-term volatility is sometimes greater, and other times less than the long-term volatility. In essence, the short-term volatility is more volatile than the long-term volatility. This relationship is depicted in Figure 17.8 which shows how the short-term volatility changes relative to the long-term volatility. The curve is upward sloping, flat, or negatively sloped, similar to an interest rate curve.

FIGURE 17.6
December 1991 coffee 20-day volatility

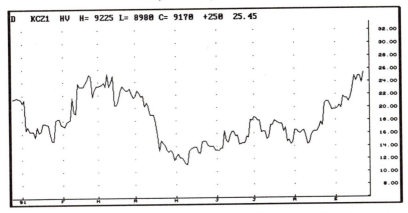

Source: Reprinted with permission, FutureSource, 955 Parkview Blvd., Lombard, IL 60148 (800) 621-2628.

FIGURE 17.7
December 1991 coffee 50-day volatility

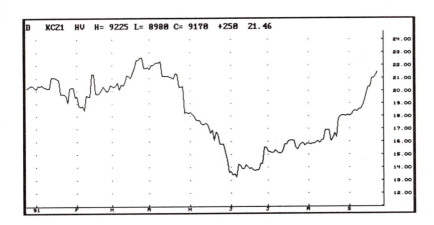

Source: Reprinted with permission, FutureSource, 955 Parkview Blvd., Lombard, IL 60148 (800) 621-2628.

FIGURE 17.8

The volatility of a market may change depending on which time frame it measured.

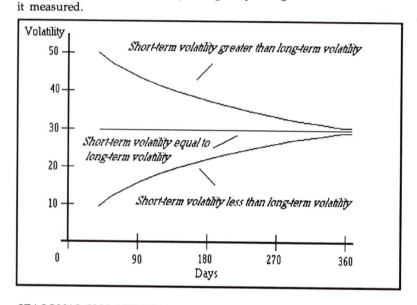

SEASONAL VOLATILITY

Certain markets tend to be more volatile at different times of the year. The grains often become more active in the summer due to possible drought and supply problems. Orange juice futures can be quite volatile during the winter when a crop freeze may occur. Notice in the 10-week volatility chart of soybeans in Figure 17.9 how the volatility increases during the summer. The summer weather is crucial to the harvest, so any bad weather may have a large influence on the price of the beans.

IMPLIED VOLATILITY

The **implied volatility** *is the volatility the option is actually trading at.* In other words, the actual market price of the option assumes a certain volatility which is termed the implied volatility. By knowing the market price we can work backward using the Black Scholes

FIGURE 17.9
Soybeans 10-week volatility

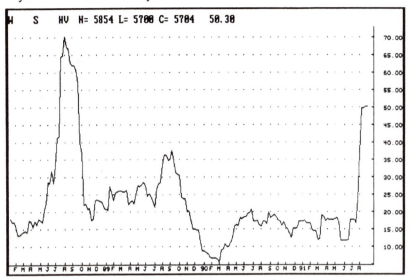

| H | S | HV | H= 5854 | L= 5788 | C= 5784 | 58.38 |

Source: Reprinted with permission, FutureSource, 955 Parkview Blvd., Lombard, IL 60148 (800) 621-2628.

model and determine what volatility the option is trading at for the given market price.

Many options traders use the implied volatility as the best guess estimate of the future volatility. They feel the implied volatility is the market volatility and the best estimate of the future volatility. The implied volatility can be different for each option. Figure 17.10 shows a set of implied volatilities for each option strike.

Sometimes the volatilities are skewed with higher and lower strikes having different implied volatilities than in the money strikes. For example, the implied volatilities for December 92 coffee under the heading ImpVol in Figure 17.10 increase with higher call strikes. The December 75 call has an implied volatility of approximately 29% (.2907), whereas the December 90 call has an implied volatility of almost 34% (.3360). This skew may occur for many reasons but one might be a bullish or bearish bias in the market. The actual 6-month historical volatility at the time was approximately 29% and the December future closed at 74.

FIGURE 17.10
Option valuation table

Option:	KC		Valuation Date:			4/14/92		Interest:	8.75	Div/For:	0.00

MY PC	Str	Qty	U	Price	Value	ImpVol	Diff	DTE	Delta	Gamma	$Theta	Vega
K2			Y		6610				1.000			
Z2			Y		7400				1.000			
Z2 C	600		Y		1505	.3293		206	.794	.0013	3	13
Z2 C	650		Y		1050	.2588		206	.740	.0020	3	16
Z2 C	700		Y		830	.3072		206	.608	.0021	5	20
Z2 C	750		Y		570	.2907		206	.494	.0023	5	21
Z2 C	800		Y		420	.3045		206	.391	.0022	5	21
Z2 C	850		Y		310	.3164		206	.306	.0019	5	19
Z2 C	900		Y		245	.3360		206	.246	.0016	5	17
Z2 P	600		Y		105	.2744		206	.125	.0013	3	11
Z2 P	650		Y		150	.2306		206	.192	.0021	3	15
Z2 P	700		Y		430	.2975		206	.342	.0022	5	20
Z2 P	750		Y		670	.2930		206	.457	.0023	5	21
Z2 P	800		Y		985	.3015		206	.563	.0022	5	21
Z2 P	850		Y		1375	.3259		206	.639	.0019	4	19
Z2 P	900		Y		1845	.3796		206	.673	.0016	5	18
Position Totals					0		0		0.000	0.0000 $	0	0
							P/L				DECAY	

Source: Reprinted with permission, FutureSource, 955 Parkview Blvd., Lombard, IL 60148 (800) 621-2628.

There may be other reasons for the skew in implied volatilities:

1. Many people like to buy cheap out of the money calls and puts but do not always like to sell them for the small amount of premium they receive. It is more difficult for option traders to hedge with far out of the money options so the premiums are sometimes greater.

2. The distribution of prices may affect the skew of option prices. If prices are lognormally distributed and there is a bullish bias to the market, out of the money calls should have higher premiums than corresponding out of the money puts. An out of the money

call has a greater chance of being in the money than an out of the money put which is an equal distance from a future if prices exhibit lognormal behavior.

3. Some traders believe markets become more volatile as prices increase. If the volatility increases as a market moves higher and declines as a market moves lower, options should have skews reflecting this.

These are some of the reasons options sometimes exhibit skewed pricing, but there is not always complete agreement as to the importance of each factor.

The implied volatility is definitely a good start in option evaluation and deriving a good estimate of what the volatility should be. But the implieds really reflect the supply and demand situation of the option much more than as a predictor of the future volatility of the market. Let's look at an example to understand this.

Assume a market has been trading in a relatively stable way with an actual historical volatility of 20%. The implied volatilities of the options will probably be trading somewhere in the same range of 20%. An unexpected news report comes out and causes the market to soar and trade around a 40% actual volatility. The implied volatility of the options may jump to levels much greater than 40%. This may happen because many investors who were short options (and therefore short volatility) may have to buy them back no matter what the price or volatility of the option. The investors may have to buy the options back due to margin calls, severe losses, or other reasons, and not necessarily because they anticipate even higher actual volatilities.

Of course the actual market volatility may increase to even higher levels, but this does not mean that the implied volatilities accurately predicted this. Instead, the typical sellers who have just been battered now require much higher premiums and, consequently, higher implied volatilities to resume selling volatility. The same type of situation occurs when the volatility bubble collapses and premiums implode. The buyers are now the ones who are hurt, and will not buy unless the premiums are low enough to justify reentering the market.

PREDICTED VOLATILITY

How do you predict market volatility? Some traders simply use the implied volatilities. Others look at a combination of the historical, seasonal, and implied to derive an estimate of future volatility. Others look at price levels and believe markets become more or less active at various price levels. Some use technical or fundamental analysis for estimates. A good estimate of volatility is essential in successful options trading and a book could easily be written on methods for predicting volatility.

FUTURE VOLATILITY

If we can figure out the future market volatility, we will know the proper price of an option and whether it is under- or overvalued. This would be somewhat equivalent in outright trading of knowing where the price of the commodity will be in the future.

FIGURE 17.11

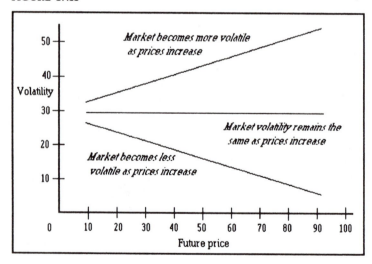

VOLATILITY AND PRICE

Another relationship is how volatility changes with price. A market may become more volatile as the price increases and large price swings occur. Other times a market may become more volatile after a decline in prices. This change in volatility is shown in Figure 17.11. Many option traders base their volatility estimates on price levels in a market, raising the volatility for pricing if markets rise and lowering it if markets drop.

CONCLUSION

Option prices are affected by various factors, but one of the most important factors is the volatility of the market. Anyone who trades options should have some understanding of what volatility is and how option prices are affected by it. Most intelligent option trading is done with a strong awareness of the volatility of the market.

CHAPTER 18

Spreads

Knowledge is power.

Francis Bacon, *Meditationes Sacrae*

Spread trading represents another way of trading the market which is somewhat different than outright buying, selling, or option trading. A trader initiates a spread by speculating on the relationship between two or more futures or securities. The trader is not usually concerned about the absolute price level of either future, but rather how both futures move relative to each other.

Almost all spreads involve one side which is buying one or more futures and the other side which is selling one or more futures. There are three basic types of spreads:

1. **An intracommodity spread** *is a spread between different months in the same commodity.* Buying July coffee and selling December coffee, or buying October sugar and selling March sugar are examples of intracommodity spreads.

2. **An intercommodity spread** *is a spread between different commodities which are usually related.* Buying March S&P500 and selling March NYSE, or selling June Treasury bonds and buying June Eurodollars are examples of intercommodity spreads.

3. **An intermarket spread** *is a spread between the same commodity on different exchanges.* Buying London sugar and selling NY sugar, or selling NY crude oil and buying London oil are examples of intermarket spreads.

Each type of spread is put on for entirely different reasons.

INTRACOMMODITY SPREADS

Intracommodity spreads are done to trade price discrepancies between different months of the same commodity. This can often be the most common type of the three listed spreads. The carrying charge from one contract month to another is often an important consideration in doing this type of spread.

For most commodities, a bull spread means buying the near month and selling the distant month. Buying July coffee and selling September coffee is an example of a bull spread. For most commodities, a bear spread refers to selling the near month and buying the distant month. Selling July coffee and buying September coffee is an example of a bear spread.

This terminology arises from the fact that when some markets rally the near term contract may rise more than the further out months. When the market drops the near term contract may drop more than the further out months. This may not always be the case, and some exceptions will be discussed later in this chapter.

DETERMINING PRICE RELATIONSHIPS

As noted in the fundamental section, a futures price is related to the cost of carry of the futures and cash price. The greater the cost of carry, the higher the future price versus the cash price. For most futures, contracts with longer expirations will have higher prices because the cost to carry increases with time. A trader may attempt to spread one month against another if a price discrepancy occurs between one month and another.

The calculations used to determine the value of a future are similar to those presented in Chapter 6, covering the basis calculations. We will use them here for spreading evaluation. The trader is now concerned with the difference between the near and distant futures prices to determine if both are correctly valued. Let's look at an example.

July coffee is trading at $0.90 a pound. What should the September future be trading at? Assume a two-month holding time and carrying costs which include insurance, storage, and interest costs of 17%.

$$\text{Cost to carry} = \text{cost of commodity} \cdot \text{interest rate} \cdot \text{holding time}$$
$$= \$0.90 \cdot 0.17 \cdot 2/12$$
$$= \$0.025$$

The September future should be trading at approximately $0.925 a pound ($0.90 + $0.025). Assume the actual future price is trading at a slightly lower price of $0.92 a pound. A trader could buy the cheaper September future and sell the more expensive July future. But there is one more important consideration the trader must be aware of in this situation.

The cost of carry represents a "floor price" for most near-term futures. The near-term future will usually not sell below a certain price relative to the more distant future. The floor price is calculated as follows:

$$\text{Floor price} = \text{further out month} - \text{carrying cost}$$

If the September future remains at $0.92 a pound, the July future should not sell below this floor price which is the September future minus the cost to carry:

$$\text{Floor price} = \$0.92 - \$0.025$$
$$= \$0.895 \text{ a pound}$$

Why does a floor price occur? An arbitrager would buy the July coffee contract at $0.895 a pound and take delivery of the coffee.

This action would be cheaper than buying the coffee in the cash market. The spread should not widen to more than the cost of carry or $0.025 a pound.

Is there a ceiling price of the near-term future? There is generally not a ceiling price because the mechanics are different. If July coffee becomes temporarily scarce due to a frost or other problems, the price of the nearby future could increase much more than the longer-term future. The longer-term future might not even increase and could in fact drop in value if the supply or demand problem is of a short-term nature. Here, the inverted spread can be much greater than $0.025 because the cost of carry does not affect the relationship on the upside. The July contract could trade at $1.00 a pound and the September could be at $0.95 a pound.

July coffee trading above September coffee would be an example of an inverted market which was discussed in Chapter 2. Temporary supply and demand problems can cause the near-term future to change much more than the longer-term future. In the opposite case, where there is an excess supply of coffee, the arbitrageur will simply buy the near-term future and create a floor price. This buying will continue until the longer-term future drops or the near term increases to the appropriate cost of carry level.

The ceiling and floor pricing in futures of different months has important implications when a trader wishes to spread one future against another. When buying a spread (purchase near term and sell further out) the risk is theoretically limited to the floor price of the carrying cost. The near-term future should not sell below the cost of carry of the distant month. However, the reward is not limited because the spread can widen to any level irrespective of carrying charges.

When selling a spread (sell near term and buy further out) the opposite applies. The risk is not limited because the spread can widen to any price. The reward is limited because the near-term future can only drop to a floor price set by the carrying cost. In the previous example, the arbitrageur could sell the July at $0.90 a pound against buying the September at $0.92 and hope to make $0.005 a pound. That is the maximum profit obtainable, whereas the arbitrageur could lose much more than this if the July increased more than the September. Perhaps this is one reason why the September is so "cheap" and the July so "expensive" in the example. If carrying costs, or more often, interest rates decrease, the carrying costs would drop and the spread difference of $0.025 would decrease. If carrying costs increase, the spread difference could increase beyond $0.025. Unless interest rates are extremely high or fluctuate greatly, the spread relationship is usually affected more by the supply and demand situation of the underlying commodity.

OTHER CONSIDERATIONS

The floor price or base level a near term future may trade relative to a far-term future can be applied to most markets. However, this relationship is different with some markets like the meats, because they are perishable, or cannot be stored easily like coffee or stocks. A hog comes to market and must normally be sold within a definite period of time. The futures contract for one month may move independently of another month because the cost of carry calculations do not readily apply. The arbitrageur may not be able to buy the near month, as in the coffee example, and inventory the commodity because it is not easily stored.

The spread between October 91 and March 92 sugar is displayed in Figure 18.1. Notice how the spread goes from a negative to a positive basis. The near-term month can rally much more than the far-term month but there is usually a floor with most agricultural commodities.

Some futures markets do not have the same types of relationships between different contract months. Many of the financial and precious metal markets do not have the same type of supply and demand problems. If the stock market rallies or drops, the near-term future should rise or drop the same amount as the further out months. The difference in prices between months are invariably determined by the carrying costs from one month to another. There is not much difference between a September S&P500 future and a December S&P500 future, whereas there can be a great difference between September and December coffee.

FIGURE 18.1
Sugar spread: October 1991 contract versus March 1992 contract.

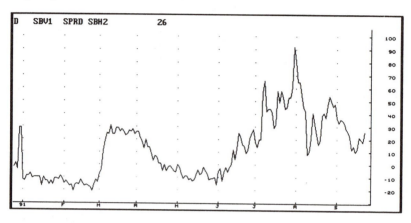

Source: Reprinted with permission, FutureSource, 955 Parkview Blvd., Lombard, IL 60148 (800) 621-2628

One other point to consider: Although spreads should never theoretically be above or below a certain level, there can always be unusual market conditions where this could actually occur. For example, July coffee might sell off sharply but the September contract might decline a lesser amount due to price limits. The July future could be much lower than the September future price, even though the theoretical price should be higher.

Another reason the spread could go beyond carry is that arbitrageurs may not be able to put on any larger position size due to margin or other reasons. Some markets may not be easily arbitraged, or some moves may be so great, the arbitrageurs may not have enough buying or selling power to overcome the discrepancies.

You might be comforted in knowing the spread should eventually get back to proper theoretical levels once the market gets back to "normal." However, your brokerage firm might take a distinctively different viewpoint and send a margin call. There is little comfort in thinking you are right but having to liquidate a position anyway. Markets may sometimes take much longer than anticipated to get back to "normal."

INTERCOMMODITY SPREADS

Intercommodity spreads are done to trade the relationship between one market and another market which are usually related to each other. These spreads are often done based on the evaluation that one market is underpriced relative to another market.

Some relationships between markets may not change greatly, such as the NYSE and S&P500 spread. Many of the stocks in the S&P500 are also on the New York Stock Exchange, so both markets tend to be highly correlated.

Some related markets vary more such as the interest rate futures. The interest rate market generally moves in unison, but shorter-term rates may change more or less than longer-term rates. It is even possible that short-term rates could go up and long-term rates go down, and vice versa. Rates of the same maturity can change with respect to each other depending on the quality of the issue. Eurodollars and Treasury bills of the same maturity might move inversely in unusual economic situations. The spread between Treasury bills and eurodollars is shown in Figure 18.2.

FIGURE 18.2
The TED spread: December 1991 Treasury bills versus December 1991 Eurodollars.

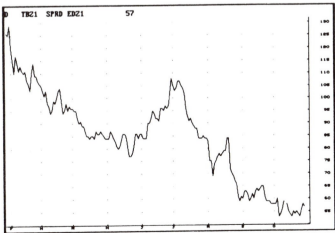

Source: Reprinted with permission, FutureSource, 955 Parkview Blvd., Lombard, IL 60148 (800) 621-2628

Other types of spreads have only a limited relationship and are not really true spreads in the sense of related markets. There may be correlations in markets over the long term, such as the gold and oil market, but buying one market and selling the other for a short-term trade in futures is more an outright position in both markets.

Another type of intercommodity spread is the crack or crush spread. This kind of spread is based on the relationship of the raw material and its constituent products. Crude oil is refined into heating oil and gasoline, and this spread relationship is called the crack spread. Soybeans are refined into meal and oil, and this relationship is called the crush spread. We will look at the crack spread later in this chapter.

MATCHING CONTRACT VALUE WITH DIFFERENT CONTRACTS

An important consideration with all of these spreads is to know the difference in contract value of one commodity with another. Let's look at an example of the S&P500 versus the NYSE. A stock index trader believes the broader market as represented by the NYSE will outperform the S&P500 averages. He decides to buy the NYSE contract and sell the S&P500. What is the proper ratio to trade?

The value of an S&P500 and NYSE contract is 500 times the index price.

S&P500 contract is trading at 365.00

NYSE contract is trading at 200.00

Value of the S&P500 = 500 · 365.00 = $182,500

Value of the NYSE = 500 · 200.00 = $100,000

If he buys a NYSE and sells an S&P500 future, he will be net short the stock market by approximately $82,500. He must determine a proper ratio by dividing the value of one contract by another:

Ratio = 182,500/100,000 = 1.83

This means the dollar value of one S&P500 is approximately equal to 1.82 NYSE contracts. Alternatively 1/1.82 = 0.55 which would mean the dollar value of one NYSE contract is approximately equal to 55% of one S&P500 contract. He must determine the minimum number of S&P500 contracts to trade since it is the bigger contract. Some ratios are:

Buy two NYSE and sell one S&P500 = $200,000 – $182,500 = $17,500.

He will be net long $17,500 of stock, and make or lose more money on the long position than the much smaller change in the relationship of the two futures. He can continue looking at proportions, and one that comes closer is the following:

Buy nine NYSE and sell five S&P500 = 9 · $100,000 – 5 · $182,500
= –2,500

He will still be net short $12,500, but now movement between the two indices will affect the profit and loss more because more contracts are being traded. The more contracts used, the more closely the dollar amounts will match, but the commissions, slippage, and risk will increase as well.

THE CRACK SPREAD

The refining margin between crude oil and its many products can partially be represented by the crack spread. Crude oil is refined or "cracked" into many different constituent products but two of the main components are gasoline and heating oil.

A barrel of crude oil yields different proportions of gasoline and heating oil depending on the crude and the refinery. Assume the percentage of gasoline is equal to the percentage of heating oil. The calculation for the crack spread follows:

One crude oil contract   = 1000 barrels
One heating oil or gasoline contract = 42,000 gallons
One thousand barrels   = 42,000 gallons

Therefore, two crude oil contracts equal approximately one heating oil and one unleaded gasoline contract:

2 crude oil = 1 heating oil + 1 unleaded gasoline

The above relationship is the basis for the crack spread. Subtracting the crude oil on both sides of the equation and dividing by 2 provides the margin or crack spread on a 1000 barrel basis:

Crack spread = [1 heating oil + 1 gasoline − 2 crude oil]/2

Assume:

July crude oil	= $21.00/barrel.	
July heating oil	= $0.56/gallon = 42 · $0.56 = $23.52/barrel
July unleaded gas	= $0.66/gallon = 42 · $0.66 = $27.72/barrel
The crack spread	= {$23.52 + $27.72 − 2 · $21.00}/2
	= $4.62

The trader might compare this to historical values or determine fundamental or technical relationships for an appropriate valuation.

As mentioned, there are different proportions of gasoline and heating oil from a barrel of crude oil. Other crack spreads are the 3:2:1 which is three crude to two gasoline to one heating oil. Another is the 5:3:2 or five crude to three gasoline to two heating oil. Gasoline is generally produced in greater amounts than the heating oil component. A 3:2:1 crack spread for the December 91 contracts is shown in Figure 18.3.

FIGURE 18.3
December 1991 3:2:1 crack spread contracts

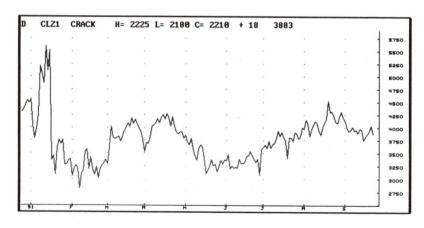

Source: Reprinted with permission, FutureSource, 955 Parkview Blvd., Lombard, IL 60148 (800) 621-2628

INDEX SPREADS

The final intercommodity spread we will look at is unusual in two respects:

1. The spread is based on the way the index is calculated.
2. The spread is initiated by buying or selling both sides.

The spread involves the US Dollar Index against some of the component currencies. This is a rather complicated spread and cannot be thoroughly analyzed, but we will look at the salient points to show how the spread is done.

The US Dollar index (USDX) is a future based on the value of the US dollar relative to ten other currencies in the following proportion:

Currency	Percent weight
1. German mark	20.8
2. Japanese yen	13.6
3. French franc	13.1
4. British pound	11.9
5. Canadian dollar	9.1
6. Italian lira	9.0
7. Netherlands guilder	8.3
8. Belgian franc	6.4
9. Swedish krona	4.2
10. Swiss franc	3.6

The index is multiplied by 500 to determine the actual cash value of the contract. If the index is calculated at 100, the value of the contract is 500 · 100 = $50,000.

The index has two important properties:

1. The USDX is quoted in European terms (foreign currency/US dollar) but settled in US dollars. A given percentage change in one currency will not equal the percentage change in the other currency because the relationship is reciprocal.

The index is inversely proportional to the component currencies. This means the index goes up if the currencies go down and vice versa. Therefore if the German mark drops by a certain amount, the dollar index will rise by a certain amount assuming the other currencies decline or stay the same. A given percentage change in one currency will not necessarily equal the same percentage change in another currency.

For example, assume 1 US dollar = 2 German marks. The European quote is a foreign currency divided by the dollar so a European quote of the dollar and mark would be 2 marks per dollar. The American quote is the dollar divided by the foreign currency so an American quote would be 1/2 dollar per mark.

	European Quote	American Quote
1 US dollar = 2 German mark	2.00 M/$	0.5 $/M
If the dollar appreciates 10% then		
0.5 · 1.1 = 0.55 but		
1/0.55 = 1.82 M/$	1.82 M/$	0.55 $/M
The percent decrease in the mark		
is 1.82/2 = 9.1%	−9.1%	10.0%

2. The index is a geometric index. A geometric average will usually increase less and decrease more than the corresponding arithmetic average. Most of us are familiar with arithmetic averages. An arithmetic average is calculated by adding all the prices and dividing by the number of prices. A geometric index is calculated by taking the nth root of the product of the prices. Therefore:

Arithmetic average $= \dfrac{1}{n} \displaystyle\sum_{i=1}^{n} x_1$

Geometric average $= [(x_1)(x_2)(x_3) \ldots (x_n)]^{1/n}$

Let's compute an arithmetic and geometric average of the combination of elements 2 and 2:

Arithmetic average $= (2 + 2)/2 = 2$
Geometric average $= \sqrt{(2 \cdot 2)} = 2$

What are the averages for elements 2 and 3?

Arithmetic average = $(2 + 3)/2 = 2.5$
Geometric average = $\sqrt{(2 \cdot 3)} = 2.4$

What are the averages for elements 1 and 2?

Arithmetic average = $(1 + 2)/2 = 1.5$
Geometric average = $\sqrt{(1 \cdot 2)} = 1.4$

When on element increases from 2 to 3, note how the geometric average goes up less from 2 to 2.4, whereas the arithmetic average goes up more from 2 to 2.5. When one element decreases from 2 to 1, the geometric average also drops more from 2 to 1.4, whereas the arithmetic average drops from 2 to 1.5. This is a normal property of the averages, but it has important implications in the dollar index versus the component currencies. A portfolio of currencies is an arithmetic average so it should outperform a geometric index.

These factors give the index option like properties similar to a straddle. If a trader buys the index and buys the component currencies, the component currencies will usually outperform the index, no matter what the prices are.

The basis is partly a function of this phenomena so there is a premium inherent in the basis calculation. The basis is partly a function of the volatility of the index and the component currencies. If the basis is too great and volatility too low, then money will be lost in buying the basis spread but made in selling it. If the basis is too low and volatility higher than anticipated, then money will be made in buying the basis spread and lost in selling it.

A trader would buy the dollar index and buy the currencies if the basis were too low for the given volatility. A trader would sell the index and sell the currencies if the basis were too high for the anticipated volatility. Although all ten currencies do not trade on the IMM, a proxy can be developed to simulate some of the currencies. Some of the currencies which are not on the IMM are highly correlated with the mark.

This type of trade can be done as an arbitrage if the cash interbank market is used. Most of the trading is still done as a spread, as opposed to a pure arbitrage.

INTERMARKET SPREADS

Intermarket spreads are usually done to trade minor price discrepancies in the same market but on different exchanges. This type of spread is in the realm of the professional arbitrageur because the price differences are usually quite small. Low commissions and margins are often required for this type of trading. There is usually not as much risk involved in these kinds of spreads and the markets are often closely watched by professional traders.

December 91 New York coffee and November 91 London coffee are shown in Figures 18.4 and 18.5, respectively. Each contract represents a different type of coffee so there is some relationship between the two, but they clearly diverge at different points. This type of spread is actually quite risky because each future represents a different type of coffee and different contract month, so the prices may not move in tandem.

FIGURE 18.4
December 1991 New York arabica coffee

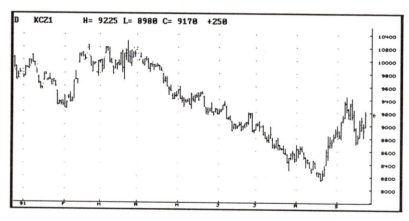

Source: Reprinted with permission, FutureSource, 955 Parkview Blvd., Lombard, IL 60148 (800) 621-2628

FIGURE 18.5
November 1991 London robusta coffee

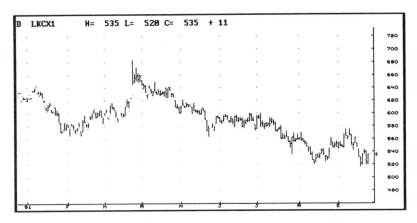

Source: Reprinted with permission, FutureSource, 955 Parkview Blvd., Lombard, IL 60148 (800) 621-2628

LEGGING A SPREAD

A leg in a spread refers to one side of the trade. In the first example at the beginning of the chapter with coffee, one leg would be the long July position and the other leg would be the short December position. Many spreads are put on simultaneously to catch a price discrepancy. *"Legging" a spread refers to buying or selling one side but not buying or selling the other side, and thus not completing the entire transaction.* Some traders do this to try and obtain better prices.

An example of legging would be buying the July coffee and waiting to sell the December coffee at higher prices. In effect the trader is now speculating on the spread as well as the absolute price in coffee. If the market sells off, the trader may lose much more than from the original spread position. If the market moves up the trader will be able to put the spread on for more favorable prices. But why not just buy the July outright in the first place? The trader is effectively outright long or short the one position until the other leg is traded. The trader is really speculating on the absolute level of the market by holding one leg of a spread.

Spreads are generally best done when the markets present price discrepancies. Legging a spread is generally not recommended. The trader must always distinguish between a good spread and a bad one. If the trader is trying to leg a spread but needs better prices, why put the spread on in the first place? There is not much sense in putting on a spread in which there is no initial potential advantage.

SPREADING—RISK AND REWARD

Many traders find spreads appealing due to their perceived limited risk, versus the supposed unlimited or greater risk of outright long or short positions. The trader must always evaluate the entire equation of risk and reward to make a proper decision. Some spreads may offer limited risk but the reward may also be much lower. Commissions and execution costs are usually greater with spreads so this partly increases the risk in them.

Spreads analyzed in a proper perspective are an excellent way to trade the market, but in a different way than outright or option positions. But, just like the outrights and options, people can lose just as much trading spreads as any other type of trading. The trader must be realistic in evaluating the risk and reward potential of any spread trade.

CONCLUSION

Spread trading is another way to approach the market without taking outright positions. Spread trading, like option trading, is no more or less risky, but the risks and rewards are of a different nature. Spreads are a means to trade the relative value of one market versus another.

CHAPTER **19**

Computers and Trading

There are more things in heaven and earth, Horatio,
Than are dreamt of in your philosophy.

William Shakespeare, *Hamlet*

Computers have rapidly become an important tool in helping the trader analyze the market. A general overview of what computers offer the trader is given in this chapter. Because the field changes so rapidly, the reader is best advised to review recent periodicals and the advice of knowledgeable consultants for information on the different types of programs and computers that are available.

Some people think computers will show you how to make money. This is totally inaccurate. Computers can aid the trader in analyzing and assimilating data. They may help good traders to become better traders but will be of little value to bad traders, except as a form of amusement in computer games when the trading is going badly.

Others see computers as a way to trade worry-free by making the decisions for them. Computers will in no way reduce the amount of stress in trading because money will still be made and lost. Computers will not provide strategies, figure out a way to make money while you sleep, or take the trading decision process away from you. In fact, computers properly used will multiply the number of decisions required to solve a problem. The analyst will be able to analyze information more quickly and therefore, generate more questions on how to improve results further.

In short, computers are a way to work much more efficiently and thereby aid the trader in making more informed and presumably better decisions.

CAN COMPUTERS REDUCE THE AMOUNT OF WORK AND DECISIONS A TRADER MAKES?

Computers can definitely reduce the drudgery work and enhance the charting and displaying of charts and graphs. Computers will unquestionably reduce the workload in this area. It will also reduce the amount of time and effort spent solving these problems. But there is another side the trader must realize.

Computers, used properly and in the most effective manner, should increase the amount of decisions the trader will make and increase the amount of work. Computers will advance the state of knowledge and level of work by tremendous amounts. This will free the user from mundane decisions, but place the person at a much higher level in asking questions and solving problems that could only be speculated on a few years ago.

HARDWARE AND SOFTWARE

Computer hardware *refers to the mechanical parts of the computer.* The central processing unit (CPU) performs the calculations; the hard disk stores information; the screen displays information; and the printer gives a hard copy or printout of information.

Computer software *consists of the programs that run on the computer.* By analogy, compact discs or tapes are "software" that "run"on the audio equipment, such as the speakers and receiver (the "hardware"). Programs can do all sorts of things to aid the user in analyzing data.

COMPUTERS AND TRADING

Computers can aid the trader in the following ways:

1. *Displaying market information:* The various software packages display various types of real time information.
2. *Performing calculations to analyze data:* Analyze different trading strategies.
3. *Options analysis:* Calculate different theoretical values and other option-related data.
4. *Computer generated spreadsheets:* Can be used to perform various calculations.
5. *Computer languages:* Can be used to develop involved programs or complex calculations.

DISPLAYING MARKET INFORMATION

Many of the studies shown in the technical analysis section were obtained from computer software packages. There are all kinds of technical studies the trader can perform and watch while actually trading. The computer has come a long way from the terminal that just flashes quotes.

TESTING MECHANICAL SYSTEMS

There are many programs that either allow you to test your trading system, or provide one that you can optimize. The decision is more one of whether you want to start from scratch and build your own system (but possibly reinvent the wheel), or use someone else's system and try to improve upon it. Most of the mechanical systems do not make money, *but some do* and should be considered by the serious futures trader. Various services rate the systems on performance and the results may sometimes be obtained through current periodicals.

OPTION ANALYSIS

Option analysis requires mathematical calculations to determine theoretical prices for options. There are many kinds of packages available depending on the requirements of the user. Different packages use different theoretical models which may affect the calculations of the theoretical options price and related information. The differences are usually minor, but more often pale in comparison to using the appropriate volatility.

DATABASE

A **database** *is a collection of information.* The brokerage statements of a trader, or the price and volume data of various futures contracts are both examples of a database. There are all kinds of databases, but the ones we will be concerned with relate to commodity information such as the open, high, low, and close of a future contract.

The manipulation of a database is of great importance to many traders. *Manipulation* is the ability to perform calculations on the data, such as a moving average of price data or any other type of study. We may then analyze the information to see how certain trading strategies compare with others.

A database language is a program designed to allow the user to access important information about the data. It is one of the most efficient ways of finding information. However, if the data require many calculations, you should look into a spreadsheet or programming language. The decision of a spreadsheet or programming language depends on the amount of data and the complexity of the calculations.

In trading, most databases consist of the price information such as the open, high, low, close, volume, and open interest. The data is usually grouped by day or some form of time. Most of the data for a data base is usually obtained either with diskettes or through modem via phone, satellite, or other source. Each computer language works with a database in different ways. Some are much more efficient than others.

A **record structure** *pertains to how the data is organized.* An individual record refers to a specific day or time of the data. For example, a typical record of futures prices may contain the date, open, high, low, close, volume, and open interest for the day. The next record will have the next day's information. The combination of all the trading days for the future constitutes a data file on the futures contract. A NYSE data file might contain the date, prices, volume, and open interest for the March 1991 contract.

A **field** *refers to a specific element of the record.* The opening price or volume figure is a field in a record. We can have all types of fields in a record.

A **key** *or primary key is a field which uniquely identifies a record.* For example, the date of January 31, 1992 uniquely identifies the opening, high, low, and closing price for the March 92 treasury bonds. A key provides a way to efficiently access large amounts of data. Figure 19.1 shows an example of a database record, field, and key.

One of the important considerations in designing a database is the way a record is structured. The structure of a record can have a great impact on how easy or hard it is to access or manipulate the data, or to work with other programs or databases. The database

FIGURE 19.1

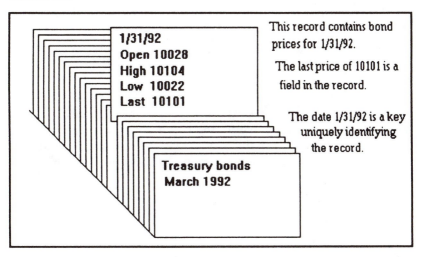

1/31/92
Open 10028
High 10104
Low 10022
Last 10101

Treasury bonds
March 1992

This record contains bond prices for 1/31/92.

The last price of 10101 is a field in the record.

The date 1/31/92 is a key uniquely identifying the record.

is the skeleton, or foundation, of the information system. A poorly designed database will have problems in speed, access, efficiency, and many other applications, no matter how well the programs are designed or how fast the computers may operate. The programmer must place crucial importance to the design of the database.

SPREADSHEETS

Spreadsheets rank in between calculators and languages in helping to calculate data quickly. They can be especially helpful in deriving trading results to see what the performance of a system was. They may also be used to test theories or do calculations on data. They do not require a tremendous amount of time to learn, and are relatively easy to get quick efficient results from.

Another benefit of spreadsheets is that they allow the display of data graphically, which allows the user to better appreciate the information. Many spreadsheets have databases included with them which allow the user to organize and manipulate different kinds of data for easier use. Spreadsheets are the choice of many analysts for quick results and easy presentations, but when the task becomes harder, due to large amounts of data and involved calculations, a procedural programming language is the next step.

COMPUTER LANGUAGES

When intensive analysis or heavy data use is warranted, computer languages are still the best way to go. If you need to develop your own complex and proprietary study, computer languages provide a way, as long as the study is objective and easily quantifiable.

The important point about programming is that learning a language is not always easy for some people, and paying top programmers to design a system can be very expensive. Another problem with using outside programmers is keeping your work secret. Be very careful in choosing programmers whom you can trust will not divulge your information.

Two important considerations, among many, when choosing a computer language are whether the language allows structured programming and how it deals with data.

Structured programming refers to writing programs for small tasks and combining them to solve bigger problems. An unstructured program is one that has no clearly defined individual tasks or groups of ideas, and can be very hard to work with. This book is written in a structured way with parts, chapters, titles, subtitles, and paragraphs, which allows the user to jump to different subjects or extract certain information easily. An unstructured book would have no chapters or paragraphs, and simply go on with no clearly defined sections, except the beginning and end, somewhat like a terribly boring speech. Structuring ideas is more natural and easier to learn from.

Certain computer languages have record structures specifically designed to deal with data. Others have a less structured way of handling data. Languages which have record structures such as "C" or Pascal make data handling much easier, and, therefore, are recommended over languages that do not.

THINGS TO CONSIDER WHEN GETTING COMPUTERS

When searching for a software package to display information some of the things to look for are:

1. *Reliability*: Software bugs can make a program with great potential a veritable nightmare to use. The computer user is always faced with the decision of using new and relatively unproven software with much better capabilities versus using older software with less features but time tested reliability. There is no hard and fast rule, but some of the greatest software packages continue to be more figments of the developers imagination versus working usable programs.

2. *Data integrity*: All kinds of data are readily available at relatively inexpensive prices. You should consider the integrity of the data first and the cost second because bad data is not just worthless but can actually be deleterious by giving invalid results to your studies.

3. *Features*: Software packages offer a wide array of features but most traders end up using a fraction of the options available to them. Keep an open mind in considering features you might

want, but remember, you are paying for the options and if you don't use them they are of little value to you.

4. *Service*: A cheap price and fast speed are some of the best selling points in both hardware and software. Without good backup service, the bargain today can become one of your worst trades in the future. Don't be lured into only considering price without service. Hardware is not easy to fix when a problem arises, and software programs are next to impossible to fix when a problem occurs, except by the group who developed the package. If the maker of the hardware or the developer of the software has packed up and decided to enter another business, the hardware or software will be virtually worthless.

5. *Data flexibility*: Be sure you can use the package with the data you have. Some packages only read certain kinds of data and are limited in use, whereas other packages read all kinds of data.

ARTIFICIAL INTELLIGENCE

Artificial intelligence (AI) *is the process of programming computers to carry out tasks which simulate the intelligence or thoughts of humans.* A computer chess game, which beats many good chess players, is an example of artificial intelligence. The computer simulates certain thought processes of humans by acting and reacting to each move. If the computer could "think" of a good trading strategy in the same way it beats chess players, there is promise in using AI. Two areas of AI being aggressively pursued in trading are natural language systems and expert systems.

A natural language in computing is more closely related to English, unlike the typical programming language which can be difficult for many people to comprehend. Many programs that test trading systems employ natural languages to assist the trader in creating and analyzing a strategy.

An expert system is another area in AI which is being actively investigated. An expert system learns information in terms of rules or factual information from experts and then attempts to make decisions from what it has "learned." A thermostat is a simple example of an expert system in that it has learned if the temperature goes below a certain amount it will decide to turn on the heater.

The *knowledge base* of an expert system are the rules, facts, and other information which it "knows." The *inference engine* interprets the information to arrive at conclusions about the problem. An expert system will learn all the trading methods of a good trader and then try to make trading decisions from this information.

Heuristics refers to programming a computer to think about how it might solve a problem, such as a simple one of determining how to play a computer game. The computer will try to get the most points, and, through trial and error, eventually arrive at a way to win.

Neural networks involve having the computer learn the different patterns of the market and then arrive at decisions to trade. It is different than expert systems in that the computer does not have the expert information "told" to it. The system arrives at a trading decision based on "learning" pattern recognition and the rules it develops. Neural networks come much closer to learning, the same way we believe we did as children (unless you had know-it-all parents, in which case it would be an expert system).

Much has been written about artificial intelligence and the promise it holds for mankind, but specifically for our purpose which is trading. AI can be valuable in many areas of trading and is aggressively being pursued in areas pertaining to pattern recognition. This area is a natural match where much money and time is being spent. But, there is still a long way to go before AI can be used practically by the basic computer user. The promise is high but the road is long.

CONCLUSION

Computers have become one of the most important tools for the trader in analyzing the market. They allow markets to be analyzed faster and more powerfully—in essence—more efficiently. They will play an increasingly important need in helping to analyze and present data, and test market strategies in the future.

PART TWO

MONEY MANAGEMENT

Do not think that what is hard for you to master is humanly impossible; but if a thing is humanly possible, consider it to be within your reach.

Marcus Aurelius Antoninus, *Meditations II*

CHAPTER 20

Risk And Reward

The most important questions of life are, for the most part, really only problems of probability.

Pierre Simon De LaPlace, *Theorie Analytique des Probabilites*

Money management *is the evaluation of risk and reward in a trade or portfolio, and determining the most efficient use of investment capital.* Money management is the study of risk and return—we are trying to get the best return for the money we risk. Money management involves:

1. Determining the different kinds of risk in any trade.
2. Deciding how much risk to take on a trade.
3. Assessing the amount of return on a trade for a given level of risk.
4. Deciding whether to accept the return and risk.
5. Implementing the entire process.

This process can be a lot of work but it will be well worth the effort.

Money management is often mentioned as important to successful trading, yet the vast majority of traders do not understand money management. Some often mentioned axioms include: cut your losses and let your profits run, or you can't go broke taking a profit. There are many more of these sayings and cliches. Most of them are well intentioned, but effectively useless without a better understanding of the goals and desires of the trader.

Money management is important to success for practical reasons. How much money should be risked on a trade? If a trader risks too much money on a good trading method, there is always a fair chance of losing all the capital in one disastrous trade or a series of losing trades. On the other hand, if the trader risks too small an amount of money, the capital will be underutilized and the trader will not achieve as high a return as possible. There is not much sense in trading commodities and obtaining returns equivalent to treasury bills because the risk is so much greater, but the return the same.

PRESERVATION OF CAPITAL

Inherent in the study of money management is the idea of the preservation of capital. Every trader must realize the preservation of capital to be a paramount consideration and a fundamental principle of money management. Futures trading is well known for high leverage which can yield fast profits and losses. Any trading strategy, no matter how well thought out and seemingly profitable, may ultimately lose money. Every trader must determine the appropriate amount of capital to risk for each trade. We will investigate what proportion of capital should be risked in the ensuing chapters. *You must always place the preservation of mind, body, and capital above all else when trading.*

THE JOURNEY

Money management is really an equity journey where you start with initial capital at point A and end with final capital at point Z. It is a simple concept to understand visually. The profits are the high points

FIGURE 20.1
An example of controllable risk. The trader determines where to place a stop to limit risk using technical or fundamental methods. The trader sells when the market breaks below the lows of the rectangle and decides where to place a buy stop. One place might be the previous highs of the rectangle.

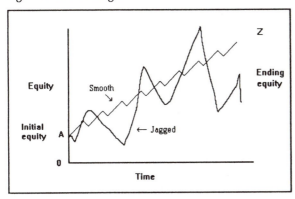

of the journey and the losses are the low points, as shown in Figure 20.1. The easiest and quickest trip is a straight line from A to Z, but every trip has its ups and downs. If the deviation from the path is too great, the journey sometimes ends abruptly at the point of no return or zero capital—"blown out" or loss of all capital.

There is one critical difference between the up and down part. There is virtually no limit to how high one may journey but there is always a limit to how far down one can go. The journey will result in a quick end if too much capital is lost. Equity increases of 50%, 100%, 1,000%, and higher are possible, but any equity drop of 100% will immediately end the journey, no matter how far the person has traveled. This is why the trader must always be concerned about losses and the preservation of capital.

What path do you desire to take—the straight and narrow, jagged and fast, or somewhere in between? This is the essence of money management and one of the most important, but least asked questions in trading. Most people believe the route is dependent on picking the right trading method, but, in fact, the route is independent of trading method. Both technicians and fundamentalists have, at times, successfully traversed the same road. This question will be continually addressed throughout the money management section by studying the two factors which affect the path—risk and reward.

RISK AND REWARD

The relationship of risk and reward is integral to trading. Every trade should be evaluated by measuring the inherent risk and associated reward. A portfolio of investments is measured by the amount of reward for a given level of risk. Money management is an attempt to determine the best risk and reward potential for a trade, as well as a portfolio of investments. Traders are not evaluated for their knowledge of technical or fundamental analysis, but on their money management skills and trading performance—how much is made versus how much is lost.

Technical and fundamental analysis provide a way to evaluate various types of risk and reward in any trade. For example, a head and shoulders pattern in technical analysis may provide indications of the amount of risk and reward in a trade. Using fundamental analysis, the cost of production yields clues as to how low prices may drop, and substitute goods help to determine how high prices might rise. Portfolio theory is an aspect of money management that deals with the risk and reward in combining investments. It is helpful in determining "efficient portfolios"—those which yield the highest return for a given level of risk.

Most people do not understand the significance or the concept of risk and reward which contributes greatly to poor trading results. Most investors have a very clear idea, or would rather think more about reward, but are less knowledgeable or concerned about risk. A balanced understanding of both risk and reward is essential in successful trading. The combination of risk and reward is the ultimate measure of any trade and trader. One of the few useful and relevant trading sayings is one which deals with risk and reward—"It's not just how much you make in trading but also how much you lose!"

WHAT IS RISK AND REWARD?

How would you define risk and reward in trading? What is a good measure of risk and reward? Which is more risky and which entails more reward—buying an S&P500 stock index future or buying a lottery ticket? These questions are actually not so easy to answer. What is risk? When most of us think of risk we probably consider the amount of loss. If we have $10,000, this becomes our risk capital and it is considered the amount that may be lost trading. Most investors view risk in this way. This is a good start, but there is another extremely important consideration—the probability of loss. What is the chance of losing the entire $10,000? It depends on the investment. The amount and chance of loss may be much different when investing in Treasury bills versus futures, but the rewards may be different too. Using the two ideas of magnitude and probability of loss, risk may be considered the amount and chance of a loss or adverse event.

There is one other important consideration when we think of risk. We usually invest in a variety of assets or the same ones over an extended time period, so we must also be concerned about a series of losses occurring. Therefore, risk may be defined in the following way: **Risk** *is the amount and probability of an adverse or series of adverse events occurring.* This is an important reference frame for determining risk in trading.

The definition of risk may be slightly altered and applied to the definition of reward. When thinking of reward we must not only consider the amount but also the chance of receiving it. **Reward** *is the amount and probability of a favorable or series of favorable events occurring.*

What is a good measure of risk and reward? Reward is normally much easier to measure but risk is another story. There are no easy answers to the question of measuring risk, but common sense and good judgment are just as valuable as any complex equation or valuation model. To consider the question, let's meet Lucky and Sharky.

LUCKY AND SHARKY

Lucky and Sharky are both trying to make money with two separate methods. Lucky buys a $1 lottery ticket that has a chance of winning $10,000,000. Sharky decides, instead, to buy an S&P500 future at 400. He places two orders—one to sell the future if it goes to 398 and the other to sell the future if it goes to 402—one order canceling the other. With this strategy Sharky will either make $1,000 if the market moves to 402, or lose $1,000 if the market drops to 398 (a 1-point move in the S&P500 future equals $500 and we will neglect slippage and commissions). Which strategy is more risky?

To answer the question we need to take two separate steps to measure risk. The first step in measuring risk is to determine the actual possible loss. In the example, Lucky is risking $1 and Sharky is risking $1,000. Sharky is clearly risking more than Lucky on an absolute basis.

However, there is more to this problem. The second step in measuring risk involves evaluating the chance or probability of the loss occurring. The probability of loss for Lucky is at least 99.99999%. The probability of loss for Sharky is approximately 50%, if random markets are assumed. By the way, if non-random markets are assumed and Sharky is a good trader, the probability of loss may be less. Therefore, if the probability of loss is viewed as the criteria for measuring risk, Sharky's risk is clearly less than Lucky's. The probability of loss is an important consideration in assessing risk and essential in making a more informed trading decision.

We have a tie for which strategy is more risky. If the total amount lost is the primary criterion, Sharky's trade is more risky. If the chance of loss occurring is the primary criterion, Lucky's lottery ticket is more risky. Although we now understand the problem better, it still is difficult to say which strategy is more risky.

There is one other consideration which has not been discussed. What if Lucky and Sharky risk the same amount? Since Sharky is risking $1,000 what if Lucky buys $1,000 worth of lottery tickets? Now Lucky and Sharky are risking the same amount of money but the probability of loss has not changed much. In this situation Lucky's chance of losing is still close to 100%, but now he will lose $1,000. Sharky's chance of losing $1,000 has not changed and is still 50%. If we multiply the total amount at risk times the chance of losing it we will arrive at an amount both may expect to lose.

1. For Lucky this number is $1,000 × 0.9999999, which is almost $1,000

2. For Sharky this number is $1,000 × 0.5, which is $500

Using these comparisons, Lucky's strategy is much more risky, both in terms of the total amount lost and the chance of losing it. This comparison illustrates the following important idea. *When we think of risk, we must always be concerned about the total potential loss, as well as the chance of the loss occurring.*

We have not definitively answered the question of which strategy is more risky if Lucky only buys one ticket, but that will be covered in the next chapter. One might also bring up an objection that Lucky's reward should also be considered because it is so much greater than Sharky's. We will address the reward side of the analysis and bring up the objection shortly, when the idea of expected outcome is presented. We will have more to say about Lucky and Sharky because there are other considerations about risk and reward.

RISKS ASSOCIATED WITH TRADING

Risk is the amount and chance of a loss, or series of losses. Let's apply our definition of risk to trading. A minimum amount of money must always be risked whenever trading. The different types of risk inherent in trading are:

1. **Avoidable risk** *is risk which can be reduced or eliminated without any reduction or compromise in reward.* Trading an illiquid market presents many risks in bad fills, which the trader can easily avoid by trading more liquid markets. Another type of avoidable risk is not being well diversified. A diversified portfolio will have less risk for the same return, or more return for the same risk than an undiversified portfolio. Diversification is a way to reduce risk without any reduction in performance. There is no reason to accept avoidable risk because nothing is gained in return. Avoidable risk usually occurs through a misunderstanding, or ignorance, of risk and return.

2. **Unavoidable risk** *is risk which cannot be reduced or eliminated without reducing or compromising reward.* We must incur some risk whenever trading, which is unavoidable in the expectation of making

a profit. There are two kinds of unavoidable risk associated with trading:

    a. **Controllable risk** *is the amount of risk which can be known and determined.* We can always know beforehand the exact amount we want to risk. For instance, Sharky decided to risk $1,000 on his trade. He has a predetermined amount to risk and will not risk any more money on one trade. Controllable risk may be determined using technical or fundamental analysis, or simply by deciding at what point to exit if a loss occurs. For example, assume Trader Vic decides to go short December 1987 Eurodollars in Figure 20.2 at 90.80 on October 14. He sets a protective stop at 91.00 to risk 0.20 points ($500). The difference between the entry and exit point would be considered controllable risk. If he decided instead to place a stop at 91.20 then his controllable risk would be 0.40 points.

    b. **Uncontrollable risk** *is the amount of risk which cannot be known and determined.* There are certain risks in trading which are uncontrollable. We cannot always determine the exact chance or amount of risk because it is dependent on many factors, not all of which are controllable or known. Uncontrollable risk is mainly a function of two different factors:

    i. *Close to open risk*: The inability to trade a market when it is closed.

    ii. *Slippage risk*: Bad fills while trading a market due to fast market conditions or volatile markets.

Each person must decide how much controllable risk to take before making a trade using technical or fundamental methods. However, each person may only estimate the amount and probability of uncontrollable risk before each trade. *Even though we may know exactly how much we want to risk, we can never be certain of how much we may actually lose when trading, due to uncontrollable risk.* The concept of controllable risk will be further examined throughout the money management section. Let's review uncontrollable risk next, to develop a better understanding so that we may be able to estimate how it will affect us.

FIGURE 20.2

December 1987 Eurodollars

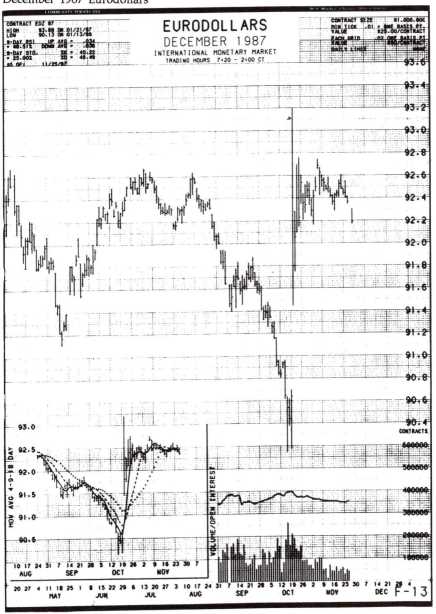

Source: Reprinted with permission, © 1991 Commodity Perspective, 30 South Wacker Drive, Suite 1820, Chicago, Illinois 60606.

CLOSE TO OPEN RISK

Close to open risk *is the risk associated with not being able to exit a position while the market is closed.* This type of risk is dependent on the inability to trade the market between the close and the open of the next period. December 87 Eurodollars, gapping approximately 2.00 points higher on October 20 in Figure 20.2, is an example of close to open risk. In the previous example the controllable risk was 0.20 points, or $500. When the market gapped higher on October 20 the risk was over 1.00 points, or $2,500—more than 5 times the amount originally risked. Any unfortunate soul caught short in this situation would face serious losses, even if a small amount of money was initially intended to be risked.

If Sharky is long the market but neither sell order is touched off, he will hold his position overnight. But what if bearish news comes out overnight and the market opens substantially lower than the intended exit point the next day? Sharky will have to exit the position at prices much lower than he anticipated losing much more than $1,000.

Sharky may decide to close out his position at the end of every day to avoid close to open risk. However, all the transaction costs incurred each day might eventually be much greater than the potential loss incurred in close to open risk. Furthermore, he will miss out on any favorable gap openings on the upside that might occur. There is no way of avoiding close to open risk through day trading, without creating other risks. Sharky has effectively traded one type of risk for other types of risks at what may be a very unfavorable cost.

Some markets, like the currencies, are open 24 hours most of the time and may not be as prone to this type of risk as other markets might be. However, the currencies are still closed on the weekend and not all traders have access to the international markets during the weekday. Other domestic markets are only open during the day in their respective country, such as the pork belly market, and cannot be hedged overseas through other markets.

We can get a good estimate of the magnitude of close to open risk by reviewing times when the difference between the close and the opening has been relatively large. This type of risk can be devastating, both financially and psychologically when it occurs, but, fortunately, it does not happen too often. A gap opening of the size which occurred in the Eurodollar example might happen once every five or ten years depending on the times and the market. When it does happen, the price move is generally not more than 5–10% of the price of the commodity, and this is in an extreme situation. Gap openings of a smaller degree will happen more often but they are not as disastrous as the larger ones. What about using options to avoid close to open risk? This will be addressed after slippage risk is covered.

SLIPPAGE RISK

Slippage risk is the risk the market will trade through a protective stop, or getting filled at prices which are worse than expected. Price slippage can occur for many reasons such as when a market becomes highly volatile and large price moves occur. Slippage may also occur under fast market conditions which may be caused by critical news events, or an imbalance of orders at certain price levels which creates a price vacuum. A fast market condition exists when the market is moving quickly and price fills may be extremely bad.

Slippage tends to be more of a problem in illiquid markets because there are not as many existing orders or market makers to absorb outside orders. There are times when even the deepest markets have slippage problems, such as the Treasury bond market which is one of the most liquid markets in the world. Figure 20.3 is a tick chart of the September 91 Treasury bond contract that shows how the market traded from the tight range of 9423–24 to 9513 in seconds. Any buy stop placed above 9424 before the market rallied would probably be filled in the 9513 to 9509 area. A loss of as much as 20 ticks, or approximately $600 per contract in slippage might have occurred. Economic news released at 7:30 caused the market to race to the higher level.

Sharky will have slippage problems too. Even if he avoids close to open risk he cannot avoid slippage risk. What if Sharky is long and bearish news sends the market tumbling while the market is open? Sharky may have stop orders to protect his position, but

FIGURE 20.3

September 1991 Treasury bond tick chart

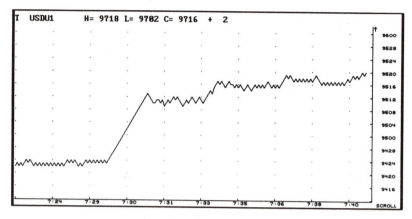

Source: Reprinted with permission, FutureSource, 955 Parkview Blvd., Lombard, IL 60148 (800) 621-2628

the market might quickly trade through the stop level, yielding bad fills at lower prices. If he uses stop limit orders, he runs the risk of not being filled at all and suffering severe losses. Using market orders will present the same problems as stop orders when markets exhibit high slippage. There is no way of avoiding slippage risk.

Slippage is not easy to determine because it may be highly dependent on the condition of the market, and the time. Markets may trade without any slippage problems; then an unexpected news event might create a "fast market" condition, causing prices to move wildly. The best way to estimate this risk is by actual trading experience. Lacking this, the trader may look at tick or intraday data to see how the market trades during the day and at certain price levels to arrive at an estimate of potential fills. Good brokers and traders who are active in the market may offer helpful information.

Slippage can be reduced by trading in more liquid markets which have relatively high trading volume. However, even the most liquid markets have periods of illiquidity so the trader cannot always avoid slippage risk.

Under normal circumstances, with more liquid markets such as the financial markets, slippage is usually not much greater than

1 to 5 ticks per contract. However, unexpected news or late breaking information can sometimes result in severe slippage. In these abnormal situations, it is possible to incur slippage as high as 10 to 50 ticks or greater, depending on the market. This amount is still not usually greater than a 5% move in the price of the contract, although there have been extreme situations where the loss may have been greater.

CONTROLLABLE AND UNCONTROLLABLE RISK: FURTHER THOUGHTS

We must always be concerned in trading of situations where we do not have control of our losses and therefore, end up losing more than had been originally risked. The previous examples of close to open and slippage risk are examples of not being able to control the amount of loss in a trade. Excuses such as, "I forgot to place the order" or "I went to lunch and got back too late" are not valid examples of this type of risk. The trader could get out but did not choose to, or did not bother to use stops.

What about using options as a means to limit inordinate loss and eliminate both types of risk? For example, being long a call and short a future in the Eurodollar example would have reduced the close to open risk to a specific controllable amount. The same idea may be applied in the Treasury bond example where being long a call before the upmove would have reduced the slippage risk.

Options will definitely reduce these two risks, but the reduction or elimination in one type of risk comes at a cost of the price of the option. For example, using options to avoid close to open risk will reduce the profitability of winning trades. If the Eurodollar market had continued in a downtrend the investor would lose money on the call. Using options to eliminate slippage risk does not always yield good results. In the Treasury bond example, most participants were aware that significant news was coming out at 7:30 and this is often reflected in higher option premiums. Once the news is released and the market makes a large move, the premiums may move back into line. Who would want to be short calls and puts if a critical news story were about to be released, without sufficient premium to compensate for the ensuing move?

In effect, two types of risk have been eliminated but another type has been created—the risk of losing the premium paid for the option or the transaction costs involved in buying and selling the option. The option premium and transaction costs may be small or large compared to the costs of close to open and slippage risk. The real issue is how much is lost in option premium and transaction costs, versus how often and severe are close to open risk and slippage risk. As mentioned earlier, close to open risk does not occur too frequently and slippage risk is generally not too severe in liquid markets. If both types of risk (close to open and slippage) do not happen too often, we will probably lose much more in option premiums and transaction costs than whatever we hope to save in eliminating the first two risks. In this case we have eliminated the risk but have paid for it in a very expensive manner. This in no way invalidates using options as valid trading vehicles to reduce risk, but there are usually much better reasons for using options.

When trading outright positions we can always limit our risk to an intended amount, but there is no guarantee we will only lose that amount. In evaluating both types of risk the trader must be realistic. Uncontrolled risk occurs and is part of the risk inherent in trading. Close to open risk, unfortunately, is often accompanied with slippage risk, which exacerbates the situation. However, as long as these situations are not too devastating, and do not happen too often, they should not seriously affect our trading performance.

In essence, if uncontrollable risk is not too great and does not happen too often, it should not affect us too much. Most uncontrollable risk can be eliminated by options or day trading, but at a cost which may be much greater than the risk itself. Uncontrollable risk is something every trader must be willing to accept, or else pay sometimes high prices to eliminate. In either case, a maximum move of 5–10% of the price of the contract beyond our expected trading point is usually adequate for most markets.

CHANCE AND AMOUNT OF A SEVERE LOSS DUE TO UNCONTROLLABLE RISK

What are the chances of incurring a severe loss and how much might be lost due to uncontrollable risk? There is no way to completely predict this, but let's go through an example to gain more insight into this problem and illustrate some of the ideas just mentioned.

Jim does not want to risk more than 1% of his $100,000 of capital which amounts to $1,000. He notes that gold has not normally moved more than $1,500 in one day in the past few years. He is bullish and buys 1 gold future at $400 setting a mental stop at $390 (a $10 move in gold is equal to $1,000). The market first rallies but then sells off and closes near $391. It opens down the next day at $376, so he sells at the market but gets filled at $370. The losses can be broken down as follows:

1. Expected loss = entry price − expected exit price
   = $400 − $390
   = $10 (i.e., an actual cash loss of $1,000)

2. Close to open loss = expected exit price − opening price
   = $390 − $376
   = $14 (i.e., an actual cash loss of $1,400)

3. Slippage loss = market order price − actual fill price
   = $376 − $370
   = $6 (i.e., an actual cash loss of $600)

The second and third losses are exaggerated and could happen in any market, but they are possible, so every trader must appreciate the fact that real losses can always be greater than what was originally anticipated. Jim lost 3% of his capital, but 2% of the loss may be attributed to risk beyond his control. Therefore, even though losses were much greater than anticipated, he still was not devastated by the severe loss because he did not risk too much initial capital. If he had risked 10% of capital by buying 10 contracts, his total losses would have been 30%, which would have been much more debilitating.

Jim ended up losing $3,000, or three times the amount he anticipated, but $2,000 of the loss may be attributed to close to open and slippage risk. He did not have a good day but there is good news in this example. Even though the market opened against him and slippage was severe, he still only lost approximately 3% of his capital. This loss was greater than expected but it occurred under extremely adverse conditions. Jim was not hurt too badly because he realized gold, or any market, always had the potential to make an extreme move well beyond his expectations.

What conclusion can be drawn from this example? When trading, we generally think of how much to risk on a trade, but must always have in the back of our mind the potential of the market to make extreme moves. If we account for extraordinary price moves and the value of the contract, we should normally not have to risk more than 5–10% of our capital on any trade. Of course, it is always possible to conjure up an even worse scenario, and sometimes these severe scenarios materialize in real time trading. But to realistically evaluate our situation we must always consider the amount and chance of a loss and a profit when trading .

We now have a way of estimating the amount and chance of a severe loss. We know from the previous section that the markets may move 5% against us in extreme situations. We also know how much we want to risk so we can now add the two and arrive at the total amount to risk. If it is greater than 10% we are probably risking too much capital. There is a good chance anyone who continually risks this much will eventually go broke, unless they are exceptionally good at trading the market. How much money should be risked on a trade? Further thoughts about this will be covered in the theory of runs and risk of ruin section in Chapter 21.

Another thing to consider when viewing a worst case scenario is that severe losses tend to be bunched or come at the same time. In the earlier example with December 87 Eurodollars, many other markets also had large gap openings or slippage problems within the same time period. For instance, the stock, currency, and gold markets also made large moves during the same time. In August of 1991 the stock, currency, and petroleum markets had significant gap openings on Monday morning after the weekend surprise coup attempt in the Soviet Union. A trader on the wrong side of any, or all, of these markets would have sustained inordinate losses. Large quick price moves and gap openings tend to occur after an unexpected news event, and may cause many markets to move in unforeseen ways. It is important to consider the possibility of a severe loss or a group of severe losses occurring together. Diversification may help at times, but each market may move in unanticipated ways when panic situations develop.

In trading, no matter how well diversified the portfolio, or how conservative the trader, there is still the chance of losing more than what was originally anticipated. Risk is inherent to trading and cannot be completely eliminated. A severe loss due to uncontrollable risk can, and probably will, happen depending on the frequency of trading, the amount risked per trade, and the type of markets traded. *However, the chances of a severe loss due to uncontrollable risk greater than 10% of the price of the contract are relatively small.* How much we should actually decide to risk on a trade will be considered in the rest of the chapters on money management.

LIMIT MOVES

Some exchanges impose limit moves which do not allow the future to trade above or below a certain price for a specific time. For example, the pork belly market cannot trade above or below $.02 from the previous close. If the market reaches the limit price, it may cease trading if no one is willing to take the other side of a trade.

Do markets which have price limits protect us from severe openings and sustaining large losses, or do they actually harm us by not allowing us to exit? The debate has been with us for a long time and will probably continue much longer. Should markets have limit moves?

Some argue that limits in markets reduce volatility and temper investor panics. A market which has limits may be less volatile during panic conditions because the absolute move is limited. Some investors may experience less panic in knowing the market can only move a certain amount, and therefore their loss is limited that day.

Others believe the idea of a limited loss due to limit moves is of questionable benefit. It is hard to imagine any solace in being short October 86 live hogs at 45 on June 23 in Figure 20.4 and watching the market rise limit up four days in a row. It is very possible that the unfortunate trader who was short might not have been able to exit the position until June 27, when it opened near 51, even if orders to buy at the market were placed each day on June 24, 25, and 26. How did the limit move protect a trader who was short the market?

FIGURE 20.4

October 1986 live hogs

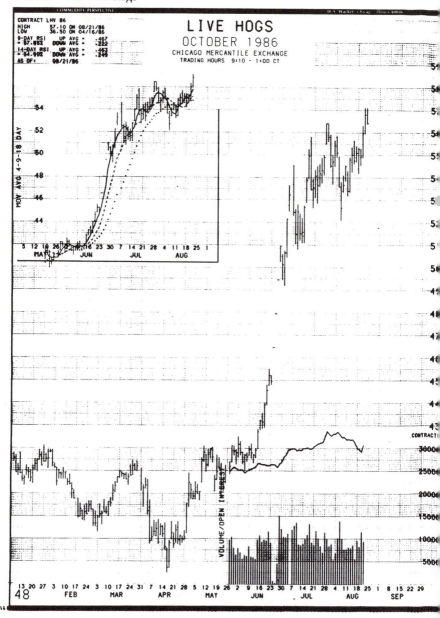

Source: Reprinted with permission, © 1991 Commodity Perspective, 30 South Wacker Drive, Suite 1820, Chicago, Illinois 60606.

Others argue that limits actually increase volatility and investor panics. Investors who are watching a market trading near a limit may be inclined to get out before the market becomes limit up or down. These actions may actually exacerbate the situation, causing the market to reach limits they otherwise might not have attained. The market may be less volatile during the day because it cannot move any further, but at what cost? The investor on the wrong side of the move usually cannot exit the position. What is to be gained from a market which is less volatile but does not trade? The possible benefit of reduced volatility, at the very real expense of near zero liquidity, is of dubious benefit.

Limit moves are really the antithesis of the idea of a market—to facilitate trade. Limit moves are a form of uncontrollable risk because the trader does not possess the ability to exit a position at a predetermined price. Any traders, comforted in knowing the market can only go against them by a certain amount because of limit moves, may not be long for the trading world.

REWARD

We have spent some time on risk, but now let's get to the part everyone has been waiting for—reward. Reward is a concept which most of us are probably more familiar with than risk since it is the foremost reason most of us enter the markets to trade. It is also much easier to understand, but, unfortunately, often harder to realize.

In the Lucky and Sharky example, Lucky's risk *was definitely* $1 but his reward *might be* $10,000,000. Sharky's risk *was definitely* $1,000 but his reward *might be* $1,000. Lucky and Sharky will always be at risk as long as they keep playing, but neither may ever attain any reward. *There is an important distinction with risk and reward—risk is always present, whereas reward is possible but by no means assured.* This has significant implications, which will be explored in Chapter 23.

Why not discuss the reward side of the market opening in our favor, or slippage occurring and getting a better fill than expected? Of course, the opposite scenario can, and does happen, but the ramifications of reward are much different than the ramifications of a loss. Profits are always desired in trading, but it is losses which we must usually be more concerned about because losses, when too severe, may bankrupt us and take us out of the game. Trading profits, no matter how great, will allow us to play one more day, but no one has ever been ruined by making great profits. It is losses, not profits, which the trader must always prevent from becoming too great. *It is poor risk control, not reward, which is the ruin of most traders.*

COMBINING RISK AND REWARD USING EXPECTED OUTCOME

The risk and reward of any trade must always be considered when evaluating a trade. Individuals who focus only on reward will probably end up ruined by risk. Individuals who are concerned only about risk would never invest in anything because there is always the chance of losing money, no matter what the investment. Curiously enough, *not* investing and placing one's money under the mattress is ironically a form of speculation because the investor has chosen to keep money in the form of cash. There is no way of getting around it, we always take on risk no matter what we do or don't do.

We have looked at different kinds and ways to measure risk and reward. The next step will be to combine risk and reward to see how they relate to each other. One of the simplest ways to look at risk and reward is by calculating the expected outcome of an event. The expected outcome in trading is important because we must not only focus on simply how much might be made or lost, but rather what the combined chances of a profit and loss are together. The expected outcome of an event is the sum of the chances of each element of the event occurring and may be calculated as:

$$\text{Expected outcome} = \sum_{i=1}^{n} w_i\,(p_i)$$

where w_i = chance of event i occurring

p_i = event i

i = period when event happens

n = total number of events

The expected outcome is easy to calculate so let's look at an example. If we expect to make \$100 on 50% of our trades and lose \$50 on the other 50%, what is the expected outcome after two trades? The expected outcome is:

Expected outcome = $100 \cdot 0.5 + 100 \cdot 0.5 - 50 \cdot 0.5 - 50 \cdot 0.5$

= \$50

After two trades we can expect to make \$50 because half the time we will make \$100 and half the time we will lose \$50. On average, we can expect to make \$25 (50/2) per trade.

Remember Sharky and Lucky? They are still playing so now we can see what the chances of winning and losing are, and the amounts each might make in Table 20.1:

TABLE 20.1

	Chance of Win	Chance of Loss	Potential Profit	Potential Loss
Lucky	0.0000001	0.9999999	10,000,000	1
Sharky	0.5	0.5	1,000	1,000

Using the equation, the expected outcome is:

Expected outcome$_{Lucky}$ = $0.0000001 \cdot 10{,}000{,}000 + 0.9999999 \cdot (-1)$

= 0

Expected outcome$_{Sharky}$ = $0.5 \cdot 1{,}000 + 0.5 \cdot (-1{,}000)$

= 0

The expected outcome in this example is zero so neither can expect to profit over the long run. In fact, the expected outcome was purposely set to zero to make the reward the same for either strategy. Our original concern regarding Lucky's profit being much greater than Sharky's is now answered since both strategies offer the same expected outcome. We can now determine in Chapter 21 if one strategy is more risky than another.

Perhaps you might have noticed that we used the expected outcome equation in a previous calculation. Remember when we determined the risk of loss for Lucky and Sharky by multiplying the amount of loss by the chance of loss? We arrived at an expected loss or expected outcome of loss for both Lucky and Sharky. Now we are looking at the expected outcome for both risk and reward.

What if Sharky is a good trader? He will then have a much better chance of making money, and in fact his expected outcome will be positive. Alas the same cannot be said for Lucky. The expected outcome addresses the original objection of not including the reward in the analysis. Which strategy is more risky? We will see in Chapter 21.

Expected outcome provides an indication of whether a strategy will be profitable in the future. Every trader must develop a trading method which will yield a positive expected outcome. Anyone developing a trading method with a negative expected outcome will eventually go broke.

Expected outcome is helpful in looking at all the possibilities of a trading event and determining whether one can make or lose money. It is a guide, but remember the key word—expected. The expected outcome is what we hope to achieve over time, assuming our input variables and assumptions are correct. It is not what we are due or will always realize.

CONCLUSION

Risk and reward is the most important relationship to consider when trading. We looked at ways of evaluating risk and reward, and investigated ways of combining them to get a better understanding of the crucial relationship of risk and reward.

CHAPTER 21

Drawdown and Return On Investment

If making money is a slow process, losing it is quickly done.

Ihara Saikaku

Chapter 20 introduced the concept of risk and reward. This chapter will continue to develop the idea, first on a practical basis through drawdown, and then on a theoretical level by the theory of runs for trading. Every trader should have a thorough understanding of drawdown because anyone who trades will experience it.

CHANCE AND AMOUNT OF A SERIES OF LOSSES

Chapter 20 dealt with one type of risk inherent in trading pertaining to a severe loss caused by uncontrollable risk. Although we can never be absolutely certain, a severe loss should never be much greater than 10% of the contract price in extreme situations. *For most traders there is another type of risk which is usually far more insidious. The trader must also be concerned about the chance of a series of losses occurring. This type of risk is far more prevalent, and usually contributes to much greater losses, than uncontrollable risk.*

The risk of a series of losses is much harder to determine because it is dependent on the losses in a series of trades, as opposed to the loss on one trade. The risk of a series of losses is also beyond the control of a trader. We can try to limit how much is lost on a trade, but there is no way to limit a series of consecutive losses. Even if we are conservative and risk 2% of our initial capital on each trade, it is very possible we could have ten losing trades in a row and wind up losing 20% of our capital. This is twice as much as the 10% amount associated with a severe uncontrollable loss, and yet we are being more conservative.

What are the chances of ten losing trades in a row, or any series of losses occurring? There is a theoretical way of developing an estimate of the chances of a series of losses occurring called the theory of runs. There is also a practical way of getting an estimate called drawdown and maximum drawdown. Let's learn about both ideas next.

DRAWDOWN

Before discussing drawdown it may be helpful to see why it is important by an analogy. The idea behind drawdown is similar to the concept of cash flow analysis in a business, or cash flow on a personal basis such as balancing a checkbook at home. Cash flow in a business is the amount of money needed to maintain day to day business operations. If cash flow becomes seriously deficient, the company may be forced to declare bankruptcy because it cannot meet its financial obligations. This could happen even if the company is profitable.

This idea applies just as well on a personal level, such as when we need to balance our checkbook. If we do not have enough cash in our checking account, our checks will bounce irrespective of how much money we make at work or have in the savings account. At the end of the year most of us will find we have deposited enough money in the account during the year to meet all our written checks. However, there may have been certain times during the year when there was a cash deficiency and there was not enough money to write a check.

Every trader faces the same problem of going through a bad trading period. No matter how proficient we are in trading, there will be times when we lose money. Let's think of drawdown as the amount of money lost in trading during a particular period of time. **Drawdown** *is a way of measuring the flow of money going into or out of an account due to trading losses and profits.*

Drawdown is determined by reviewing the winning and losing trades over a period of time. Money withdrawn or deposited to an account is not included in the computation of drawdown. Drawdown is calculated using the following three steps:

Steps to Calculate Drawdown:

Step 1. Scan from the beginning of the period for the first losing trade while disregarding any profitable trades. The first losing trade becomes the drawdown.

Step 2. After identifying the first losing trade and drawdown, add every subsequent trade to the drawdown (a winning trade reduces the drawdown and a losing trade increases the drawdown). Continue this calculation until the drawdown is zero or positive. If the drawdown is positive reset it to zero.

Step 3. If the drawdown reaches zero again, scan the subsequent trades for the first losing trade while disregarding any profitable trades as in step one. The first losing trade becomes the new drawdown and continue as in step two.

Assuming 1 trade per month, the following series of trades and calculations for drawdown are presented in Table 21.1.

The drawdown is calculated in the following way:

Step 1. January—The first trade is profitable so it is disregarded.

February—A losing trade of $900 occurs so the account is debited or "drawn down" by $900, making the drawdown –$900. You may be wondering why the $4,300 is not included in the calculation, but this should soon become apparent. Since this is the first losing trade we go on to step 2.

TABLE 21.1

Trade	Month	Net Profits	Cumulative Profits	Drawdown	Calculation for Drawdown
1	Jan	4,300	4,300	0	0
2	Feb	–900	3,400	–900	–900
3	Mar	1,200	4,600	0	–900 + 1,200
4	Apr	100	4,700	0	0
5	May	–2,400	2,300	–2,400	–2,400
6	Jun	–800	1,500	–3,200	–2,400 – 800
7	Jul	1,000	2,500	–2,200	–3,200 + 1,000
8	Aug	–1,600	900	–3,800	–2,200 – 1,600
9	Sep	1,500	2,400	–2,300	–3,800 + 1,500
10	Oct	–400	2,000	–2,700	–2,300 – 400
11	Nov	3,600	5,600	0	–2,700 + 3,600
12	Dec	1,000	6,600	0	0

Step 2. March—A winning trade of $1,200 occurs so we add $1,200 to the –$900 drawdown and obtain $300. Since the drawdown is now positive it is reset to zero and we go on to step 3.

Step 3. April—The next trade is a winner so it is disregarded.

May—A losing trade of –$2,400, so the drawdown is now –$2,400.

June—The losing trade of –$800 is added to the drawdown of –$2,400 so the new drawdown is –$3,200. Since the drawdown is negative we continue adding trades until the drawdown is zero or positive.

July—The winning trade of $1,000 is added to the drawdown, reducing it to –$2,200.

August—The losing trade of –$1,600 is added to –$2,200, increasing the drawdown to –$3,800.

September—The winning trade of $1,500 reduces the drawdown to –$2,300.

October—The losing trade of –$400 increases the drawdown to –$2,700.

November—The winning trade of $3,600 decreases the drawdown to zero.

December—The next trade is ignored since it is positive.

FIGURE 21.1
Drawdown is the amount lost at a specific time from the previous
equity high. The underlined numbers represent the drawdown at the
specific time from the previous equity high.

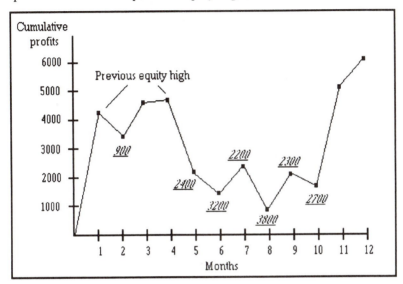

The cumulative profits in the table are graphed in Figure 21.1
to depict the drawdown. Notice how a drawdown begins whenever
a loss occurs after a new high in cumulative profits is reached. For
example, a drawdown occurs in the second month with the –$900
loss, and also in the fifth month with the –$2,400 loss. However,
a drawdown does not occur in the fourth month, even though a
new equity high is reached in the third month because there was
a profit in the fourth month. From this observation we can develop
the following definition for drawdown. **Drawdown** *refers to the
amount of equity lost or drawn down at a particular time from the
previous equity high point.*

Why do we need to understand drawdown? To fully answer
this question we need to explore one more concept—maximum drawdown.

MAXIMUM DRAWDOWN

Maximum drawdown is much easier to determine. **Maximum drawdown** *is the largest drawdown which has occurred to date.* Every new high in the drawdown becomes the new maximum drawdown.

Using the previous results the maximum drawdown is presented in Table 21.2.

TABLE 21.2
Maximum Drawdown Calculations

Trade	Month	Net Profits	Cumulative Profits	Drawdown	Maximum Drawdown
1	Jan	4,300	4,300	0	0
2	Feb	-900	3,400	-900	-900
3	Mar	1,200	4,600	0	-900
4	Apr	100	4,700	0	-900
5	May	-2,400	2,300	-2,400	-2,400
6	Jun	-800	1,500	-3,200	-3,200
7	Jul	1,000	2,500	-2,200	-3,200
8	Aug	-1,600	900	-3,800	-3,800
9	Sep	1,500	2,400	-2,300	-3,800
10	Oct	-400	2,000	-2,700	-3,800
11	Nov	3,600	5,600	0	-3,800
12	Dec	1,000	6,600	0	-3,800

Some other results are:

Total profits = $12,700
Total losses = $6,100

The net profit is $6,600

Winning trades = 7
Losing trades = 5

Beginning in January, the maximum drawdown is zero because the drawdown is zero. The maximum drawdown is -$900 in February when the drawdown becomes -$900. It remains at -$900 in March and April, even though the drawdown is zero because the largest drawdown in the first four months was -$900. In May and June the drawdown reaches new highs so the maximum drawdown increases to -$2,400 and -$3,200, respectively. In July, the drawdown declines but the maximum drawdown remains at -$3,200. In August, the drawdown reaches the highest amount and the maximum drawdown becomes -$3,800 and remains there for the rest of the year.

From this example we may infer that drawdown is a continuous calculation or flow of capital, whereas maximum drawdown is a snapshot or static picture of the largest drawdown that has occurred during the period. **Maximum drawdown** *is the largest drawdown during the entire period and therefore the worst case scenario.* Maximum drawdown is also called largest drawdown, maximum peak to trough, and maximum retracement. Figure 21.2 shows the cumulative profits and depicts the maximum drawdown.

FIGURE 21.2
Maximum drawdown represents the greatest equity drawdown that has occurred to date. The underlined numbers represent the maximum drawdown to date.

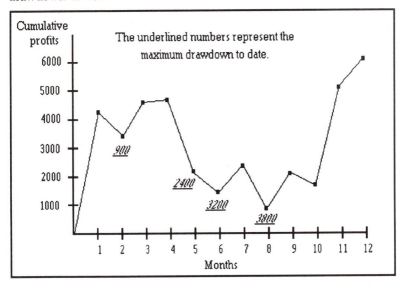

Drawdown may be measured on either a real time or theoretical basis. If drawdown is measured on a real time basis, it provides a picture of how much money was required to actually trade under the most adverse conditions. If drawdown is measured by theoretical trades with a mechanical trading method, it provides an indication of the absolute minimum amount of capital that might be required to trade the system in the future. However, additional capital will more likely be needed when actually trading a mechanical trading method based on theoretical drawdowns. A thorough and prudent analysis of maximum drawdown is a good start in determining the initial amount of money required to trade.

TWO SCENARIOS

You may be wondering why the first trade of $4,300 is not included in the drawdown calculation. Remember the concept behind drawdown—the amount of money required over a particular period of time to retrace back to the highest point. It is irrelevant how much money is in the account before a losing trade occurs. It is also irrelevant if money is deposited or drawn out of the account. We are only concerned with the amount of money lost in trading after one or more losing trades occur. Why is this so important? To answer the question, let's look at the situation from two different perspectives.

Scenario 1. Assume in February a friend suggested that you invest your money with him in a good trading program. You instead decide to take a prudent approach and wait to see some of the results. He casually mentions his profit of $4,300 in January. You hesitate and see him lose $900 in February, but then he goes on to make $1,200 in March and $100 in April.

By now you are totally convinced of his trading prowess and decide to give him $7,000 which is more than six times the amount he has lost so far. He begins trading in May and loses $2,400. You are upset but assure yourself that the $4,300 trade is just around the corner. You watch him lose $800 in June and begin to have serious doubts since you are now down $3,200.

If you lose 50% of your capital you will get a margin call from the brokerage firm and will be forced to stop trading. You breathe a sigh of relief in July when he makes a $1,000 profit, but you are still down $2,200. In August your hopes are dashed as you lose $1,600 and have to stop trading as you have no more funds to put up and even less enthusiasm to resume the trading. You have lost a total of $3,800 and a lot of sleep.

Scenario 2. Donna has developed a technical trading system which had theoretical results similar to the yearly trading results presented in Table 21.2. She now wants to trade the system real time and decides to commence trading in January. She feels the overall results this year will be similar to the results last year, but realizes there is no way of predicting when a profitable or losing trade will occur in any month.

If the trading in January starts off just as well as last year, she will not need much money to initiate the trading. The first amount she makes will probably cover some of the ensuing losses. But what if the trading starts off as it did in May and she immediately loses money? In this case, she may need a reserve amount of money to weather the losses.

Perhaps you now realize that both scenarios ask the same question. What is the worst case scenario? In the first scenario the loss is exactly the same as the drawdown amount for the first year. In the second scenario the drawdown in the beginning of the new year may be similar to the drawdown amount in the previous year. You might counter that hitting a maximum drawdown period is a case of bad luck. Possibly it is, but you might be surprised how often "bad luck" occurs in trading.

WHAT DOES MAXIMUM DRAWDOWN TELL US?

The -$3,800 maximum drawdown represents the minimum amount of capital required to continue trading without liquidity problems. Trading is a continuum of winning and losing trades, where we never know if the next trade may bring untold wealth, severe loss, or, usually, something in between. We would all be much happier to start the new year with a $4,800 profit as in the previous example.

However, we can never know when initiating a trade, whether it will go for or against us. Drawdown provides a clue, or what to expect, if things do not go well.

Why not add the total losses and use this as a measurement of how much capital might be required? Isn't it possible to have all five losing trades in a row and therefore sustain a maximum drawdown of –$6,100? In fact, we could do this, and if we trade often, there is a very real chance of not only five, but ten or more losing trades in a row. But it is unrealistic to use all the losing trades sustained in a long time period or during a large number of trades. If the period spans a long time or contains hundreds or thousands of trades, the losses would be staggering and not portray a realistic view of potential drawdown. However, the maximum drawdown would probably be larger over a longer time period or large number of trades because there is a greater chance for a large series of losing trades to occur.

Is it appropriate to assume that the maximum amount of money required to trade the previous method will be the calculated –$3,800 maximum drawdown? The answer is a resounding no. Maximum drawdown is a guide which yields an indication of how much we might possibly lose in a series of trades, but never guarantees against losing even more. The first year is a small test period and the results could be much better or worse in another market or year.

There have been situations where actual maximum drawdowns have exceeded theoretical or historical figures by as much as two to three times. This by no means invalidates using maximum drawdown as a good estimate for initial capital requirements. What this does suggest is to use a multiplying factor of at least 3, 10, 20 or perhaps 50 times the theoretical or historical maximum drawdown, depending on your risk tolerance and how accurately the previous drawdown might reflect current conditions.

In the example, the maximum drawdown is –$3,800 so a trader would need at least $3,800 to trade this strategy. Although the chances of hitting a bad streak of losing trades might be small, frequent trading increases the chances of hitting a severe period of losing trades. Every trader will hit a maximum drawdown, but, more importantly, every trader must always face the possibility of a new maximum drawdown. Therefore, every trader must consider ways to reduce the chances of a large and potentially debilitating maximum drawdown. Maximum drawdown provides us with an indication of how much we might lose employing a certain trading strategy. Now, to finally answer the question—What does maximum drawdown tell us? If we have a long enough real time track record, or a realistic theoretical track record, maximum drawdown will provide an indication of the following:

1. Maximum drawdown provides us with an indication of how much we might lose on one or a series of losing trades.

2. Maximum drawdown will provide us with an indication of how often a large loss or a series of losing trades might occur.

Does this sound familiar? *Since risk is the amount and probability of an adverse or series of adverse events occurring, maximum drawdown is one of the best ways of assessing risk in trading. In essence, maximum drawdown is one of the best ways to measure risk in trading.* Maximum drawdown indicates the amount and chance of a series of losses. There are other means to assess risk, but evaluating drawdown and maximum drawdown is an excellent start.

We usually know how much we intend on risking for one trade. We now have an idea with maximum drawdown how much might be lost on a series of losing trades. Maximum drawdown is an important link in showing us the risk inherent in trading.

RETURN ON INVESTMENT (ROI)

Let's take a break from risk and look at reward. How should we measure reward? If you guessed return on investment then you are right! What is ROI?

Return on investment (ROI) *is the amount made or lost in a certain period of time divided by the amount invested.* We often look at reward on a relative basis using the ROI calculation:

ROI = profits/investment

If an investor buys a stock for $100, and sells it one year later for $120 while also collecting a $5 dividend, the ROI is:

$$ROI = [(120 - 100) + 5]/100$$
$$= 25\%$$

ROI annualized is the return calculated on an annual basis. Since the investor held the position for a year the annualized return is also 25%. If the investor held the stock for only six months with the same return, the annualized return would now be:

$$ROI_a = [(120 - 100) + 5/100] \cdot [12 \text{ months/year} \cdot 6 \text{ months}]$$
$$ROI_a = 50\%$$

Why not use a reward calculation similar to the maximum drawdown calculation? What is the chance of a series of winning trades to get an optimistic viewpoint in trading? A series of winning trades is actually not relevant to a traders performance. For example, a trader who has a streak of 11 winning months in a row will still have poor annual performance if all the profits are lost in the twelfth month. A series of winning trades is great and desired, but they will never hurt the trader like the maximum drawdown will. No one leaves the trading business in distress after experiencing a series of winning trades. One or a series of losing trades can and have done this.

Return on investment is one of the best measurements of reward. ROI is an important calculation in judging performance because it tells us how much we have made for a given amount of capital invested. It tells us how efficiently our capital is used because a relatively high ROI will mean a high return for the amount of the investment.

MAXIMUM DRAWDOWN AND
RETURN ON INVESTMENT

Return on investment is a good measure of reward. Maximum drawdown is a good measure of risk. The combination of the two provides us with one of the most important relationships in trading—the risk/reward ratio, or the relationship of how reward varies with risk. The link of ROI and maximum drawdown provides an indication of the risk reward ratio of a trader or trading method.

In the previous example a profit of $6,300 is achieved at the end of the month. Since the maximum drawdown of –$3,800 shows the minimum capital required to trade the strategy, we now possess a risk and reward relationship. In other words, we need at least $3,800 to make $6,300. Multiplying the maximum drawdown by a multiple amount provides a more realistic indication of how much money might be required to trade a strategy. Let's use three for now to get:

$$\text{Capital} = 3 \cdot \$3,800$$
$$= \$11,400$$

Capital of $11,400 should provide a fair cushion to "comfortably" trade the strategy. But notice how the ROI changes:

$$\text{ROI}_1 = (\$6,300 \cdot 100)/\$3,800$$
$$= 166\%$$
$$\text{ROI}_2 = (\$6,300 \cdot 100)/\$11,400$$
$$= 55\%$$

The ROI drops dramatically from 166% to 55% and it is still uncertain if 3 is a good multiple or perhaps even a larger multiple should be used. This can only be resolved when we fully cover total amount to risk on any trade in the ensuing chapters. We will actually need more money to trade the strategy because of margins. Drawdown calculations usually only refer to trading amounts so margins must be added to the amount to get a better idea of the initial capital requirements.

Maximum drawdown provides us with one of the best ways of measuring risk in trading. The trader should be willing to risk at least $3,800 or the maximum drawdown in trading the strategy. Maximum drawdown gives us an indication of what the chance of loss, as well as what the amount of loss might be when we trade. Let's look at Tables 21.3 and 21.4 on the next page to see how maximum drawdown is helpful in evaluating two different trading methods.

Both trading methods yielded cumulative profits equal to $5,000 and the same number of winning and losing trades, but the way the profits and losses were achieved differed radically. The profits were much greater in method 2 but the losses were more severe.

TABLE 21.3
Method 1

Trade	Net Profits	Cumulative Profits	Drawdown	Maximum Drawdown
1	-900	-900	-900	-900
2	1,800	900	0	-900
3	-1,100	-200	-1,100	-1,100
4	2,400	2,200	0	-1,100
5	-1,000	1,200	-1,000	-1,100
6	1,900	3,100	0	-1,100
7	-1,300	1,800	-1,300	-1,300
8	1,700	3,500	0	-1,300
9	-1,200	2,300	-1,200	-1,300
10	2,700	5,000	0	-1,300

TABLE 21.4
Method 2

Trade	Net Profits	Cumulative Profits	Drawdown	Maximum Drawdown
1	2,000	2,000	0	0
2	-2,000	0	-2,000	-2,000
3	-1,500	-1,500	-3,500	-3,500
4	4,700	3,200	0	-3,500
5	-3,000	200	-3,000	-3,500
6	2,100	2,300	-900	-3,500
7	-4,100	-1,800	-5,000	-5,000
8	4,000	2,200	-1,000	-5,000
9	-2,000	200	-3,000	-5,000
10	4,800	5,000	0	-5,000

The results were not as exaggerated in method 1 as in method 2, which is reflected in the lower maximum drawdown in method 1. Figure 21.3 portrays the cumulative profits and maximum drawdown for methods 1 and 2, respectively.

FIGURE 21.3

The profits and losses are more exagerated in method two versus method one so the drawdown is greater in method two.

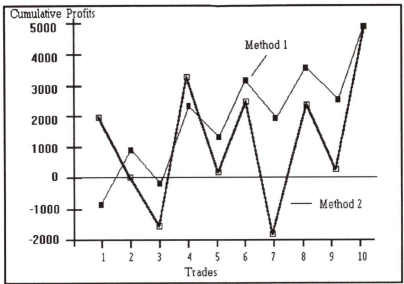

Which method would you prefer to trade, or are they the same? The only material difference between the methods was the maximum drawdown because the absolute return was the same. Assume you can expect similar results in the future. Using the maximum drawdown as a guide for risk, we only need to risk $1,300 with method 1, whereas we need to risk $5,000 with method 2. The maximum drawdown in method 2 is almost four times the amount as in method 1. In essence method 2 is almost four times as risky as method 1.

If we multiply maximum drawdown by three to get an idea of our initial capital requirements for both methods:

$$\text{Capital}_1 = 3 \cdot \$1,300$$
$$= \$3,900$$
$$\text{Capital}_2 = 3 \cdot \$5,000$$
$$= \$15,000$$

The ROI for each method will then become:

$$\text{ROI}_1 = (\$5{,}000 \cdot 100)/\$3{,}900$$
$$= 128\%$$
$$\text{ROI}_2 = (\$5{,}000 \cdot 100)/\$15{,}000$$
$$= 33\%$$

Method 1 is a much better, and less risky way to trade than method 2, since we can risk less capital and may achieve higher returns. Since ROI is a good measure of reward and maximum drawdown is one of the best measures of risk, we now have a most important way of relating risk and reward together. *Maximum drawdown is often used in conjunction with ROI to measure the performance of a theoretical trading system or the real time results of a futures trader. The importance of the relationship of maximum drawdown and ROI cannot be underemphasized because we now can evaluate the risk and return in trading. The combination of ROI and maximum drawdown is certainly one of the most important relationships in analyzing reward and risk in trading.*

Maximum drawdown and ROI provide an indication to the following questions:

1. How much money is required to initiate a strategy?
2. What is the risk/reward ratio?
3. Is this a good trading strategy?

STERLING RATIO

The Sterling ratio is a measure of the relationship between ROI and maximum drawdown. The Sterling ratio is calculated as follows:

Sterling ratio = ROI/maximum drawdown

A high ROI and low maximum drawdown are always desired, so the higher the Sterling ratio the better the performance. The Sterling ratio for the previous set of results is calculated as follows:
For method 1:

Profit   = \$10,500
Maximum drawdown = \$1,300
Sterling ratio$_1$ = \$10,500/\$1,300
                          = 8

For method 2:

Profit   = $10,500
Maximum drawdown = $5,000
Sterling ratio$_2$ = $10,500/$5,000
                        = 2

The Sterling ratio is 8 for method 1, or four times better than method 2, so method 1 is better by providing an equal return with less risk. This confirms our conclusion in the previous section that method 1 is a better strategy.

USING ROI AND MAXIMUM DRAWDOWN FOR DETERMINING CAPITAL REQUIREMENTS

The previous example shows that we can improve the ROI if we know how to reduce the maximum drawdown. The examples were idealized and most of us would prefer to trade the first method. But is it really possible to have results similar to method 1, or are we totally at the mercy of the market? Is maximum drawdown strictly a function of chance, or can we somehow develop a strategy that yields results similar to method 1? We will look at ways to do this in the optimization section.

Why not just be safe and multiply maximum drawdown by 100? You can, and some conservative traders may do this. But risking too little capital is not always the best strategy either because your capital is then underutilized. ROI drops off as you increase your initial investment, so the key is to find an ideal range where you are comfortable with the amount of reward given the level of risk.

PROS AND CONS OF MAXIMUM DRAWDOWN

There are some weaknesses in using maximum drawdown as a measure of risk when testing a theoretical trading system:

1. *A series of losses is arbitrary when testing a theoretical trading method and therefore maximum drawdown is an arbitrary measurement.* Assume you have just tested two systems which yield the results in Table 21.5:

TABLE 21.5
A Comparison of Trading Systems

Trade	Net	System 1 Cumulative Profits	Drawdown	Maximum Drawdown
1	100	100	0	0
2	-50	50	-50	-50
3	100	150	0	-50
4	-50	100	-50	-50
5	100	200	0	-50
6	-50	150	-50	-50
Trade	Net	System 2 Cumulative Profits	Drawdown	Maximum Drawdown
1	100	100	0	0
2	-50	50	-50	-50
3	-50	0	-100	-100
4	-50	-50	-150	-150
5	100	50	-50	-150
6	100	150	0	-150

The cumulative profits of $150 are the same for both systems but the maximum drawdown is three times greater in system 2 because of the consecutive losses experienced in system 2. The consecutive losses in system 2 might be considered bad luck, so neither system may be judged better than the other. Maximum drawdown (as well as any other performance measurement) is a meaningless measurement in this example because the sample size is small. What if there were 1,000 trades and 500 losses occurred in a row? Perhaps this string of losses might instead indicate something wrong about the trading system.

The real question is how well does a theoretical drawdown portray the possible future drawdown when actually trading? Actual drawdown, like any other performance measurement such as profits and losses, or percentage winning trades, may vary greatly from theoretical results. The idea in testing theoretical methods is to have a framework from which to develop a crude approximation of risk and reward. When large sample sizes are used, a simulated maximum drawdown becomes a reasonable approximation of what may happen in the future.

It is true that maximum drawdown is somewhat arbitrary (similar to life), but this is not an argument against using drawdown as a measure of risk. Any measurement has some amount of randomness inherent because every market has an element of randomness. Maximum drawdown is a very real concern when actually trading. We cannot tell our broker to disregard how much has been lost so far—it will eventually be made up in the long term.

2. *Greater maximum drawdowns yield a greater ROI.* This idea is simply not true. Some traders ardently believe greater profits come at the expense of larger maximum drawdowns. In fact, some argue that the greater the drawdown the more potential for profit of a trading system. These two ideas are blatantly false. It is true that some trading methods yield a higher ROI and concomitantly higher drawdowns. However, there are other systems which yield a higher ROI and lower drawdowns, and still other systems which yield high drawdowns and low or negative returns. When actually trading, a person who is aggressive and risks more capital will probably have higher drawdowns and potentially a higher ROI, but this is a function of capital risked and independent of the trading method.

There is simply no mathematical theorem which proves that higher drawdowns yield higher returns, or that a higher ROI comes at the expense of higher drawdowns. To suggest greater maximum drawdowns yield a greater ROI assumes that risk is always exactly proportional to return, and this is not true. In other words, the relationship of risk and reward does not have to be linear. Sometimes a much greater risk must be taken to obtain a slightly higher ROI. Look at the performance of Commodity Trading Advisors (CTAs) and note how some have consistently higher ROI to maximum drawdown ratios than other CTAs. The CTAs which had a higher ROI and lower drawdowns may have been "lucky," but I'll still put my money with them.

3. *The chance of a severe loss due to uncontrollable risk is a better estimate of risk.* A severe loss is always a concern but is really independent of any trading method. Any trading method, irrespective of how well it has performed in the past, may yield a trade in the future which incurs a severe loss due to uncontrollable risk. A late breaking news event may occur after the markets close, which could turn an overnight position into a severe loss before the trader has a chance to exit. Even during the trading day, the market may make a violent move which makes it difficult to exit without incurring a severe loss. The chance of a severe loss is the same for any trading method, but partly dependent on the market because some markets have greater dollar moves than others. It is wise to appreciate the possibility of a severe loss, but it is equally important to understand the chance of a series of losses.

4. *The amount of a severe loss due to controllable risk is a better estimate of risk.* Some traders believe reviewing the history of a theoretical method and singling out the largest loss is a good way to measure risk. This is one good way to determine risk but the probability side of risk is missing. What is the chance of one large loss or a series of large losses occurring? A trader will have to prepare for a much greater series of losses if there is a reasonable chance for a string of large losses.

5. *Each trade is an independent event, so drawdown can vary greatly.* A series of losses may occur which are related. For example, an increase in the inflation rate might cause the bond market to sink and gold to rally. A trader long the bonds and short gold would not perceive both losses as independent events. Large drawdowns may occur all at once because a sudden change in bullish or bearish perception may cause many markets to change direction immediately. A trading method may yield signals concurrently, creating the potential for large profits or losses to occur at the same time. This would be reflected in the drawdown estimate, especially when more than one market is analyzed.

Summary of Drawdown

One thing is quite clear about drawdown. A maximum drawdown of 100% means the trader must stop trading and look for another way to make a living. Any other performance measurement, no matter how enticing or provocative, is meaningless when all the trading capital is lost. As mentioned in Chapter 20 the preservation of capital is of paramount concern to the trader. Maximum drawdown is a very clear and precise way to measure the preservation of capital. *The good trader will always appreciate the importance of being able, both financially and mentally, to trade tomorrow no matter how bad today was.*

THEORY OF RUNS

What are the chances of a series of bad trades happening? The question of a string of bad trades occurring is ignored by some traders. Many more traders answer the question with Murphy's Law—Anything that can go wrong will go wrong. Although this is a pessimistic way of viewing the problem, it's probably a good start, especially when it comes to trading. However, we will try to be more objective and look at what the possibilities are of a series of events occurring.

We first need to know what the chance of one event is to determine what the chance of a series of the same events may be. If a coin is flipped the chance of a tail or head appearing is 1/2. What are the chances of flipping two tails in a row? *The probability of a series of events happening is the product of the probability of each independent event occurring.*

Probability of a series of independent events occurring = p^n

where p = probability of the event happening

n = number of times the event occurs

What are the chances of heads occurring 3 times in a row when flipping a coin?

The chance of a head is 1/2 in any one flip. Therefore, the chance of heads coming up 3 times in a row using the equation is:

$$\text{Probability of a series of events occurring} = (1/2)^3$$
$$= (1/2 \cdot 1/2 \cdot 1/2)$$
$$= 1/8$$

TABLE 21.6
Possible Combinations for 3 Tosses of a Coin

1	H	H	H
2	H	H	T
3	H	T	H
4	T	H	H
5	H	T	T
6	T	H	T
7	T	T	H
8	T	T	T

There is a 1 in 8 chance of this happening. We could also say the event had a 12.5% chance of occurring (i.e., $1/8 = 0.125$). Table 21.6 presents the matrix of possibilities each having a chance of 1 in 8 of occurring.

If heads came up 3 times in a row, what is the chance of a head appearing on the next toss? The answer is 1/2, no matter how many times heads or tails has come up before because the flipping of a coin is an *independent event*. An independent event is one which is not affected by any other event. Therefore, the coin has no memory of what occurred before. What are the chances of flipping a head 4 times in a row? Using the equation the chance is $(1/2)^4 = 1/16$ or a 1 in 16 chance of heads occurring 4 times in a row.

APPLICATIONS TO TRADING

The theory of runs has quite useful applications in trading to determine the chance of a series of winning or losing trades in a row. Some traders seem to be more concerned with the chances of a series of profitable trades occurring in a row. Many profitable trades are always welcome, but they will not put the trader out of business or deplete the trader's funds. Instead, we *should be keenly aware of what the chances are of a series of losing trades in a row*. This stems from the fact that too many losses will ultimately bankrupt the investor. This is certainly one of the reasons that many people must cease trading careers, but there is also another reason. More often, traders will become so psychologically battered from a series of losing trades that they will no longer want to, or be able to, trade.

Let's see how we can use the equation in a trading example. Joe has devised a trading system which yields approximately 50% winning and losing trades. What are the chances of having 5 losing trades in a row? Using the theory of runs the answer is:

$$\text{Chance of 5 losing trades in a row} = (1/2)^5$$
$$= 1/2 \cdot 1/2 \cdot 1/2 \cdot 1/2 \cdot 1/2$$
$$= 1/32$$

There is a 1 in 32 chance, or almost a 3% chance, of 5 losing trades in a row. Pretty remote chance—or is it? First, remember this is an estimate and by no means a guarantee. He could have 10 losing trades in a row for a variety of reasons. Secondly, if he trades often, the 1/32 chance becomes very possible because the frequency of trading is great. If he makes 100 or more trades, there is a reasonable chance that 5 losing trades could occur in a row.

If Joe has $10,000 and risks $2,000 on each trade, there is a 1 in 32 chance of losing the entire $10,000. If he does not want to take this kind of risk what can he do? Reduce his risk on each trade to an amount he is comfortable with. If he only risks 10% on a trade, or $1,000, what is the chance of losing the entire $10,000? A series of 10 losing trades in a row would exhaust his capital therefore:

$$\text{Chance of 10 losing trades in a row} = (1/2)^{10}$$
$$= 1/1,024$$

There is approximately a 1 in 1,000 chance of losing all his capital. This is better than before but still may be on the high side. What is the right percentage? There is no exact amount because it is contingent on other factors but we will continue exploring this question in further chapters.

The **theory of runs** *is a way of measuring the chance of a series of runs going against or with you.* We are generally more concerned with the chance of a series of losing runs. This will help you in determining the proper amount of capital to risk for any one trade or series of trades. The theory of runs is a theoretical way of viewing the chance of a series of bad trades occurring. We

438

Chapter 21

should risk less than 5% of equity on any trade due to the possibility
of a series of losing trades. We will have more to say about this
in Chapter 26.

LIMITATIONS WITH THE THEORY OF RUNS

There are some constraints with the theory of runs which should
be understood before applying it for trading. They are:

1. *Independent events*: The chance of a series of two or more
events occurring assumes the events are independent. The coin has
no memory. Some trades are independent of each other but there
are other trades which are dependent, or have some relationship
to each other. For example, markets which are highly correlated
may not yield trades which are independent of each other. Similar
trades in the S&P500 and the NYSE will probably both prove profitable
or unprofitable, because both markets are highly related. Trading
the NYSE and orange juice futures would be a better example of
relatively unrelated trades and independent events.

If some markets are highly related does this imply the theory
of runs is not applicable? Not really. The theory of runs must be
used with caution (as any other trading measurement should) when
evaluating risk. If markets are somewhat related then there is a
greater chance of having a larger string of losses, but the theory
of runs is still a helpful guide.

2. *Probability of a losing trade*: The chance of heads or tails is
1/2 and always known. Although we may have a fair approximation,
we can never be certain of the chance of a losing trade in the
future. Markets and traders go through various phases which will
affect the percentage of losing trades. The percent of losing trades
may be very high one month and quite low another, and at least
appears to go beyond mere chance sometimes. The chance of a
losing trade is a function of the trader, method, and market and
not always precisely known like a coin toss.

3. *Amount of loss*: We can strictly regulate the amount of risk
and loss incurred on any trade. But we can never guarantee the
amount we might lose due to uncontrollable risk. Markets may race

beyond our protective stops or open limit against us, and we will not get filled at our intended price. These limitations do not mitigate the usefulness of the theory of runs. The trader should understand the benefits and liabilities of using the theory of runs in helping develop a trading plan. The theory of runs is a good start in determining the chance of a series of losses occurring. In general, it is always safer to estimate conservatively, partly due to the above limitations. For example, if there is a 20% chance of 5 losing trades in a row using the theory of runs, assume there actually may be a 30 or 40% chance depending on the above limitations. The experience of the trader will go a long way in dealing with these limitations.

LUCKY AND SHARKY

Hopefully you have not forgotten about Lucky and Sharky. Perhaps now we may be able to answer which of their strategies is more risky by looking at risk in terms of maximum drawdown and the theory of runs. What should the maximum drawdown of Lucky and Sharky be? Part of this answer will depend on how much money they risk, and how often Lucky buys a ticket and Sharky makes a trade. Let's assume they both risk $100,000 in a ten year period. Recall:

The chance of loss for Lucky = 0.9999999
The chance of loss for Sharky = 0.5

What are Lucky's chances of sustaining a $100,000 drawdown in a series of small $1 bets placed 100,000 separate times. Using the theory of runs the chance of losing the $100,000 is:

Chance of Lucky losing $100,000 = $(0.9999999)^{100,000}$

= approximately 1

There is a very high chance that Lucky's drawdown will be $100,000, resulting in him losing all his capital.

What are Sharky's chances of sustaining a $100,000 drawdown in a series of $1,000 losses? Since Sharky must lose $1,000 in 100 trades to lose $100,000, he must have 100 losing trades in a row. Using the theory of runs the chance of losing the $100,000:

Chance of Sharky losing $100,000 = $(0.5)^{100}$

= a very small number
but close to 0

Therefore, the chance of Sharky sustaining a $100,000 drawdown is very small. This could happen if Sharky trades a lot but it does not really matter. Sharky's theoretical drawdown will always be lower because of the theory of runs. Lucky may win three lotteries in a row but this will not affect the subsequent drawdown calculation.

Although the original question concerned risk, what is the reward or ROI for either person? If you recall, the expected outcome for both players was zero so the ROI is zero for both, and neither may expect to make money over the long run.

Is either strategy better? There is a subtle but salient difference between the two strategies even though the expected outcome is zero for each. Lucky's chance of losing all his capital is much greater because his drawdowns will be larger, so there is a better chance he will eventually have to stop playing. Sharky's chance of losing all his capital is so small because his drawdowns will be less so he can virtually continue playing forever. While neither may expect to make money Sharky can at least expect to continue playing indefinitely, whereas Lucky will more likely get "blown out" of the game.

The risk is much greater for Lucky than for Sharky because the chance of a large drawdown is greater. Since the reward is the same, which strategy would you choose? Sharky's strategy would always be better even if the expected outcomes were the same for both strategies because his risk would always be less than Lucky's.

If neither of them can win in the long run, why should either try? The odds are always against the lottery player and can be against the futures trader too. But, unlike the lottery player, the futures trader may be able to change the odds in his favor. The same cannot be said for the lottery player. Poor Lucky will always be unlucky.

CONCLUSION

This chapter reviewed different ways to measure risk and return. ROI and maximum drawdown provide some of the best indications of risk and reward in trading. There are many more simple and elaborate formulas to analyze trading performance. There are limitations with any measurements, including the ones just presented. Maximum drawdown is a practical, or real time, way of looking at risk. The theory of runs is a theoretical way of looking at risk. The combination of the two give us a powerful, theoretical, and practical way of evaluating risk in trading.

Reward is usually much easier to define and measure than risk because most investors view reward in the same way, but each investor has a different perspective about risk. Maximum drawdown, variance of returns, chance of a severe loss, and other indicators are all ways to measure risk. However, every trader must understand drawdown because every trader will experience drawdown.

CHAPTER 22

Other Measures
of Risk and Reward

Do I contradict myself?
Very well then I contradict myself,
(I am large, I contain multitudes.)

Walt Whitman, *Song of Myself*

We have looked at two ways to develop a perspective on risk and reward using expected outcome and the combination of maximum drawdown and ROI. This chapter will introduce other measurements which may be used to measure risk and return in trading. The chapter will also show how risk and return may be viewed when combining investments via portfolio theory.

STANDARD DEVIATION AS A
MEASURE OF RISK

The traditional means of viewing risk has been to measure the change in returns of a portfolio by calculating the standard deviation of returns. The calculation for the standard deviation was covered in the options section to measure the volatility of a security. Portfolios with larger standard deviations exhibit greater risk than those with smaller standard deviations. Risk is measured by viewing the consistency of returns. This measure is covered more fully in the options section.

CORRELATIONS

Another way of viewing risk is to observe how one investment correlates with another investment. Correlation refers to the way one variable relates to another variable. The correlation coefficient measures the relationship of two variables and may vary anywhere in the range between –1 and 1, depending on how the two variables are related. Three types of correlations within the range are:

1. *Perfect positive correlation*: Variables with perfect correlation have a coefficient equal to 1. The relationship of variable a and b in Figure 22.1 is an example of perfect correlation because both variables move in unison with each other.

2. *Not correlated*: Variables which are not correlated have a coefficient equal to 0. The relationship of variables b and c in Figure 22.1 is an example of behavior which is not correlated because the movement of one variable is unrelated to the movement of the other variable.

3. *Perfect negative correlation*: Variables exhibiting perfect negative correlation with each other have a coefficient equal to –1. The relationship of variable c and d in Figure 22.1 is an example of perfect negative correlation because the movement in c is exactly opposite to the movement in d.

Notice in Figure 22.2a, how combining a positively correlated investment with another positively correlated one tends to exaggerate profits and losses. When a positively and negatively correlated investment are combined in Figure 22.2b the losses from one are mitigated by the other, so the equity increase is much smoother. This is the ideal portfolio (though not so easily attainable) because there are virtually no drawdowns, but a high ROI.

FIGURE 22.1
Markets 1 and 2 exhibit perfect positive correlation. 2 and 3 are not correlated, and 3 and 4 exhibit perfect negative correlation.

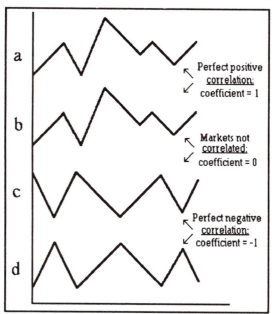

a

Perfect positive
correlation:
coefficient = 1

b

Markets not
correlated:
coefficient = 0

c

Perfect negative
correlation:
coefficient = -1

d

FIGURE 22.2
A portfolio of highly correlated investments will exhibit greater variations in equity than a portfolio of negative or uncorrelated investments.

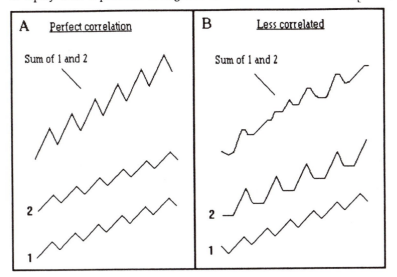

A   Perfect correlation

Sum of 1 and 2

2

1

B   Less correlated

Sum of 1 and 2

2

1

In trading, we often need to know how one market interacts with another market. We can use the correlation coefficients to measure the degree of relationship one market has with another. Markets often exhibit relationships somewhere between the extremes of perfect positive, negative, or zero correlation. A market with a 0.5 correlation would move in a similar manner with another market approximately 50% of the time. A market with a –0.5 correlation would move in an opposite way with another market about 50% of the time.

Correlations between markets are useful to know because they are helpful in determining portfolio diversification. A diversified portfolio is best achieved with markets which have correlation coefficients near zero, because the movement in one market will be unrelated to the movement in the other. Markets at the extreme end of the correlation spectrum such as –1 and 1 are closely related to each other and do not provide good diversification. In statistics correlations for linear regression models are often measured using the coefficient of determination (r^2) or the coefficient of correlation (r or $\pm\sqrt{r^2}$).

It may often be hard to find markets with zero correlation so the trader must choose ones which show as little correlation as possible. Other important considerations such as liquidity and volatility must also be assessed in deciding which markets to trade. It may be much better to trade a liquid market which has a coefficient of 0.5, versus trading an illiquid market which has a coefficient of 0.

One fundamental point of portfolio theory is that investments held together may offer less risk and more reward than investments held separately. This is the fundamental idea behind diversification, which will be covered in Chapter 23.

EFFICIENT FRONTIER

The traditional method of analyzing risk and reward has been through portfolio analysis. Markowitz developed some of the early ideas of portfolio theory such as efficient portfolios. Risk is defined as the variation in returns from an investment and is measured by the standard deviation of returns. An investment with a large deviation

FIGURE 22.3
A and *B* lie on the efficient frontier because they provide the highest reward for a given risk. The efficient frontier contains all optimal investments; *A* has less risk for the same reward as *C*; *B* has more reward for the same risk as *C*.

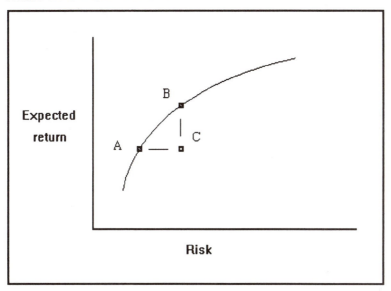

in returns would be considered more risky than an investment with a small deviation. Return is measured in the standard form as ROI.

Each investment has an expected risk and reward which may be depicted on a graph, as shown in Figure 22.3. Investment A provides a lower risk and lower return than investment B. Investors may choose one or both investments depending on their risk and return preferences, but neither investment is superior to the other. Investment C is not a good investment because it yields the same return with greater risk versus A, and a lower return with the same risk as B. No rational investor would prefer investment C to A or B, so A and B represent optimal investments.

A line drawn through all optimal investments is called the efficient frontier and represents the best investment for a given level of risk. *The efficient frontier depicts the relationship between risk and reward.* The relationship is normally a positively sloping curved line, as shown in Figure 22.3. The idea is simple—the greater the risk the greater the return. The curvature of the line may change or the line may shift depending on various economic factors. The efficient frontier may also be considered as a portfolio of assets. A portfolio containing investments on the efficient frontier would be termed an efficient portfolio because it yields the highest return for a given risk or lowest risk for a given return.

One important result of this relationship is the idea of marginal returns. The reward increases at a decreasing rate as the risk increases. In other words, we do not get double the reward for double the risk. This is a concept that most investors should be familiar with because many investments do not yield substantially higher returns with higher risk. In fact, some investments offer greater risk and less return and would be considered inefficient. As risk increases the increase in reward becomes marginal, or negligible, relative to the amount of risk incurred. Investments may become a lot riskier but they may not necessarily offer much more reward.

EFFICIENT FRONTIER AND
RISK-FREE ASSETS

Sharpe added to the study of portfolio theory by developing the capital asset pricing model (CAPM), which introduces risk-free assets on the efficient frontier. If risk-free assets, such as Treasury bills, are included then the efficient frontier line changes and becomes more linear, as shown in Figure 22.4. The inclusion of risk-free assets extends the efficient frontier beyond the initial boundaries.

Indifference curves are shown in Figure 22.5 and depict differing views regarding risk. Joe seeks more return for even a greater amount of risk—he is a risk seeker. Mary Beth looks for the same increase in reward for a given risk—she is risk indifferent. Theresa needs much more reward for a proportionate increase in risk—she is risk averse. Each individual has an indifference curve. Combining the indifference curves with the CAPM provides an idea of what type of risk and reward an individual should expect.

FIGURE 22.4
A has more reward for the same risk than B because risk-free assets are included in the A portfolio. The investment opportunities lie on the CAPM line when risk-free assets are included in a portfolio; this provides more reward for the same risk.

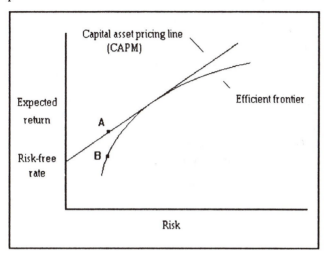

FIGURE 22.5
The indifference curves depict the type of risk profiles for each person.

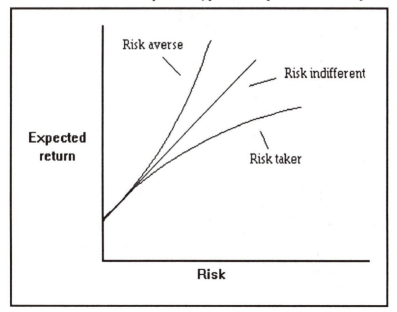

THE EFFICIENT FRONTIER
IS DYNAMIC

The efficient frontier is dynamic because investors' perceptions about each point on the line may change. Markets change because people require different investments during different times. Some investors want securities which offer more risk and return when economic conditions are favorable, but seek safer securities when the economic climate is uncertain or bad.

Securities may become under or overvalued for many reasons. The prospects for new securities may be difficult to determine, so there may not be reliable measures for their risk and reward characteristics. After a period of time, investors are better able to assess the benefits and liabilities regarding new securities. The risk and reward may change quickly because market fundamentals may change quickly.

SHARPE RATIO

The **Sharpe ratio** *is a measurement of the consistency of returns of a trading method or trader.* Returns that are highly variable cannot be relied upon as well as returns which are more steady. This can be an important consideration in choosing a CTA or developing a trading method. The Sharpe ratio is calculated as follows:

Sharpe ratio $= (r_a - r_f)/s$

where r_a = average return

   r_f = risk-free return

   s   = standard deviation of returns

Let's look at an example to determine the Sharpe ratio. Assume the risk-free rate is 6% so the monthly rate is $6/12 = 0.5\%$ per month. What is the Sharpe ratio for the series of returns in Table 22.1?

The average return of 5% is the same for both methods but note how method two exhibits much steadier and consistent returns than method one. Method two is preferable is the Sharpe ratio is the criterion for judging

TABLE 22.1
Percent Returns per Month

Month	Method 1	Method 2
1	10	0
2	40	10
3	–50	20
4	0	–10
5	100	10
6	–30	10
7	–40	–20
8	20	10
9	60	–10
10	–70	10
11	10	20
12	10	30
Average	5	5
Standard deviation	48	15
Sharpe ratio	(5–0.5)/48	(5–0.5)/15
	0.09	0.30

FIGURE 22.6
The variation in returns is much greater with method 1 versus method 2.

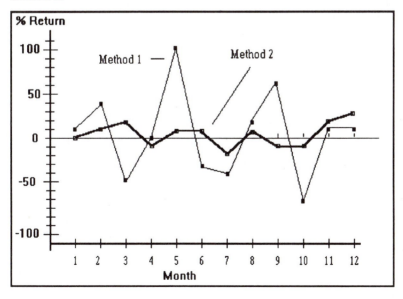

THE RISK OF RUIN

The risk of ruin calculation is related to the theory of runs, by providing an indication of the chances of a trader losing all initial capital under a given set of conditions. Assume the same amount is made or lost on every trade. The risk or chance of ruin can be determined by the formula:

$$R = \text{risk of ruin} = [(1 - A)/(1 + A)]^c$$

where p = probability of a winning trade

$1 - p$ = probability of a losing trade

$A = p - (1 - p)$ = is the trader's advantage

c = trading units of capital at the beginning

$p > 0.5$

$0 \leq R \leq 1$

The trader's advantage is an indication of the odds in favor of the trader, and must always be positive because p must be greater than 0.5. If p is less than 0.5, the risk of ruin will always be 100% because the amount won equals the amount lost. c is the number of equal capital units available for trading. If the trader has $100 and risks $10, c would equal 10.

Example. A trader has $90 and risks $30 on each trade. The chance of a winning trade is 55%. What is the risk of ruin?

$p = 0.55$

$c = 90/30 = 3$

$A = 0.55 - (1 - 0.55) = 0.10$

$R = [(1 - 0.1)/(1 + 0.1)]^3$

$\quad = 0.55$

Therefore the risk of ruin is 55%.

There are more complicated formulas to deal with unequal losses and profits, which is closer to the real world. The calculations become more complex, but they do not necessarily provide any substantial advantages because every equation has constraints and drawbacks when simulating the real world. These are not criticisms of the formulas. The equations are worthy attempts to determine what types of risk might be encountered in trading. However, the trader must realize markets reflect the actions of people which may not always be easily analyzed with mathematical models.

MARTINGALE APPROACH

Martingale approached the theory of runs and risk of ruin from a different perspective. He developed his theory for gambling but it is easily transferable to the trading arena. He suggested doubling the bet after each consecutive losing wager until a winning trade occurs, recouping all the money lost. One winning trade would eventually compensate for all the previous losses, no matter how many losing bets occurred. A gambler would need to observe the number of times a bet might go against him to develop an idea of how much capital would be required to sustain a losing streak.

The problem with the Martingale approach is when the bets get doubled the sums begin to get enormous. The Martingale method will work with virtual certainty if the trader has an infinite amount of capital and time. No matter how great the string of losses, there should be at least one winning trade which will negate the losses. The Martingale method is highly recommended for those who have unlimited wealth and time. For the rest of us, this approach is one of the best ways to disaster and beyond. It is mentioned because people do use it in trading, but generally not for too long.

A REVIEW OF PERFORMANCE MEASURES
IN MONEY MANAGEMENT

The following section summarizes and includes a few more important performance measurements in trading. Assume the following results of a trading strategy:

$$
\begin{aligned}
\text{Investment} &= \$10,000 \\
\text{Profits} &= \$10,000 \\
\text{Losses} &= \$5,000 \\
\text{Net profits} &= \$5,000 \\
\text{Total trades} &= 25 \\
\text{Winning trades} &= 10 \\
\text{Losing trades} &= 15 \\
\text{Maximum drawdown} &= \$2,500
\end{aligned}
$$

Some of the performance measurements include:

1. *Return on investment:* Return on investment (ROI) is the amount made or lost in a certain period of time divided by the amount invested:

ROI = net/investment
ROI = $5,000/$10,000
ROI = 50%

2. *Profit to loss ratio:* The profit to loss (P/L) ratio is simply, total profits divided by total losses:

P/L = profits/losses
    = $10,000/$5,000
    = 2

The profit to loss ratio is a good indication of how efficiently one trades. For example, assume $5,000 is made with a different trading strategy, but total profits are $100,000 and total losses are $95,000. The profit/loss ratio is then 11% (100 · 100,000/95,000). Although there may be other merits to this strategy, the first method is probably a better and less risky way to trade.

3. *Percentage winning (or losing) trades to total trades:* This ratio is the number of winning trades divided by total trades:

Percent winning trades = winning trades/total trades
                        = (100) · 10/25
                        = 40%

This ratio can vary greatly among different traders. Many people believe that the best traders have a high percentage of profitable trades, but this is not necessarily true. Some of the most successful traders have percentages which may range from around the 10% level to the 90% range. This will be explored further in the optimization sections.

4. *Dollars per trade:* Dollars per trade is the amount of money made on average in any trade:

Dollars per trade = total net profit/number of trades
                  = $5,000/25
                  = $400

This ratio provides an indication of the average profit or loss per trade, which is helpful when considering commissions and slippage. It is not calculated so you will know what will be made on the next trade. Some trading systems which give frequent signals actually work, but when slippage and commissions are included the dollars per trade ends up zero or negative.

5. *Drawdown:* Drawdown refers to the amount of capital required in trading to retrace to the previous high. Drawdown indicates how much money might be required during bad trading periods, and how often they have occurred in the past.

6. *Maximum drawdown:* Maximum drawdown refers to the largest drawdowns observed in a trading period. Maximum drawdown is one of the best measures of risk, and is often used in conjunction with ROI to measure the performance of a trader or trading system.

7. *Sterling ratio:* The Sterling ratio is the ROI divided by the maximum drawdown:

Sterling ratio = ROI/maximum drawdown

= $5,000/$2,500

= 2

This ratio is often used in evaluating the performance of commodity trading advisors (CTA). A CTA is a money manager of commodity funds. The ratio is one of the best ways of assessing risk and reward, since it measures reward with ROI and risk with maximum drawdown.

8. *Sharpe ratio:* The Sharpe ratio is the average return divided by the standard deviation of the returns. Assume:

Average return = 5%

Standard deviation in returns = 0.10

Sharpe ratio = average return/standard deviation in returns

= 0.05/0.1

= 0.5

The higher the Sharpe ratio the less the change in returns has been, which means there is less variability in returns. The Sharpe ratio is helpful in assessing the deviation in returns for a trader or a trading system.

CONCLUSION

There are weaknesses in every measurement but this is not because the formulas are inaccurate or unrealistic. Behind the performance measurements of any real time trading result is a person. *We must never lose sight of the fact that the individual is the ultimate measure of how well he or she will do in the future.* The measurements are just guides as to how well the person has done in the past. They can never tell us exactly how well the person will do in the future.

Chapter 23 will look at the elements of risk more closely to see how we can maximize return and minimize drawdown.

Methods of Reducing Risk and Increasing Reward

It is easier to stay out than get out.

Mark Twain, *Pudd'nhead Wilson*

Losing money is the least of my troubles. A loss never bothers me after I take it. . . . But being wrong—not taking the loss—that is what does the damage to the pocketbook and to the soul.

Edwin LeFevre, *Reminiscences of a Stock Operator*

This chapter will cover some of the factors which affect risk and reward in trading. Our goal is to determine how to change the risk and reward factors in our favor, to reduce the risk and increase the reward in trading.

FACTORS THAT AFFECT RISK AND REWARD

Risk is a function of the amount of uncertainty that exists in a system or event. The more uncertain the outcome of an event the greater the risk. Some elements that affect uncertainty and contribute to risk in trading are:

1. Time.
2. Volatility.

3. Diversification.
4. Liquidity.
5. Bid and ask spread.
6. Slippage.
7. Market closed for trading.
8. Political and economic conditions.
9. Default of a company.
10. Limit moves in a market.

These factors may also affect the reward in a trade but in a different way. Let's review how each of these may affect risk and reward.

TIME

Time is one of the most important factors affecting uncertainty precisely because we can never be certain about the future. Time affects risk in trading in the following two ways:

1. The amount of risk in a security is partly a function of the life of the security. A 3-month Treasury bill should be less risky than a 20-year Treasury bond partly because the risk of default is much greater for a 20-year bond than a 3-month bill.

2. The amount of risk in a trade is partly a function of the amount of time the position is held. Holding a Treasury bond contract for three minutes should be less risky than holding a Treasury bill contract for three months.

The relationship of time versus risk is depicted in Figure 23.1. Risk increases with time but at a decreasing rate. This graph is similar to the normal yield curve in interest rates. The graph can change and become more linear or curved, and also shift with time.
Risk and time are inseparable. The longer a trade is held the greater the chances the market will go against the position, so risk increases with time. As soon as a trade is initiated, and until the time of exit, the trader is always at risk of the market going against

FIGURE 23.1
The relationship of risk versus time shows that risk increases with time at a decreasing rate.

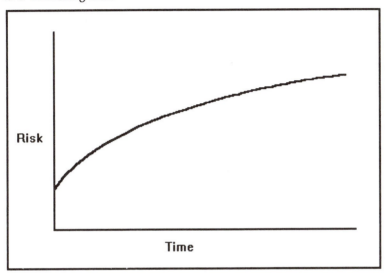

Risk

Time

the position. This is true irrespective of whether a profit or loss has been made. If there is a profit, it can always turn into a loss with time, and, of course, a loss can always become greater.

We may limit our losses by employing various strategies such as options, but this actually proves the point. Options may be used to limit our risk in time but we must pay for this protection. The risk of time is inherent in part of the price of the option.

The shorter the holding period for a trade the less the risk, but there is another factor which must be considered which is the potential for reward. We should seek to hold onto a trade for as short a time as possible to reduce risk, but as long a time as possible to realize a potential reward.

Reward does not necessarily increase with time, unlike risk, and this distinction is crucial. For example, a position held for a long period of time may simply lose more money, and may never realize any type of reward, but risk will always be present. The reward would definitely not increase, or even be present with time, for an investor who stayed short the stock market from 1932 and held for ten or more years. The stock market had a major bottom in 1932 and has been in a sustained uptrend ever since. Anyone short this market from 1932 may find a reward in heaven, but certainly not in this world.

If reward is not a function of time, then what is? The potential reward increases with time in a trade but the actual reward may not. Anyone long the stock market from 1932 would face potential rewards for being on the right side of the market. What is reward a function of? *Reward is a function of the timing of entry and exit as opposed to the length of time a position is held. This has extremely important implications in trading.* A reward should result for someone long the stock market in 1932 because timing of entry was correct. Even properly timed short selling during the same period could have yielded reasonable profits.

Many people hope and believe that the longer they hold a trade, the better their chance for reward, but this may simply not be true. The potential reward is a function of time but the actual reward is not. *Risk is always present with time whereas reward may not be. Therefore, the risk in holding a position too long may negate any actual profit.* How often have you held onto a trade which was initially profitable in the hope of realizing further profits, but later watched it go against you?

What is the proper time to hold a trade to achieve a reasonable reward and not incur too much risk? There are no hard and fast rules in determining how long to hold a position. Most of the trades we do initiate are profitable at some time, whether it be for a minute, day or month. Some of the factors to consider are:

1. *Mechanical indicators*, such as technical or fundamental analysis, can provide us with clues as to good entry and exit points.

2. *Market personality*: Each market exhibits trends of varying size and duration. We may want to hold onto trades longer in markets which trend for longer periods of time. The currencies have manifest relatively large and broad trends, versus other markets which have been random or trendless.

3. *The era or time we are in*. As noted in the technical analysis section, the 1970's and early 1980's manifest large and broad trends

FIGURE 23.2
Sugar monthly chart

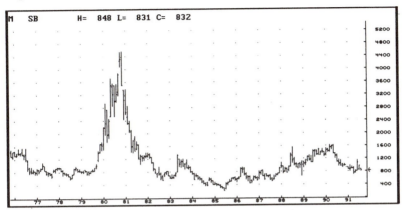

Source: Reprinted with permision, FutureSource, 955 Parkview Blvd., Lombard, IL 60148 800 621-2628

in many markets. The inflationary times had a lot to do with this phenomena. People believed prices would keep going higher and jumped onto the trend so as not to miss the move, which contributed to markets trending even more. When a new era of lower inflation began, many of the markets quieted down and became trendless and random. Without high inflation and the belief that prices would go even higher, commodities did not move with the characteristic urgency reminiscent of the previous era. Traders were still trying to catch the big trends in the late 1980's but they were not as prevalent because many other traders did not believe the markets would trend as greatly.

The monthly sugar chart in Figure 23.2 is an example of one market which was very active in the late 1970's and early 1980's. Note how much quieter it became toward the end of the 1980 decade. The trends were of a much greater magnitude in the early part of the decade.

4. *Money management*: Good money management can help in the timing decision. Timing of entry and exit, as well as an awareness of all types of risk in trading, will allow for more informed and better decisions. We will look into this in the diversification section.

5. *Psychology of the trader*: Perhaps most often the decision on how long to hold a position really becomes a function of the psychology of the individual. Many people simply cannot mentally or physically tolerate watching a position move for or against them for too long a period, while others dislike short-term trading. This will be investigated more fully in the psychology section.

Much more work needs to be done in the area of risk, reward, and time. Perhaps if we learn more about what time is, we will have a better idea of ways to work with it. Such a simple question as "What is time?" is actually a difficult, if not unanswerable, question. It is interesting to note that time has such a profound influence on our life, and yet, we know so little about it.

VOLATILITY

Volatility *refers to the change in price or return of the investment.* The simplest way of measuring volatility is by observing the absolute change in price. A much better way to analyze volatility is by measuring the percent change in price. This eliminates the distortion of a higher priced security, which may move more in absolute terms but less in percentage terms. For example, which security in Table 23.1 is more volatile?

TABLE 23.1

Security	Price	Change	% Change
A	10	1	10
B	100	5	5

The absolute change in security B is greater than security A. However, the percent change of A is greater than B, so A is more volatile than B.

The calculation of volatility is normally done using the standard deviation of prices which is covered in the options section. We will look at volatility in this section to see how it relates to risk and trading. Markets which exhibit a high volatility are generally more risky than markets which manifest low volatilities. October 90 heating oil in Figure 23.3 is an example of a market which rapidly undergoes a dramatic transformation from low volatility to extremely high volatility. The moves on an absolute and percentage basis were much greater, which increased the risk in trading.

Markets exhibiting a low volatility can change into highly volatile markets rather quickly. Markets which become volatile often do so because of important news events or unexpected developments. Unexpected or crucial news items can create huge increases in volatility, and dramatically change the fundamentals and character of the market. The petroleum market became quite volatile in one month when Iraq invaded Kuwait in the summer of 1990. The market stayed volatile for months and finally dropped in volatility as the war situation changed.

Highly volatile markets may quickly drop to lower volatility levels, but the transition sometimes takes longer. Markets often decrease in volatility after an important event, so longer periods of time may be required for the market to find a proper trading level and settle down. Therefore, increases in volatility may happen quite quickly, but decreases may be dragged out over longer periods of time.

Some markets tend to exhibit cyclical or seasonal volatility as mentioned in Chapter 17. The soybean market varies in activity but when weather problems such as a drought arise the market can go through a transformation from low to high volatility. These changes can often appear in the agricultural commodities because the weather can be highly unpredictable but greatly affect supplies.

Risk increases with more volatile markets because there is a greater chance of suffering larger losses. The potential reward is also greater with more volatile markets, but again, as with the time example, actual reward does not necessarily increase. Increased volatility will entail increased risk but may not assure more profits.

Trading markets which exhibit low volatility may reduce the risk in trading, but there can be problems with this approach. Markets which exhibit extremely low volatilities may also have poor reward potential, because there may not be enough movement for an adequate reward. Therefore, markets with low volatility may not necessarily offer good risk reward trading opportunities.

FIGURE 23.3
October 1990 heating oil

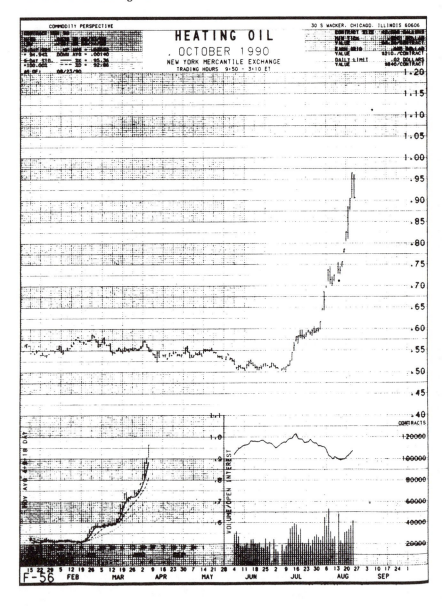

Low volatility markets often exhibit random or highly congested market patterns which may be very hard to trade. A random market will not afford any real possibility of profit. Congestion markets may be traded with counter trending methods, but the results may not always be good enough to merit continued trading. For example, even if we are successful in predicting these markets, the potential profits are often nullified by other real trading considerations. Problems of slippage, commissions, bid and ask spreads, and lack of movement will tend to reduce the already small profits typically offered by these markets.

Reward is generally much greater in higher volatility markets because there is much larger dollar movement. But again there may be a tradeoff in highly volatile markets. Although the reward may be greater, the risk is also much greater in markets of high volatility.

Slippage can be a serious problem in markets with higher volatility. Bids and asks may disappear in violent markets, and consequently fills can be quite costly. Trends are often more prevalent in markets with higher volatility but this is not always the case. The market may make large moves without any significant trend, but still maintain a high volatility. This can happen, especially after a large trending move has occurred. November 91 soybeans in Figure 23.4 became much more volatile in the middle of July, but the market ended essentially unchanged after the move. There is clearly more risk, but the reward seems less assured.

The soybean move is also a good example of how timing is important in reward. Anyone long soybeans near the bottom in July around 530 did not realize any greater reward by holding beyond August 2, though the risk was always present. Reward was actually reduced by holding for a longer period of time.

The trader must strike a balance. A market trading at a low volatility level with a small risk, but too small a reward, will probably yield small profits in the best case. The mental frustration in watching these markets do nothing, and getting chopped up in the process, can make them even less attractive for trading. A possible higher reward with a guaranteed higher risk and anxiety level can be found in high volatility markets. Holding positions in these situations where the slightest news can send the market wildly in any direction can be shear agony. The novice trader is best off choosing markets between

FIGURE 23.4

November 1991 soybeans

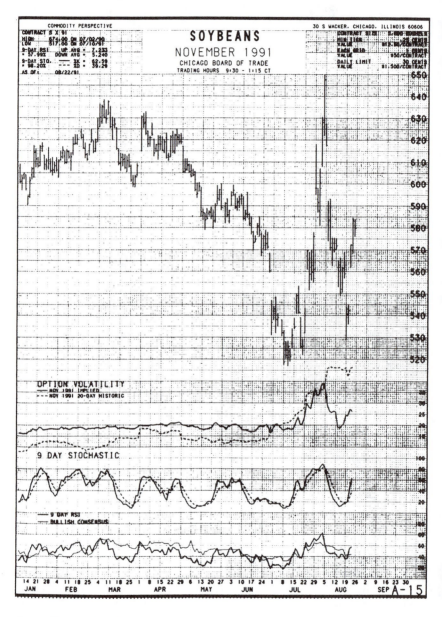

Source: Reprinted with permission, © 1991 Commodity Perspective, 30 South Wacker Drive, Suite 1820, Chicago, Illinois 60606.

these extremes, and leaving the high or low volatility ones for those who have experience with them.

What is too high or low a volatility? Volatility is a relative concept and partly a function of the price of the commodity. Volatility estimates should not be used in an absolute sense of being too high or too low. Volatilities should be compared on their current level, versus where they were in the past.

The base price of the commodity will also affect the volatility. Since volatility is a relative concept, a market may exhibit high volatility even if the absolute price moves are small because the price of the commodity is low. On the other extreme, a market may exhibit a low volatility, but large price moves because the base price is high. Common sense is again one of the best ways in determining how high or low the volatility is, and whether there are good risk reward characteristics in the market.

DIVERSIFICATION

Diversification is a way to achieve higher returns with the same or less amount of risk, or a way to reduce risk and achieve the same return. In essence, it is the best of all possible worlds if implemented correctly, so it is wise to see how diversification can help you. Even if you only trade one market or contract, there are still benefits which may be derived from diversification.

Before delving into diversification, we need to take a side trip and mention the concept of correlation.

Correlations

Market diversification is ideally achieved with securities which are not highly correlated. The September 91 S&P500 in Figure 23.5 and September 91 NYSE in Figure 23.6 are examples of markets which are highly correlated. Trading both of these will not provide much diversification because both markets will often yield similar signals which will ultimately result in similar profits and losses. However, September 91 soybean oil in Figure 23.7 might be a better choice for diversification since it is much less correlated with the stock market.

FIGURE 23.5

September 1991 S&P500

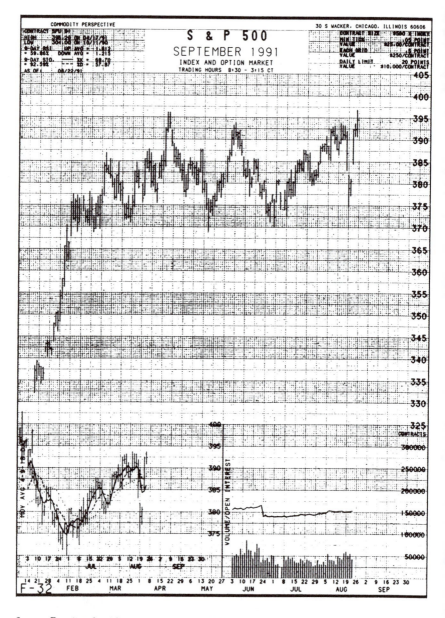

Source: Reprinted with permision, © 1991 Commodity Perspective, 30 South
Wacker Drive, Suite 1820, Chicago, Illinois 60606.

FIGURE 23.6

September 1991 NYSE composite

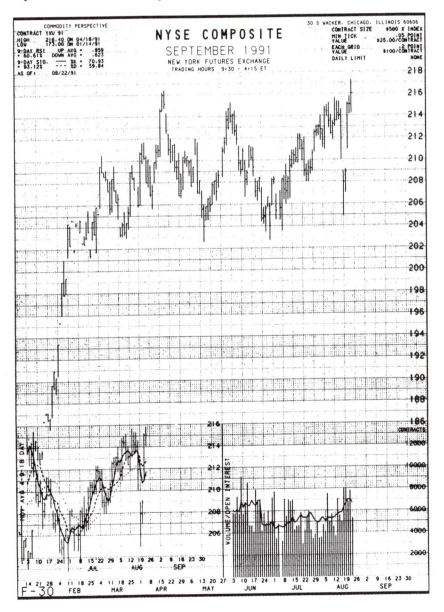

Source: Reprinted with permision, © 1991 Commodity Perspective, 30 South Wacker Drive, Suite 1820, Chicago, Illinois 60606.

FIGURE 23.7

September 1991 soybean oil

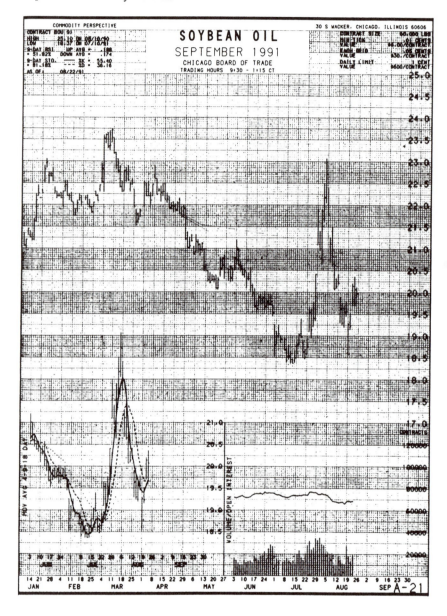

Source: Reprinted with permision, © 1991 Commodity Perspective, 30 South Wacker Drive, Suite 1820, Chicago, Illinois 60606.

Correlations are a guide but not a final answer in trade diversification. Markets can have more complex relationships with other markets that might not be apparent from the correlation coefficients. Coefficients may change with time, or one market may lead or lag another market. For example, two markets may exhibit highly correlated movement with each other at one time, but move in an unrelated or even opposite fashion another time. The stock and bond markets will often move in a highly related manner with each other. There are other times when the two markets will move in an unrelated manner, and still other times when the two markets move in the opposite direction to each other.

Certain markets may sometimes lead other markets, so a relationship is not always easy to discern. The bond market sometimes leads the stock market. This can occur during the early stages of an economic recovery when the bond market rallies first and the stock market follows. Leading and lagging relationships may not always be so easy to discern with correlation coefficients. There are other relationships which can be even more complex. The bond market may be affected by the crude oil or gold market because of inflation fears, but other times may not show a strong relationship with the same markets. Markets are sometimes correlated due to specific events or times and then resume trading with little or no correlation to each other.

The financial markets tend to be correlated with each other to certain degrees depending on the market and time. Many of the financial markets are interrelated with each other. Interest rates may have a great impact on the value of a currency or the stock market. Exchange rates can in turn affect the level of interest rates or the stock market. All the financial markets are affected by the state of the economy, and may react in a similar or different way to important news.

Some of the basic commodities such as the grains are related with each other, because a drought might cause all the grain markets to rise. Other commodities may not be as closely related with each other. For example, a rise in the price of coffee does not necessarily affect the price of live hogs. However, a severe drop or increase in the dollar may cause many commodities to rise or fall in unison, such as during the late 70's and early 80's when inflation was severe.

Ways to Diversify

The idea of diversification is easy to understand, but sometimes much harder to implement on a practical basis. It is clearly an important aspect of money management. Different ways to diversify include:

1. *Different market*: Trading different markets should tend to reduce risk and is probably the most familiar and widely used way of diversifying. Trading markets with low correlation coefficients is a good start in proper diversification, as mentioned in the correlation section.

How many markets should be traded to have a well diversified portfolio? Diversification increases with more markets but at a decreasing rate, as shown in Figure 23.8. Note how risk is substantially reduced with a few markets, but is only marginally reduced as more markets are added. The benefits of greater diversification by trading more markets drops substantially after only a few markets are chosen.

FIGURE 23.8
Risk versus diversification: Avoidable risk decreases with increased diversification at a decreasing rate.

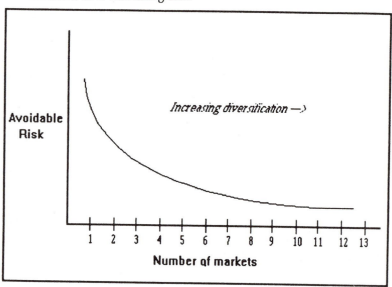

The number of contracts for proper diversification does not have to be too great. Diversifying with greater than 8 commodities does not provide any substantial difference in reducing risk. Where did the 8 come from? Different theoretical studies suggest as few as 3 or as many as 15 unrelated markets are enough for a well diversified portfolio.

There are other practical reasons why diversifying into too many markets can actually increase risk and reduce return. One important consideration is liquidity. If the markets presently traded are liquid, and the trader seeks to diversify into less liquid markets, problems can easily materialize. Trading more markets which are less liquid can actually negate, or even reduce, any of the benefits of increased diversification. Benefits obtained in diversification can easily be lost in slippage costs with the less liquid markets.

Another important consideration is time. The trader must now devote more time to more markets, which can actually reduce overall performance. The trader will have to watch and spend a greater amount of time on more markets, at the expense of losing concentration in the original markets. This can be both costly and frustrating.

Initial diversification in a few markets with low correlations should reduce risk and possibly increase reward. However, too much diversification can actually be detrimental to trading performance. In essence, the benefits of increased diversification comes at a cost which becomes greater with increasing diversification. Therefore, risk may actually be increased with too much diversification. A proper balance, as usual, is required.

2. *Different time frames*: One often overlooked, but important way to diversify is by changing the entry and exit times in the same market. A trading system may work well in one time frame but badly in another, even in the same market. This type of trading is especially helpful when trading more than one contract in the same market. This is an ideal way to diversify for someone who only trades one type of contract in one market.

A trader may decide to stagger the entry or exit points by adding more, or reducing the number of contracts with time. Long term position trading in the June 91 Swiss franc in Figure 23.9 might have caught the nice move in February and March, which short-term trading may have missed. However, short-term trading

FIGURE 23.9
June 1991 Swiss franc

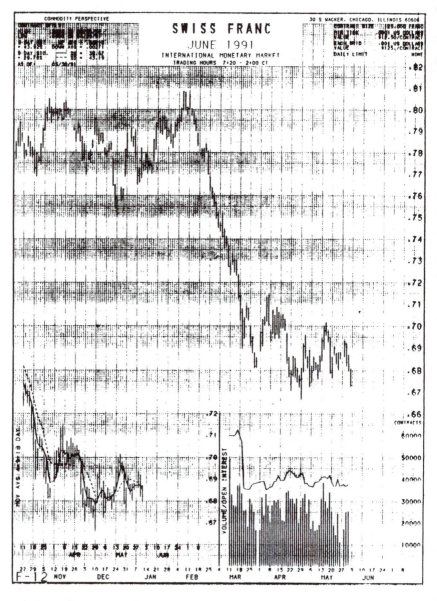

Source: Reprinted with permission, © 1991 Commodity Perspective, 30 South Wacker Drive, Suite 1820, Chicago, Illinois 60606.

might have provided better opportunities than long-term trading before January and after March, when the market exhibited choppy behavior.

When getting out of a trade a person may decide to exit based on different risk and time parameters. This is a way of pyramiding and will be further covered in Chapter 25. For now, a simple example should suffice. After selling three Swiss franc contracts you might hold one contract for a day trade, one for a week, and another for a longer time frame.

3. *Different methods*: Employing different methods is one way to trade disparate market conditions. Some trading systems work well in trending markets, others excel in countertrending markets, while others seem never to work no matter what the market. Some markets trend better than others but all markets undergo various periods of trending, counter trending, and random behavior. However, keep in mind, no trading system works well in a random market.

In Figure 23.9 the June 91 Swiss franc exhibited a strong downtrend in February and March, which would have been caught by many trend following methods. However, as noted, the market was congested before January and after March. A counter trend method may have been able to catch some of the moves while in this congestion phase.

Another Thought on Diversification

On October 13, 1989, Robert thought his portfolio of commodities was well diversified. He had profitable positions in unrelated futures markets such as pork bellies and coffee, but had no position in the stock market. At 3 PM on Friday the stock market crashed. Though he was bearish and missed shorting the market, he was still content with the profits which had accrued from other positions.

On Monday morning virtually every profitable position went against him. He exited every market at a loss because the stock market crash affected all the other positions. Supposedly, these markets were not highly correlated with each other, but the thinking at the time was if the stock market crashes, a depression or recession could follow. This would cause most of the other commodities to fall in price.

On that day, many of the normally unrelated commodities were highly correlated with the stock market. When the stock market reversed course and rallied on Monday, the commodities went on their merry way generally independent of the stock market. Markets can become highly correlated for brief, but crucial, periods of time. He learned a lesson about diversification and markets. The cost was high, but hopefully worth it.

In this example, a crash in the stock market caused many other commodity prices such as crude oil to fall. However, there have been other occasions where the opposite has occurred. In August of 1991, the stock market dropped sharply on Monday morning after the coup attempt in the Soviet Union. However, oil prices opened sharply higher because the Soviet Union was a large producer of oil, and there was concern a supply problem would develop. Other commodity markets, such as coffee, remained unaffected by the incident.

Diversification, when used properly, is an effective way to reduce risk, but markets can become correlated or not correlated rather quickly depending on the fundamentals at the time. For example, the bond market will normally move independently of certain commodities such as orange juice. A frost in Florida may affect prices of orange juice, but should not tend to move bond prices. However, if broad inflationary trends develop, sending many commodities such as orange juice higher in price, bond prices will probably drop. In this scenario, bond prices would show a negative correlation with orange juice prices. Every trader must understand the fundamentals behind each market before applying correlation measures for diversification.

LIQUIDITY

Liquidity *of the market refers to the volume and open interest of the future.* Volatility and diversification must be viewed from a balanced perspective. Too much or too little will usually entail more risk in trading. Liquidity does not present this trade-off. The more liquid the market the lower the risk with no decrease in reward. Liquidity is best measured with volume figures as opposed to open interest numbers with most markets. A market with high volume and relatively low open interest is generally more liquid than a market with low volume and high open interest.

Open interest does become an important consideration with very large traders because they need to know how much their trading will impact the market. If a large trader comprises a good part of the open interest, who will take the other side when the trader decides to exit the position?

The currencies are the most liquid markets but even they have periods of illiquidity, such as when important news events or reports roil the market. Liquidity has a potential to build on itself. Traders choose to trade more liquid markets and ignore the less liquid ones. The more liquid markets become more liquid, while the less liquid markets become even less liquid.

THE REST

The other elements of risk will be briefly covered in this section. The *bid and ask spread* is the difference between where the future may be bought or sold. The greater the spread the greater the amount which is given or "donated" to the market and lost in entering and exiting a position. More liquid markets provide tighter spreads than less liquid markets.

Slippage is the amount one loses when markets trade through buy or sell levels and was covered in Chapter 20. Slippage is usually a function of the liquidity and volatility of the market. Slippage is generally less in more liquid and less volatile markets. Slippage varies with each market, and the same market may exhibit different slippage factors at different times. Significant news reports can change a market from utter quiet to a violent nightmare, thereby increasing the chance of slippage.

Political and economic situations affect trading risk. The more unstable the situation the more risky. Certain currencies can become more risky to trade than others due to an unstable political or economic environment. This is one of the reasons why many of the markets in the United States are less risky to trade than other markets in less stable countries.

Default of the coupon or dividend is a risk always inherent in any security that pays one. Default is not a serious problem in futures unless the underlying contract, such as treasury bonds, default. It is a much more serious subject with individual issues in other markets such as junk bonds.

Limit moves are constraints placed on markets by some exchanges which dictate the maximum amount a market may move in a day or trading session. Limit moves are intended to reduce risk by reducing the amount of loss in a time period. However, limits can severely limit liquidity or stop trading altogether, and therefore, may tend to effectively increase liquidity risk. Limit moves are a frustrating way of dealing with risk. Each camp has their proponents for and against limits but one thing is clear—limit moves reduce liquidity, which increases risk.

There are other factors which affect risk in certain markets, such as systematic and unsystematic risk in the stock market.

MEASURING RISK

We have looked at variables that contribute to risk and reward but is there a way to measure all of them, and develop an idea of what the total risk is for a position? For example, let's look at two elements of risk in security A and B in Table 23.2:

TABLE 23.2

Security	Holding Time	Volatility
A	2 years	20%
B	5 years	40%
C	1 year	50%

Security A has a shorter holding period and lower volatility, so it is clearly less risky than B based on the two elements of time and volatility. But when security C is introduced the comparison becomes more difficult. If the volatility measurement is the only criteria, security C, which has a higher volatility, has more risk than A or B. But, if time is the criteria, security C, which has a shorter holding period is less risky than A or B. It is really hard to say which one is more risky unless we place special importance on one element.

The question of which security is more risky becomes even more complex when other variables such as liquidity are considered. The problem here is that we are trying to compare different forms of risk with dissimilar measurements of time, volatility, and liquidity—in essence, a case of comparing apples to oranges.

It can even be difficult to compare risk when using the same measurement. For example, how should we measure volatility? Should we use an absolute or percentage amount? If the percentage change is used, what time frame should be analyzed? Should the closing price or a combination of the high, low, open, and close be included? There is no right method because each possibility has its own benefits and drawbacks. There is a way to combine some of these elements and answer some of these questions using option valuation models, and this was covered in Chapters 14 through 18.

IMPORTANT DISTINCTION BETWEEN RISK AND REWARD

When considering money management techniques, always remember an important distinction between risk and reward. Whereas risk is always present, reward is not. Risk must be assumed for a potential reward but the reward is by no means guaranteed. In any trade both parties assume a certain amount of risk but neither party is guaranteed any reward. Both parties may reap a reward, one party may win and one may lose, or both may lose. This can occur in a zero-sum game as well because both parties may exit at different times; so even though their entry price was the same, their exit prices may vary. Therefore, there is always risk of loss but not always the realization of reward. Risk is always present whereas reward can be much more elusive.

PRACTICAL TRADING RISKS

1. *Number of contracts to trade*: You must look at the maximum drawdown and theory of runs to determine your risk. Determining the number of contracts to trade is not a function of how much you plan to make on a trade, but a worst case scenario if things go wrong. *Contract size is not determined by profit objective but by the amount of risk incurred on any trade or series of trades.*

2. *Real risk*: It is usually hard to determine your actual risk because any market may exhibit unusual behavior in a particular day, quite unlike anything it may have done in the past. On the other hand, always thinking the worst case scenario and risking too little, will generally mean you are not using your capital as efficiently as possible. You must have a balanced approach when it comes to considering all aspects of risk.

3. *Diversification*: If the S&P500 moves three times as much in dollars as crude oil does should three crude oil contracts be traded for each S&P500? This is a very hard question to answer because there is always the possibility the crude oil market might open limit up or down, not allowing you to exit a losing position. In this situation, you might lose just as much on one crude oil contract as you would on one S&P500 contract.

CONCLUSION

This chapter dealt with practical ways of looking at factors which affect risk and reward. You must always consider ways to reduce risk and increase potential return in trading, to better the risk/reward ratio.

CHAPTER 24

Considerations in Developing a Trading Method

Take calculated risks. That is quite different from being rash.

George Patton

The game isn't over till it's over.

Yogi Berra

This chapter will cover some of the ways to change certain performance measurements to see how the risk and return ratio varies. Every trader must make these important decisions either actively or by default.

PERCENT PROFITABLE TO TOTAL TRADES

Can you vary the percentage of profitable to total trades, or is it something immutable depending on the study or method? For example, assume the percentage of profitable trades is 50% in an objective or subjective trading method. Can this percentage be increased to 60% or higher, or reduced to 40% or lower? The answer is yes, even if the market is random. Let's see how this is possible with the following example. Assume:

1. *No bid or ask spread, no slippage, and no commissions*: This allows the trader to buy or sell wherever the market is currently trading.

2. *The market is random*: This means most traders should breakeven over the long term because they have no advantage or edge in trading.

We must make these assumptions about the market to better understand the example but will relax the restrictions later on for a real world situation. Let's meet three traders Barney, Bob, and Bart. All three start off buying one contract at 100. Their strategies and results follow:

Barney. Barney loves to go for the home run. He trades the old fashioned way by cutting losses short and letting profits run. He buys at 100 and sells at 90 if the market goes against him. If the market goes in his favor he sells at 120 and therefore makes twice as much of a profit as a loss. Sometimes he allows profits to run much more, but he will exit at 120 in this example for simplicity.

What kind of results should he expect? A profitable trade will be 20 points but a losing trade will be 10. There will be approximately twice as many losing trades (remember random markets) as winning trades because 120 is twice as far away as 90 is from 100. Therefore, the chance of getting to the 120 level is 1/2 that of reaching the 90 level. The percent profitable trades should be approximately 33%.

Bob. Bob is a singles hitter. He does not try to make big profits, but instead tries to make a reasonable reward without risking too much. He buys at 100 and sells at 90 just like Barney if the market goes against him. But unlike Barney he does not go for the big profit. He sells at 110 if the market goes in his favor and makes as much as he loses.

What are his results? The profits and losses will both be 10. The number of winning trades will be approximately equal to the number of losing trades because 110 and 90 are the same distance from 100. The chance of hitting either level will be the same in a random market so the percent profitable trades will be approximately 50%.

FIGURE 24.1
Barney, Bob, and Bart all buy and place stop loss orders at the same level but they have different profit objectives so their percentages of winning and losing traders will vary.

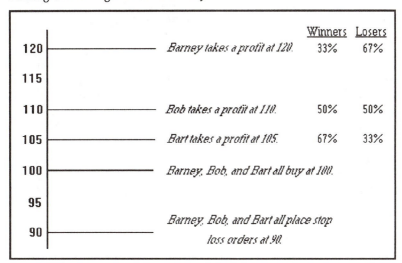

		Winners	Losers
120	Barney takes a profit at 120.	33%	67%
115			
110	Bob takes a profit at 110.	50%	50%
105	Bart takes a profit at 105.	67%	33%
100	Barney, Bob, and Bart all buy at 100.		
95			
90	Barney, Bob, and Bart all place stop loss orders at 90.		

Bart. Bart refuses to let a profit get away. He believes in the adage that you won't go broke taking a profit. He buys at 100 and sells at 90 if the market goes against him. If the market goes in his favor he sells at 105 and makes one half of what he loses.

What are his results? Many traders would find Bart's style "incorrect" because losses are greater than profits but in fact the overall results are no different. He will make a profit of 5 points and lose 10 points. The number of profitable trades should be about twice as many as the number of losing trades because 105 is half the distance to 100 as the 90 level. The percent of profitable trades will be approximately 67%.

All three trading styles are shown in Figure 24.1. How do the scenarios change if the assumptions are relaxed?

1. A bid and ask spread, slippage, and commissions would tend to reduce the number of winning trades and increase the number of losing trades, which would reduce the profitability of all three.

2. If markets trend and are not random, then it will be possible to change the probabilities for each trader. If all three have a good trading method, they will have an edge on the market and all will be able to make a profit. This edge will allow them to overcome the bid-ask spread, slippage, and commission problems.

Let's assume the edge will improve their percentage of winning trades by 5%. Their profit objectives will be the same, so Barney, Bob, and Bart will now have 38%, 55%, and 72% winning to total trades, respectively. Furthermore, they will have trading methods which allow them to profit irrespective of their percent profitable to total trade ratio.

This example demonstrates the following idea. *Traders can change the percentage of winning to losing trades by changing their profit and loss objectives.* Barney, Bob, and Bart may use the same trading method but vary their entry and exit points to successfully achieve different percentages for winning to total trades.

This example also demonstrates how maximizing one variable will tend to reduce the effects of another. Increasing the percent of profitable trades will tend to decrease the number of big winning trades. Decreasing percent profitable trades will tend to increase the number of big winning trades. We would all like to have the big winning trades and high-percentage profitable trades. For most of us this is an unrealistic expectation except for a very small number of traders who have an exceptional feel for the markets.

PERCENT PROFITABLE TRADES
AND THE THEORY OF RUNS

When developing a trading method we will consciously or subconsciously decide percent profitable to total trades by going for the big profit, or accepting the smaller one. It would be nice to have many large profitable trades but this usually comes at a cost of lower percentage of profitable trades.

The theory of runs provides an indication of the chances of a series of losing trades occurring when the percentage of losing trades to total trades is known. What are the chances for a series

TABLE 24.1
The Probability of a Series of Losing Trades Occurring as a Function of the Percentage of Losing Trades to Total Trades.

Number of Trades	Percentage of Losing Trades/Total Trades (%)		
	25%	50%	75%
2	6.3	25	56.3
3	1.6	12.5	42.1
4	0	6.3	31.6
5	0	3.1	23.7
6	0	1.6	17.8
7	0	0.8	13.3
8	0	0	10

of losing trades when the percentage of losing trades to total trades is changed? Table 24.1 shows that the chance of a series of losing trades increases dramatically the higher the percentage of losing trades to total trades. For example, if the percentage of losing trades to total trades is 50%, there is a 3% chance of having five losing trades in a row. If the percentage of losing trades to total trades is 75%, the chance of having five losing trades in a row increases to 24%.

This table clearly demonstrates why many successful traders only risk 2–4% of their capital on one trade. Some of the best traders have a high proportion of losing trades, but they do not run the risk of losing all their capital if only a small amount of money is risked per trade. Traders risking more than 10% of their capital stand a very good chance of losing all of it, unless their proportion of losing trades is very small.

A trader should adjust the amount of risk capital according to the percent losing trades which may be expected in the future. How do you know what to expect in the future? By analyzing the theoretical returns from a trading method you plan to trade or your actual historical performance. If neither are available then plan for the worst and expect 75% or higher. You must risk less per trade if you expect to take many small losses, because the probability of a series of losses increases dramatically with a higher percentage of losing trades.

GOING FOR LARGE OR SMALL
PROFITS

Why would anyone consciously opt for a high percentage of losing
trades when the risk of losing all of one's capital is so much greater?
Part of the answer is psychological. Many traders desire to go for
the big winner, and feel one of the reasons they are in the futures
business is to make a big play or not play at all. They have no
desire to take small profits and losses and consider it a waste of
time. The reasoning is acceptable and there are traders who have
made big fortunes in this manner.

Another reason is not so obvious. The markets and times may
determine the optimal trading tactics. You may want to trade in a
certain manner but the markets may not allow you the courtesy.
For example, markets change and may at times exhibit periods with
large trends, and other times exhibit congestion or random phases.
In times when the market is trending, it may be preferable to try
for a big profit and have a smaller percentage of profitable trades,
because the chance of making a big profit is greater. In times when
the market does not exhibit strong trends traders must often be
content with taking small profits and have a larger percentage of
winning trades, because the big move seldom materializes. When
the markets are random, no method will consistently work.

Markets may tend to make large price moves during certain
times of the year such as the agricultural commodities during important
growing periods. The possibility of an extreme price move is an
important reason many traders go for big profits, and, hopefully,
smaller losses. If a market is making extreme price moves, there is
a better chance of making a big profit and consequently taking a
high percentage of small losses. There is no correct percentage of
profitable trades, but instead, the number is arrived at by the market,
the era, and most importantly the person. We will look into this
last aspect in the psychology section.

The monthly coffee chart in Figure 24.2 shows periods of large
trends in certain years, and quiet congested trading in other times.
Trading for large moves in the early 1980's and 1986 would be
justified due to the large moves, whereas taking smaller profits in
1985 and 1990 would be more appropriate. A trading method which

FIGURE 24.2
Coffee monthly chart

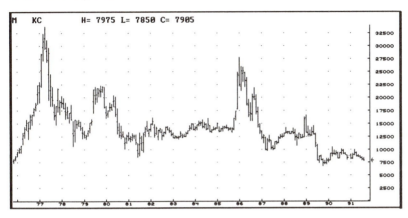

Source: Reprinted with permission, FutureSource, 955 Parkview Blvd., Lombard, IL 60148 (800) 621-2628

worked well when the market trended, might not work so well in another time. Commodity prices have made large price moves in the past and there has been a tendency for markets to trend quite strongly during certain times.

The fact that markets change brings up another point. You cannot design a system and expect outcomes to always be close to historical results. Markets change but when the system doesn't, the results can be quite different than expected. You must always adjust the system to the market and not vice versa—never expect the market to adjust to your particular system.

OTHER PERFORMANCE MEASURES

Profit to Loss Ratio

This ratio is a good indication of the overall profitability of a system, or historical track record. The higher the ratio the better the performance, but do not be misled into thinking going for big profits will invariably increase this percentage. Some traders take small but consistent profits and have excellent profit to loss ratios.

Sharpe Ratio

The Sharpe ratio will be partially affected by the percentage of profitable trades to total trades. More consistent profits with no significant losses will tend to increase the ratio.

Return On Investment and Maximum Drawdown

A high ROI and low maximum drawdown are two important goals for the trader. They are dependent on trading method, market, and, sometimes, each other.

ENTRY AND EXIT POINTS

Where should an entry and exit point occur on any trade? Each trader should consider this question thoroughly because there is much at stake in the correct answer. An entry and exit point may be defined as:

1. *The* **entry** **point** *is where the risk is low and the potential reward is high.*

2. *The* **exit** **point** *is where the risk is high and the potential reward is low or uncertain.*

From these definitions it should become clear that entry and exit points are not necessarily the same points. Markets sometimes exhibit random behavior, and, therefore, are best left alone or not traded as much as trending or consolidating markets. A market which changes to random behavior should be exited if a trade is in place, and no entry should occur until better opportunities exist.

Entry points in technical trading are often based on two different reasons. Trend following systems generate two different entry points:

1. Buying occurs on strength after resistance has been broken.

2. Selling occurs on weakness after support has been broken.

Counter trend following systems generate two different entry points:

1. Buying occurs on weakness into support.

2. Selling occurs on strength into resistance.

Trend and counter trend following methods may be combined to yield a unique trading method. For example, buying on weakness in a bull market, or selling on strength in a bear market is an example of using both types of methods.

It is interesting to note that exit points are usually given less importance than entry points in trading. Many people with clear hindsight will say where they were going to enter a position, but seldom mention where they planned to exit the trade. The exit point in any trade is at least as important as the entry point, because the exit point determines whether a profit or loss is made. The next section on stop placement will look into ways to evaluate entry and exit points, and these issues will also be investigated in the psychology section.

STOP PLACEMENT: DECIDING ENTRY AND EXIT POINTS IN TRADES

A stop is a point where you enter or exit a trade. The placement of stops will refer to both entry and exit points in a trade. There are two kinds of stops:

1. *A* **price stop** *is the price where the trader will enter or exit the market.* A price stop is the most commonly thought of stop. When a price objective has been reached the stop can be used to enter or exit the trade by using a buy stop, limit order, or mental stop in conjunction with a market order.

2. *A* **time stop** *is a time when the trader will enter or exit the market.* A time stop is not often considered a stop but in fact time stops are used as often, and, sometimes, more often by default. Determining a time to enter a market can be just as important as determining a price to enter. If a price objective is not met, the trader may exit the position and play another day. Another frequently used time stop by default is the use of options, where the option trader has a specified time to reach a certain price objective.

Placement of stops for both entry and exit is one of the most important decisions you can make in trading. Entering a position too soon or late can lead to being stopped out or missing the move. Exiting too soon or late can mean missing a large part of the move or watching a profit go to a loss. Using too tight a stop will get you continually whipsawed, while too large a stop is really not a stop at all, and serves little purpose.

How often have you heard someone complain or have actually experienced the frustration of entering a market and being stopped out for a loss, and then watch it trade effortlessly in your direction? "They went after my stops" is a commonly heard expression that may actually be true at times, but more often is false.

Many people think in terms of buying and getting out at higher prices, never considering the possibility the market could drop. *Before you enter the market you must always know where you plan to exit.* Your exit point may be price or time, or the combination of both. Everyone trades on stops consciously or subconsciously, but if they don't their FCM will eventually stop them out by forced liquidation.

Is there a way of entering at the exact bottom and exiting a trade at the top to catch the entire move? Probably not, except with excellent hindsight, but there is a way of catching part of a move, which is a more realistic objective in developing a trading system.

Let's look at an example to see how stop placement can affect trading results. We will use a trend following method and buy on strength as shown in Figure 24.3, but the same principals will apply for counter trend trading. This is a question that virtually every trader asks—Should you buy and enter at A which is below the resistance level, at B which is the resistance level, or at C which is above the resistance line? If using a counter trend trading system, A, B, and C would be sell levels. These are some of the considerations:

- *Entry point A*: Entering below the line will produce more false breakouts but give better initial prices. This is the best price to enter if the market continues higher, but if it reverses, as in Figure 24.4a it is not such a good entry point with hindsight.

- *Entry point B*: Entering at the resistance line will give fewer false breakouts than A, but will come at a cost of a higher

FIGURE 24.3
Should the buy order be placed below the resistance line at A, at the resistance line at B, or above the resistance line at C.

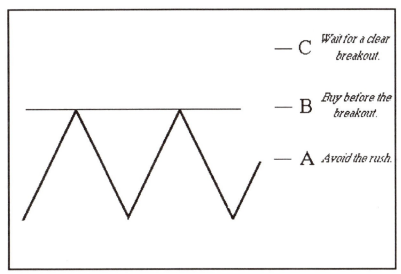

entry price. This level will avoid the losses incurred in Figure 24.4b, but there could still be a false breakout, as in Figure 24.4a.

- *Entry point C:* Entering above the line will provide the fewest false breakouts, but will come at a cost of the highest entry price. This point will avoid the losses incurred in the previous methods, but there could still be a false breakout, as in Figure 24.4c.

Entry at A will always generate more trades and more false breakouts than C. However, this will be partly compensated by the fact that A will have better entry prices on almost every trade, versus C. Why almost? Because some trades will yield a buy at A and be stopped out, and then yield a buy at C but missed by A (assuming no reentry by A). The same analysis applies for B. The trader is again faced with a trade-off of better entry points and more false breakouts.

FIGURE 24.4

Buy points A, B, and C will yield different performance measurements

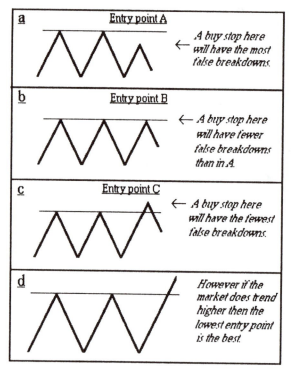

Many people feel there is one best level to enter or exit a market. My work in testing trading methods and actual trading experience over an extended time period, suggests performance results should not differ significantly *with minor variations* in entry and exit levels. Any method that yields substantially different results with a slight change in order placement or parameters must seriously be questioned regarding the reliability of results. This will be further explored in the sensitivity section in Chapter 25.

The extremes in entry and exit ranges are important to consider. If the entry point is too low, the amount of false signals generated will be too great and will entirely negate any benefit of better entry prices. If the entry point is too high, the bulk of the move will be missed, fully negating any benefit of fewer false breakouts.

The decision then comes down to a practical one. The two important considerations:

1. *The frequency with which the trader wants to be in the market*: People who want to trade frequently and have low commissions will find themselves entering at point A. They must accept the frustration of more false breakouts but better entry prices. On the other hand, people not wanting to trade as often, or those with higher commissions will find themselves at C. Of course, that leaves many others somewhere in between.

2. *Liquidity*: A very practical problem of liquidity arises after a market gets through B and C and into an extreme price level. Liquidity and bad fills may be a problem anywhere, but can be more severe the further from A because technical resistance may be reduced as the market moves to higher levels. This can especially be the case in markets making new highs because there may not be many orders to sell above the market. There are generally fewer sell orders as the market rises and more panic buying. Trading beyond certain breakout ranges may create problems in fills.

PROTECTIVE STOPS

We have looked at entry points, but what about exit points? Interestingly enough, similar principles for protective stops apply, but now there is the added consideration of when to exit. Timing also becomes more important, because the longer we hold onto the trade the greater the risk we incur. Let's look at protective stops first.

A range of prices will yield somewhat similar results. Using too small a stop will almost surely guarantee being stopped out of a trade. Using too large a stop is somewhat similar to not using a stop at all. We may also have a time stop, which will get us out if the trade never reaches either our profit objective or stop loss.

If the trade is profitable, should price objectives be set or should profits be allowed to run? This is somewhat of a personal decision and there is no correct answer. Some traders cannot accept having a loss turn into a profit and will get out as the trade turns a profit. These traders are usually the first to complain—Why didn't I hold on longer and catch the big move? Others will let the trade run, but may face the prospect of a nice profit going to a small one, or even a loss. They may complain—Why didn't I get out sooner?

Why not use the best of both worlds and set trailing stops? This is between both extremes but in fact may not be any better or worse than either. Some profitable trades will reverse and hit the protective stops, then continue further while others will simply keep reversing.

My work suggests letting profits run, but not to an extreme. How much is extreme? This question brings us back to the previous discussion of the distribution of prices. If the markets are running and trending, it is best to let profits run. However, if the markets are choppy, going for small profits may be much more profitable than going for elusive big profits. I have had the frustrating experience of watching great trades go to losses (but never bad trades go to great profits). My frustration is somewhat relieved when I occasionally watch markets go well beyond my expectations.

CLOSING, OPENING, OR INTRADAY PRICES
FOR ENTRY AND EXIT

Should closing or intraday prices be used to generate buy and sell signals? Many analysts suggest waiting for one, or a series of consecutive closes as a more valid indication that a trend has begun, instead of using intraday penetrations.

Figure 24.5 of the December 89 NYFE shows how using intraday or closing prices can affect trading results. Assume a sell signal is generated on October 13 at 198. If an intraday signal is used, the trader will have a substantial profit. If a closing or opening signal is used, the trader will have a severe loss. The intraday signal was clearly the better one to use.

Figure 24.6 of July 91 crude oil shows why many traders use closing prices to trade. Crude opened lower on January 9, which set off many intraday sell stops in the 21 to 22 level, then rallied and set off a series of buy stops above 24 to end virtually unchanged for the day. Anyone using intraday stops might have suffered severe losses, whereas anyone using closing prices probably did not even trade that day.

FIGURE 24.5

December 1989 NYSE composite

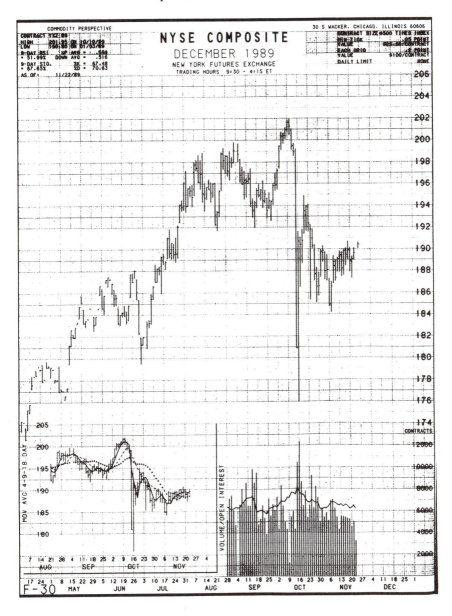

FIGURE 24.6

July 1991 light crude oil

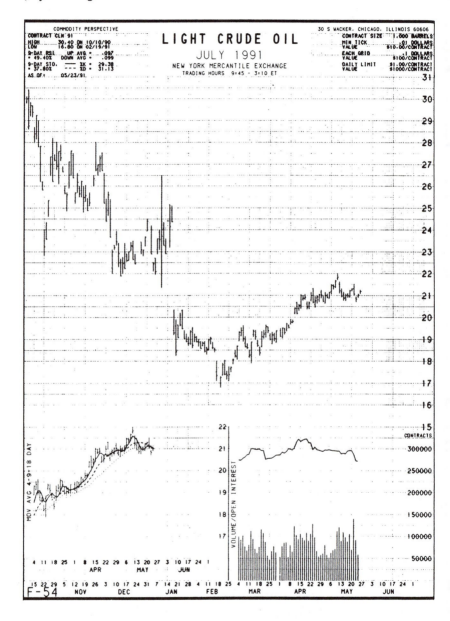

Source: Reprinted with permission, © 1991 Commodity Perspective, 30 South Wacker Drive, Suite 1820, Chicago, Illinois 60606.

Let's look at some of the pros and cons of using opening, closing, or intraday entry or exit points:

Intraday prices:

1. Using intraday entry or exit will allow for faster execution, and probably better initial prices.
2. Slippage will probably be the worst with trend trading, but will not be greatly affected with countertrend trading.
3. More false breakouts.

Closing prices:

1. Considered by many to be the best reference of market valuation and therefore market direction.
2. Slippage will generally not be as bad with trend trading, and will not be significantly affected with countertrend trading.
3. Less false breakouts.
4. May not be able to execute due to limit moves.
5. Closing prices may not necessarily represent market direction, but, instead, the desire of traders to exit a position at any price on the close.

Opening prices:

1. Considered the least representative of the true direction of prices, but, instead, more an emotional or first response to overnight news or information.
2. Slippage should not be as severe as intraday, but may not be as good as closing prices.

As shown in the previous examples there is no best price to use. Two or more closes may seem to confirm a definite trend, but they can just as easily yield a false breakout. Intraday signals get you in quickly, but clearly there are times when you wished you were out instead of in the market. You must decide which entry and exit points to use, and which ones are most comfortable with your mentality.

IF YOU WANT TO USE CLOSING PRICES
AS BUY OR SELL POINTS

Many people believe closing prices are the most important or accurate assessment of the market. They believe it represents the balance of buying and selling at the end of the day, and is a final price upon which both the bulls and bears agree. However, there are certain problems inherent in using buy and sell orders on the close. These problems do not detract from using these orders, but they must be understood or execution problems may arise. Some of the problems are:

1. *Closing range*: The settlement price or closing price is usually an average of the last trades for a certain time period, designated as the close depending on the exchange and market. For example, one exchange uses the last minute of trading to determine the closing or settlement price for the contract. Let's see how this can affect whether an order is executed or not.

Assume a trading method generates a signal to sell on the close if the market closes below 99.50. At the beginning of the close the market is trading at 99.60 and trades down to 99.30 in the last minute. The settlement is designated by the exchange as the average of the closing prices which is 99.60–99.30 or 99.45. Therefore, a sell signal is set off. However, the trader does not know this till after the close and cannot enter an order.

If the trader decides not to wait, and places an order to sell market on close at 99.45 another problem may arise. The market trading at 99.60 may sell down to 99.45 electing the order, but rally to 99.75 and settle at 99.60. In this case, the trader has sold the market on the close, but in fact should not have sold it because the market did not close below 99.50.

These may seem like minor points, but if many signals are generated in many markets, the problem can become significant. The performance results should not vary too greatly over the long run, but you should be prepared to deal with this situation in the short term. Two possible ways of getting around but not solving the problem are to:

   a. Use an entry on the open the next day if the market closes above or below a point and generates a signal. This solves one problem but may create another. For instance, what if the market closes up generating a buy signal and the next day opens much higher or even limit up? In this case, it may be impossible to enter the market or may not be prudent. Of course, in other cases, the market will sometimes open lower in the traders favor, in which case a better price may be obtained than on the close. But, this does not necessarily balance out, and is not much consolation when the trader is in the first situation debating on whether to carry out the trade.

b. Use the closing ranges instead of the closing price, and if a signal is generated on the closing range, then buy or sell. This is one of the best ways of getting around the problem, but also one of the hardest ways to back test. Closing range information for all futures is not always readily available, even if tick data is used.

c. Hope for the best. Actually, this is not normally advised, but, in this case, unless the signals occur frequently there is not much else to do.

2. *Limit days*: Some markets have limit moves. Though the trader may want to enter or exit a position on the close, it may be impossible because the market is limit down or up. The only way of resolving this is to enter or exit on the open the next day, but there may be problems with this tactic as mentioned in 1a.

WHERE TO PLACE STOPS:
A SECOND THOUGHT

Where are good places to put exit points? One rule of thumb for the novice trader is to relate risk and reward on a one to one basis initially. For example, if you expect to make $10 on a trade, risking $10 may or may not be appropriate depending on what the chances of a winning trade are. Remember Barney, Bob, and Bart? Risking $10 to make $5 is ok as long as there is a very high chance of making the $10. If the chances are approximately 50%, you must expect to make at least as much as you risk.

If using a subjective trading method, it is helpful to think in terms of the pattern being broken or losing significance. For example, assume you are trading a rectangle formation, and the market breaks the bottom of the rectangle, yielding a sell signal. An appropriate buy stop might be in the range of the middle to top of the rectangle pattern. If the market does reverse trend and convincingly penetrates the top of the rectangle, the pattern has lost its shape and significance. There is probably not much sense in holding on in hopes the market will continue lower. Get out and try again. This can be said for any subjective trading pattern, such as the triangle or head and shoulders pattern. In this case, the top of the rectangle may have been an entry point for a trade and now served as an exit point.

If using an objective trading method, you must always consider price above signal. For example, assume an oscillator provides a sell signal and you enter the market placing a protective buy stop when the oscillator yields a buy signal. This can be deadly. What if the oscillator never yields a buy signal but the market reverses trend and incessantly moves higher, resulting in a severe loss? The stop should be placed on a technical point, such as an important high or low. If you must use the oscillator for a reversal signal, consider when it changes direction or other movement which must always happen.

If the trade is profitable, consider how much was risked to develop a base for possible reward. Set reward objectives based on technical or fundamental points.

OTHER CONSIDERATIONS

Some other practical considerations in money management include the following:

1. *Changing price risk*: How much should be risked on a trade? Some people use the market to derive an answer by choosing important technical points to place stops. Others decide on a certain amount of money to risk and place a stop at that point. This is a personal decision but there is one thing to remember—the market does not know, or care how much you plan to risk. If the market is making $2,000 moves each day, do not expect to risk only $250 on a trade.

If you only have $250 to risk, trade another market where the daily moves are not as great. It is prudent and smart to risk as small an amount of money as necessary, but don't expect the market to comply with your objectives. My preference is a technical stop because the market does not care how much each trader is willing to risk. Markets seem to respect important technical points because they are part of the market.

2. *Changing rules*: The first rule to consider is whether to use trending or countertrending methods. Most futures traders employ some trend following rules, but markets do not always trend, and, consequently, more studies are being designed to go against the trend or fade the market. The stock market is one market where some traders like to buy weakness in a long-term bull market and sell strength in a long-term bear market.

The rules you decide upon have to be compatible with your psyche. Some people cannot buy strength and others cannot buy weakness, whereas others simply don't care either way. You have to integrate the rules with your frame of mind and feel comfortable about the trades you make. You may never feel comfortable about any trade, but you must at least be at peace with the decisions you make. If not you will find yourself in constant turmoil, and, possibly, not be able to execute your trades at all.

LIMITING LOSSES

Testing strategies provides us with a good reason why it is always necessary to limit our risk. Certain patterns may be predictive and profitable, but all will generate losing and sometimes disastrous trades if stops are not well placed. We do not always want to hold onto a position, no matter how well a method has worked in the past, since there is always a chance the market may go severely against us.

Any market may make a tremendous move at any time, and it is nice to be on the right side of the move when it does happen. However, if you are on the wrong side of the move, it is necessary to protect yourself by placing some type of technical or dollar stop to exit the position. You must always have a point where you exit the position to preserve your capital.

PYRAMIDING

Pyramiding is the act of adding on to an existing position. Buying one or more contracts when you are already long is an example of pyramiding a position. Pyramiding done on a larger scale can quickly affect the profit and loss potential tremendously. There are two kinds of pyramiding:

1. *Adding to winning positions*: Increasing position size as the market goes in your favor. For example, you initially buy five lots at 100 and then decide to buy five more lots when the market reaches 105, and five more lots if the market reaches 110. Figure 24.7a is an example of pyramiding a position when buying.

FIGURE 24.7
There are two types of pyramiding—when the market goes with or against you.

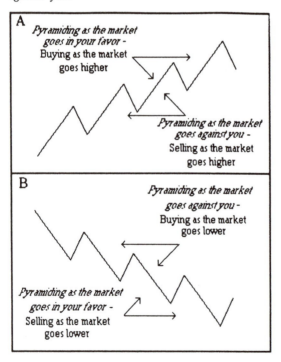

2. *Adding to losing positions*: Increasing position size as the market goes against you. In this case you buy five lots at 100 and then buy five more lots if the market goes down to 95, and five more at 90. Figure 24.7b is an example of this type of pyramiding. In either case you may buy less, more, or an equal amount of contracts when pyramiding.

Many investors wonder if it is good to pyramid positions irrespective of whether the market goes with or against you. This is a question best answered in asking another—Why are you adding to your position? If you are entering a position using valid trading methods and pyramid in the process, then it becomes part of your strategy. For example, if you believe the market will find support in the 100 level and stagger orders to buy at 105, 100, and 95 with a stop loss at 90, then you have a coherent trading strategy. This simulates buying at the 100 level and is a valid trading method. If the market is at 90 and you believe that if it reaches 100 it will probably trade to 120, then pyramiding by buying at 100, 105, and 110 is another valid strategy.

However, if you are pyramiding because you have a loss and want to double your size to break even if it goes back up, then you are probably getting yourself into trouble. The latter decision is being made on emotion or poor judgment as opposed to proper trading judgment. In the same way adding to position size just because you have profits can lead to disaster if the market makes a quick break against you.

Pyramiding is not recommended for the novice trader. Some of the most experienced traders never pyramid. However, other successful traders do pyramid but only after having much experience with trading the markets. Pyramiding is appropriate only within the constraints of proper amount of capital to risk.

KNOW THE THREE TRENDS OF THE MARKET

Whenever trading, it is important to know the three trends of the market. First, discern the long-term trend; next, the intermediate trend: finally, the short-term trend. One person had an incredibly profitable trading system which seemed too good to be true—and

FIGURE 24.8
Money management is really a study of how equity changes from point
A to Z; is the path linear or jagged?

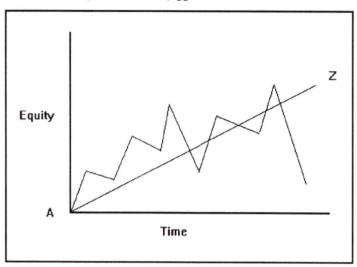

was. Buy the Swiss Franc on Monday and sell it on Friday. He
had gone back a year and found the strategy would have made a
lot of money with approximately 52 trades. The problem was he
chose 1986 which was one of the biggest bull markets for the currency.
The same strategy employed in 1984 would have bankrupt him
because the franc was in a severe bear market, as depicted in Figure
24.8.

Know the three trends of the market. This seems like such an
obvious statement; and yet so many people lose money because
they try to fight the trend.

SUBJECTIVE ANALYSIS: A SECOND LOOK

If using subjective analysis, you must identify simple patterns such
as rectangles or triangles, and then move on to the more complex
head and shoulders or wedges. At this stage it is helpful to be

general and flexible so don't look for an exact replica of a pattern, but the general idea. Look at the charts and try to recognize recurring patterns. Keep in mind, the trading formations can be the standard patterns outlined in the book or ones you develop yourself. Also remember, patterns are not restricted to price. Look for the combination of price and time (recall Gann) for possible trading signals.

An important consideration is that the more specific you define the pattern, the harder it is to look for past and future occurrences of the pattern. Too simple a pattern will suggest randomness or not be predictive, while too complex a pattern will not be meaningful to trade. There is simply not enough data on the formation to justify whether it yields a buy or a sell signal. Even if these rare patterns are excellent indicators of market direction, they are not realistic to trade because they occur so infrequently. If you plan on trading actively, it is more practical and profitable to look for more common formations than rare and exotic ones which hardly ever develop.

DAY TRADING

When developing a trading method the question of day trading often arises. Day trading can be seductive to many people because it offers quick profit potential with precise loss limits. A great amount of day trading is done by professionals on the exchange floor. More off-floor traders are beginning to day trade with the advent of easily accessible quote services and powerful computer charting systems.

Some things to consider when day trading are:

1. Slippage and commissions are always important in trading, but are critically important in day trading because you are generally working on smaller profit and loss margins.

2. Day trading can be very emotionally and physically draining because you are trading more often. The benefit is that you do not have to hold positions overnight and therefore can walk away from the job.

3. Day trading can only be done in certain markets due to liquidity and dollar movement, unless you intend to trade directly on the floor.

4. Day trading requires intense concentration and few distractions. Don't expect to day trade while watching television and listening to the baby cry.

5. Day trading requires special equipment, such as a real time quote service, to constantly know where the market is trading.

6. The decision to day trade on or off the floor is generally made off floor unless you live near one of the exchanges. If you do have access to floor trading then the decision is a personal one to remain upstairs (off-floor trader) or be a floor trader. Don't naively think that if you become a floor trader you will be able to buy the bid and sell the offer. There are a lot of floor traders with the same idea who have been there a lot longer than you have.

7. Day trading is one of the hardest ways of trading, but it can also be very lucrative and rewarding.

FIGURE 24.9
September 1991 S&P500 30-minute bar chart

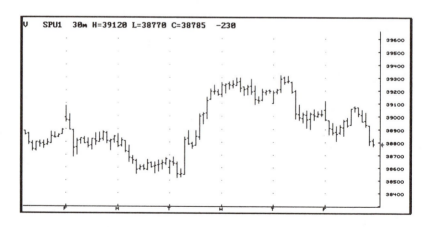

Source: Reprinted with permission, FutureSource, 955 Parkview Blvd., Lombard, IL 60148 (800) 621-2628

Trading methods which work on a longer-term basis can also be applied for day trading. It may be more difficult to use continuous studies, such as a 60-minute moving average, because there will often be gaps from the close to the open each day. However, subjective formations, such as a rectangle, apply just as well on short-term charts as on long-term charts. Figure 24.9 is a 30-minute bar chart of the September 91 S&P500 that shows some of the movement on a shorter-term basis.

CONCLUSION

This chapter looked at ways to change performance results, and some of the trade-offs involved in changing trading methods. This should be a good prelude for Chapter 25, which is concerned with the process of optimization.

CHAPTER **25**

Optimization

In completing one discovery we never fail to get an imperfect knowledge of others of which we could have no idea before, so that we cannot solve one doubt without creating several new ones.

Joseph Priestly, *Experiments and Observations on Different Kinds of Air*

Optimization *is the process of changing different parameters or trading rules to see which yield the best trading results.* Optimization, used properly, is an excellent way of determining how a method may have performed in the past and which methods may yield potentially good results in the future. If used incorrectly, optimization results are essentially useless, and potentially dangerous, by not providing a realistic idea of the performance of a method. Optimization is essential to develop a good trading method, and also provides a practical way to study money management techniques.

Optimization is not limited to mechanical trading systems. The ideas can be applied equally well to either objective or subjective methods, because the fundamental principles apply to any method. The following examples will be done with purely objective methods to present the ideas more clearly. We will look at how to apply optimization concepts to subjective methods later in the chapter.

THE OPTIMIZATION PROCESS

The optimization process involves three separate steps as shown in Figure 25.1:

FIGURE 25.1
Optimizing is a three-step process of determining the overall goal, determining the intermediate results, and determining the methods and parameters.

Optimization process

1. Determine the overall goal

2. Determine the intermediate results

3. Determine the methods and parameters

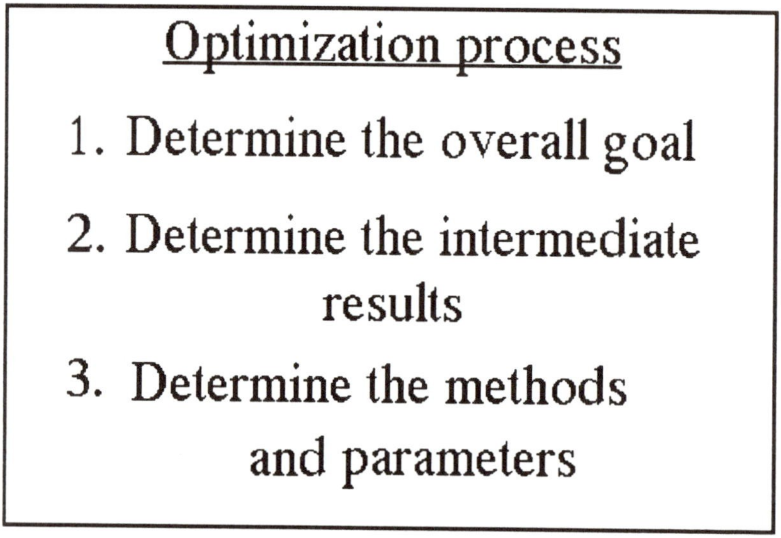

1. *Setting the overall goal*: The optimization process is a study in achieving the best risk reward ratio for a trading method using statistically significant results.

2. *Determine the intermediate results*: What criteria are used in evaluating the overall goal? Profits, profits divided by losses, maximum drawdown, and other performance measurements may yield different intermediate results.

3. *Testing the methods and parameters*: What methods or studies should be used and which rules and variables should be tried? The studies and parameters will have a large impact on the intermediate results.

Let's learn more about all three steps.

Overall goal

The following items should be considered when developing the overall goal of the optimization process:

1. *Attaining the best return for a given level of risk*: Realistic profits and reasonable drawdowns are a good starting objective. Profits should be obtainable in different types of markets such as bull and bear and cover a relatively long period of time, thereby not simply arising out of chance. For example a system which was highly profitable by catching the 1987 stock market crash may have lost money ever since and may not be so good. The user may have to wait another 50 years for the next crash and there is no guarantee the system will catch the move. The higher the profits the better, but high losses may also detect a good trading method if the rules can be reversed.

2. *Statistical significance*: The study should be statistically significant. It is easy at inception to have systems with huge profits but then why don't the systems work afterwards? Sometimes the systems don't perform well in the future because the methods are not thoroughly tested over an adequate period of time to determine the consistency of the results. Perhaps these systems never really did work in the first place.

Intermediate Results

The **intermediate results** *refer to the measurements used in attaining the overall goal*. Should the performance criteria be profits, ROI, maximum drawdown, or a combination of many different measurements? The performance measurements reviewed in Chapter 23 are a good start, but they seldom give a definitive answer.

We generally have a clear idea of what results we hope to achieve—profits! It is equally important to obtain these rewards with as little risk as possible, because we will soon see profits are not the sole criteria in evaluating a system. Many people forget that profits come as a result of risk. If the risk is too great the trading system will eventually fail.

Interpreting the intermediate results can be one of the hardest parts of the process because improvement in one result may cause another result to be worse. For example, a higher ROI might come at the expense of a higher drawdown, so it may not be easy to determine which method is better.

Methods and Parameters

A **method** *is the type of study and a* **parameter** *is a number or rule which affects either the price or time of entry and exit.* An example of a method is a moving average system or trendline analysis. Let's assume the method being optimized is a 20-day moving average system. The 20 days would represent a parameter. Switching to a 30-day moving average would be an example of changing the parameter. Another parameter would be the rules in the method. Assume one of the rules is:

Buy if the price closes above the moving average.

We can change the rule:

Buy if the moving average turns up.

Or:

Sell if the price closes above the moving average.

Changing the parameters can greatly affect the results. There are an infinite number of parameters so we must be selective in testing. In the initial phase of testing, we normally do not know much about which parameters to use in a study. Which is better a 20- or 30-day moving average? Which is the better rule—buy if the price closes above the moving average, or buy if the moving average turns up? In other words, the reason we optimize is to find out which combination of parameters provides the best results. The terms parameter and variable will be used interchangeably in this book.

Which methods and parameters should we use? Of course that is the ultimate question. A tome could be written and it would only begin to adequately cover some of the possibilities. We will look at a few of the more common parameters, but ultimately the question must be left to you. But, if you have some good ones, feel free to let me know!

Further Thoughts

We generally know less about each succeeding step. For instance, the overall goal should be clear—a good return given the level of risk. The way of achieving the overall goal is through the intermediate results. But which type of intermediate results will satisfy the overall goal? High profits and low drawdowns are a good start, but what is high and low? This is a much harder question to answer than at first might appear. Assuming we do know what intermediate results to attain, what parameters do we test for? This is the least known part of the process because it is not always so clear how the parameters will affect the results.

The optimization process is performed until we are satisfied with the results, or, more often, cannot think of any other ways to improve the results. Optimization is a continuous process because the parameters and rules may often change as the market or person changes. Let's review each step of the process next.

HOW A CHANGE IN PARAMETER AFFECTS
THE INTERMEDIATE RESULTS

Most of us are probably aware that the trading method will have a great impact on the intermediate results. A moving average will often yield different intermediate results than a stochastic study, but how does a change in parameters employing the same method affect the results? For instance, how does a change in the number of days affect a moving average method? Assume:

1. A 10-day moving average is used.

2. A buy occurs when the price closes above the moving average.

3. A sale occurs when the price closes below the moving average.

The 10-day parameter is changed to a longer-term parameter of 30 days. These are some of the intermediate results which will be observed when changing from a shorter- to a longer-term parameter:

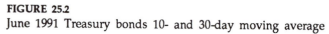

FIGURE 25.2

June 1991 Treasury bonds 10- and 30-day moving average

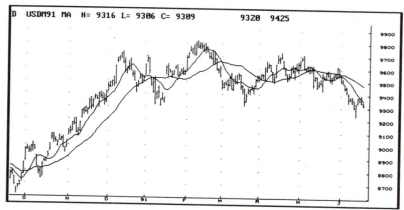

Source: Reprinted with permission, FutureSource, 955 Parkview Blvd., Lombard, IL 60148 (800)621-2628

1. *The price level for entry and exit may change.* A 10- and 30-day moving average are overlaid on the June 91 Treasury bonds in Figure 25.2. Note how the price levels will usually be higher in buying and lower in selling if a longer-term moving average is used. This should have a great impact on profitability.

2. *The timing of a trade may change.* Note how the holding period of the trade will usually increase because there will be fewer buy and sell signals generated with the longer-term average.

3. *The frequency of trading may change.* The frequency of trading will decrease because there will not be as many signals generated with the longer-term average. The frequency of trading is usually inversely proportional (i.e., if one goes up the other goes down) to the holding period, but this is not always the case.

Certain types of risk will increase, while other types will decrease when changing to a longer-term parameter. A position will generally be held for longer periods of time with longer-term parameters. Recalling that risk increases with time, the longer-term parameter will incur more risk with respect to time. The loss per trade may also be higher with longer-term parameters, because the signals to enter and exit are not generated as often. Some risks decrease with longer-term positions. There are usually fewer trades; so the slippage and transaction costs are lower with fewer trades. The longer-term parameter may not yield as many whipsaw trades because it does not generate as many signals. The person does not have to spend as much time actually trading with longer-term moving averages, because the frequency of trades has decreased. A trader's time is a very real cost which is not always considered when evaluating a method. These are some of the trade-offs a person must consider when determining which parameters to use.

Parameter changes are often done to filter out certain trades. A longer-term parameter filters out more of the short-term noise to capture the longer-term trends. In the process the longer-term parameter may miss profitable or unprofitable short-term trades.

We generally have a better idea of what the three factors—price of trade, time of entry and exit, and frequency of trades—should be by looking at a price chart. We generally have less of an idea of what parameters to use. For instance, we usually have an idea of where and when to buy or sell the future by looking at a chart of the market. But what combination of parameters will yield good buy and sell signals? This is not so easily discerned.

WHAT TO OPTIMIZE?

One of the most obvious, yet deceptively hard parts about optimization is determining what to optimize. "Easy," you say, "just give me big profits!" But there is much more to consider. For example, going for huge profits or the big winner will probably mean fewer winning trades and watching small profits dwindle to losses. On the other hand, taking profits quickly will probably yield many winning trades but generally no real big winners. The short-term trader is often heard complaining—"I got out too soon, if I only held on for the big one." The long-term trader is often heard complaining—"I held on too long, if I only got out sooner." Both may always complain, but neither can have it both ways!

Why not just optimize for the largest profits in a certain time period? Let's look at Table 25.1 for the trading results in one year to gain better insight into answering this question.

TABLE 25.1

	Profits	Losses	Net	Maximum Drawdown	Trades
1. System 1	50,000	35,000	15,000	10,000	25
2. System 2	15,000	25,000	–10,000	2,000	20
3. System 3	20,000	10,000	10,000	5,000	5

If the sole criterion in judging a system was profits, the choice would be easy. We would immediately rule out system 2 because it loses money. The profits in system 1 are greater than in system 3, so the clear choice is system 1.

If maximum drawdown were the sole criterion, the choice would not be so clear. System 2 has the lowest drawdown but it does not generate any profits, so it must still be ruled out. System 3 is the choice in this case since it has a lower drawdown than system 1, and also shows a profit, unlike system 2.

We are deadlocked at a decision between system 1 and 3, so another criteria is required to arrive at a decision. How about number of trades? The results of system 1 would probably be more statistically valid than 3, because there are more trades with 1. Maybe only one trade made the entire $20,000 in system 3 and the other 4 trades were losers? Perhaps system 1 generated a consistent set of 50% winners and losers. It now seems system 1 may be the better choice.

Here is the wrench. When the systems were further tested for 10 years, system 2 provided the best profits and lowest drawdowns of all 3 systems! Unfortunately, it was also the most inconsistent. Maybe system 2 is the best of all of them.

The other performance measurements, such as the Sharpe and Sterling ratios and percent winning trades, would also help in the evaluation. But do not think using any set of performance measurements will give definitive answers. The process of optimization should be considered a guide for testing strategies and answering some questions, but it often elicits as many questions as it answers. There is seldom one best system over any other because each system has strengths and weaknesses. *Most importantly the person trading the system must also be considered in the optimization process because the method must be compatible with the person.* There will be much more to say about this in the psychology section, but this matching method with psyche can be the most difficult aspect of the optimization process.

OPTIMIZATION: A QUESTION OF BALANCE

One kind of risk or reward should always balance another kind. In the previous example, the use of longer-term moving averages entailed holding onto trades for a longer period of time. There is a greater risk the trade will become a loser because the holding time is longer. This risk is partly compensated by the lower frequency of trades generated with longer-term moving averages. Fewer trades may yield fewer whipsaws and lower slippage costs. If the risks did not balance then no one would chose a system where one type of risk was greater without corresponding decreases in another type of risk.

The rewards also balanced one another. The trades were fewer in number and longer in holding time because there is anticipation for bigger rewards. The longer-term moving average system is employed to catch broader and larger trends. The shorter-term moving average system is employed to catch the small-term trends but possibly miss a long-term move.

The optimization process is really a study in balancing the benefits and drawbacks of one variable against another. There are seldom any obvious answers. To summarize:

1. *Parameter size*: Using too small a parameter value will probably catch virtually every move, but also many more false breakouts. Trading will be quite frequent and often frustrating with many whipsaws. Using too large a parameter will result in missing a large chunk of a major move and missing out on many potentially profitable but smaller intermediate moves. Trades will be infrequent because

major moves do not occur too often. Risk per trade is generally greater but the number of trades is not as great, so total risk is similar.

2. *Changing time to hold*: Holding for too short a time can be frustrating and costly. The shorter a trade is held, the more commissions, slippage, the bid and ask spread, and randomness will negatively affect profits. Catching big moves usually implies holding onto a trade for longer periods of time, although this is not always the case. For example, the entire stock market drop in October 1987 occurred in approximately three weeks.

If you plan on holding on for longer-term moves, be prepared to sometimes watch winning trades turn into losses. Using trailing stops will have the effect of locking in hard-earned profits, but it creates another problem. Raising or lowering a stop can also mean getting filled and taking a small profit or loss, but then watching the market resume trending in the anticipated direction.

CONSIDERATIONS WHEN TESTING

The following items should always be considered when optimizing:

1. *Relationship of one parameter on the results*: One consideration when beginning the optimization process is to change only one parameter at a time while holding all other parameters constant. If four parameters are changed simultaneously, the results may prove excellent but we do not have a clue as to why the results were better. Did changing three parameters or four parameters cause the better results to happen? Or perhaps only one parameter caused better results and the others did not matter, or actually made results worse? Whenever testing, change one parameter while holding all others constant. This is the best way to know how one parameter affects the results.

2. *Interrelationship of one parameter with another*: After identifying some potentially promising parameters the next step is to see how they relate with each other and how this relationship affects the results. Assume the following four parameters are tested:

1. 10-day moving average (faster than a 30-day).

2. 30-day moving average (slower than a 10-day).

3. Buy if the market makes one higher close above the moving average (faster than 3 closes).

4. Buy if the market makes three higher closes above the moving average (slower than 1 close).

The combination of parameters 1 and 3 will yield the fastest signals while 2 and 4 will yield the slowest signals. The combination of parameters 1 and 4 or the combination of 2 and 3 will yield different, and, sometimes, unpredictable results. *At this point it may be necessary to change more than one variable at a time to see how both variables affect results.* Parameters 1 and 4 may yield mediocre results but 2 and 3 may yield much better results, and vice versa.

     3. *Backward and forward test*: Backward testing refers to optimizing a trading system using historical data. Forward testing refers to testing the trading system using the optimized parameters in the future. For example, assume the period being optimized is 1980–1990 for Treasury bonds. A backward test from 1980 to 1988 might be performed to arrive at a good set of parameters for a trading system. Once the parameters are determined, a forward test can be done using historical data from 1989 and 1990 to see how the system performs during a time the parameters were not optimized.

     4. *Guarding against curve fitting*: Curve fitting occurs when a method is tested over a limited time frame, or with specific parameters to yield the best results. Some trading systems are curve fitted to show excellent theoretical results. These curve fitted systems may have superb theoretical results for a specified time but the performance tends to "break down," or degrade during other times not tested or when actually being traded. The results should be monitored over an extended length of time to see how a method performs in bull, bear, and congestion markets. Short-term testing is a frequent reason why actual trading results fall far short of theoretical results. While performing an optimization, you must always be concerned about the dangers of over optimizing or curve fitting.

     Forward testing is one way of guarding against curve fitting. This yields clues as to how the system "might" perform in the future, and also may help to detect if too much curve fitting occurred when back testing. Another way to guard against curve fitting is to avoid parameters or methods that only work under very specific conditions—conditions that too often don't recur in the real world of trading.

5. *Deciding on the parameters to start testing with*: One of the best ways to begin choosing a parameter is to look at a chart and determine where you want to be long or short. Then observe what parameter will allow you to enter the market at that point. This is a starting point but by no means an ending point.

SENSITIVITY

A natural question arises when testing trading methods—What is the best parameter to use? To answer this question another question should be asked—What is the sensitivity of the results when changing the variables? Sensitivity *refers to how the results vary with a change in the parameters*. If the results change dramatically, with small changes in the parameters, the method of testing or sampling may not be statistically reliable. If the results do not vary as much with small changes in the variables, the results may be more realistic and consistent in real time trading.

Method 1 in Table 25.2 is a summary of profitability results when a moving average parameter is changed by a few days. Some might think the 10- or 20-day moving average is the best and decide not to use the 15- or 25-day moving average. It is possible that certain moving averages will work more consistently than others in various markets. It is more probable, in this instance, that there was not enough testing done to develop statistically adequate results. The results are simply not dependable.

TABLE 25.2
A Comparison of Trading Methods

	Results				
Number of Days in Moving Average	5	10	15	20	25
Method 1	$ 0	$10,000	–$7,000	$8,000	–$1,000
Method 2	1,000	5,000	4,000	4,000	2,000

FIGURE 25.3
Method 1 is much more sensitive to a change in parameters than
method 2.

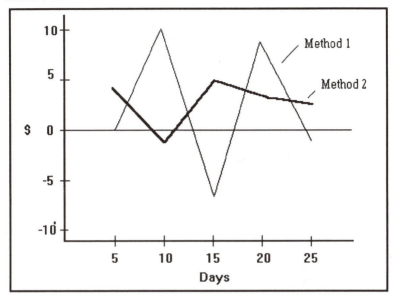

Method 2 in Table 25.2 is another summary of results with
different rules, but the same change in days for the moving average
over the same time period and market. The results may not be as
good as the 10-day moving average but they are more dependable
because there is less variation in results. For example, the 5-, 10-,
15-, 20-, and 25-day moving average all yield profits. Theoretically,
this method may not make as much money as the first method,
but it is probably more realistic and will probably be more consistent
in real time trading.

The results of both methods are depicted in Figure 25.3 to see
how the profits vary with a change in the number of moving average
days. The less the change in results, the lower the sensitivity and
more reliable the results. The results in method 2 are less sensitive
to a change in parameter, so they may be considered more reliable
than method 1.

Recall the example in Chapter 24 regarding where to place stop levels? The concept of sensitivity is the reason the results should not vary significantly with a minor change in stop placement. If the results do vary considerably over a relatively small range of stop placement, the trading method or test may be suspect.

AN EXAMPLE IN OPTIMIZATION

We will perform an actual optimization example to demonstrate the various steps in the process. There is no "correct" way to do an optimization, but there are steps that should be followed to ensure statistical reliability and realistic results. The following ideas for optimizing apply with any type of trading method, whether it be objective or subjective analysis.

Recall the three parts of the optimization process:

1. The overall goal is to attain the best return for a given level of risk, and have statistically significant results.
2. Determine the performance measurements such as ROI and maximum drawdown to achieve the overall goal.
3. Decide which parameters and studies to test.

First Step

The first step is creative and requires you to decide which trading method and parameter to test.

Let's test a moving average system using the following parameters:

Rule 1: Buy market on close (MOC) if the market closes above the 4-, 9-, and 18-day moving average.

Rule 2: Sell market on close (MOC) if the market closes below the 4-, 9-, and 18-day moving average.

These two simple rules form the basis of a trading system that can be easily tested. This type of trading system would be an example of a stop and reversal system which would always have a position in the market. The Treasury bond futures will be tested because they are liquid and have good dollar movement. Why choose these parameters? These are popular ones and it would be interesting to see how well they perform, but any number of moving averages or days for the study could be tested.

Second Step

The second step is more methodical and requires you to test the market for trades which occur in using the parameters to obtain a performance profile. The strategy may be tested by reviewing price charts or writing computer programs to determine the theoretical trading performance in the past. Although a computer is not essential, you will find it to be of enormous benefit in performing an optimization. Many of the following calculations and simulations were done with the aid of a computer. The same test by another person may yield different results due to varying assumptions such as when to switch contract months, but the overall results should be similar.

The following performance measurements are some of the more important ones to analyze:

1. Profits.

2. Losses.

3. Net profits and losses.

4. Maximum drawdown.

5. Profit to loss ratio.

6. Percent of profitable trades to total trades.

The theoretical results trading one Treasury bond contract using a 4-, 9-, and 18-day moving average for 1990 were:

Profits	Losses	Net	Max Draw	Profit/Loss	% Winners	Trades
$17,856	$11,435	$6,421	–$4,257	1.6	36	25

This performance is okay, but how can we improve on these results? Higher profits and lower drawdowns are obvious goals for

better results, but before changing the parameters, let's test over a
longer time period to see how the results vary in time. The results
for 1989 follow:

Profits	Losses	Net	Max draw	Profit/loss	% Winners	Trades
$5,244	$15,025	–$9,781	–$9,781	0.3	12	24

Testing over longer time intervals clearly demonstrates the importance of statistically significant results, and guarding against the
possibility of curve fitting.

Third Step

*The third step leads to a difficult question: Should you test the same
market over a longer period of time, or test a different market with the
same method and parameters over the same time interval?* This question
will be addressed later on, but for now, let's try some variety and
determine the performance in other markets. Table 25.3 shows how
other markets performed under the same rules and includes the
Treasury bonds for comparison:

TABLE 25.3

Market	Year	Profits $	Losses $	Net $	Max Draw $	P/L	% Win	Trades
Bonds	89	5,244	15,025	–9,781	–9,781	0.3	12	24
	90	17,856	11,435	6,421	–4,257	1.6	36	25
S&P500	89	26,782	66,330	–39,548	–43,011	0.4	34	26
	90	48,342	60,790	–12,448	–26,025	0.8	31	29
D-Mark	89	18,189	9,681	8,508	–3,299	1.9	42	21
	90	13,502	21,777	–8,275	–11,299	0.6	20	35
Coffee	89	32,122	18,445	13,677	–7,442	1.7	40	27
	90	15,848	11,827	4,021	–5,710	1.3	37	27

Our first impulse might be to trade the markets with the best results but be careful—they may be the next ones with poor results. The markets with bad performance may continue yielding poor results in the future, or they may be the next great performers.

What is considered good or bad performance? Bad performance is usually much easier to determine than good or better performance. The S&P500 exhibited poor performance because both years showed large losses and drawdowns. But which performance is better—coffee or D-mark? Coffee had higher profits, but also higher drawdowns than the D-mark in 1989. Sometimes higher profits may be accompanied by higher drawdowns, but not always.

One question which naturally arises: What are the results over longer time frames and more markets? More markets or time frames may be tested to see how the method performs under a variety of circumstances.

Fourth Step

The fourth step leads to the next question: What parameters should you change to obtain better results? For example, you may ask—Why be in the market all the time? Some would object to this trading system because a position is established all the time. Many traders want to be in the market only part of the time, both for financial as well as mental reasons. By adding one more rule we can create a system which is in the market only part of the time:

Rule 3: Exit the position if the 18-day MA turns flat.

What are the results with rule 3? We can now begin to see the clear advantage of working with a computer. The results of a parameter change, testing different markets, or testing longer periods of time can be ascertained more quickly and easily when a computer is used. Another example of a parameter change might be trying different days in the study, such as a 30-day average.

Fifth Step

The fifth step leads to the toughest question: Which method and parameters do you use? This is a difficult question because obvious choices seldom arise. Part of the answer to this question lies in the psychology of the person. Do you want to trade trend following methods? Which market do you prefer trading? Are you comfortable with the method? More of this will be indirectly addressed in the psychology section. For now, it should become apparent that the question cannot be answered in a simple way.

QUESTIONS WITHOUT ANSWERS

Four important questions need to be addressed (but may not be definitively answered) about the optimization process:

1. *When is a result statistically valid?* There are tests which provide an indication of statistical significance. The trader must realize that a good performing theoretical study with statistically valid results is no guarantee of actual real time trading profits. Markets change and a model which performed well during one time may do poorly under new circumstances. For example, a model which showed good performance in a bull market, may not do as well in a bear market or one in a congestion phase.

Why not test a system over an extended period of time to see how it performs in bull, bear, congestion, and random markets? You can, but problems still exist. On a practical level, older data is often more difficult to obtain and cannot always be equally compared with newer data. For example, the COMEX changed the futures contract in copper in 1989, so later futures contracts may not be easily compared with older ones. Another problem is that the data may not always exist. There is plenty of historical data for the grains and meats in the 1970's, but there is no data for stock index futures before 1982, which is when they began trading.

Testing over extremely long periods of time may seem appropriate, but the results may actually be just as useless as testing over too short a period of time. Basic economic conditions may change over time, which can affect the fundamental structure of the market. For example, the stock market is a more mature market now than it was 50 years ago, partly because the US economy has matured. Inflation was a critical factor in many markets in the 1970's and early 1980's, but became much less a factor toward the end of the 1980's. Testing for patterns which occurred long ago may have no relevancy to today's patterns because the fundamental structure of the market has changed. Sometimes it is actually best to limit the period studied to a small amount of time. This is especially true for short-term traders, who may see patterns consistently develop for a short period of time and then break down and not become reliable any more. The patterns for a short time interval may provide excellent signals but then may break down for various reasons, such as when the market changes phase and turns from a bull to a bear phase. The extent of the testing period is partly a function of your holding period. If you are a short-term day trader, the past year may be all which is required for trading studies. A long-term trader who holds positions for a month or longer will need to study price behavior over a much longer time frame, such as five to ten years.

Sometimes the time span is not as important as the number of trades analyzed. Any valid study should have a minimum of 20 to 30 trades. More samples will add greater validity to a study, but a large sample size with great results will not guarantee positive results in the future.

When it comes to trading, statistically valid results can be a difficult and relative concept to grapple with, but there is definitely a minimum number of trades which should be reviewed. Anyone casually looking at only five or six trades for a good idea of possible future movement may be disappointed. Anyone placing too much emphasis on total number of trades as being more valid may be equally disappointed. Again, a balance between too few and too many trades is usually the best path to pursue.

2. *Should different parameters be used with each market?* Quite often a specific set of parameters yields excellent results in one market but poor results in another market. In the previous example, the coffee market showed profitable results using the moving average system but the S&P500 showed losses during the same time frame. Should the 4-, 9-, and 18-day parameters be used for coffee, and a different set of parameters such as a 20- and 50-day moving average be used for the S&P500?

Each market has its own personality and characteristics, which might account for better performance with one set of parameters, versus another. Some markets seem to exhibit longer-term trends than other markets, so possibly a different parameter will consistently provide better results. This can be a strong argument for using separate parameters for each market. There is an equally convincing argument which suggests that markets have many common traits, so a well optimized system should work reasonably well in a variety of markets with the same parameters. Markets change. Perhaps the 4-, 9-, and 18-day moving average will work well in the S&P500, and poorly in the coffee market in the following year.

Some traders use the same parameters in every market and trade each market in the same manner. Others believe each market should be traded in a unique manner because each market has unique characteristics. There is no right or wrong answer, but, instead, a philosophical question of how you believe markets trade. You must decide which way to approach the subject or find some middle ground.

3. *What are good theoretical results?* Is there a best performance? Should you strive for highest profits or lowest drawdowns, or some combination of performance measurements? You must ultimately determine which performance results are the most important to you. Having a high percentage of winning trades will probably come with a low amount of large winning trades. There is usually no easy combination, but, instead, a trade-off of one performance measurement for another.

Obtaining incredibly good theoretical results is actually easy if small samples or time frames are used. The hard part is having consistently good theoretical results and most importantly realizing the same results in real time trading.

What is a good indication of reasonable results? A very good benchmark is other traders—the commodity trading advisory funds which actually trade the market and publish their results. Their results are representative of what kind of real time performance is possible in the real world. In some years the average return might be 50% or higher, but in other years the returns could be negative with drawdowns of 25% or more.

4. *Why optimize?* How valuable are the results of a study? The past results will not necessarily be repeatable, but wouldn't it be nice to know how well a trading system has done over time? If a

moving average with certain parameters has never made money in the past, would you want to place much money on it now? *In trading we should be looking for probable instead of definitive answers.* If a market has exhibited certain behavior in the past what are the chances it will continue exhibiting the same behavior in the future? This question is similar to the one asked earlier in the beginning of the book regarding the validity of technical analysis. Markets do not necessarily repeat their past behavior, but it still is nice to know how they have moved in the past.

Optimization is a valuable way to analyze the market but it should now become clear—optimization is an involved process which asks at least as many questions as it answers. *The key is not to have excellent results every time in every market, but instead to try and obtain reasonable results over an extended period of time.* Sometimes it is much better to have results with reasonable profits and low drawdowns, rather than big profits and high drawdowns. For some unknown reason the huge drawdowns always seem to come before the elusive big payoff.

OPTIMIZING RESULTS WITH MAXIMUM DRAWDOWN AND ROI

If a good measure of risk and reward is maximum drawdown and ROI, why not use these numbers as the ultimate goal when optimizing? These performance criteria can be used, but the trader must realize the inherent problems in using these numbers for theoretical testing. Here are some considerations:

1. *Maximum drawdown is a function of a series of one or more losing trades.* An extended series of bad trades or one severe loss may be a bad stroke of luck that might never occur again, but don't count on it in trading. A serious trader would usually consider this question quite often: What are the chances of a series of losing trades, or one severe loss occurring, and how do I mitigate the resulting consequences? This is generally a much better way of trading than ducking your head in the sand and thinking it won't happen to you.

2. *Profits and maximum drawdown are absolute measurements and do not consistently measure results over time.* For instance, the crude oil market changed dramatically in July and August of 1990, from a relatively quiet moving market to an extremely volatile market, as shown in Figure 25.4. The daily moves in March 91 crude oil comprised 10- and 20-cent moves before July, whereas the daily moves afterward turned to $1 and $2 moves. The drawdowns and profits during the volatile period would probably be much larger, and possibly overwhelm the results for the rest of the year. The weekly chart at the bottom of the figure shows the change in the market on a longer-term basis.

3. *Profits and maximum drawdown do not consistently measure risk and reward between markets well.* A market like the June 91 S&P500 in Figure 25.5 which had large dollar moves, will dominate the performance results over a market with smaller dollar moves, like July 91 sugar in Figure 25.6. One of the largest day moves in sugar occurred on April 8, when it opened near 875 and closed near 925, which is approximately a $560 move. One of the largest day moves the S&P500 future made during the same interval occurred on February 6, when it opened near 354 and closed near 363, which is a $4,500 move. The profits and drawdowns for the S&P500 will consistently overwhelm the results for sugar.

The number of sugar contracts may be increased to compensate for this variation, but this comes with the benefit of hindsight. This is similar to curve fitting which can give unrealistic results. On a practical trading basis it can be difficult balancing the number of contracts with one market against another market. The sugar contract may become more active and the S&P500 may quiet down (which is actually what happened for a few months).

One way around some of these difficulties is by measuring profits as ROI, and maximum drawdown as a percentage of investment capital to discern performance on a relative basis. For example, if the total amount invested is $10,000 and the profits are $5,000, the ROI is 50%. If the maximum drawdown is $3,000, the maximum drawdown to investment ratio is:

Maximum drawdown/investment = $3,000/$10,000
                            = 30%

FIGURE 25.4
March 1991 light crude oil

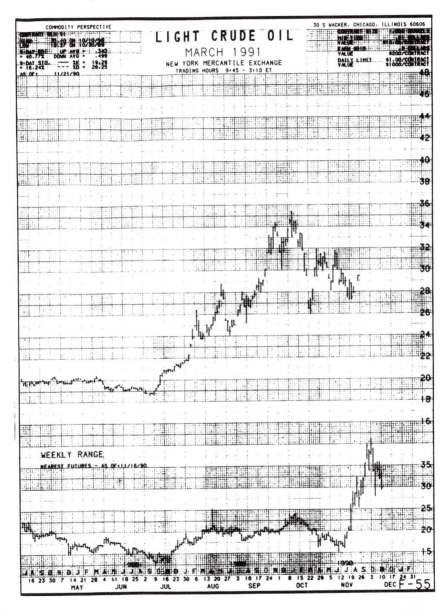

Source: Reprinted with permission, © 1991 Commodity Perspective, 30 South Wacker Drive, Suite 1820, Chicago, Illinois 60606.

FIGURE 25.5
June 1991 S&P500

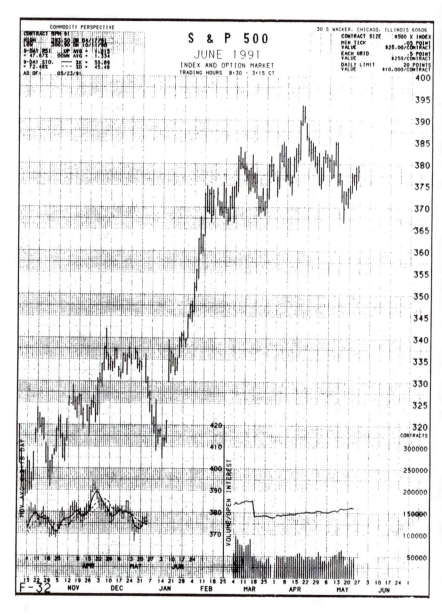

FIGURE 25.6

July 1991 sugar

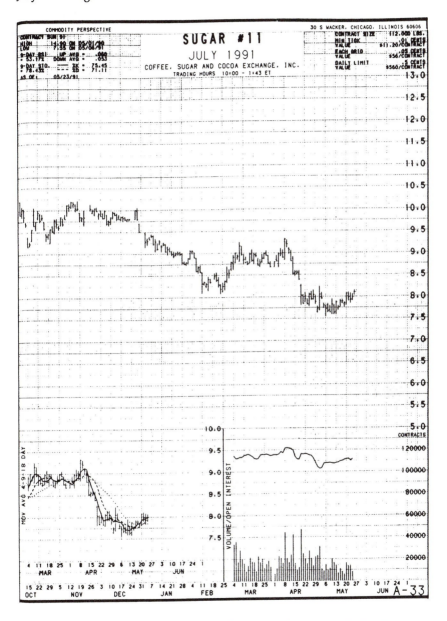

Source: Reprinted with permission, © 1991 Commodity Perspective, 30 South Wacker Drive, Suite 1820, Chicago, Illinois 60606.

The Sterling ratio, which measures ROI versus maximum drawdown, provides a similar result. If the ROI and maximum drawdown numbers suffer from certain weaknesses in theoretical testing, don't they suffer from weaknesses in real time results? Not really. If a person has a poor ROI and high maximum drawdown, there is no explaining away the results. A trader can try to rationalize why the low ROI or large maximum drawdown occurred in real time, and say it will never happen again. But these results will always be there, and the performance will reflect this. What's more, a high drawdown can often mean financial ruin—there's simply no escaping that fact.

OPTIMIZATION AND SUBJECTIVE ANALYSIS

The concepts of optimization can be readily applied to subjective analysis. The overall goal and intermediate results remain the same but the subjective trading methods now become the parameters and rules. For example, the results of testing a rectangle pattern may be compared with those of a head and shoulders pattern. It is more difficult to test these methods objectively, but simple rules can be devised to identify the more common patterns.

Recalling the ideas of sensitivity, it is not so critical to identify an exact pattern or results, but instead to have a range of possibilities. Remembering the ideas on pattern recognition, we are not looking for identical formations, but identifying features. Family members and friends do not always look exactly the same. We look for a few identifying characteristics to recognize people we know.

To apply these ideas to trading we might test a rectangle pattern. For example, a rectangle pattern may be identified by two relatively equal tops and bottoms, which would also be the first parameters. Where would a buy order be placed? Before the breakout from the resistance level, at the resistance level, or above the resistance level? Perhaps it does not make a critical difference, as long as the levels are not too far apart as discussed before. Computer testing is more difficult with subjective analysis but some of the ideas in objective optimization may be borrowed, such as sensitivity analysis.

HOW REALISTIC IS YOUR TRADING SYSTEM?

There are some good theoretical trading systems that may make money over time, and some bad ones that probably never will, but all system testing must include:

1. *Commissions*: Unless you trade for free, include all fees and commissions associated with each trade. This can be substantial if you day trade.

2. *Slippage*: Probably one of the biggest factors in why some systems don't work, and one good reason why many traders get frustrated. Even the most liquid markets undergo periods of illiquidity and resultant bad fills. Sometimes the slippage is not too bad, but it is possible in extreme cases to lose more than $1,000 per contract just on bad fills in supposedly liquid markets. Fortunately this does not happen often, but it can happen. Some markets are more illiquid than others and the reader should be forewarned about illiquid markets.

It is equally incorrect to exaggerate bad fills and use huge slippage factors, because no trading system will work if fills become too bad and unrealistic. You should become familiar with the behavior of the market which is being tested to arrive at a proper slippage factor. Tick data is helpful in reviewing market pricing at the entry and exit points of a theoretical trade, especially if you have no prior experience in trading the market.

3. *Limit moves*: Don't assume you will get filled selling a market if it is limit down, or buying one if it is limit up. Some trading decisions based on Market On Close (MOC) orders assume you can buy or sell the close if it is limit up or down. If you have gotten this far you should know better by now.

4. *Bid and ask spreads*: So many traders need to buy the bid and sell the offer. Leave that for the market makers. If your trading system really works, it shouldn't need the benefit of doing better than the market, simply because it's not possible to always buy the bid and sell the offer.

CONCLUSION

This chapter introduced the concept of optimization and how it applies to money management. Optimization is a way to test a theory, and at least have an idea if you are on the right track. It is no guarantee of future performance, but neither is any other method.

CHAPTER 26

Developing a Comprehensive Approach to Money Management

The sharp edge of the razor is difficult to pass over; thus the wise say the path to Salvation is hard.

Katha, *Upanishad*

Tomorrow will be a new day.

Miguel de Cervantes, *Don Quixote de la Mancha*

The chapters on money management have covered ways to view and measure risk and reward but how much should be risked in trading and what reward should be expected? We will combine many of the ideas previously mentioned to develop a comprehensive approach to determining proper risk and reward in trading.

THE JOURNEY CONTINUES

Remember our equity journey from A to Z? We now see that profits lead to higher elevations whereas drawdowns lead to even lower depths as shown in figure 26.1. We have seen how drawdowns identify various points on the path where losses occur and maximum drawdowns show areas of particular danger. These maximum drawdown areas often occur when too much capital is risked or markets

FIGURE 26.1

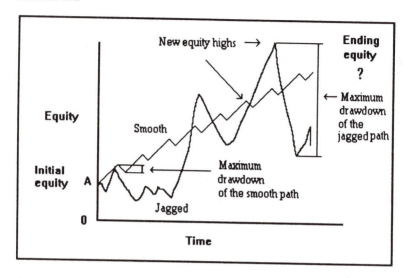

make extraordinary moves against us causing extreme losses. We can only anticipate so much when trading and though the path is sometimes familiar we always tread anew over unknowable terrain because each trading day is a new day.

Everyone would like to get from A to Z as quickly and safely as possible but it should now become apparent that this is seldom an easy task. If the route is too jagged then it is probable the person will never make it to Z even though there were initial signs of promise. If the route is too slow then the person will make it but will the risk and time be worth all the effort? Most of us would like a path somewhere between the 2 extremes of slow but steady growth and fast but wild and dangerous growth. The 2 characteristics of the path are:

1. The steeper the slope the faster the growth.

2. The straighter the path the safer the growth.

We would all like a straight and steep path—is it possible? This path is one of the most sought after but least found paths in all of history. How do we find it? By asking another question—How much capital should be risked on a trade? Before trying to answer the question let's take a quick side trip and see how winning and losing trades affect capital growth.

EFFECT OF WINNING AND LOSING TRADES ON EQUITY

One of the most perverse truths of trading is the mathematical fact that a 10% loss cannot be made back by a 10% gain. For example assume initial capital of $100. A 10% loss or $10 would reduce the capital to $90. However a 10% gain on the $90 of capital would result in a $9 profit with resulting equity of $99. A profit of $10 requires a gain slightly greater than 11% to break even from a $90 equity base.

We can determine what percentage gain is required to recover a loss using the following equation:

$$G = \frac{L}{(1-L)}$$

where G = percent gain necessary to recoup the loss
       L = percent loss incurred

If a 20% loss occurs then what gain is required to break even?

$$G = 0.2/(1 - 0.2)$$
$$= 0.25$$

A 25% gain is required to break even from a 20% loss.

A graph of this equation is shown in figure 26.2. What becomes all too apparent from the graph is that losses beyond 40% of equity become increasingly difficult to recoup. This is one of the reasons it is hard to come back from a severe loss and another reason why losses can be so devastating in trading. A trader who loses 50% of initial equity must make 100% to break even. This may be quite difficult because margin requirements and proper risk control may not allow a trader to take greater risks to achieve higher returns. Returns greater than 100% percent can be extremely difficult to obtain

FIGURE 26.2

Percent gain required to recoup a loss

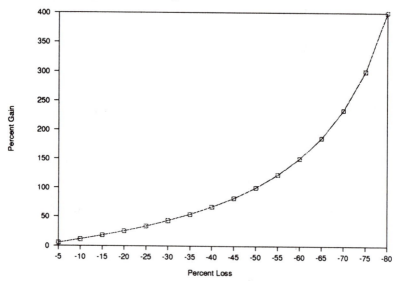

except in the best market conditions when every trade seems to be a winner.

This graph should provide a good reason why every trader must show extreme caution when trading. Lost money is more difficult to recover. It becomes even more difficult psychologically because after a large amount of money is lost it can be emotionally hard to trade and recoup the loss.

WHEN SHOULD POSITION SIZE BE CHANGED?

One key to accelerating on the path from A to Z is by increasing the number of contracts traded at the right time. When should position size be changed? This can be a difficult question for many traders but is one of the most important ones to answer. Increasing position size at the wrong time can lead to severe capital loss while not increasing position size at the right time will mean underutilization of capital. "I never have enough contracts when I am right and always have too many when I am wrong" is a common lament of many traders. How do we determine how much risk to take on a trade and thereby know the number of contracts to trade?

After a Severe Loss?

Some argue it is best to increase trading size after a large drawdown because a winning streak is imminent. There are serious problems with this idea. If most trades are independent of the previous trades then there is no reason to believe the next series of trades after an extended losing streak will be winners. In fact the next large drawdown may be lurking right around the corner. Increasing position size at that juncture could result in finan cial ruin. This idea also conflicts with our original rule of risking less than 5% of capital on any trade. If capital has been depleted by 20–50% then increasing contract size will invariably mean risking a much larger percentage of capital. A trader may get away with this strategy once or many times but eventually there is a very good chance increasing trading size after a severe drawdown will probably result in financial destruction.

After a Profit?

A more pleasant scenario to contemplate is determining when to increase position size after a sustained winning streak. Assume a trading method yields winning trades of $2 and losing trades of $1 each occurring approximately 50% of the time. This method will quickly yield tremendous profits if used consistently. However if position size is increased at the wrong time then the trader may actually only hope to breakeven in time even if using a highly successful method. To see why, suppose initial capital is $10 in the following scenarios and assume:

1. All capital is risked in fractional amounts. If capital is $12 and 10% is risked then $1.20 may be risked. Although we cannot trade fractional amounts of futures this assumption does not substantially affect the final results. Profits and losses are rounded off in Table 26.1.

2. 50% winning trades
3. Profit to loss ratio of 2:1. A winning trade makes twice as much as a losing trade. If $1 is risked and a losing trade occurs then $1 is lost. If a winning trade occurs then $2 is made.
4. A losing trade always follows a winning trade and a winning trade always follows a losing trade. Since there is a 50% chance of either occurring this is a reasonable assumption. This will of course not happen in the real world but it should not affect the final results of this example in the long term.

   Scenario 1. This is the reference scenario where no change in investment capital occurs. The position size does not change and 10% of initial capital is risked per trade (this is a high percentage but is used only for illustration).

   Scenario 2. This scenario is similar to the person who risks profits to trade. Position size increases immediately after a winning trade by risking the entire amount of profit. For example if a $2 profit occurs then the entire $2 is risked on the next trade. No more than 10% of initial capital is risked on any trade.

   Table 26.1 shows the results of the 2 scenarios. Risking profits is clearly not the way to go. Risking profits will always be mired

TABLE 26.1
Capital Growth as a Function of Position Size

	Scenario 1 No Change in Position Size		Scenario 2 Increase in Position Size After a Profit	
Trade	Net	Capital	Net	Capital
		10		10
1	2	12	2	12
2	–1	11	–2	10
3	2	13	2	12
4	–1	12	–2	10
5	2	14	2	12

in a breakeven situation. In fact scenario 2 will probably end up losing all the capital because there will eventually arise a string of losses which will cause the equity to drop to zero. What about always risking a certain percentage of equity?

Position Size as a Function of Percentage of Current Equity?

Let's use a percentage of current or available capital as a way to determine position size. Assume the following 3 scenarios:

Scenario 1. This is the reference scenario where no change in investment capital occurs as in the previous example. The position size does not change and 10% of initial capital is risked per trade.

Scenario 2. This scenario examines how capital grows when capital risked is a function of currently available investment capital. Position size increases as a function of percentage of available capital. Risk per trade is never more than 10% of currently available capital. For example if initial capital is $10 then only $1 may be risked. When capital increases to $20 then $2 may be risked (.1 × $20 = $2).

Scenario 3. The same scenario as 2 but now 50% of available capital is risked. All numbers are rounded to $1.

Table 26.2 shows the results: As can be seen a successful trading strategy is also strongly dependent on how position size is increased. Scenario 1 and 2 will eventually yield profits whereas scenario 3 will always be mired in a breakeven situation. Any trading scenario in a sustained breakeven situation stands a good chance of eventually losing all capital as mentioned earlier.

What may be disturbing is the fact that there is no apparent difference in risking 10% of initial equity in scenario 1 or 10% of available equity in scenario 2. The results are the same but this is only in the short term. In the long term, risking a percentage of available capital will be far superior than risking a percentage of initial capital as may be seen in Figure 26.3.

TABLE 26.2
Effect of Increasing Position Size on Capital Growth

	Scenario 1 10% Initial Equity		Scenario 2 10% Current Equity		Scenario 3 50% Current Equity	
Trade	Net	Capital	Net	Capital	Net	Capital
		10		10		10
1	2	12	2	12	10	30
2	-1	11	-1	11	-15	15
3	2	13	2	13	15	30
4	-1	12	-1	12	-15	15
5	2	14	2	14	15	30
6	-1	13	-1	13	-15	15
7	2	15	2	15	15	30
8	-1	14	-1	14	-15	15
9	2	16	2	16	15	30
10	-1	15	-1	15	-15	15

FIGURE 26.3
Capital growth as a function of risking 10% of initial
or available equity.

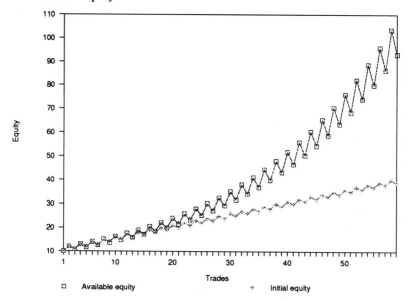

Conclusion

There are 2 important conclusions which may be drawn from these examples:

1. Position size is a function of available risk capital and independent of whether a profit or loss has been made. Traders must risk a small percentage of capital on each trade.

2. These examples show why money management is so important to the overall trading strategy. A highly successful trading method will ironically yield a bad performance if poor money management techniques are employed. *Proper money management techniques will greatly enhance the performance of a good trading method whereas poor money management techniques may yield bad results even with a good trading method.* A bad trading method combined with poor or excellent money management techniques will invariably yield disastrous results.

HOW MUCH CAPITAL SHOULD BE RISKED IN TRADING?

How much capital to risk on a trade is one of the most important questions a trader will continually ask. There can be much debate about this question and part of the answer depends on the risk tolerance of the trader. The amount of money which can be risked is a function of the risk in any trade or series of trades:

1. The chance of a severe loss due to uncontrollable risk may be as high as 10% of the price of the future but it is generally less than 5%. Anyone risking 10% or more of equity in controllable risk should probably rethink the trading method.

2. A loss of 10% or more of capital may easily occur when 1% of initial capital is risked and 10 or more losing trades occur in a row. Furthermore there is a good chance of this occurring especially if you trade often. If 10% is risked per trade on initial capital and 10 losing trades occur then all capital will be lost.

Recalling the theory of runs, the chance of a series of independent trades occurring is the product of the chance of each trade or:

Chance of a series of losing trades occurring = $(1/p)^n$

where p = chance of a losing trade

= number of trades

What percentage should be used in real time trading is dependent on each person's trading style. As we have seen some traders have extremely low percentage losing trades whereas others have high percentage losing trades and both may be successful. Most traders have percentage losing trades in the 50–70% area if we include breakeven trades as losers. Remember traders may have theoretical percentage losing trades closer to 50% or less but slippage and commissions reduce this percentage to usually greater than 50%. We also need the percentage losing trades over the long term because a series of losing trades may occur at any time. This percentage could even be higher during bad periods. Let's assume a 60% losing trade percentage. What are the chances of 10 losing trades in a row?

The chance of a series of 10 losses   = $(0.6)^{10}$

= 0.006

There is approximately a 0.6% chance of having 10 losing trades in a row. Pretty remote? Don't count it out. If you actively trade then it is certainly possible for this to occur. Even if you are not an active trader it may be very possible to sustain a series of 10 losing trades because every trade may not be an independent event. As previously shown markets sometimes move in unison and a trader may be on the wrong side of many seemingly independent trades all occurring at the same time Every trader should respect the possibility of having at least 10 or more losing trades in a row.

Since a series of 10 losing trades in a row is quite possible then traders risking 10% of initial capital on each trade will probably lose all their capital. The exact amount to risk on any trade is partly a function of the risk profile of the trader. Anyone risking more than 5% of equity stands a good chance of losing 50% or more of their capital which is quite damaging and hard to recover. Most seasoned traders tend to risk between 1–4% of capital on a trade. Novice traders should risk less than half that amount or less than 2% of equity on any trade.

Capital risked should be a function of currently available equity and not initial equity. For example someone who starts with $10,000 and makes $100,000 should not base equity risk on the initial $10,000. This point will be dealt with later when the optimal f and the Kelly equation is discussed. For now let's assume risking less than 5% of equity is a prudent approach to money management.

EFFECT OF RISKING DIFFERING PERCENTAGES OF EQUITY

Is there a way to determine exactly how much to risk to increase capital in the fastest way? It should become apparent that the amount risked as a percentage of available capital is the key to the fastest capital growth. The more capital risked the greater the equity increase but only up to a certain point. In Table 26.3 are presented 3 scenarios with the same assumptions as in the previous example.

TABLE 26.3
Capital Growth as a Percentage of Capital Risked

Trade	Scenario 1 10% of Available Equity Risked		Scenario 2 25% of Available Equity Risked		Scenario 3 40% of Available Equity Risked	
	Net	Capital	Net	Capital	Net	Capital
		10		10		10
1	2	12	5	15	8	18
2	-1	11	-4	11	-7	11
3	2	13	6	17	8	19
4	-1	12	-4	13	-7	12
5	2	14	6	19	9	21
6	-2	13	-5	14	-8	13
7	2	15	7	21	10	23
8	-1	14	-5	16	-9	14
9	2	16	8	24	10	24
10	-1	15	-6	18	-9	15
11	3	18	9	27	11	26
12	-2	16	-7	20	-10	16
13	3	19	10	30	13	29

Scenario 1: 10% of available capital is risked
Scenario 2: 25% of available capital is risked
Scenario 3: 40% of available capital is risked

Notice how the equity lows are the same when 10% or 40% of capital is risked but different when 25% of equity is risked. For example the equity is 15 for the 10% and 40% method but 18 for the 25% method on the tenth trade. Figure 26.4 is a continuation of Table 26.3. Notice how capital growth based on equity lows is the same if 10% or 40% is risked but actually increases if 25% is risked. *Capital growth increases as a greater percentage of capital is risked but after a certain threshold level it then decreases and eventually drops to zero.* Is there an optimal area for capital growth and if so can it be determined?

FIGURE 26.4
Capital growth as a function of 10, 25, and 40% of available equity risked.

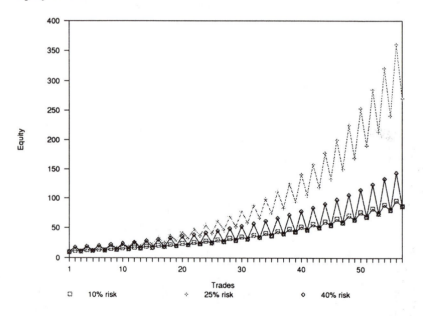

THE KELLY FORMULA

An inevitable question arises from the preceding example—What is the exact amount to risk on a trade? Risking too little will imply slow capital growth but risking too much will invariably yield disastrous results. In between is an area where capital growth will skyrocket. There is an optimal region where capital growth is greatest and then declines on either side of this area as shown in figure 26.5. How can this optimal area be determined?

The optimal f method is a way to determine the amount of money to risk and relies on equations developed by John L. Kelly. The amount of capital risked should be based on the maximum loss which might be sustained. A trader might look through the theoretical trading method or real time results after ascertaining the greatest loss and use this to determine the optimal f. Kelly developed

FIGURE 26.5
The optimal f value curves upward and peaks and then drops off depending on the percentage of profitable trades and profit to loss ratio.

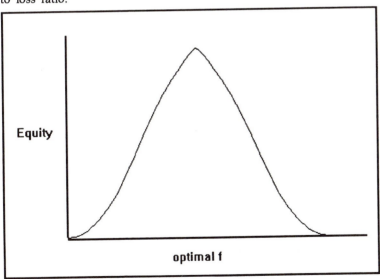

Equity

optimal f

this formula while working on data transmission problems but it can be applied to capital growth in money management:

$f = \{p(R + 1) - 1\}/R$

where R = profit to loss ratio

p = chance of a winning trade

The f in the equation represents the optimal fractional amount which yields the greatest capital growth and hence the term optimal f. The optimal f is a calculation to determine how much capital to theoretically risk on a trade. This equation is appropriate for situations where profits and losses are always the same amount but not necessarily equal. For example assume a coin toss where you win \$2 if heads appears and lose \$1 if tails appears. The probability of a head or tail is 1/2 and the profit to loss ratio is 2/1 = 2. Determining the amount of capital to risk is a 2 step process:

Step 1. First we'll calculate the optimal f:

$f = \{0.5(2 + 1) - 1\}/2$

$= .25$

Step 2: Determine the amount to risk. Take the largest loss and divide it by the optimal f to derive the amount which may be risked. The largest loss is \$1 so:

Amount which may be risked per contract = \$1/.25

= \$4

One contract may be bet for each \$4 of capital. For example if you have \$20 then \$20/\$4 = 5 implies you should bet 5 contracts or \$5 in the coin flip toss.

If the optimal amount of capital traded is dependent on the largest loss a trader may take then how can we relate that to the equity in an account? In other words what percentage of capital may be risked on each trade? The answer is simple. The optimal f indirectly provides an indication of how much capital to risk as a function of equity. In the previous example 1 contract may be bet for each \$4 of capital so 25% of equity may be wagered for each bet. The optimal f indicates what percentage of equity may be risked on each trade.

One interesting thing about optimal f is that betting more money after a certain level will not result in making more money. Recalling Figure 26.4 notice how 25% of capital risked resulted in the fastest capital growth. This is no accident since the optimal f is also .25. When the profit to loss ratio is 2.1 and the chance of a winning trade is 50%. The optimal f varies depending on profits to losses and the percentage of profitable trades. For example if profits to losses are 4 to 1 and the percentage of profitable trades is 50% then the optimal f will be approximately .38. The optimal curve will shift to the right in this case.

How does the Kelly formula apply in the real world of trading where profits and losses are invariably not the same, percentage of winning trades varies and trades may not be independent events? The solution is possible but more difficult and will not be presented here but for our purposes the general idea is of more importance. Optimal f can be used as a guide to capital risk as opposed to a rigid number which must be adhered to when trading.

WHICH PATH?

In the previous example risking 10% or 40% of capital yielded the same capital growth. Is there any difference in risking 10% or 40% of capital? Yes. Intuitively we might think it better to risk 10% especially if no great er capital growth may be achieved risking 40%. The 10% and 40% capital growth is depicted in figure 26.6. What is the difference? Remember the other characteristic of the path—the straight and narrow way. The 10% risk yields a line which is much straighter than the 40% risk. This means the 10% risk is less risky because there will be less variation in returns.

This figure also shows that drawdowns can be controlled up to a point. Each equity drop represents a drawdown and new maximum drawdown therefore drawdowns are significantly greater when more capital is risked but the returns remain unchanged. Risking capital on the right side of the optimal f will always yield drawdowns greater than the corresponding ones on the left side of the optimal f. In other words the drawdowns should be much lower when risking 10% than 40% of capital. Though the eventual results may be the same the way they are obtained are vastly different. Greater gyrations in

FIGURE 26.6

The difference in capital growth as a function of 10% versus 40% of available capital risked.

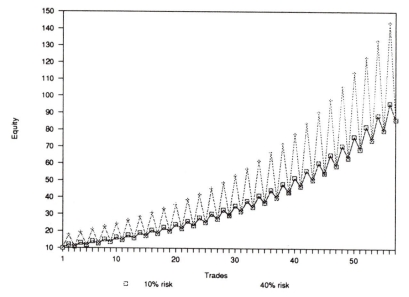

equity imply more risk. The right side of the curve is always more risky than the left side.

The optimal *f* shows that risking too much capital will not yield greater capital growth but instead result in total loss of capital! This is where many traders go wrong losing much or all of their capital even if they have a good trading system. It is far better to err on the left side of the curve than the right. Not risking enough will mean slight underutilization of capital but still result in equity growth as long as the trading system is profitable. Risking too much will more likely result in total loss of all capital—a much different and far more serious problem. Optimal *f* decreases as winning to losing trades decreases and percentage of profitable trades declines. Straying too far to the right can bring grave consequences.

HOW MUCH CAPITAL TO RISK USING
THE OPTIMAL F

The optimal f for a trading method which has profits of 2 to 1 and 50% winning trades is .25. We may risk 25% of capital on each trade but this is well above our maximum of 5% of capital derived using the theory of runs. Why the discrepancy? The percentage of profitable trades was 40% (60% percent losing trades) in the theory of runs example but much lower in this example where the percentage of winning trades is 50%. Is the difference that important? Let's develop an optimal f for what might be expected in real time trading.

What kind of profit to loss ratio and percentage of profitable trades can be expected when actually trading? Theoretical results may yield optimistic but unrealistic future results. Slippage, commissions, and the bid and ask spread decrease the performance of any trader. Some traders may have extraordinarily high ratios such as 3 to 1 or better profit to loss ratios or 55% or better profitable trades. However most successful traders have overall profits to losses between 1.5 to 2 and percentage profitable trades in the 25–50% area. Let's assume the average profit to loss is 1.8 and average percentage of winning trades is 40% (remember this is over the long term and not stellar performance in one year). The optimal f in this scenario is:

$$f = \{0.4(1.8 + 1) - 1\}/1.8$$
$$= 0.067$$

Notice how the optimal f declines precipitously as the profit to loss ratio and percentage of winning trades drops. This shows why traders must risk such a small percentage of capital. The optimal f agrees with the theory of runs calculation (it should since the basic ideas are similar). One year with breakeven results (1:1 profit to loss ratio and 50% winning trades) will yield a total loss of capital if too much equity is risked. If some trades are not independent which is the case sometimes then the optimal f will have to be reduced even further. Remember it is always best to be to the left of the optimal f curve so a 0.01–0.05 f value may be more appropriate depending on your risk tolerance.

DETERMINING AMOUNT OF CAPITAL TO RISK

If the optimal f is 50% then 50% of equity may be risked. In the previous section the optimal f was calculated to be .067. But also recall it is always preferable to be on the left side of the optimal f. Furthermore if the optimal f is actually lower because the profit to loss ratio or percentage of losing trades is lower then trading at .067 may prove disastrous.

In the long term we may all make money but it is the short term which is the bane or joy of every trader. A period of losses or breakeven situations over too long a period will result in a total loss of capital because the optimal f approaches 0 under these circumstances. Since 0.067 is a reasonable approximation for good traders, half the optimal f or 0.02–0.04 is probably appropriate for most traders.

Reinvestment of profits or increasing position size should be a function of available investment capital and independent of previous trading results. Risking only a small fraction of capital is essential in the preservation of capital. Risking only 1–4% of capital will slow the growth of capital but remember this is an idealized example. Every losing trade will not be fol lowed by a winning trade and there will be a string of losses which slows the process even further. Poor trading results with the expectation that a good trade is just around the corner is a poor reason to increase position size.

As a general rule we should never risk more than 1–4% of our capital on one trade because of the chance of a severe loss or series of losses occurring. The amount of risk is partly a function of the risk profile of the trader. We must always err on the conservative side when it comes to risking money because if too much is risked the person will end up losing everything. If not enough is risked we may not make as much as quickly but at least we will be able to stay in the game and play tomorrow. If 10% of initial equity is consistently risked per trade and the person is an active trader there is a very good chance of complete financial (as well as mental) ruin. Anyone risking 10% of initial equity will lose all capital if 10 losing trades occur. As shown with the theory of runs it is certainly possible to have 10 or more losing trades in a row. These risks are with the trader at all times so it is wise to thoroughly understand them.

A trader will never theoretically lose all equity if 10% of available capital as opposed to initial capital is risked. However, there will still be a large amount of capital depleted after a string of losses when risking 10% of available capital. For all practical purposes, a large amount of equity will be exhausted and the trader will find it difficult to maintain any type of position due to margin requirements.

What if you have never traded before and do not have a good reference frame for risk and reward? Use the greater of uncontrollable or controllable loss in a trade (approximately 10%) and less than 50% for percentage profitable trades. The optimal f or theory of runs should provide similar results. The same results can be obtained using the theory of runs because the same ideas are used—percentage of winning trades and amount of loss. Risk or drawdown is a function of the percentage of losing trades and the profit to loss ratio. Since the theory of runs is theoretically related to drawdown then either may be employed in determining amount of capital to risk. When the optimal f, theory of runs, or actual or theoretical drawdowns are used, they quite frequently yield the same low percentage of 1–4% of capital being risked.

WHAT ABOUT EXCHANGE MARGINS?

Why not use exchange margins as a good indication of how much money to allocate for a trade? Futures margins are initially set by the exchange as minimum deposits to trade. Various factors go into devising the margin and one important factor is volatility. Margins are an estimate for a wide array of traders but do not provide insight into the chance of a severe loss or series of losses. Maximum drawdown, the theory of runs, risk of ruin, and optimal f all provide a much better indication of risk.

WHAT TYPE OF REWARD SHOULD WE EXPECT
IN TRADING?

Once risk can be estimated we can proceed to determine if the reward is sufficient to trade. Reward must be based on risk and alternative investments. Risk-free assets such as Treasury bills are often considered the benchmark for determining reward. Stocks and bonds follow with futures considered to be the most risky but providing the most reward. You must determine how much reward to expect for a given level of risk and then see if the risk is worth taking.

TRADING IS A GAME OF PROBABILITIES

Trading is a game of probabilities. We must understand all the possible and probable outcomes of any trade. The probable rewards must outweigh the risk exposure incurred otherwise the trade should not be made. Trade when the risk reward ratio is in your favor so a positive expected outcome is attain able. *Trading is that simple and that complex.*

THE PATH NEVER ENDS—
TRADING IS A CONTINUOUS PROCESS

Trading should be viewed as a continuous process. Many people desire to initially make a large amount of money in order to risk a greater percentage of capital and make even more money. This is poor money management and will probably lead to ruin.

We now have an idea of how to find the path from A to Z. There is no exact amount to risk but there is clearly a danger area where the risk of ruin becomes quite possible if too much equity is risked. The irony of the path is that it is continuous and never really ends. Of course some traders traverse this path and build tremendous wealth but if they continue trading they must follow the same rules and begin the journey again. It is irrelevant how much money has been made in the past because in reality we are always at the beginning of the equity curve in terms of amount of equity to risk. In other words you must always risk a small percentage of your equity (no greater than 5%) or there is a high probability all of it will eventually be lost. This can be shown using either the optimal f, risk of ruin calculation, or the theory of runs.

CONCLUSION

Traders should become more familiar with money management concepts because it is the cause of many peoples' failure in trading.

The amount of money to risk and the potential reward are the cornerstones of money manage ment. Preservation of capital is also another integral consideration in trading and money management.

A good money management system will enhance the profitability of a successful trading method whereas a bad money management system will retard or even turn a winning trading method into a losing method. A bad trading method cannot be helped with a good money management system but combined with a bad money management system should allow for quick exit from the trading world and therefore be less painful!

Trading methods are important but proper money management techniques must be incorporated into the overall trading strategy. Everyone uses a money management technique consciously or subconsciously. It is best to determine which one you employ especially if it is too risky.

PART THREE

PSYCHOLOGY

The heart has its reasons which reason knows nothing of. . . .
We know the truth not only by the reason but by the heart.

Blaise Pascal, *Pensees*

CHAPTER 27

Psychology
and Trading

Our greatest glory is not in never falling but in rising every time we fall.

Confucius

The trading methods and money management techniques form the theoretical or cerebral aspects of trading. The psychological part of trading deals with how we develop our strategies and interact in the entire trading process. Psychology is the heart of trading.

PSYCHOLOGY AND TRADING

Let's assume you have thoroughly read and learned the first two parts of this book on trading methods and money management. Armed in one hand with a well tested and potentially profitable trading method, and in the other hand, with sound money management principles, you are now ready to begin trading. And yet, you feel something is not quite right. You feel uncertain and uncomfortable and aren't quite sure why. You are at the brink, but for some reason cannot take the plunge. *You have advanced to the hardest part of trad-*

ing—being able to live with your trading decisions. Experienced traders are finally realizing that a proper psychological attitude is essential to successful trading.

The psychology of a trader refers to the following three behavioral factors:

1. *Emotions:* Emotions are extremely important in trading. How a trader deals with emotions when trading will play a large part in the success or failure of the person.
2. *Philosophy:* The outlook on life, and beliefs the person holds will have a large impact on trading success.
3. *Intelligence:* The intelligence of the trader can help in understanding trading methods, money management principles, and the market, which may help in trading success.

Trading is much more than simply applying a trading method and watching profits grow in your account. It is a constant struggle where the battleground is not the market but always within you. You will face the stress over losses in trading and not the market. You will be in turmoil in deciding whether to enter or exit a trade and not the market. Trading will place many demands on you, and will force you to think of who you are and what you are trying to accomplish.

One of the first books which dealt with a trader's mental state was *Reminiscences of a Stock Operator* by Edwin Lefevre. It is one of the best books ever written regarding trading, and is highly recommended reading. The stock operator in the book was supposedly the great stock speculator Jesse Livermore. Jesse reportedly made and lost many fortunes in his lifetime, trading mainly stocks and commodities in the early and mid 1900's. The book provides insight into the way a trader thinks, and is a valuable resource on trading.

WHY TRADE?

One of the first questions to ask is—Why trade? The most obvious answer—to make money—may not be the right one. The question and answer may both seem naive, but there is more here than meets the mind. There are plenty of other ways to make money. So why choose trading? *Trading is a mental and physical game which provides an intellectual, physical and emotional challenge of the highest order.* Trading is a more involved process than simply making money or "playing the market."

Many people lured by tales of big profits do not comprehend that trading is a demanding business, and not a simple pastime to make money. The amount of information and time required for trading can be enormous. Trading is one of the most deceptively easy and accessible businesses to start—all you need do is put up some money and open an account. But the price of tuition is one of the highest of any field of study, if one considers the amount of money lost each year in trading. *Losing money when you begin trading is the tuition paid in learning how to trade and enter the business. But do not be misled into thinking the higher the tuition paid the better the education. This is clearly not the case in trading.*

Why trade? Maybe it's not such a dumb question after all. In fact you will probably be asking yourself this question for as long as you trade whenever you find yourself losing money and wondering why you even considered trading in the first place.

THE PSYCHOLOGY OF THE TRADER DETERMINES
THE TRADING STRATEGIES

How does a trader arrive at choosing a trading method and proper money management techniques? By deciding on the best trading method and money management principles. But there is no best trading method, and there is no best money management technique! *The psychology of the trader ultimately determines the answers to the questions of which trading method and money management technique to use.*

Why do some traders use mechanical trading methods such as a moving average system, while others swear by more subjective methods such as rectangle patterns? Why do some traders rely on only technical studies, while others work exclusively with fundamental information? Either or all of these traders may be equally successful or unsuccessful, irrespective of the method employed. Each one of us has developed a unique outlook about trading and life that is ultimately based on our beliefs about the universe. Our belief structure is the core of who we are.

Assume trading method X was tested for 10 years and found to be profitable every year. Would you use it? Some would immediately reject it because they might feel the past has nothing to do with the future, but there are others who would still be interested. Assume method X was a technically based trading method. Some would reject it because they might only use fundamental analysis, but there are others who would still be intrigued. Now assume method X was based on astrological observations. Many of the believers who have followed so far would now unequivocally reject it, because they would feel stars and the planets have nothing to do with the market. But there would still be some who are interested. Would you accept any type of trading method as long as historical results were impressive? *The acceptance or rejection of any trading method is really a function of a person's philosophy, because no trading method can be proven to work in the future.*

Many would prefer to use a method which makes logical sense such as fundamental analysis, even if the historical performance were not as good as a more mystical or abstract method. A moving average study that worked well in the past may never work well again, but many are willing to continue using it because they feel the past will repeat. They believe the probabilities are in their favor because of past performance. Markets trended in the past and will continue to trend in the future. This idea may seem grounded in logic, but it is not. The core idea is not that patterns repeat, but the *belief* that patterns repeat. *Belief that the market follows certain rules or patterns is the heart of trading.*

There is no trading strategy that is guaranteed to work. In fact, a method which one person may successfully trade may yield terrible results at the same time by someone else. How is this possible? Because one person believes in the method while the other person considers it a mechanical tool. Trading is not a science where laws and rules apply, but an abstract arena of emotion and ideas. *Our beliefs and emotions about ourself and the world ultimately determine what we want, how we approach, and what methods we use in trading.*

PSYCHOLOGY IS THE CRUX OF TRADING

If the psychology of the trader ultimately determines the choice of trading method and money management technique, it should now become clear that psychology plays a crucial role in trading. Since no method is guaranteed to work, your choice of method is a function of your belief in which one will outperform the others. Therefore, you ultimately determine the success or failure of your trading, and not necessarily the trading method.

Cunning, savvy and a host of other traits will be helpful in trading, but all these abilities pale in comparison to your entire psychological profile. Many people believe the only key to success in trading is intelligence and finding the right trading method. There are many extremely intelligent people who have devised excellent trading methods, but have never made, or have even lost substantial sums of money trading. Trading is not simply an intellectual exercise, but a total mental and physical involvement in a complex and extremely challenging high stakes game. *Trading will test your emotions, stamina, feelings about yourself, and many other things—in essence, it will provide you with an excellent and thorough evaluation of yourself.*

We have looked at the intellectual and philosophical part of psychology. What about emotion? Let's say you have found a method which is intellectually and philosophically compatible with you. You must now deal with the most difficult part of trading—the emotional aspect.

Assume you are trading a method which is long the market. You are initially excited and optimistic about the prospect of making money and winning at this game. However, the market begins selling off and then takes a sharp break turning your profitable position into a breakeven. Should you get out, or stay in and endure this temporary setback? The market rallies slightly, but then spirals downward with lightning speed, turning your profit to a loss. Your hands begin to sweat, there is a pain in your stomach, and you become lightheaded. You freeze and refrain from selling at the market, hoping the market will bounce back even though your method has provided a sell signal. You are scared—your emotional side is now in control. The market rallies again and a glimmer of hope surfaces anew. But the resurgence of optimism is misplaced as the market renews its free fall plunging to new lows. You are now weak and have lost all desire to trade or hope in salvaging the position. You are now thinking, "Get me out I don't want to play anymore"! Your optimism has turned to apathy as you exit the trade.

Once intrepid, you now cringe with fear. You finally realize the need to rely on your primal instincts for survival. You have experienced the emotional battlefield of trading and you are now terrified. It is a frightening but vivid picture of yourself. You are scarred but have survived—congratulations and welcome to the world of trading!

All those intellectual exercises and philosophical discussions are thrown out the window. Your method told you to get out a long time ago, but you waited, and now it is too late. Maybe emotion does affect a person's trading success!

Your psychological makeup—emotions, philosophy, and intelligence—will ultimately determine how successful you are in trading. The search for the great trading method that always works should now be over with—it is within you. Does this mean that you can trade any method and be successful? Of course not. There are many terrible trading methods which will not make money, and it is quite difficult to develop a reasonably profitable trading method. But, there are some trading methods which do make money, and yet, many people cannot trade them because they do not believe in them. It is not enough to develop a trading method which works—you must develop one you are compatible with and believe works. This is much harder, but necessary, for successful trading. *You must develop a successful trading method, but you must also believe in and live with the method you develop which is just as difficult if not harder.*

CONCLUSION

The relationship of psychology and trading is ultimately the most difficult aspect of trading. Successful trading methods are hard to develop but they do exist. Money management strategies can be developed to enhance the trading results. A proper psychology may take years to develop and for many may never be attainable. *Psychology is the crux of trading.*

CHAPTER 28

Character Traits
for Successful Trading

A man's character is his fate.

Heraclitus

Trading is a very personal experience; what works well for one person may be disastrous for another. There are some common traits which the more successful traders have. Though trading is a unique experience, the following is a list of some of the important character traits some of the better traders possess:

1. Self-control.

2. Accepting responsibility for your actions.

3. Ability to function in an unstructured environment.

4. Ability to think independently and creatively.

5. Willingness to accept risk and take losses.

6. Acceptance of the inability to control and comprehend the market.

7. Ability to adapt quickly to a constantly changing environment.

8. Ability to act on your decision.

9. Ability to withstand stress.

10. Emotional detachment.

11. Patience.

12. Enthusiasm, commitment, and focus.

13. Self-direction.

Even the best traders do not possess all these attributes but many try to continually develop them. Some of these traits may conflict with each other, or do not always blend well together. There is not always a logic in this area because we are not only dealing with logic, but emotion and belief as well. Let's look carefully at each of these traits.

SELF-CONTROL

Self-control *or* **internal control**, *is the ability to control your thoughts, emotions, and actions.* It is one of the most important character traits required for successful trading. However, it is also one of the hardest character traits to develop, and one attribute we struggle with our entire life.

An example of self-control is not eating that dish of ice cream at night when you have a craving for it. Ice cream may not be your weakness but there must be other situations where you are not in total control of your emotions and actions. In essence, you have temporarily lost control of yourself.

Discipline is often mentioned as an important character trait to possess in trading. There are two kinds of discipline. The first is self-discipline, which may be used interchangeably with self control. The second kind of discipline is external discipline. External discipline refers to control from an external authority which is imposed on an individual. An example of external discipline might be a soldier in the army. The soldier must listen to and obey all orders from an external authority.

Internal discipline and external discipline are two entirely different—and in fact quite opposite—types of discipline. Internal discipline requires the ability to control oneself internally. External discipline requires the person to surrender all or most control of oneself to an external authority. The authority may then control the person.

One might argue that external discipline requires self-control to carry out orders, but there is an important distinction. In external control the individual becomes an automaton, or robot, for another power. When not under external control, you must determine the course of action and become self-directed. The difference between deciding a course of action and an authority ordering you to one is crucial and more difficult.

The distinction between internal and external discipline is crucial in trading. The type of discipline required for trading is internal discipline, or self-control. When trading, you will always be required to have strong self-control over your actions and not listen to, or be dissuaded in any way by suggestions or tips from other people. Trading requires you to have total control over yourself, unlike external discipline where you surrender or subordinate control to a higher authority.

Traders are certainly a varied group, but one of the most common threads running through the more successful traders is the amount of self-control they possess. Good traders create a set of rules and are able to follow them because they possess self-control. They are not persuaded by others, but resolve to carry out their own ideas.

Why is self control so important in trading? A trader is often required to make many important, and usually critical, decisions in a short period of time. Each decision is based on a set of rules developed by the trader which must be followed. It is very easy for a trader to become impulsive and abandon the trading plan or rules. For example, the trader believes the market is going higher, but there is a rumor out that the market will soon drop. What to do? The trader cannot simply abandon a course of action and follow every new rumor and news tip which comes forth. There is so much conflicting and contradictory information that is continuously generated. Any trader heeding all this information would become so indecisive that no decision or course of action could ever be taken.

Of course, most traders need to be well informed and aware of current events. But, there is a critical difference between being aware and being persuaded by external information. The trader must assimilate the information but not be swayed into making an impulsive decision.

There is another reason self-discipline is so important. Trading will require going through difficult periods. Whether it be a bad trade or series of losing trades, trading will continually put a person through emotionally and physically jarring times. It will be easy to abandon trading at these times, or bet the whole stake to take the easy way out and make or lose a fortune. This is when self-discipline is essential to avoid quitting or a potential disaster.

You will need self-discipline to continue with your trading plan and not give up during tough times. You must have a clear idea and trading plan, and know how to selectively incorporate information into the entire trading process. You must have the discipline to develop a course of action and follow it through to fruition.

ACCEPT RESPONSIBILITY

An important consequence of self-control is that you are totally responsible for your actions, and therefore must assume all responsibility for improper or incorrect action. Many people cannot accept responsibility for their actions. There is no one to blame but yourself if trading is going poorly, and this can be a very hard and lonely thing to accept.

One of the hidden benefits of external control is that we do not have to accept responsibility for our actions. Many people search for ways to hide or absolve themselves from any form of responsibility. We can blame any of our actions deemed improper on the external authority which issued the order. Many people live in an environment where they feel they are controlled, and therefore feel relieved not to have responsibility for their actions. Passing the buck is a way of not assuming responsibility, but trying to place it to someone else. When we do not believe we are responsible for our actions, we often do not consider the consequences of our actions. Trading demands that we understand the consequences of our actions, or we may be very sorry of the outcome.

When trading we can give all kinds of excuses as to why we are not successful, such as the tip sounded good, or I should have known better. However, all the reasons anyone might dream up, and more, really don't matter, because you still must take responsibility for the results of your actions. Your profit and loss statements will not listen to your excuses. You do not have to explain your reasons to a higher official to escape censure. You have a far harder task. You must instead justify your actions to yourself. *There is nowhere to hide when trading, because you always stand alone.*

OPERATE IN AN UNSTRUCTURED ENVIRONMENT

Trading requires you to operate in an environment with few rules and little structure. Most people need order and rules for guidance. Many of the orders and rules that help to maintain our sense of security in society are imposed from an external authority. We feel there are laws and rules of conduct to protect us if our well being or security is threatened. We can try to change these laws through a governing body if we believe they are wrong. We feel assured the group assigned to carry out the laws will protect us. Finally, we can turn to the court system if we have not received justice.

There are clearly defined rules in the mechanics of trading, such as contract size and expiration date of the contract. However, there are no rules regarding movement of the market. The market is free to trade wherever it pleases. The society of trading (i.e., the market) has no governing body to create rules, no policing body to enforce rules, and no judicial body to interpret rules. This nebulous environment can be an unsettling situation that most of us are totally unfamiliar with. If we think the market should go up when instead it goes down, we cannot petition or complain to our elected officials, call the police, or go to court and appeal the decision. The market does not even care if you make or lose money. The market can trade in the most irrational manner, but it never has to explain its actions to anyone. When trading, we are never far from anarchy, and just around the corner from chaos.

You must create your own reality and rule system, and that in itself can be a formidable task. We are more familiar with accepting the rules of our society, or trying to change those which are unfair. Most of us are inadequately prepared or equipped to create, from the beginning, an entire rule system or paradigm for trading. This process is involved, and not simply an everyday occurrence we casually do. Yet each trader must develop his or her own unique view and reality of the market.

Many people look to books or gurus for tips on how to trade. Many become quickly frustrated because there is so much contradictory advice and theories on how to trade. There is no place or authority to determine the "proper" course of action—except the arena of the market. You must ultimately determine which trading method and money management system is right for you—not which one is the "best" or makes the most money. It is not enough to create a paradigm, because many theorists do this but never actually test it. The rule structure or reality must work, or it will be brutally uncovered as wrong by the market. *A strategy must be created, tested, and constantly applied, but most importantly, it must work.*

The game of trading has very few external rules, and as a consequence, many people find themselves helplessly lost in an ocean of conflicting and generally vague advice. The market can be an overwhelming and nebulous enigma. What worked yesterday may not work today, but may work tomorrow, or may never work again. What strategy should be followed in this type of environment where there is so much uncertainty?

Information and advice from well meaning sources can easily be contradictory and misleading. Anyone actually trying to follow this advice can end up being even more confused after listening and trying to comprehend all the information. This can happen because a few basic rules in trading are obvious. There is no court or judge to resolve contradictions; so any statement can appear true or false and there is no way of confirming it. There are few trading truths because the trading world has few absolutes, but an infinite number of possibilities and maybes.

ABILITY TO THINK INDEPENDENTLY AND CREATIVELY

Independent thought *is the ability to think for yourself and develop ideas separate from anyone else.* This allows one to think creatively, and sometimes contrary to other people to attain goals many might have otherwise considered impossible. Independent thought allows you to think in a contrary way but contrary thought for its own sake is of little value. You must think independently and if necessary in a contrary way.

From infancy we are taught to get along with other people. We learn that the benefits of socialization and getting along with others far outweigh the other extreme of isolation and loneliness. Many of us tend to develop beliefs and opinions which are in the mainstream partly due to our socialization process. People with contrary or strange ideas and actions are often ridiculed and sometimes ostracized. The trading world is much different from our "normal" world. Unlike many other occupations, where work is done in a team fashion, trading success is strictly up to the individual.

Trading requires a different view about the world. Markets generally go down when most people are bullish, and up when most people are bearish. There is a simple reason for this. If everyone is bullish and long the market, there is no one left to buy. If there are no buyers left, the market can only drop, because people will begin to lose enthusiasm and start to sell. The same holds true when everyone is bearish and disenchanted with the market.

Though the concept of being contrary may be easy to understand, it can be hard to implement. It is difficult to take the opposite side of a trade when everyone around you is giving excellent reasons why you are wrong. You will immediately question your decision and find it hard to maintain your position in the face of obvious opinion against you. Trading requires you to make decisions and take positions contrary to commonly accepted ideas, and this naturally makes you question the validity of your ideas.

Traders do not, and should not, take a contrary opinion just for the sake of being contrary. A trader must instead possess independent thought, which fosters our ability to think clearly and separately from the crowd mentality. Independent thought allows the individual to pursue ideas and possibilities that most people might find unusual, or simply not possible.

Independent thought is a way to think creatively, or in ways which many others might have considered unimaginable. Excess and extremes are quite possible in the market because emotions such as fear and elation may run high and low in good or bad times. The market moves in ways which are inconceivable for many but possible for some.

Creativity is thinking in terms of possibilities, as opposed to impossibilities. Trading requires creativity because you must always think in terms of what the market may possibly due and the chances of such a move occurring. Being able to anticipate certain moves of a market can spell the difference between disaster or opportunity for a trader.

The life of a trader is closer to that of an artist. It is a struggle of ideas, within and without, which are continually tested by a different judge. The trader creates ideas and has them tested, sometimes brutally, by an uncaring but usually efficient market.

WILLINGNESS TO ACCEPT RISK
AND TAKE LOSSES

A trader must be willing to accept risk and take losses. An inevitable consequence of reward is risk. To strive for reward implies the necessity of incurring risk. More risk does not always imply a commensurate reward but risk is inherent in any process where reward may be expected. Anyone not willing to accept risk cannot trade and should look for another endeavor. A person searching for a riskless trade should reconsider: Who would take the other side of a trade which offered risk but no reward? No rational person would, and anyone else who did would not be trading for long.

Risk taking does not necessarily imply taking on tremendous risks to make a fortune. Many traders are actually some of the most risk conscious people—they have to be or else they won't last too long. They are in the business of taking on risk for profit and must thoroughly understand risk and reward.

Other people enter the trading business to make money and cannot accept taking a loss. If a losing trade develops they might decide to put on a spread that has no real chance of being profitable, or simply refuse to exit the position to turn a trade into a long term "investment." These rationalizations and many others result from a simple fundamental problem in which the person will not accept a loss. *One of the ironies of trading is that the more successful you are as a trader the more money you will lose.*

Many people enter the business to make money but cannot accept taking a loss. There are many reasons for this. Some people believe they cannot be wrong and will not accept the fact the market does not agree with their view of the world. They decide to hold onto the losing trade and wait until the market sees the error of its ways, which will eventually make the trade profitable. Others simply refuse to trade, because they perceive a losing trade as a failure in themselves or an aspersion on their integrity. Even though these perceptions and attitudes are incorrect, they are beliefs many cannot come to grips with.

There are usually two kinds of losses which occur. Some losses are the result of human mistakes for a variety of reasons. You must be willing to accept the fact that you will make many mistakes in trading. Mistakes are an inevitable consequence in any learning process. There is always so much to understand about the markets. Never be afraid to make mistakes as long as the errors are not severe and are part of the lessons of trading. You will soon learn to minimize the impact of these mistakes which inevitably occur.

As the trader becomes more proficient the losses will still occur. However, these happen more often from the probabilities of the market, and are simply part of the business of trading. Any trade, no matter how well thought out, has a chance of becoming a loser. Many people think the best traders don't lose any money and have only winning trades. This is absolutely not true. The best traders lose a lot of money, but they eventually make even more over time. Trading is a business of making and losing money. Anyone wanting to make money must accept the fact they must risk and possibly lose money in the process.

Trading is a lot like boxing. A good boxer is someone who can throw a good punch, and, just as important, someone who can take a lot of good punches. Be prepared to take a lot of hits in trading. They are an inevitable part of the process of winning. Part of the joy and appreciation of life comes from the awareness and experience of sorrow. Just try to keep the hits minor and not knockouts.

ACCEPT THE LACK OF CONTROL AND UNDERSTANDING OF THE MARKET

Trading requires that you not necessarily control or understand the market, but instead react to it and accept what it does. We often try to make sense out of life and look for cause and effect in events. Most of us learn to think logically as children. We extend this logical education through religion, philosophy, science, or other ways by believing there is an inner logic and order to the universe. Interestingly enough, our precept of logic and order is not based on logic but on belief, which is outside the realm of logic.

We employ the same rationale of logic and order to trading but find it impossible to understand why the market moves in certain ways. It is not always possible to rationalize or understand the mind of the market because it does not always act in a rational manner. We have been taught that investment decisions should always be based on rational and prudent behavior. But when investors begin to make or lose money we often see emotion takes precedence over rationality.

Others find trading agonizing because they are not in control of the situation. Many people are accustomed to, or need to control the environment they live and work in. Although trading demands total self-control of your thoughts and emotions, it also demands that you accept and surrender yourself to the flow of the outside power of the market. You cannot impose your logic and beliefs on the market, but instead must try to understand or appreciate the underlying forces which drive the market—emotion and rationality. We may not always understand the market, because the market is a reflection of peoples' emotions which cannot always be comprehended. You must learn to flow with the market, as opposed to changing or controlling it.

Markets may seem irrational, wrong, incorrectly priced, unfair, and a host of other incomprehensible things. But you must accept the fact that the market is more powerful than you or any group or government. If you cannot accept this fact, you should not trade.

The market battlefield is littered with people who felt they could manipulate or control the market. These people are invariably unsuccessful or ruined in their attempt to control the market, or belief they were right and the market was wrong. You must surrender your ego and feelings to a more powerful entity—the market.

ADJUST TO A CONSTANTLY CHANGING ENVIRONMENT

You finally develop a method that makes money and—pow!—the market changes and you find yourself losing money again. *Trading requires that you be flexible and adaptable to the ever changing market environment.* The only constant in life is change, and this applies equally well to trading.

A strategy that worked well one year may prove disastrous the next. The markets continually change, but most peoples' trading methods usually stay the same. It is hard to change a method that worked just a short time ago, but complacency in the markets is often a prelude to disaster.

Brains is a bull market is an apt description of the mentality of some traders about a market. Some people can only buy and appear to be fantastic traders in bull markets, but when the bull market turns into a bear phase they often lose their touch and their money. Others can only sell and wait for bear markets to trade. Others don't seem to care either way and are adroit at making or losing money in either phase.

Traders may have good winning streaks and then begin losing money for no reason at all. What usually happens is a method that was successful before does not work now because the market has changed. We would give almost anything to see the market trade as it did in the past, but it is senseless to think this way. Instead, we must learn to adapt to the market and change the method or find a different market where the method may have a better chance of working.

You may be wondering if there is a contradiction brewing. A trader needs to be disciplined and follow rules; yet the trader also needs to be flexible and know when to change the rules and surrender to the flow of the market. There is a crucial difference. The trader does not follow rules to prove he possesses self control. Instead, the trader believes following the rules will produce beneficial results in the long run. Flexibility is the ability to adapt to a constantly changing environment. The trader must realize the rules are not inviolate, but may change because the market changes with time.

The trader must understand the rules may need to be changed in order to obtain the beneficial results again.

The trader does not surrender internal control to the market, but realizes the market is more powerful. Therefore, the trader does not try to impose his control or set of beliefs on the market.

For example, assume you are following a trading method. You notice every time a buy or sell signal occurs the market often goes the opposite way, and the trade results in a loss immediately. In this situation, self-discipline in carrying out the trading signals will only prove disastrous. What you really need is the flexibility to change the original system. This is the difference between being flexible to the changing market, versus following the whims or utterances of rumors and news reports.

There are always times when you are better off not following the rules of your trading system and breaking your self-discipline. But what you have to determine is whether you are consistently better off following or not following the rules. If you are better off not following the rules, it is not the discipline which must be broken, but the rule system that is not quite as good as you originally thought.

Therefore, you must follow your rules, and this requires self-discipline. But, you must also be flexible in adapting to the constantly changing environment of the market. The dinosaurs did not survive because they could not adapt to the change in their environment. You must be able to adapt to the market or you will not survive. You need the flexibility to adapt to a situation and develop a versatile trading method, along with the self-discipline to carry out your plans.

ABILITY TO ACT ON YOUR DECISION

Many analysts pride themselves on calling the market, or predicting what the market will do. The analyst gets paid for calling the market. *The trader gets paid for trading the market. Therefore, the trader must be able to decide the proper action but more importantly be able to act on and live through the decision.*

The trader can be wrong about a prediction and still make money trading, whereas the analyst gets paid to predict but not to trade. Some analysts can predict markets accurately but may not be able to trade them successfully. Some traders can trade successfully, but be poor at prediction because they change their opinions so quickly.

The distinction between analysis and trading is crucial. The trader must act on the trade, live through the position, and accept the consequences. The trader puts money on the line; the analyst puts recommendations on the line. Recommendations may be explained away or forgotten, whereas a trade cannot. It is simply not enough to call the market—you must also trade it.

For example, assume the market is breaking out of a long rectangle formation and you feel it is time to go short. The market takes a severe plunge so you wait to sell a rally to obtain better prices. But the hoped-for rally never comes and the market plummets to new lows. The decline finally ends and the market begins to rally. Should you sell now? Or is this the beginning of a bottom? You missed the move but called the market correctly. What reward does a trader receive for this? Nothing.

Countless times people brag how they would have bought the bottom or sold the top, but never actually trade. Some traders are correct about market action, but enter or exit at the wrong time and end up losing money. This can be a frustrating situation every trader has experienced.

Carrying overnight positions can be nerve wracking, especially when there is the possibility of important news coming out at any time. For example, being short coffee during the drought season can be disastrous if the market opens limit up the next day due to crop damage. Being long can be just as agonizing to watch the market crash if the rains do eventually develop. Living through these times with a position is much more difficult than looking back at a chart and reviewing obvious entry and exit levels.

It is totally different to say what you would have done after the fact, versus what you actually would have done. It is often much easier to know what should have been done after the fact, but much more difficult to determine a proper course of action beforehand. It is so much harder to trade with your hand to the fire and the markets moving quickly for and against your position. Rapidly disseminated bullish and bearish information can cause the market to change direction immediately. It is very easy to question your original position. Monday morning quarterbacks are not limited to just sports, but their post predictions after the fact are of no use in trading today.

Trading demands you make clear and quick decisions, then execute them without delay. No Hamlet need apply.

ABILITY TO WITHSTAND STRESS

Trading is one of the most stressful endeavors imaginable so a trader must endure a tremendous amount of stress. Trading is physically and mentally punishing. Probably the toughest time any trader experiences is during a large loss, or a series of sustained losses resulting in a large drawdown period.

Taking losses day after day with a strategy that, just a short while ago was working well can be a terrible experience. The trader watches hard-earned profits or original investment capital erode quickly into thin air. Another frightening experience is to build a profit in a trade, only to see it vanish and turn to a loss when the market moves swiftly against your position.

These are just a few of the many ways the market can batter your psyche and gnaw at your soul. These kinds of experiences will never end as long as you trade. You must learn to live with them, or find some acceptable compromise. *But remember that the market makes no compromises; so you must.*

Trading is a nurturing ground for internal conflict. The combination of a limited rule structure and constantly changing environment is fertile ground for all kinds of inner turmoil that surface in trading. Contradictory experiences, as well as seemingly illogical and cruel markets, somehow bring out emotional conflicts within us. Contradictions arise in trading all the time and the trader must try to continually resolve these conflicts. These are not easily resolved and often are the seeds for quitting the market altogether.

Conflicts make it hard to concentrate. Focus and attention in the market is important. Internal conflicts and external contradictions seem to steal attention away, making it difficult or impossible to trade.

Trading is not an occupation, but a love/hate relationship in which the trader constantly struggles with not just making and losing money, but his own gain and loss of identity. This may not even be in the sense of ego, but more in the creation or destruction of ideals and dreams. It is more closely related to the artist's world, although the benefits and drawbacks are much more tangible.

It is imperative you thoroughly understand trading will be a grueling, grinding process that can easily wear you down. You must not allow the market to affect the way you feel about yourself. Trading the market is a never ending struggle which emanates from within rather than without. The stress will always exist, but the trader must learn how to avoid or channel it away.

You might feel that you have to deal with conflicts and contradictions all the time at work, so why is trading any more demanding? You are correct but there is one important point not considered. You are paid for your work, so even if there is much stress and frustration at the job the compensation makes it much more bearable. In contrast, when trading, you may have to suffer through a great amount of stress, conflict, and contradictions. But to make things worse, the trader may lose a lot of money in the process. Imagine working very hard and not getting paid, or even losing money for your labor. That makes all the difference.

EMOTIONALLY DETACHED

You must look at trading as a business, and emotionally detach yourself from the results of the trades. Many traders tend to personalize their trades and equate their self worth or measure their ego with the amount of money or number of winning trades they make. This can happen any time but is especially prevalent when a trader goes through a heavy winning or losing period. An individual needs to keep an even temperament because one of the requirements in trading is to not get swept up in unbridled optimism, or blown away in the depths of despair.

Trading can be a highly emotional experience because profits and losses can tend to be exaggerated. Unlike many other businesses where revenues may be more steady, trading performance can be consistently volatile with good and bad times highly magnified. These highs and lows bring out the emotional side in all of us, which can prove destructive if left unbridled.

It is easy to become elated after a great trading period and live it up to the fullest. After all, the trader has most likely worked hard for this and deserves to celebrate and enjoy every minute of the happiness. Savoring success is part of living, but in trading you must realize that the higher highs may be accompanied with lower lows. If a trader becomes too emotional, losing periods may lead to depression while winning periods may produce a dangerous over-confidence. Whether trading is going badly or well, you must remember that a series of winning or losing trades may be just around the corner.

It serves no purpose to be too optimistic or pessimistic in trading. Too much optimism leads to focusing on profits, but not being concerned with losses. Too much pessimism may make a person dwell on risk, never believing an opportunity for reward will arrive.

Trading is a business. The more emotional you become on the upside, the easier it is to become emotional on the downside. You must temper your elation with the sobering fact that after every new trading profit or equity high is the possibility of a new and even greater maximum drawdown, with a subsequent emotional drawdown.

PATIENCE

Trading requires patience because you must wait until the appropriate time to act. Markets do not always offer good trading opportunities because they may be in congestion or random phases some of the time. Anyone trading a random market will be fortunate to break even because they have no advantage or edge. Patience is required to stay out of a sleepy market or seek more active ones.

There are other times when markets become too volatile and risky to trade. It can be especially enticing to trade during these times because large moves seem to offer quick and easy profits. However, risk may be much greater but not commensurate with the potential reward. These times may be equally difficult to wait out.

The monetary cost can be secondary compared to the emotional costs a trader must suffer in these types of markets. Being whipsawed in trendless or high risk markets can be quite frustrating and crush any lingering desire to resume trading. After such an experience, a trader may become mentally broken and ill prepared or incapable to act at the appropriate time when real opportunities do arise.

People often trade out of sheer boredom or for the excitement of just doing something to pass the time. Others will stake a position just to make sure they do not miss the next big move. This is not really trading but more a form of entertainment which can be very expensive but of questionable value. Still other traders believe that as soon as they put a position on, the market must begin moving in their direction. The market may have other ideas. Even active short-term traders do not always trade but wait for opportune times to unfold.

A trader must not confuse activity with profitability. Many traders watch others become involved in a market and feel they are somehow being left out of the action. Some feel they must constantly trade to catch all the moves or believe the market must make large moves instead. Others hear stories of people making big money and fear being left out of the gravy train. Keep in mind that the train is sometimes empty or even becomes derailed.

ENTHUSIASM, COMMITMENT, AND FOCUS

Enthusiasm *implies a true enjoyment and excitement for something.* **Commitment** *is the ability to dedicate yourself to an endeavor.* Enthusiasm and commitment are necessary because trading can be so difficult and demanding. You must develop an ardor and passion for trading. Traders are often highly motivated individuals. You must be willing to devote yourself to the business of trading. After a series of losing trades there will be times when you wonder if it is all worth it. You must maintain your commitment to the business because there will always be many good reasons to quit trading.

Focus *is the ability to concentrate on the task and finish the job.* Trading requires tremendous focus because it is easy to become distracted. Most trading is not a physically active endeavor (except floor trading) but instead, requires one to watch and sit through sometimes agonizing experiences. It will be tempting to wander and try to forget about trading when losses develop, but this will be precisely the time when focus is required. Trading demands an intensity of purpose.

SELF-DIRECTION

Self-direction, *akin to insight, is the ability to understand and know the right course of action.* There are few obvious answers in trading, and questions frequently arise. Good traders must develop a sense or feel for the proper course of action. They may not always be right, but they are willing to act on their intuition and are usually more right than wrong.

Should a technical or fundamental trading method be employed, or can they be incorporated into a universal approach? How do you know when to buy support for the next move higher, or sell support in the expectation the market is headed lower? How do you know when to change your trading method when the market has really changed, or continue with the same method and withstand the recent losses? Trading requires you to possess a keen insight into knowing what should be done, and, when the proper time occurs, to do it.

The ability to know when to change a strategy, or which trading method to use partly comes from self direction. It is not enough to learn all the trading methods and money management techniques. You must really understand the underlying ideas and be able to apply them in sometimes frightening and uncharted waters. No one can provide the "right" answer because it does not exist. Working in an unstructured environment requires that the individual have a sense of knowing what to do, or creating a game plan to succeed. Independent thought demands self-direction and the ability to know what to pursue and explore.

Trading does not necessarily require that you read many books on trading, but it does require that you write your own "book" and develop your own ideas.

CONCLUSION

There are other character traits which are helpful in trading but the ones mentioned will go a long way in helping you become more successful. How are these traits developed? We will investigate this in Chapter 29.

CHAPTER **29**

Three Qualities

This above all: to thine ownself be true.
And it must follow, as the night the day,
Thou canst not then be false to any man.

William Shakespeare, *Hamlet*

How do we obtain the traits outlined for successful trading? All of the necessary traits are a function of the three most powerful qualities a person may have:

1. *Introspection:* The ability to see into and know yourself.

2. *Confidence:* The belief in yourself.

3. *Perseverance:* The courage and spirit to carry out your plan.

INTROSPECTION

Introspection *is the ability to look within and see yourself as you really are.* The first step in any endeavor in life is introspection—know yourself. You must acknowledge who you are then ask yourself,

"What do you really want in life? What do you expect to gain from trading, and how will trading help you achieve what you desire from life?"

A thorough introspection will determine if you possess the 13 character traits for successful trading. Do you have self-control, and are you willing to accept complete responsibility for your actions? Do you have the proper traits requisite for trading? If not do, you really want to go through the process of obtaining them?

You must see if you possess the enthusiasm and dedication necessary for trading. Trading may appear exciting and highly rewarding, but it can also be a very painful process. Most people think only of making money when trading, but losing money is an integral and difficult part of trading as well. Trading will require tremendous dedication, because whenever we begin losing money and suffer pain we will want to stop trading. Losing periods provide a good indication of how dearly we really desire to trade.

Trading will be an enlightening experience because it will draw out aspects of your personality, some of which you would rather keep locked away and forgotten. How can trading be so revealing? Whenever faced with a difficult situation such as losing money, we will immediately question how we got involved and determine how to expeditiously get out. In essence, we question who we are (Why am I in this situation?), and whether we possess the requisite abilities to extricate ourselves from the predicament (How do I get out?). We will learn what is truly important to us. *Trading will be quite revealing because it will present many difficult and painful situations.* It will be a true test of our mettle. Trading will strip your soul, force you to examine every corner of your mind, and bring out the essence of who you are.

Trading demands a hard and truthful introspection of yourself. You must possess an ability to look at yourself as truthfully as possible. Introspection is the ability to know yourself. What could be a more powerful force than the possession of knowledge? One of the most important reasons I enjoy trading is that I must continually learn about myself and the world. I do not always like what I see, but must either change it or learn to accept it. Introspection is the key to developing confidence and perseverance which are necessary to continue trading.

CONFIDENCE

Confidence *is believing in yourself.* Confidence is essential in any endeavor, because you need to believe you can succeed at the task. Confidence can be developed through introspection. Once we know who we are, we can proceed to unwaveringly carry out our goals because we believe we can succeed. Confidence is the belief you can succeed.

Confidence must not be confused with haughtiness. Haughtiness is ignorance of oneself and false overconfidence—an improper introspection. Too much confidence or a haughty attitude can be a sure means to destruction. Realistic introspection is a way to guard against haughtiness.

Confidence helps you in many ways:

1. It strengthens your self-control because you now believe you possess the power to control yourself. This helps provide the power to act on your decision.

2. It helps you to accept responsibility and the results of your actions, and tolerate stress because you believe in what you are doing is correct.

3. It provides you with the ability to think independently of others and take a contrary view. Independent thought requires that you possess a strong belief in yourself. You need not be swayed by others because you believe in yourself.

5. It helps you to accept the insecurity that may arise in not understanding the market.

6. It provides the security of functioning in an insecure and changing unstructured environment.

7. It helps you to be emotionally detached and accept losses, because you realize short-term trading results are not a reflection of your ego.

8. It builds patience because you can wait for the proper time to act.

9. It reinforces commitment and enthusiasm, and helps you focus and work to improve yourself.

Confidence implies belief. All trading methods and money management techniques are based on the belief they will work in the future. You must possess confidence in your trading methods and money management techniques otherwise you will not trade. Confidence and introspection are critical to success but there is one more essential quality which is needed—perseverance.

PERSEVERANCE

Perseverance *is the courage to endure.* Trading will be very difficult. There are stories of how people have made easy fortunes in the market, literally overnight, starting out with next to nothing in capital. Some of these stories are true, but many more are not. The majority of successful traders toil long hours and many years in achieving success. Even the best traders probably experienced one or more crises sometime in their career. Some of these dark times might have derailed others, but the better traders withstood the pressure because of their perseverance.

What can make trading even harder is that you may have a valid trading strategy, but an outside event may cause it to perform badly. Unforeseeable events totally outside of your control can have immediate and devastating impacts on the market. These events can immediately affect your profit and loss statement and ultimately your psyche. There is little consolation knowing you have a good idea but bad results, and certainly even less consolation in your trading account.

No matter how well thought out your plan, no matter how much you believe in yourself, there will come a time when you will wonder if all the stress and turmoil is worth going through. Trading will physically and mentally batter you, so it becomes all the more necessary to persevere. Perseverance rekindles your fervor to trade and keeps you in the game when others quit. Perseverance provides the power to continue your introspection and strengthen your confidence. *Perseverance is the light that illuminates the path in dark and difficult times.*

It is not enough to just introspect and have confidence; we must also be able to accept or change whenever we look within.

Otherwise we will refuse to look again. This is not such an easy task. We must go through a three-step process:

1. Work to find out who we are.
2. Accept ourself for who we are.
3. Work to change ourself for the better and accomplish the task.

Introspection, confidence and perseverance are required for this process because they provide the key in finding out, accepting, and changing who we are. *From introspection arises confidence and perseverance, and the ability to pursue your goal.* If you believe you have the necessary attributes and enthusiasm for trading, you will develop confidence and perseverance, and fervently pursue trading. Introspection and confidence provide a most potent combination in accomplishing a task, but perseverance is the essential third element required to overcome a difficult task. Trading demands great effort.

INTERACTION OF THE THREE QUALITIES

The proper interaction of these three qualities is a most powerful force. People of vision such as Columbus, Michelangelo, Beethoven, and da Vinci are great because of their ability to think and act beyond the present. They knew that what they were doing was right. Their introspection permitted them to realize who they were and what they could accomplish. Their confidence reinforced the belief they could accomplish their task. Their perseverance allowed them to continue when others would quit. Their vision was partly fostered by introspection, and their actions were realized through the confidence or belief in themselves and their courage to persevere. *No great effort could have ever been achieved without confidence, introspection, and perseverance.*

The interaction of confidence, introspection, and perseverance is essential in any endeavor. You develop confidence and perseverance through proper introspection. Confidence strengthens your courage to persevere because you believe you will succeed. Perseverance rejuvenates your confidence when it has been shattered.

CONCLUSION

You must always know who you are and your strengths and weaknesses to possess the confidence and perseverance of what you desire from life. You must work to believe in your ideas and learn to change the ones you find do not really work.

Through introspection you understand who you are, through confidence you believe in what you do, and through perseverance you possess the courage to endure and carry out your plan.

CHAPTER 30

Developing a Trading Mentality

I sometimes think that speculation must be an unnatural sort of business, because I find that the average speculator has arrayed against him his own nature. The weaknesses that all men are prone to are fatal to success in speculation—usually those very weaknesses that make him likeable to his fellows or that he himself particularly guards against in those other ventures of his where they are not nearly so dangerous as when he is trading in stocks or commodities.

The speculator's chief enemies are always boring from within.

Edwin LeFevre, *Reminiscences of a Stock Operator*

The list of 13 important character traits previously cited reveals only part of the reason why psychology is important in trading. To understand why psychology is so crucial to successful trading, recall in Chapter 1 the three important components of trading:

1. Trading method.

2. Money management.

3. Psychology.

The first two aspects of trading are logical concepts and therefore can be understood by most people. Take for example trading methods. Most people should be able to understand how a moving average is calculated, and the trading rules employed when using them. The same idea applies with money management techniques. Although maximum drawdown may be an unfamiliar concept, most people can learn how to calculate it and apply it in trading. Therefore, you can logically learn trading methods and money management techniques and employ or not employ them at your discretion.

Whereas the first two components of trading are logical, the third is not, and this is why the psychology of the individual is so critical for successful trading. Developing a proper psychological attitude for trading is far different, and much harder than learning logical concepts for the following reason. You may agree that the 13 character traits are important for trading. You may ardently strive to learn and develop these traits. *But the reality is that you may never be able to possess these traits, because they cannot simply be learned or developed. Why? Specific personality traits that will improve your trading cannot necessarily be learned logically and implemented as you please, because they are also a function of your emotional state. These traits, or lack of them, are the product of a variety of factors such as the interaction of our environment, genetics, and biology. You cannot learn these traits and integrate them into your psyche, without first changing your entire emotional stability, and in the process, yourself.*

Emotions cannot easily be learned or turned on or off to ease the trading process. Emotional qualities often take a long time to develop—and there is still much debate on how our emotions develop, or how to change them for the better. Let's review the 13 character traits:

1. Self-control.
2. Accepting responsibility for your actions.
3. Ability to function in an unstructured environment.
4. Ability to think independently and creatively.
5. Willingness to accept risk and take losses.
6. Acceptance of the inability to control and comprehend the market.
7. Ability to adapt quickly to a constantly changing environment.
8. Ability to act on your decision.
9. Ability to withstand stress.
10. Emotional detachment.
11. Patience.

12. Enthusiasm, commitment, and focus.

13. Self-direction.

Who can learn any of these traits today and expect to master them in a few days? Consider the character trait of self-discipline. Many people yearn for greater self-control yet the development of self-control requires self-control. *You may agree that self-discipline is essential to successful trading, but you may never be able to possess or acquire the self-control necessary for trading.* This trait is a part of your emotional state and has developed from infancy, and possibly earlier in your genetic imprint. It cannot simply be learned logically like a moving average. For example, many people face the problem of being overweight. Losing weight is really quite simple on a logical level—just eat less food and the overweight person will eventually lose weight. But why can't most overweight people do this? Because eating is not just a logical response to survival, but is tied to emotional needs as well. The overweight person knows eating too much is not healthful but cannot stop eating. We do not eat just because we are hungry. Eating satisfies many other needs besides hunger, such as love and anger. We also do not trade just to make money. Trading is an attempt to satisfy many desires within us, some of which we may not be consciously aware of.

Emotions are involved in trading, so we cannot simply use or dispense with them at will. Tremendous conflicts arise in trading because we are constantly torn between being in or out of the market, increasing or decreasing the size of our position, and a host of other critical decisions. Enormous sums of money can be made and lost quickly, which can immediately affect our emotions.

The three qualities will help in developing these character traits. Introspection will allow you to see if there is a strong desire and dedication to trade. Do you have the requisite traits to trade? Do you really want to trade? Or do you just want to make money irrespective of how it is made? Do you possess the confidence and perseverance to change yourself, and believe what you are doing is right and that you will eventually succeed at it?

Developing a successful trading method and proper money management techniques is difficult. But developing a proper trading mentality can be far more challenging, and sometimes impossible.

It should now be apparent why some of the most brilliant minds and well educated individuals have been totally humiliated and lost substantial sums of money trading the market. It should also be clear that there is no easy way to learn these proper mental traits for trading. *Finally, you must answer these questions from deep inside of you: Do you possess the proper traits for trading? Can you acquire these traits? If so, do you want to acquire these traits? In essence, do you really want to change who you are?*

This is why trading is so hard.

THE FIGHT FROM WITHIN

Trading can be difficult and confusing because some of the character traits and impulses considered normal in society may tend to be opposite those which are necessary for trading. This does not imply that trading is immoral or antisocial in any way, but that it requires special talents that few people possess. For example, civilizations developed to establish an order and structure that people could live by and understand. This order allows us to have some reasonable expectation about the future—we can expect some certainty in life. Most people shun an unstructured environment and desire the security of a structured one, but in trading we must be willing to not only operate but also live in an unstructured environment. We know not the future, cannot rely on the past, but can only go forward in the present believing in ourself.

The traits of independent thinking and contrary opinion can sometimes be the antithesis of normal social behavior such as following the crowd or doing what everyone else does. We learn from an early age not to go against the grain and try to be like everyone else. This is fine in most social situations but in trading, going with the crowd can be disastrous as was pointed out earlier.

Encountering pain is something every human instinctively avoids and yet we must continually accept pain and stress as part of the routine of trading. Taking a series of losses or a big loss can always be a painful experience no matter how seasoned the trader. These painful experiences become deeply etched in our mind making us try to avoid them in the future. Trading demands that we accept pain to realize pleasure.

The timeless traits of hope and fear are natural feelings which the trader must particularly control. The trader must never fear a loss but always fear the market and the possibility of a loss becoming too great. The trader must not hope that the market will bail out a losing position but always have hope that a position will become a winner.

And so in trading we are caught by many tendencies which are not considered normal. Trading requires that we unlearn or subdue these natural tendencies which we inherently possess or have developed from infancy. This is no easy task. Trading is an extraordinary occupation because it demands unusual traits. But remember the potential rewards may be worth the risk for some people. This continuous battle from within makes trading all the more difficult.

SOLVING A PROBLEM

Let's see if we can develop some of the character traits for trading. We will approach this in the same way we might try to resolve any other type of problem by taking the following steps. The ability to successfully solve a problem is dependent on these factors:

1. *Become aware of the problem.* The person must acknowledge that a problem exists. Many people cannot even reach this first step. For example, many drug abusers do not even realize they have a problem, because they feel drugs are a necessary part of life. In trading, many people do not even realize that psychology has anything to do with their performance and trading ability. They blame their bad results on fate, bad luck, irrational markets, bad trading methods, and a host of other factors. They cannot even make the connection that the problem may be them, and not due to external reasons.

2. *Understand the problem.* The person must understand the problem. Some people believe they have a problem but do not know what it is or how to solve it. A stomachache may be temporarily

relieved with medicine, but if the root cause of the ache is stress, the problem will not be solved until the stress is eliminated. Many traders are not happy with their results and blame it on the trading method, such as a moving average system or chart formations. If they had a better trading method they would surely make money.

3. *Learn whether it is possible to solve the problem.* The person must know if it is possible to solve the problem, and if so, what methods are available to solve it. A person who suffers from depression may realize there is a problem, but unfortunately may not be able to resolve it satisfactorily. If self-control is lacking, is it possible to acquire or develop this trait? Are certain traits latent or totally absent from the person? A person must realize that certain character traits may never be developed beyond a certain level. Others believe they may be able to change, and must then determine how to do so, either by learning more about solutions to the problem, therapy, or other approaches.

4. *Realize the implications of solving the problem.* What are the ramifications of solving the problem? The solution to the problem may be worse than the problem. The pesticide DDT solved an immediate problem but created many more environmental problems. Changing one character trait will change the person. Developing more self-discipline may improve the trading performance but this personality change may cause the person to feel worse than before. The person may be more unhappy now because he or she is less impulsive and carefree. Will the person be happy with the new change?

5. *Decide whether it is worth solving the problem.* After reviewing the first four factors, the person must decide whether to solve the problem or leave things as they are. The person must decide whether the transformation will be more or less beneficial. Is the person really better off changing?

6. *Commitment and willingness to resolve the problem and accept the consequences of change, or simply continue living with the problem.* If the decision is made to resolve the problem, the person must commit all resources and accept the insecurity of change. Many dieters get to this point but cannot bring themselves to forego that

extra piece of delicious cherry pie. The person must also realize that no matter how well thought out the plan, one can never fully know the implications. Change implies both hope and fear. No matter how hard or easy the first five steps may be, the sixth step of execution is usually the most difficult.

INTROSPECTION: A SECOND LOOK

Introspection and Psychological Problems

The solutions to psychological problems present special difficulties to anyone. It is not possible to analyze yourself objectively because you will naturally have a subjective perspective. Therefore, the six-step problem solving process previously outlined may not be possible to perform because of an inadequate introspection. For example, the first step—an awareness of a problem—may not be apparent because of improper introspection. How can any problem be solved if the person is not aware of it? *Without proper introspection the solution to any psychological problem becomes impossible.*

Solving a problem can be further complicated or blocked by neuroses or other mental dysfunctions. For example, a person may sincerely want to trade but may not be able to accept risk. If an overt or latent fear of risk taking cannot be overcome, the person will never be able to trade. This may seem like an obvious problem to overcome, but it is not. Trading, like life, is quite complex so there are many "blocks" which do not allow us to easily attain our goals.

The Hunt Brothers thought they could control the silver market in 1980. They bought huge amounts of silver which helped to push the price up to exorbitant levels. They were forced to exit their positions at much lower prices, which resulted in losses of millions of dollars on their positions. The Hunt Brothers had the confidence and perseverance to succeed but not the introspection. They lacked an understanding of who they were and what they could accomplish. They believed they were bigger than the market and tried to corner it. Their introspection was wrong, which proved to be their undoing. Improper introspection is the cause of failure for many people.

Exploration of Yourself—Terra Incognito

You must be willing to delve inside of you and see yourself. This can be difficult and painful. The process of introspection implies the person must have the ability to accept the results of introspection. Anyone who cannot accept a self-evaluation cannot adequately perform an introspection. This is one of the reasons why introspection is so important in solving individual problems. You need an awareness of who you are and an understanding of your goals—in other words, you need proper introspection to understand the direction you are heading in.

You cannot sit back in passive contemplation and think—I want to be a trader and make money. You and many other people in the world share the same thought. Trading implies accepting risk and stress and frequently losing money. It will involve experimentation and exploration of who you really are. You will need to clearly determine whether you want to trade and whether you will be able to tolerate the emotional and physical turmoil which trading engenders.

Trading is an active and involved process of discovering yourself. If the introspection process is beginning to seem long and involved, then you are finally getting the message. This is not a cursory 30-minute meditation, but a rigorous exploration which must be done the rest of your life.

IS THERE NO HOPE?

Some of the previously mentioned character traits are quite difficult, if not impossible, to acquire. Some problems may not be solved because we are not even aware they exist. Is there no hope? Should a trader deficient in some important character traits give up all hope of trading and find another endeavor? Some people do not have the ability and may have to leave the business, but some of us can still get by with what we have.

All of us have physical and mental disabilities to varying degrees, which prevent us from attaining everything we desire. The more severe the disability the more limited in what we may achieve. We must overcome the disabilities that can be conquered and learn to accept those that we believe are insurmountable. In effect, we must either change ourself or our goals to attain our happiness.

You must determine your strengths and weaknesses and decide how this will affect your trading. This is similar to reviewing a trading method and determining the good and bad points of a moving average system, or analyzing a money management technique such as diversification, which is always ideally beneficial but much harder to implement in practice. You must understand the inherent benefits and limitations of each method and try to improve upon them, but realize they will never be perfect.

The same analysis holds true when reviewing our psychological makeup. You should not immediately expect to attain every character trait or just give up in frustration. You must understand how to use your strengths to their fullest and determine how to overcome or compensate as much as possible for your weaknesses. We may strive for perfection, but we should not expect it in an imperfect world.

You have inherent strengths and weaknesses and may not possess all the required character traits for trading, but neither does anyone else. The more traits you possess, the greater your advantage, but the more you work at obtaining these traits, the better your chances for success. What will help in attaining these traits—introspection, confidence, and perseverance?

WHY IS TRADING SUCH A PAINFUL PROCESS?

For those new to the business, trading appears exciting, fast, and fun. In fact it is. However, trading is much more than this—it is a painful process as well.

Losing money can be a hellish experience but it can also make us feel insecure and frightened. Seeing money we struggled so hard to make vanish instantly into thin air as a market moves against us can be an agonizing and gut-wrenching experience. Our ability to trade will come into question. We may doubt ourselves and become angry and disillusioned. Trading can be an emotional roller coaster where we may soon grow weary of the ride.

Trading can be stressful because you will be constantly barraged with decisions that only you can answer. In fact, trading is an excellent study of the decision process. Trading will present many difficult decisions that will produce anxiety and tension. Should you enter now or stay out? Should you hold on or exit? Should you risk more money or less? These are but a few of the many questions that will incessantly gnaw at you.

Trading can be painful for other reasons that may not be so obvious. *We all have psychological chains that are far more powerful and difficult to break than any physical ones that bind us.* It will be very hard and sometimes impossible to sever these psychological chains. For example, someone who is insecure may have an inordinate fear of losing money and will not be able to risk any money to trade. A person with this problem may ardently strive to develop confidence to eliminate this block or chain of insecurity but the efforts may prove totally fruitless. *We like to think our environment imposes these blocks or chains, but more often than not we set them ourselves. More often than not, we are the only ones who can break them.*

Trading will demand that we become mental and physical athletes to overcome many of these blocks. But unlike the athlete who can clearly improve through training, we will find it much more difficult to improve ourselves for trading. Why? We may not understand why we cannot bring ourselves to make a trade—Are we afraid of losing money or not sure of ourselves? How do we resolve this conflict if we don't even understand the cause? How do we become confident if we doubt ourselves? How do we avoid the anguish and frustration of repeating the same mistakes but not knowing how to avoid them? We may find ourselves struggling where we don't even know who or what the opponent is. How do we train for an event we know so little about?

Trading places our frailties in a cold revealing light forcing us to confront the truth about ourselves. To break these chains will prove a tremendous and painful struggle. Trading is a series of battles—it is a war we must wage from within. Are we up to the task? We may face a formidable opponent—ourself.

INSIGHT

Insight *is the ability to look deeply into a problem and comprehend ways of solving it.* Insight is intuition and a powerful means of solving problems. Some people possess the power of insight much more than others. Whereas some traders may spend years searching for an elusive trading method, some people with insight seem to know immediately what works best for them.

Insight can go a long way in seeing who we are and determining solutions to difficult problems. But insight is not something that seems to be easily learned or developed. It will definitely help in this process of changing the psychological profile of a trader.

HOW DO YOU DEVELOP A PROPER MIND SET FOR TRADING?

The first requirement is that you know you want to change. Realize that you will become a different person and ask yourself if that is what you really want. For example, why do many dieters abandon their regimen and regain weight? One reason is that some will find themselves more unhappy being thinner but feeling deprived than being heavier but feeling satisfied They would rather be overweight and "happy" than thinner and "unhappy." They become someone they do not want to be when thinner. They may truly want to change but cannot accept all the implications of the change. Many of us want to change—few of us ever do. There is no sense in becoming someone you do not want to be or feel you should not be. You will ultimately end up unhappy with yourself and life, irrespective of the monetary reward involved.

Many people fear change. Change brings on insecurity. The markets constantly change. Some people may believe there is a strict order to life and simply cannot take the confusing chaos the market sometimes becomes. They will avoid trading the market because it frightens them and does not conform to their reality.

Self-control is mentioned as one of the most important traits, and there is also another reason for this. Good self-control is essential in trying to achieve the other 12 character traits. If you have excellent self-control you may be able to improve upon some of the other character traits. Since changing yourself is a delicate process, it is best to do this one step at a time. Remember, you may hope for something, you may realize your hopes, but you may not actually want what you get. No matter how well thought out your plans, there is no way of knowing the full implications until the transformation occurs. And sometimes you cannot go back to the original state. Be careful of what you wish for!

GOALS—CHANGE AND ACCEPTANCE

We go through a three-step process in life:

1. *Develop an overall goal:* The main goal is to seek happiness and serenity for ourselves.

2. *Set intermediate goals to attain the overall goal:* Making money is an intermediate goal that many believe will provide happiness. Whether this is true is another question. Intermediate goals such as financial independence and the challenge of trading are a means of fulfilling our main goal which is happiness.

3. *Carry out actions to achieve the intermediate goals:* Trading or starting a new business are actions to attain the intermediate goal of financial independence.

This process should look familiar. It is similar to the one discussed in the optimization section on money management. We usually have an excellent idea of our main goal. We have a reasonable idea of how our intermediate goals will help us attain the ultimate goal. However, we know less about how our actions will ultimately affect our intermediate and overall goals. There is one crucial difference—the analysis is on ourselves—a far more delicate and critical study.

Our actions will clearly affect our happiness or lack of it. The inability of our actions to meet our expectations or intermediate goals can lay the seeds of frustration—exactly what we originally hoped to avoid. For example, many believe financial independence will help in achieving the ultimate goal of happiness and security. Assume the action chosen to obtain financial independence is trading. But what happens when we begin trading and losing money? Losing money can make life become a nightmare, but even worse, it is exactly the opposite of our intermediate goal of financial independence.

Our action of trading has subverted rather than fulfilled our intermediate goal and furthered us from our ultimate goal of happiness.

We must realize that the actions designed to achieve our intermediate goals may often cause us to endure painful experiences that are exactly the opposite of our ultimate goal, which is happiness. Our action, trading, can yield exactly the opposite results (pain versus pleasure and financial insecurity versus independence) of what we originally desired. This presents a dilemma within every trader. If the anguish and uncertainty become too great, trading will be abandoned because it will not provide the contentment originally intended. It should be relatively apparent why so many people quit trading. We hope trading will foster happiness—but it may not, and even worse, it may cause anxiety and grief.

We have to determine which actions will help us achieve our ultimate and intermediate goals—and this is the hard part. We must decide if the action of trading will help us obtain our ultimate goal. Even successful traders may abandon trading because the conflict and torment become too much to endure.

Actions effect change. Our trading may require that we try to change our psychological framework for trading. We may be willing to change certain traits to achieve our goals. But change will effect uncertainty which will beget insecurity. We may change ourselves, but will we end up being satisfied with the results?

GOALS AND OBJECTIVES

Another consideration is determining how you plan on realizing your actions. For example, it is important to define your objectives and see how they relate to your ultimate goals. Do they help to accomplish your goal, or are they independent or even hinder your goals? The following is an example.

When Theresa first started trading, her objective was to develop a trading system that would catch every major move in the futures markets. She tested the standard systems and then began to create her own trading systems, finally developing one that actually fulfilled her objective. At first she was happy when the method worked, but then she quickly realized all was not well. Why not? Because the trading method not only caught every major move, but also caught every losing move, every whipsaw, and breakeven trade as well! After being chopped up in the market for a few months, she stopped trading the system and resumed her search for a better trading system.

She had fulfilled her objective and still was not satisfied. *This is because her objective, which was to catch every move, was not consistent with her intermediate goal, which was to develop a profitable trading system.* She had to change her objective from catching the big moves to developing a trading method which made money. Her trading strategies changed and so did her profit and loss statement, from negative to positive. She learned that the business of trading can be quite different than devising a system which caught most of the big market moves in the past.

It may seem hard to imagine, but there are many people who are more concerned with catching big moves or other objectives than simply making money. It is important when developing your objectives and actions to define your intermediate goals and be certain they are in synchronization with each other. Otherwise you will never be able to reach your ultimate goal.

LOSE YOUR EGO: SELFLESSNESS

Many people involve their ego in trading. They believe they can outwit or are more powerful than the market and think it is their reputation or self versus the market. This type of attitude is a prelude to disaster. In fact, it is the opposite attitude, or the reduction of the ego in the trading process which will prove to be more successful.

The more our egos are involved in a trade the greater we will become emotionally attached to a trade and biased in an opinion. Trades will be initiated because of an emotional love for the market, instead of a realistic appraisal for the chances of success. Anyone who falls in love with a trade will not exit, even if the probabilities are no longer favorable. Trading is a game of probabilities. Trades must be made in a cold and dispassionate manner.

Selflessness *is the reduction or elimination of the ego, and is an important concept to learn for trading.* Remember the character trait of emotional detachment? A big ego or the involvement of the ego in the trading process is in direct contrast to being emotionally detached. Our ego often comes to the forefront, but we must continually try to subdue it. We must become selfless to view a market in a proper perspective. The less your ego is involved, the better your chances for success. We are not trying to beat the market or prove our intellectual superiority, but simply to take calculated risks for a given reward which will yield positive returns in time. You should enter a trade because the probabilities are in your favor, and exit or stay out when the probabilities are against you.

One of the biggest reasons people are unsuccessful in trading is that they impose their belief and reality on the market. They believe the market must act in the way they think. They are sorely mistaken. The better traders try to learn how the market thinks.

You must subdue your ego and realize the battle is not between you and the market, but within yourself. The fight is always from within, because it is control of yourself which is always the most difficult battle. It is the garnering of your strength and emotions and the inherent power of selflessness which will prove the greatest force.

Selflessness is a means of losing one's ego and is practiced in some Eastern religions such as Zen Buddhism. It is a way to lose the ego and become part of a process as opposed to an observer of it. The stronger the ego the more the person will be distanced from the market. Once the loss of ego occurs the person is better able to become one with the market. What better way to try and understand or be in touch with the market than by losing your ego and becoming part of the market? Selflessness cannot be covered in depth in this book because it is an involved process as well as a way of life. The interested reader can review some of the books recommended in the bibliography under the psychology section for further enlightenment.

DEVELOP A TRADING STYLE

You must find a trading method and money management technique which is compatible with your personality. This will require experimentation and the testing of different methods to see which ones are most appropriate. This is one of the reasons there is no one correct trading method. For example, some people are not comfortable with the trend-following method, while others cannot trade against the trend. Some people cannot hold positions for long periods of time and must day trade on a short timespan. Others get frustrated day trading and look for the big move, not wanting to be bothered with the short-term fluctuations in the market. These attitudes have nothing to do with a correct approach to trading, but instead reflect the personality and philosophy the person has toward trading.

Trading is a learning process about the market, trading methods, and yourself. Instead of determining which methods work best, try to determine which methods you work best with or try to accommodate yourself to methods that show promise. Be prepared to spend time understanding what methods are most appropriate for your style. Try to develop a deep and abiding respect for the market.

Trading will elicit many naked truths about ourself precisely because it is an enigma. Why?—The less we know about something the more we will learn about ourself.

Find methods which are logically compatible, or ones which you philosophically believe in. This is why trading is like an art. Some artists exhibit various techniques and styles with great beauty and imagination. Traders can also employ totally different techniques, such as fundamental or technical analysis. As a trader, you must be willing to create and develop your own unique style which works for you. Imitators are often not successful in art or trading. They do not possess the same personality as the originator, and therefore, cannot understand or believe in the trading method. Trading is not just an understanding of the market but an understanding of your method and how you work with it. This is a very complex process.

PLAYING THE PROBABILITIES

You must look to play the probabilities, instead of searching for the infallible system which always works. We are studying human nature, so looking for certainties or the Holy Grail will prove fruitless. Many people want a good trade which is a sure winner. We must realize that in order to achieve a reward, we must assume risk.

The key is to assume intelligent risk, or risk which will provide good potential rewards.

Think in terms of positive expected outcome. You do not need more profitable trades than losers, but profits must be greater than losses. As we have seen, it is not enough to have a positive expected outcome because a large drawdown will spell disaster. Furthermore, we know that too large a percentage loss will probably mean never recovering to resume an equity uptrend. Not risking too much capital is a way to avoid large drawdowns and big losses.

Trading can be most difficult when the markets continually go against us. This is when we need to really understand our trading method and ourself.

CONCLUSION

You must find a successful trading method which you are comfortable with. This will be one of the hardest parts of trading. Once you have found one, the next step will be to improve upon the method, which will become an eternal search for most.

The next step is to understand how money management techniques will affect the trading method. In the money management section we learned about the equity journey. The journey in psychology is one inside yourself. It is more involved and difficult but the rewards are much greater.

CHAPTER **31**

Practical Considerations in Psychology

> *The recognition of our own mistakes should not benefit us any more than the study of our successes... But I will tell you something curious: A stock speculator sometimes makes mistakes and knows that he is making them. And after he makes them he will ask himself why he made them; and after thinking over it cold-bloodedly a long time after the pain of punishment is over he may learn how he came to make them, and when, and at what particular point of his trade; but not why.*
>
> Edwin LeFevre, *Reminiscences of a Stock Operator*

The markets constantly change. Be prepared to go through a transformation for yourself. Assuming you are still ready, let's get prepared for some of the psychological hurdles and considerations facing a trader.

DEVELOP A GAME PLAN

Try to create a plan you can follow. This will help you from being swayed by the conflicting reasons to buy or sell. You do not have to create a highly structured or rigid game plan, but at least think in terms of a cohesive method for dealing with wins, losses, and in between. You must believe in your plan or you will not follow it.

Here are some steps to follow in developing a game plan:

1. The first step is knowing who you are through introspection. This is the one step many people ignore, which leads to an infinite number of ensuing problems.

2. The second step is to analyze your strengths and weaknesses. If you possess mathematical abilities, perhaps studying an objective trading method such as a moving average system might be one direction to start. If you are more abstract, perhaps reviewing a subjective technical study such as chart patterns is a better start. If you are extremely creative, learn some of the basic ideas of technical and fundamental analysis and develop your own unique methods. Do not look for the "best" method, but the one most compatible with your way of thinking.

3. Review the money management principles and apply them to your trading method. For example, changing entry and exit points can change the percentage of profitable trades. Are you willing to wait long periods of dry spells for the big winning trade, or would you rather take quick small profits?

4. Determine how much money you can afford to risk and always risk a small percentage of capital (less than 5%, 2% for novices) on any trade. If paper trading is possible, it may help in simulating some of the potential pitfalls with your trading methods. You can never simulate the real experience of trading, but paper trading can help to alleviate some of the minor ones which add up to major ones.

5. Trade markets that do not present tremendous risk, such as lower volatility markets or ones without huge dollar swings. Trading can be a time consuming business, so be prepared to spend quality time trading. It can be beneficial, at least initially, to observe how markets move to develop better trading methods.

6. Learn to stick to your game plan, but realize the importance of flexibility, especially when starting out. Many traders complain if they had only stuck to their original plan they would have made money, but they quickly forget the times they would have lost money had they stuck to their plan.

7. Learn to accept mistakes and losses. You will often find your biggest advances in knowledge arise from serious mistakes of the past.

You must develop a rule structure to follow when trading the market. You cannot just trade in a state of anarchy, but must make a few assumptions and rules in such an unstructured environment. Rules provide a solid foundation for growth, but they inherently limit you as well. You must be prepared to create new rules, or revise existing ones, in order to grow in the ever changing trading environment.

EMOTIONAL DRAWDOWN

Just as there is a financial drawdown there is also an emotional drawdown that contributes to the demise of many trading careers. A trader will experience an emotional, as well as a financial drain after a series of losses or one big loss. This drain can extinguish any remaining desire to trade and make you wonder why you entered the madness and torment of the trading environment.

Severe or unexpected market moves may cause substantial losses which can devastate a person's financial and mental well being. Some never recover. A series of small losses can be equally damaging by emotionally battering a trader. It seems as though you have lost your touch and will never make a winning trade again. These and other real or imagined ideas rip at your insides draining you physically and emotionally.

What is the best course of action when going through a series of sustained losses? Should you continue trading with the expectation things will improve or stop trading and perhaps take a vacation? These are tough questions that only you can answer because there is no "right" answer. If markets go through periods of trending and random behavior then there is no reason to assume a good trade is overdue because the last 10 were bad. Markets may stay in random patterns or strongly trend for extended periods of time, so an inappropriate trading method may yield disastrous results no matter how conservative or skilled the trader is. On the other hand, the market may be ready to trend and a rainbow of profits may be just around the corner.

It is hard to make money trading and just as hard to keep it. Profits which may have taken years to gain can suddenly vanish. Much of what you have worked for can suddenly disappear. We are clearly in a tenuous situation. Prudence and patience is required at all times in trading. You must be prepared to suffer and accept pain. Between 5–15% of all commodity traders are successful. Most successful traders have probably experienced serious emotional drawdown at some time. In essence, even the ones who "make it" suffer and go through emotional turmoil.

Losing money is no fun. Most normal people do not want to lose money. We may work very hard and try to learn about the markets. We may think we deserve to make money. The market does not know, nor care about our concerns. We may not get what we think we deserve. Trading implies making and losing money. It also implies suffering financial and emotional losses that can be quite devastating.

THE HIGHS AND LOWS
OF TRADING

You must be able to deal with long periods of time without making money and then possibly making a great deal of money in a short period of time. Both circumstances can be difficult to deal with. It might seem that making a lot of money in a short period of time is easy to take, but it can actually be hard to accept. Moral questions sometimes arise as to whether it is right to make so much money and not even "work hard" at it. Many people tend to cut their profits and exit trades because they have made what they "deserve" rather than basing their trading decisions on proper technical or fundamental analysis.

Even if large profits are easy for you to accept, it will probably be quite difficult accepting dry spells of breaking even or losing money. Waiting for the elusive big profit can be agonizing during these extended periods of not making money. Trading can be very frustrating during these intervals, and you will begin to wonder if the "good times" will ever return.

The opposite scenario can be equally frustrating, when money is made slowly over an extended period of time and then a large sum is agonizingly lost in a relatively short time span. Both scenarios seem to happen more often in trading than simply making a constant amount of money and not losing much. Trading is far removed from our normal lifestyle of collecting a paycheck on a consistent basis. This occurs because markets may consolidate for long intervals and then make large rapid moves. Remember that markets reflect peoples' emotions and can be wild or mellow depending on the time. They seldom make consistent or moderate moves; so your profits and losses will reflect these exaggerated moves.

LACK OF RESOLUTION

As soon as you begin creating your rules you will find contradictions occur, and plenty of reasons to scrap what you have developed. But one of the things many find hard to accept is that the nebulous trading environment never really allows for a resolution of arguments or rules. Sometimes knowing the outcome, no matter how bad, is better than being kept in suspense and not knowing at all.

Most traders want a simple means to consistently make money. They want to resolve the mysteries of the market, but what they are really asking is to consistently understand human behavior. This is much harder than it might seem. The stock market crash of 1987 provides an example. The fundamentals of the economy had not materially changed before, during, or after the market crashed. The only thing which changed was peoples' perception about the fundamentals. Fundamentals will ultimately affect the prospects of a market, but investors' reactions to the *perceived* fundamentals or reality is what drives the price of the market.

A lot of our frustration in life does not always result simply from failure or disappointment. Our frustration is often due to uncertainty or not knowing what the outcome will be, which brings about the agonizing worry and waiting we dread. In essence, it is part of human nature to seek resolution, and in fact many religions and philosophies are based on the resolution of what we believe to be unanswerable questions. Trading seldom answers but more often creates questions. Which is the better technical study? What is properly diversified? These questions are but a few which are integral to trading and have no clear answers.

DISTINGUISH BETWEEN CHANGING MARKETS AND CHANGING STRATEGIES

Some people have a fear of success, or possess destructive personalities which may impede their success and not allow them to make money. However, the vast majority of traders want to succeed and be profitable. Many traders make money and then lose it, not because they don't really want to succeed, but because they rely on methods which worked in the past but no longer work now. In other words, the trader has not changed but the market did; so the trader is left confused as to the next course of action.

Other times traders do consciously try to change successful methods, because they believe the market will change and the method will no longer be valid. It is very easy to say, "stick with your trading style because it has worked in the past and you know it makes money." The problem is *you do not know* if the method will continue making money, and it is natural to assume that the results might change. We live in a world of constant change, and find it easy to rationalize the markets will change too.

ENVIRONMENTAL INFLUENCES

Our upbringing and religious background can have a tremendous influence on how successful we are in trading. Some of us may like to think we are not influenced by outside events, but even that attitude is partly fostered by our environment and time. People had a much different outlook on life during the Middle Ages than now, and even today people from other cultures may have widely dissimilar attitudes about life. Our surroundings have a considerable effect on how we think about ourself and the outside world.

Various experiences can be deeply etched in our mind and affect our subconscious thoughts. These experiences and beliefs can affect our trading and we may not even be aware of them.

Many people reject or feel uncomfortable trading for a variety of moral reasons. Some people believe trading is a useless occupation or a form of gambling. Others cannot see a tangible benefit to society in trading unlike the construction worker who physically toils to build a structure. Others feel it is wrong to make so much money so quickly, because it somehow goes against their perceptions of the laws of nature. Still others believe it is not right to make a lot of money without "doing any work."

Trading is a valid and useful occupation benefiting society as much as any other occupation. All these arguments against trading suggest ignorance about trading and life, and need not be addressed. The issue here is not to defend trading, but to see why some traders have mental blocks or problems in trading or making money. If a person subconsciously feels trading is a disreputable occupation or of no benefit to society, this unease and guilt will often be reflected in the person's performance and reluctance to improve.

TRY TO BE AS UNBIASED AS POSSIBLE

When trading, you will find it easy to develop a bias about the direction of the market. Some traders holding a position will try to find people or information which agrees with their opinion about the market. For example, a trader who is long may try to reinforce this opinion by looking for any kind of corroborating bullish information, and dismiss any contradictory bearish information. This process of searching for corroborating information and dismissing conflicting information is called *reinforcement* and *selective perception*. It is something that is very natural for humans to do. But it can be dangerous because a trader may block information which is important in making an intelligent decision about the market. Looking for a consensus to reinforce a decision is fraught with disaster in trading.

Other traders who wish to initiate a position or hold a position may look for reasons to not enter a market or get out of an existing position. For example, many traders may feel that as soon as they buy the market will automatically head lower, as if the market knows or cares what they are doing. Many traders feel the market is unfair to them and should treat them with more respect.

Some traders can be swayed by the opinions of analysts who may articulate persuasive arguments and flawless reasons for having a certain position in the market. The market is not a debating session where the most eloquent argument wins, but a fair arena where supply and demand are judged. The trader may simply have no rebuttal to the arguments except for the minor fact that the market does not agree with the analyst either. However, the market cannot be as easily convinced of any argument, unlike the trader. The trader must maintain a distance from others and realize the arguments of others may be irrefutable, but the market still does not have to agree and follow the logic.

Biased attitudes are unhealthy in trading because you need to maintain a clear perspective of the market. The better informed and less opinionated you are, the better the chance for a good decision when entering or exiting a position. Markets may change quickly; so it is wise to maintain a clear and unbiased view.

DO NOT TRY TO BEAT THE MARKET

Traders cannot beat the market, nor can the market beat the trader. Many traders try to force trades by trading for the fun of it, or trading and then hoping the market will move. Remember, the fight is always within; so you must not try to beat the market because you will only end up beating yourself. The market never beats any trader, because the trader must always consciously or subconsciously enter and exit the market. The market never tells the trader when to put on or take off a trade so the market never makes the trader do anything.

PSYCHOLOGY OF ENTRY AND EXIT

The decision to exit a trade is very different from the decision to enter a trade. Why? You can wait until the market is in a condition where you feel the time is right to enter, and a good trade can be made. Before entering, you do not have to risk any money, except opportunity cost. When exiting you cannot simply watch. Once in the market, you must accept whatever the market does or get out immediately. You can no longer wait, but are now at the mercy of the market.

If the market moves in an unexpected manner you may lose substantial sums of money. You must always decide whether to stay with a position or get out. This is not the case before entering a position.

When is the stress and the pressure greatest when trading—before entering, while a trade is on, or after exiting? Most traders would probably agree stress is greatest while holding a position and less before a position is put on or after it is taken off. This is why many people reject paper trading as not realistic. There is no way to simulate the amount of pressure you must undergo when holding a position. Even if a loss is experienced after a trade, there is at least a sense of resolution, which is an important way for most people to reduce stress.

The entry decision is indeed important, but you can always walk away and wait for another time to play. You are not allowed this luxury when exiting and must follow and sometimes suffer through the trade. Of course, some traders can walk away and forget about their positions by having the brokerage firm send them a margin call, but this is a passive decision to avoid pain and responsibility as well as a means of denial.

Many traders equate longer holding times for a trade as a way to make more money in an attempt to squeeze the last penny of profit. We are often brought up to learn to work long and hard to complete an endeavor. Trading is different. Markets can make extreme moves quickly and then do nothing. Markets may move in exaggerated ways, but this is simply the reflection of the participants in the market.

A good way to develop a trading method is to try to draw the movement of the market. You may find it difficult to simulate the jagged and confusing moves of a market, but this will help to see how the market actually moves.

THE IMPORTANCE OF KNOWING WHEN
TO STAY OUT OF A MARKET

When developing a trading strategy and assessing entry and exit points, always appreciate the benefit of *staying out* of the market as much as possible. *In trading it is equally important to know when to enter, when to exit, and when to stay out.*

Some traders feel they have to be trading all the time because they equate the occupation of trading only with the actual process of buying and selling. Since everyone else works a full day, they should be "working" too. The act of trading requires intense concentration and knowing when to be in or out of the market. Inactivity in trading should never be confused with not working; it is just as much a part of the trading process. Others feel that as soon as they enter the market it should now begin moving. Remember that markets do not always present good trading opportunities because they may be inactive or random much of the time. There is no sense in trading a market when there is no clearly defined trend or movement; the trader has no advantage during these situations.

An even more important reason to avoid overtrading is to keep your strength and health. You must know when to stay out of the market to maintain a proper perspective, but most importantly to avoid burning out. Trading saps your mental and physical energy. Staying on the sidelines at the right time allows you to build up your stamina for the next trade. Overtrading can not only be financially ruinous, but also mentally and physically debilitating. Stay in shape mentally and physically by not trading too much.

ABILITY TO SEPARATE THE PRESENT FROM THE PAST AND THE FUTURE

The trader must focus on the present condition of the market and determine whether it is right to be long, short, or out of the market. Many traders make trading decisions about the market based on their current positions. For example, a trader holding a long position may buy more contracts because there is already a profit from the original position. Others take positions because they believe the market will go higher or lower and do not want to miss out on the move, irrespective of the current condition of the market. These are poor reasons to take positions.

The trader must take a position based on the present condition of the market. If the present environment does not hold good trading opportunities, the trader should not have a position. For example, if you are long the market and have a profit, you should buy, sell, or hold based on the condition of the market and not on your current position. Of course, you must trade within the limits of the amount of risk you can incur.

Execution costs are relatively small in futures, compared to the amount that can be lost in a trade. The trader must make a conscious decision whether to be in or out of the market all the time.

IS THE MARKET RIGHT OR WRONG?

Is the market right or wrong? If the market appears overvalued but continues to rally is the market wrong? Many traders believe the market is trading at the wrong price by being too overvalued or undervalued. It will soon learn the error of its ways, and drop or rise to the "right" level.

There is a problem in assuming that the market is right or wrong. The market does not have to meet margin calls, the market does not have to rationalize what it does, the market does not make or lose money, and the market does not care. The market simply exists for itself. You, on the other hand, have to meet the margin calls and have to rationalize your behavior. *The market may be wrong to the trader, but that is because the trader is viewing it from the wrong perspective and not because the market is wrong.*

Whenever a trader asks whether something is right or wrong, a moral question is implied. The market cannot be judged in this way because the market does not have to answer to any moral code. It is wrong to ascribe moral concepts to the market, because the idea of right and wrong is uniquely human. The market may have a mind, but this does not imply it possesses a conscience. The market is a natural phenomenon, no different from any other natural process. A natural process, like a snowstorm or a rabbit eating a carrot, is not wrong, and neither is the movement of the market.

There have been many times in history where masses of people have been deluded into believing incorrect things. The consequences have sometimes been disastrous. A market may be overvalued and it may be that investors are totally mad in their perceptions of valuations. The people may be crazy but this does not imply the market is wrong, but only a reflection of the madness of the people. *The trader should attempt to understand the dynamics of the market and dispense with a morality as it applies to the movement of the market.* It is pointless to assume whether the market is right or wrong because our ethics are only applicable to humans, and not an entity like the market. It is also futile to assume the market is wrong on a practical basis, because there is nothing we could do about it even if it were wrong. If the market is wrong, can we complain to our elected official, call the police, or take it to court? Can we appeal to its conscience to change the error of its ways?

If the market is never wrong, then what about times when the market was valued at one price and then quickly changed to another price, such as the stock market crash of October 1987? Was the stock market wrong in being overvalued in September and undervalued in November? "Right" and "wrong" assume a morality that the market does not have to follow. The market was neither right nor wrong, but simply was valued at whatever the mass of investors believed it should be. The market is a reflection of the hopes and dreams of its participants, and therefore neither right nor wrong.

Your concern is not whether the market is correct, but whether your analysis of the market is correct. If you felt the market was overvalued and sold in September, and also believed the market was undervalued and bought in November, then your analysis was correct. So you should concentrate on the correctness of your analysis of the market, and not whether the market is right or wrong.

GOOD AND BAD TRADES

There is an important distinction in trading between a good and a bad trade. A good trade is made with the probabilities in your favor; no matter what the outcome the right decision was made. An investor may make a good trade, and it can still result in a loss. A bad trade is made with the probabilities against you; no matter what the outcome the wrong decision was made. A bad trade can result in a profit. Good trades should eventually yield profitable results over time, while bad trades should provide unprofitable results.

If making money in the short term is the only criterion, then good and bad trades don't matter. But if you consider trading a business and attempt to keep the probabilities in your favor, it is important to determine whether you make good or bad trades. The same bad trade which makes money once or twice will eventually cause much more money to be lost.

Trading is a marriage of ideas and emotions. Sometimes the marriage appears to be an excellent mix, but other times the ideas and emotions conflict. Trading methods are embraced and well thought of when they make money. But when times get tough the trading rules often get abandoned because they are no longer considered of any use. One of the ironies of trading is that most enter with grand ideas of untold wealth, but the more successful stay with prudent visions of possible loss.

MAKING GOOD OF A BAD SITUATION

When experiencing a losing period it is important to make it as constructive as possible. Question your trading rules to determine if they are still valid or see if they can be improved. What about your money management techniques? Are you experiencing an extended series of losing trades, or was it one bad trade which caused the loss? Is your mental state contributing to the losses?

Adverse periods are certainly the hard part of trading, but they also may prove to be the most rewarding. Each bad period should make you question your existing strategies and cause you to develop even better trading methods and money management techniques.

We seldom have the desire to change strategies that work. Don't fix a clock that's not broken. But this kind of mentality discourages change and ultimately improvement of ourself. Of course, we should not look forward to the next bad time to improve ourself. Bad times may help to accelerate change and improvement, whereas complacency sometimes reigns when good times occur.

CHANGING YOUR STYLE

Changing your style of trading can have drastic effects on the results. The slightest change in trading method, money management, and psychology can affect you greatly. Let's look at an example to see why.

Philip, a trader, works alone from his office and decides to share space with a group of traders at a trading desk. He has been successful but does not enjoy being alone, and also looks forward to sharing ideas and being better informed about the market from the other traders. He moves in with the group and gets along well with everyone. He becomes bullish on the market and is ready to buy, but notices his friend who appears more knowledgeable is bearish and is short the market. Phil questions whether it is prudent to buy, especially in light of going against a better trader, and decides to sit this one out.

The market rallies and his friend covers his shorts and goes long. But Philip does not want to go long here, reasoning that he could have bought at lower prices and feeling that the market is overdue for a correction. The market continues higher; so he finally enters in frustration that he will miss the move. His friend bails out of the position five minutes later and the market drops shortly after. Philip is left with a loss and confused about what to do next. His next decision was easier: He returned to his original arrangement and resumed trading successfully. He could not trade when others were offering opinions. This does not imply every trader must be alone but every trader must find an appropriate environment for trading.

Many factors go into the decision to trade, and we should try to be aware of as many of these factors as possible. Our environment and our social surroundings will also affect the way we trade and consequently our performance. Chapter 25 shows examples of how changing one variable, either with the trading method or money management technique, can dramatically affect the results in trading. The same effect may occur with the psychological and sociological part of trading. You must be aware of this and try to make your trading environment as amenable to your needs as possible.

CHANGING YOUR STYLE: ANOTHER THOUGHT

For a time Philip traded his own capital. He reached a point where people were willing to give him money to trade for them because of his excellent performance record. This was a great opportunity so he accepted, but there was only one catch—he would have to change his trading style slightly. The commissions the client had to pay were slightly higher than his own. This meant he would have to hold onto a trade longer and not enter and exit a position as quickly as before. He felt this was a minor concession, because he would only have to hold onto positions for a few days longer and take slightly more risk in each position.

He commenced trading with the client, and both initially made a small amount of money. However, he subsequently lost what was made and later ended down 10% for the year, which was his first losing year. He was shocked and could not understand how such a small change in method could affect performance results so much. Only later, with the benefit of more research, did he realize how changes in style can vastly affect trading performance.

You need to understand how changes in the market or changes in the trading rules impact your results. Knowing how different scenarios will affect results will assist you in reacting appropriately to market changes. You will have more confidence in your trading methods if you know how changes in the market might affect the results.

As a postscript, Philip went back to his original trading style. He felt much better because he preferred the style, but also because his profit and loss statement looked better.

TRADING IS AN EVOLUTIONARY PROCESS

Some traders become comfortable with a trading system and see no need to try to improve upon it. Other traders constantly attempt to develop a better system by improving on the existing one or creating a new one.

Trading is an evolutionary process, no different from any other life experience. Most trader are always looking for a better trading method because we are also looking for a better way of life.

TRADING BY FEEL

One of the first ways many people begin trading is by feel. They watch the market and then try to sense an opportunity to buy or sell and take a plunge. This experience probably originates from our primal instincts, and often stays with us no matter how experienced we get. In fact, some good traders never go beyond this stage by looking for intellectual or complex trading methods, but instead have a good feel or sense of the market.

The few traders with this gift have a hard time teaching it to others, partly because it is instinctual and not easily learned. Either you possess this quality of feel or you don't, and most people don't.

It is important to acquaint yourself as much as possible with the market or markets you plan to trade because each market has its own personality. Some good traders do not believe this and feel all markets are the same. But operational factors can change the character of the market. For example, the currencies are a 24-hour market but the stock market is generally traded during normal domestic business hours. This can dramatically affect how a market trades. Currencies tend to open with large gaps more often than stocks because they have been trading continuously.

In between trading by feel and rigidly following a purely mechanical system is a vast realm of possibilities for which most traders strive. The trader may decide on using chart analysis, but only after observing the signals given by a mechanical system and trying to develop a sense of where the market is headed.

MECHANICAL TRADING SYSTEMS

If mechanical trading systems work, why don't more people use them? Or if they don't work, why do so many people want them? Certain mechanical trading systems can and do make money if traded by the right person, but more often the investor gets frustrated using the system and eventually ends up abandoning it. Bad results may not necessarily be the fault of the person or the system. The person may be incompatible with the system.

Mechanical trading systems require certain concessions from the trader. *The trader must yield to the signals of the system and surrender control of the trading, but accept responsibility for the resulting profits and losses of the system.* This relationship of lost control, but responsibility for actions, is fraught with conflict and will prove tenuous at best.

We do not want to consciously lose control of our actions when trading, especially in an environment which can be so chaotic and confusing. Of course, anyone using a mechanical trading method has ultimate control and may always override the trading signals, but doing this too often eliminates the need for the system in the first place.

A trader wanting to use a mechanical system will find a better chance for success with a system with rules which are compatible with the way the trader thinks. How can a system think? It can't, but a trader should look for a system that provides trading signals similar to the way the investor would view or trade the market. For example, a trader who is used to fading the market (buying weakness and selling strength) should not look for a trend-following system (buy strength and sell weakness), but instead investigate countertrend systems.

Most people pick the system with the best track record and then try to live with it. This is no different from choosing a blind date who looks great, but you know nothing more about the person than what your friend told you. Appearances can be deceiving. What are the chances of success or a long lasting relationship?

There is another choice. We can change the way we view the market. If you are used to fading the market and are currently using a trend-following system you can try to learn to trade with the trend. This requires *you* to change and not the system. It is much easier to change a trading system, or find one compatible with you, than it is to change your personality to fit the trading system. However, it is possible for some to change, and may be quite beneficial as well.

Assuming you have found a match made in heaven, why can it still be hard to actually use the system? There are many practical reasons for this. For example, assume the market opens at 301 and a trend-following system yields a sell signal if the market declines to 300. An hour later a bearish news report sends the market crashing to 300, but you do not want to put a sell order in because of fear of a bad fill. The market continues to drop to 299.50 where you place an order to sell at 300 on a limit. The market trades up to 299.90 but then promptly collapses, never to see the 300 level for the rest of the day.

Is this a worst case scenario that usually doesn't happen? Yes, but trading methods, systems, and traders do not get abandoned because they make money consistently. They fade away because bad periods and the loss of money also entails the loss of confidence.

There is a misconception that mechanical systems take the emotion out of trading. Anyone who becomes too emotional in making trading decisions may not necessarily find solace in mechanical systems. A trader using a trading system will not magically abandon all feeling and emotion and automatically begin dispassionately trading by the dictates of the system. The individual trying to subdue or eliminate emotional feelings will have to consciously work on this, irrespective of which trading method is chosen.

There is another reason why some people find mechanical trading systems troubling. When the system is profitable, who made the money—the system or the person? Perhaps there is more to trading than simply making money. Many of us seek success in what we have done—not what someone else, or something else, has done. And for those who are only in it for the money, they will end up abandoning the system as soon as it begins to lose money and renew their search for the next great hope.

TRADING SYSTEMS: A SECOND LOOK

Kristin is a practical person who simply wants to make money with a mechanical trading system. She decides to invest in a trading system that has a good track record. She follows the signals religiously and makes a little money at first. However, the system begins to lose money and experiences drawdowns close to the level of the historical maximum drawdown. Kristin begins to wonder if the system is valid anymore. She reasons that the markets have changed and questions if the system will not work as well under the new conditions. She feels uneasy about risking any more money on the trading system.

The markets will always change in that there will always be reasons to wonder if the present conditions are similar to the past. For example, the money supply numbers were important in the interest rate markets in the early 1980's because inflation was a large concern. However, as inflation abated the money supply numbers lost importance and hardly affected the interest rate markets in the late 1980's. This change, and a host of others in the market environment, could affect the results and performance of a system. Therefore, anyone using a system will question if the new market environment will produce results as good as the previous one. But many traders do not want to risk their money to find out the results.

Even if the trader feels the changing market environment should not affect the performance of the system, there are other questions which recur. How statistically valid are the results? Are more people using the system, which may tend to reduce the performance? There are all kinds of questions that might arise as to the reliability of the method, and all of them are perfectly reasonable, especially considering the amount of money at stake. Historical results may be excellent, but there is simply no guarantee that future results will come close to historical, or even be profitable. Therefore, there is tremendous uncertainty in trading a system which you cannot trust. This is all the more reason to find a method you are comfortable with and believe works under many situations.

IF TRADING SYSTEMS ARE SO GOOD, WHY GIVE AWAY A SECRET?

Traders often wonder why anyone would want to sell a good trading system to the public. The amount of money the developer of the system could make from trading the signals would potentially be so much more than the relatively small amount of money received from the sale of the system. Other traders are concerned with the effect of revealing the secret rules of the system to the public, which could possibly ruin the performance of the system. These are some of the reasons that many traders are skeptical about mechanical trading systems.

There are people selling products of dubious benefit to the public but this happens in any business, not just in the trading industry. There are definitely some bad trading systems which will not make money, and others whose secret is not far from the fairly well known and simple moving average systems. It is also true some methods have become so well known that the system has lost its effectiveness for a variety of reasons. For example, widely followed trading methods can produce a bunching of stop orders at the same price level, which can lead to terrible fills. Another problem with a system becoming too popular is that if too many people use the system, the signals will tend to lose their validity.

There are good trading systems which are developed by sincere people who may or may not choose to trade them. Some people are good theorists but do not apply the theory well. A close analogy occurs in science. Physicists work in a theoretical world and think about all kinds of ideas, but do not usually apply the ideas to real world applications. The engineer works with the theoretical idea of the physicist and applies it to practical use. The same may hold true in trading. System developers may create good trading systems, but they may not be able to trade them for many reasons. Traders must be practical, and may be able to apply the ideas of the system developer to the market.

CONCLUSION

There are many useless trading platitudes, such as:

1. Cut your losses and let your profits run.
2. You won't go broke taking a profit.

The list goes on ad nauseam. Though there is some truth to the lines, there are as many false notions and much ambiguity to effectively invalidate or provide little help or substance in using them. The three qualities and 13 traits previously outlined show there are not always easy answers to the complex idea of trading. Anyone peddling easy answers should be approached with great caution. The sayings at the beginning of the chapters should provide more help in developing a trading strategy.

CHAPTER 32

Advantages and Benefits of Trading

No profit grows where is no pleasure ta'en;
In brief, sir, study what you most affect.
William Shakespeare, *The Taming of the Shrew*

For there was never yet philosopher
That could endure the toothache patiently.
William Shakespeare, *Much Ado About Nothing*

Certain advantages in trading should be exploited to the fullest. Some of these are:

1. You can choose when to trade, or not to trade at all.
2. You do not have to rely on others to complete your work.
3. The market and trading opportunities will always be there.
4. You only need to focus on trading.
5. The pressure is only as much as you place on yourself.
6. You do not have to answer to any authority but yourself.
7. The cost to enter is low.
8. You have access to a lot of information.
9. Individual versus the crowd.
10. Create any theory and easily test it.

YOU CHOOSE WHEN TO TRADE

You always have the final say in deciding when to enter or exit the market. This is an important advantage because you can trade when the probabilities are in your favor. You can wait when the market is in an uncertain condition, and then trade when the market presents opportunities. Equally important, you can decide to trade when you are mentally and physically at your best. In essence, you determine when and how to do battle, which is a valuable option.

YOU NEED ONLY RELY ON YOURSELF

Trading is a very private experience. You must make the decisions to buy or sell. Trading by consensus, or relying on others, is usually an excellent way to lose money quickly. You do not have to wait for other people to be ready, or hold meetings to get second opinions. You can act when you want to, and at the most appropriate time.

THE MARKET WILL BE THERE TOMORROW

Even if a great trade or big move was recently missed in the market, you must realize the market will be there tomorrow. There will eventually be another good trading opportunity in the same or another market. You always have a second chance, as long as you preserve your capital.

The Voyager mission, which explored some of our solar system, could only happen approximately every 200 years with our present technology because of the way the planets were configured. If the scientists missed this opportunity they would have to wait quite a long time for the next mission. However, as a trader, you only have to wait till tomorrow to get back in the game.

Although it is always helpful to look back and see how a strategy may have been improved, do not use retrospection to brood over missed opportunities. The market may not be forgiving, but it does provide the chance to try again.

Some exceptional trading opportunities occur infrequently such as the massive bull market in gold in 1979–1980, or the stock market crash in 1987. But do not think these moves were so easy to catch, and in any case there will be big moves in markets in the future.

FOCUSED ATTENTION

One of the great benefits of trading is that you only have to focus on the business of trading. You can marshal all your power and efforts into becoming a more successful trader, instead of being distracted by other considerations such as fame or credibility. The market may be severe in dealing with ignorance and bad trading, but at least it is open minded about trading ideas.

NO OUTSIDE PRESSURE

You do not have to face deadlines or the pressure of getting something done for an outside group. Of course, there is internal pressure, but that can be varied by reducing your position size and learning to live with the stress of trading.

YOU ONLY HAVE TO ANSWER TO YOURSELF

You do not have to justify your actions to a higher authority or seek acceptance in a group because of your beliefs. For example, the theories of scholars and professors have to be judged by their peers. Careers can be made or broken depending on how these ideas are received at the time, irrespective of whether the ideas prove to be true or false. Galileo had to suffer through the ignorance of higher authorities and publicly renounce his hard work and brilliant ideas. Of course, he was vindicated after his death, but this provided him with little solace at the time!

Many traders can be ridiculed for their ideas, such as the supposedly ridiculous notion of following astrology to determine market prices. But the last laugh is always on the trader. If the ideas prove accurate, the trader can laugh all the way to the bank, while the skeptics and experts try to make their money in a more "respectable" way.

COST TO ENTER IS LOW

All that is required for trading is an initial sum of money and a brokerage house to execute your orders. Sophisticated and expensive equipment is available to enhance your trading, but do not be misled into thinking that more expensive equipment will guarantee profits. Trading still comes down to understanding human nature, and some better traders have made money simply watching the market and developing a feel for it.

INFORMATION ACCESS

The amount of data and information available to the trader is staggering. The problem with data analysis is generally not in accessing, but in filtering out what is important or irrelevant. The analyst must focus specifically on what is needed and perform the studies. Much of the data is readily available, except for some fundamental information which may either be kept secret or sometimes used in misleading ways.

INDIVIDUAL VERSUS THE CROWD

The market is a reflection of peoples' expectations—their hopes, dreams, and fears. It is a fascinating display of the psychological and sociological forces of humanity. The market measures, in a coldly analytical way, the degree of optimism and pessimism of people, and so it is an excellent barometer of how people feel about the world and themselves.

Many people are frightened by the markets because they fear there are so many intelligent whiz kids using high powered computers that make them superior in analyzing the market. How can a novice investor expect to win when there are experienced traders who have access to secret or confidential information, and know when and where the market is going?

Since markets may at times be driven by the mass of investors, then it possesses a mind of its own. Gustave LeBon studied crowd psychology and noted that the mind of a crowd often reflects the behavior of the lowest common denominator in the crowd. Therefore, crowds do not often exhibit highly intelligent behavior, which can be an important advantage when trading.

You are not competing against an individual, but a composite of people and ideas which exhibits crowd mentality. How could there be any advantage of one person against an entire crowd of people? Isn't a crowd so much more powerful than an individual? Yes and no. If, as an individual, you plan to do physical battle against a crowd, you will most likely fail. This analogy is similar to one person or a group of people trying to manipulate or control the market; ultimately they will be unsuccessful. But you should not choose to fight the crowd on this battlefield.

A crowd can be very dangerous but it is not necessarily smart. An idea, on the other hand, can be a powerful force too. The individual has the power of thought but the crowd does not, and there is the tremendous advantage. The market represents the mass of peoples' ideas or crowd mentality, and not the individual's thoughts. Therefore, you have an advantage in trying to beat the crowd on a mental level instead of a physical level.

CREATE A STRATEGY AND TEST IT

You can develop all kinds of theories about trading, and can usually test them by entering the market and trading the position. A physicist might have to wait for a government grant, which could take years to get. You can act immediately, and thereby advance your knowledge so much more quickly.

BENEFITS OF TRADING

There are more benefits to trading than just making money. Trading provides a way to financial independence. A successful trader will have the freedom to choose a lifestyle many people might only dream of. Trading allows an individual complete freedom of expression and creativity by testing methods and ideas without being ridiculed or denigrated by others. The market, which is the only judge, is entirely impartial and fair, though it may not always be understood and sometimes works with brutal honesty.

Trading allows you the freedom and the ability to realize the full potential to develop yourself. How many people complain about not doing what they want or not being appreciated for their talents? You are limited only by yourself in trading. What more could a talented person desire?

Trading encourages and demands the exploration and understanding of yourself. This in itself can prove the greatest reward.

CHAPTER **33**

A Separate Peace

God grant me the serenity to accept the things I cannot change, the courage to change the things I can, and the wisdom to know the difference.

Reinhold Niebuhr

Trading is:

1. Developing a successful trading method that you also believe will work.
2. Incorporating money management concepts with any trading method, and understanding how they affect your trading methods.
3. Developing a proper psychology for trading and understanding yourself in the process.

You must ultimately come to terms with whatever trading strategy or rule structure you develop. You must be able to live with the rules you create, the resulting signals these rules generate, and the performance of the trading strategy. If you can live with these rules, accept the trading signals, and are comfortable with your performance, you will be able to trade by your rules even if they do not give profitable signals. As strange as it might seem, it is much easier to use a trading method that you believe in but yields continually unprofitable results than it is to use a trading method that you do not believe in but continually yields profitable results. Why? Many people continue to lose money every year using the same unprofitable method. They cannot switch to a better method because they do not believe the better method will work.

Trading is by no means a peaceful experience, but the decisions you make must be acceptable to you or you will never be comfortable trading. In essence, you are the ultimate judge of any trading system and money management technique because you must be able to live with it. *You must find a separate peace where you can accept your trading strategy for its good points and inherent limitations, and, just as importantly, accept yourself for who you are in all your strengths and weaknesses.*

Trading is a reflection of life. This is why there are so many contradictory ideas and shades of gray, instead of black and white answers. It is a journey, a voyage of discovery within and without you. It is the study of the human condition in the aggregate, as well as an intimate portrait of yourself. Our hopes and dreams and joys and sorrows are reflected in trading. How you approach and perform in trading will reveal a great deal of information about yourself and life. What could be more challenging? What could be more rewarding?

No man is an island, entire of itself; every man is a piece of the continent, a part of the main; if a clod be washed away by the sea, Europe is the less, as well as if a promontory were, as well as if a manor of thy friends or of thine own were; any man's death diminishes me, because I am involved in mankind; and therefore never send to know for whom the bell tolls; it tolls for thee.

John Donne, *Devotions Upon Emergent Occasions*

Epilogue

The artist and scientist both try to understand and explain reality but ultimately create another illusion.

Bibliography

The classification at the end of each book indicates which subjects are covered:

TM: Trading method

MM: Money management

PS: Psychology

Arnheim, Rudolf, *Art and Visual Perception*, Berkeley: University of California Press, 1974. TM

Bartlett, John, *Familiar Quotations*, Boston: Little, Brown, 1980. TM, MM, PS

Bernstein, Jacob, *The Handbook of Commodity Cycles*, New York: Wiley, 1982. TM

Bookstaber, Richard M., *Option Pricing and Investment Strategies*, Chicago: Probus, 1987. TM

Capra, Fritjof, *The Tao of Physics*, New York: Random House, 1975. TM, PS

Cox, John C. and Mark Rubenstein, *Options Markets*, Englewood Cliffs, NJ: Prentice Hall, 1985. TM

Crabel, Toby, *Day Trading with Short Term Price Patterns and Opening Range Breakout*, Greenville, SC: Traders Press, 1990. TM

Davis, Morton D., *Game Theory*, New York: Basic Books, 1983. TM

Douglas, Mark, *The Disciplined Trader*, New York: New York Institute of Finance, 1990. PS

Edwards, Robert D. and John Magee, *Technical Analysis of Stock Trends*, Boston: John Magee, 1966. TM

Fink, Robert E. and Robert B. Feduniak, *Futures Trading*, New York: New York Institute of Finance, 1988. TM

Frost, Alfred J. and Robert Prechter, *Elliott Wave Principle*, Gainesville, GA, 1984. TM

Gann, W. D., *How to Make Profits in Commodities*, Pomeroy, Washington: Lambert-Gann, 1976. TM

Gastineau, Gary L., *The Stock Options Manual*, New York: McGraw-Hill, 1979. TM

Gehm, Fred, *Commodity Market Money Management*, New York: Wiley, 1983. MM

Gleick, James, *Chaos*, New York: Viking Books, 1987. TM

Guillen, Michael, *Bridges to Infinity*, Los Angeles: Tarcher, 1983. TM

Herrigel, Eugen, *The Method of Zen*, New York: Vintage Books, 1974. PS

Herrigel, Eugen, *Zen in the Art of Archery*, New York: Vintage Books, 1971. PS

Hofstadter, Douglas R., *Godel, Escher, Bach: An Eternal Golden Braid*, New York: Vintage, 1980. TM, PS

Jones, George Thaddeus, *Music Theory*, New York: Barnes & Noble Books, 1974. TM

Kaufman, Perry J., *The New Commodity Trading Systems and Methods*, New York: Wiley, 1987. TM

Kondratieff, Nikolai, with a translation by Guy Daniels, *The Long Wave Cycle*, New York: Richardson & Snyder, 1984. TM

Le Bon, Gustave, *The Crowd*, New York: Penguin Books, 1977. PS

LeFevre, Edwin, *Reminiscences of a Stock Operator*, Burlington, VT: Books of Wall Street, 1980. TM, MM, PS

Lorie, James and Richard Brealey, *Modern Developments in Investment Management*, Hinsdale, IL: Dryden Press, 1978. TM, MM

Mackay, Charles, *Extraordinary Popular Delusions and the Madness of Crowds*, New York: Farrar, Straus and Giroux, 1932. PS

Mansfield, Edwin, *Economics: Principles, Problems, Decisions*, New York: W. W. Norton, 1974. TM

Maugham, W. Somerset, *The Razor's Edge*, New York: Penguin Books, 1979. PS

McConnell, James V., *Understanding Human Behavior*, New York: Holt, Rinehart and Winston, 1974. PS

McFadden, Fred R. and Jeffrey A. Hoffer, *Data Base Management*, Menlo Park, CA: Benjamin/Cummings, 1988. TM

McMillan, Lawrence G., *Options as a Strategic Investment*, New York: New York Institute of Finance, 1986. TM

Minsky, Marvin, *The Society of Mind*, New York: Touchstone, 1988. PS

Moore-Ede, Martin C., Frank M. Sulzman, and Charles A. Fuller, *The Clocks That Time Us*, Cambridge: Harvard University Press, 1982. TM

Murphy, John J., *Technical Analysis of the Futures Markets*, New York: New York Institute of Finance, 1986. TM

Natenberg, Sheldon, *Option Volatility and Pricing Strategies*, Chicago: Probus, 1988. TM

Neter, John, William Wasserman, and G. A. Whitmore, *Applied Statistics*, Boston: Allyn and Bacon, 1978. TM, MM

Nison, Steve, *Japanese Candlestick Charting Techniques*, New York: New York Institute of Finance, 1991. TM

Pirsig, Robert M., *Zen and The Art of Motorcycle Maintenance*, New York: Bantam Books, 1974. PS

Rand, Ayn, *The Fountainhead*, New York: Signet, 1971. PS

Resnick, Robert, *Basic Concepts in Relativity and Early Quantum Theory*, New York: Wiley, 1972. TM

Resnick, Robert and David Halliday, *Physics*, New York: Wiley, 1966. TM

Ritter, Lawrence S. and William L. Silber, *Money*, New York: Basic Books, 1981. TM

Schwager, Jack D., *Market Wizards*, New York: New York Institute of Finance, 1989. TM, MM, PS

Simpson, Thomas D., *Money, Banking, and Economic Analysis*, Englewood Cliffs, NJ: Prentice Hall, 1976. TM

Sklarew, Arthur, *Techniques of a Professional Commodity Chart Analyst*, New York: Commodity Research Bureau, 1980. TM

Smith, Adam, *The Money Game*, New York: Vintage Books, 1976. PS

Smith, Adam, *Paper Money*, New York: Summit Books, 1981. PS

Smith, Adam, *Powers of Mind*, New York: Ballantine Books, 1975. PS

Smith, Adam, *Supermoney*, New York: Random House, 1972. PS

Steidlmayer, J. Peter and Kevin Koy, *Markets and Market Logic*, Chicago: Porcupine Press, 1986. TM

Stevens, Peter S., *Patterns in Nature*, Boston: Little, Brown, 1974. TM

Stock Market Institute, Inc., 715 East Sierra Vista Drive, Phoenix, AZ 85014. (Wyckoff course) TM

Taylor, Joshua C., *Learning to Look*, Chicago: University of Chicago Press, 1957. TM

Teweles, Richard J. and Frank J. Jones, *The Futures Game*, New York: McGraw-Hill, 1987. TM, MM

Thomas, Gordon and Max Morgan-Witts, *The Day the Bubble Burst*, New York: Penguin Books, 1980. PS

Tompkins, Peter, *Secrets of the Great Pyramid*, New York: Harper & Row, 1978. TM

Vince, Ralph, *Portfolio Management Formulas*, New York: Wiley, 1990. MM

Watts, Alan M., *The Wisdom of Insecurity*, New York: Pantheon, 1951. PS

Weston, J. Fred and Eugene F. Brigham, *Managerial Finance*, Hinsdale, IL: Dryden Press, 1978. TM

Williams, David, *Financial Astrology*, Tempe, AZ: American Federation of Astrologers, 1982. TM

Zukav, Gary, *The Dancing Wu Li Masters*, New York: William Morrow, 1979. PS

INDEX